intermediate
BUSINESS

intermediate
BUSINESS

MARIA WILLIAMS & HELEN NEEDHAM

Hodder & Stoughton

A MEMBER OF THE HODDER HEADLINE GROUP

© 1995 Helen Needham and Maria Williams

First Published in Great Britain 1995

Impression number   10 9 8 7 6 5 4 3 2 1
Year   1999 1998 1997 1996 1995

A Catalogue for this title is available from the British Library

ISBN 0 340 61859 0

Typeset by GreenGate Publishing Services, Tonbridge, Kent
Printed and bound in Great Britain for Hodder and Stoughton Educational, a division of Hodder Headline plc, 338 Euston Road, London NW1 3BH by the Bath Press, Bath, Avon.
Cover artwork by Paul Bateman

CONTENTS

INTRODUCTION

WHAT IS A GNVQ?

A General National Vocational Qualification is a broad-based qualification which tests understanding of a vocational area – in your case, business.
GNVQs are currently available at three levels:

- Foundation
- Intermediate
- Advanced

How is the Intermediate GNVQ structured?

The intermediate qualification is split into six units or subjects, four of the units being mandatory (compulsory). These are:

- Business organisations and employment
- People in business organisations
- Consumers and customers
- Financial and administrative support

Everybody works towards these units. In addition you will need to work towards two optional units. The choice available will depend on which awarding body your school/college is using to run the GNVQ qualifications, i.e. BTEC (Business and Technology Education Council), The City and Guilds of London Institute or the RSA (Royal Society of Arts). This book deals with options offered by each awarding body (as well as the mandatory units).

ELEMENTS

Each unit is broken down into elements. For example, Unit 1, 'Business Organisations and Employment' has three elements:

Element 1.1 'Explain the purposes and types of business organisations'

Element 1.2 'Examine business location, environment, markets and products'

Element 1.3 Present results of investigation into employment'

'These are broad headings which explain what you will be expected to be able to do, understand or achieve.

PERFORMANCE CRITERIA

Each element is then broken down into smaller parts. For example, Element 1.1 'Explain the purposes and types of business organisations' has four performance criteria:

1 Describe developments in industrial sectors
2 Explain the purposes of business organisations
3 Explain the differences between types of business ownership
4 Explain the operation of one business organisation

These are the **specific** things you will be expected to do, understand or achieve in each element.

RANGE

The range is the range of knowledge you should demonstrate an understanding of for each performance criterion. For example, for the performance criteria for Element 1.1 given above the range of purposes will include profit making, public service, and charitable.

How do I go about proving that I can do, understand or achieve these performance criteria?

The way you meet the requirements of each unit element and performance criterion is by gathering **evidence**. This means that you will carry out activities or tasks to meet each criterion until you have sufficient evidence for each unit. All the evidence is then filed in a special portfolio (or folder). You may be given assignments or guidance by your tutors to help you gather the evidence. Alternatively, you may decide the best ways to collect it yourself (after negotiation with your tutors).
Examples of evidence are:

- written reports
- diaries
- statistics
- video or audio cassettes
- presentations
- written statements/testimonials
- photographs

- letters/memoranda
- evidence of oral work
- assessment of previous achievements and qualifications
- evidence from work experience/part-time employment

WILL I GET A GRADE FOR MY EVIDENCE?

If your evidence successfully meets the requirements of each performance criterion you will pass. In order to achieve a **merit** or **distinction** your tutors will be looking for evidence of the following:

1 **Planning** This is how well you outline the way you are going to go about specific tasks to achieve the evidence requirements and the way you monitor your plans as you go along.
2 **Information seeking and handling** This is the way you identify the information required for evidence collection and how well you use the information.
3 **Evaluation** This is the way you look back on the work you have done, reflect on your progress, identify problems you have encountered and explain how you have overcome them.
4 **Quality of outcomes** This is the quality of the work or evidence you actually produce, including the knowledge and skills you demonstrate and the language you use.

A grade may be awarded once you have submitted *all* your evidence. At least one third of the evidence must meet the required standard to achieve a grade. Your tutors may ask you to prepare a detailed plan for each piece of evidence to assist with the grading process.

ARE THERE ANY TESTS?

There are three external tests you must pass to achieve the GNVQ qualification (in addition to the successful collection of evidence). These are in three of the mandatory units:

- 'Business organisations and employment'
- 'People in business organisations'
- 'Consumers and customers'

The tests are set and marked by the awarding body. They last for one hour and are made up of multiple choice questions. There are a number of testing opportunities during the year and if you don't pass a test the first time, you will be able to retake it until you do.

Core skills

In addition to the mandatory and optional units you will also be asked to gather evidence for core skills units. The compulsory core skills units are:

- 'Communication'
- 'Application of number'
- 'Information technology'

Each core skill unit is broken down into elements and performance criteria in the same way as the other units.

Core skills are important, basic skills which we use everyday whether we are at work or in education. Because of this in most cases you will find that you do not need to gather separate evidence for them but can simply identify which core skills you have achieved in the process of gathering the evidence for your mandatory and optional units. For example, for Element: 1.1 'Explain the purposes and types of business organisations' you may decide to prepare a presentation with a friend to meet the performance criteria. Your presentation could involve some of the following core skills.

COMMUNICATION

- taking part in discussions with a range of people on routine matters – discussions with your friend to plan the presentation and discussions with your tutor for guidance
- preparing written material – your presentation could be accompanied by a handout
- using images – your presentation could include diagrams presented on an overhead projector or flip chart

APPLICATION OF NUMBER

- interpreting and presenting mathematical data – your presentation finding could be supported by statistics

INFORMATION TECHNOLOGY

- selecting and using formats for presenting information – your accompanying handout could be produced using a word processor.

How do I put together my evidence portfolio?

First buy yourself a large, strong folder and some subject dividers. Then organise your folder as follows:

- a section for each mandatory and optional unit
- a subsection within each of these to include the evidence for each element
- a section for each of the core skills
- a subsection within each of these for each core skills element (included in these may be cross referencing sheets to evidence for mandatory and optional units instead of actual evidence for core skills – see below)
- a section for any forms or documents which your school

or college or awarding body may require you to complete

- a contents page

It is important that the people checking through your portfolio can find their way through it as easily as possible and are able to check that there is sufficient evidence to meet all of the performance criteria.

CROSS REFERENCING

As we indicated when we were talking about core skills, an individual piece of evidence can often meet the requirements of the performance criteria of more than one unit. If this is the case you can photocopy the work and include it under each relevant section in the portfolio, so that a copy of the presentation for Element 1.1 we discussed earlier could be filed in your portfolio under Unit 1 'Business organisations and employment' and each core-skills unit. Alternatively you could

develop a suitable system to cross reference your work as in the following example:

Communication
Element 2.3 Use images

Evidence submitted: Tutor feedback, visual aids and written copy from presentation on purposes of organisations

Range covered: Images produced by the student, people familiar with the subject who know the student

Location of evidence: 'Business organisations and employment' Element 1.1

By following this information, anyone checking your folder could look under 'Business organisations and employment' Element 1.1 and see the evidence (including tutor feedback) which meets some of the requirements of Element 2.3 of the 'Communication' core skills unit.

HOW TO USE THIS TEXTBOOK

This book has been written to cover the range of knowledge you will need for the mandatory units, as well as some of the optional units for each of the awarding bodies. It should be particularly helpful when you are revising for your external tests.

We have included lots of practical activities to help you understand and apply the things you are learning about business. You will find many of the activities useful when deciding how to gather your evidence.

The following symbols have been included to make the book easier to use:

 indicates an activity and a possible opportunity for evidence gathering

 indicates that work produced could involve the use of a computer (or other form of information technology) and be used as evidence towards the 'Information technology' core-skills unit

 indicates that work produced could be used as evidence towards the 'Application of number' core-skills unit

 indicates that work produced could be used as evidence towards the 'Communication' core-skills unit

At the end of each unit we have included some revision questions to assess your understanding and prepare you for the external tests in the mandatory units.

At the end of each mandatory unit we have also included some evidence-gathering projects that will enable you to meet all the requirements of the performance criteria for these units. The projects are identified by the following symbol:

ACKNOWLEDGEMENTS

The authors would like to thank the following people for their assistance in producing this book:

- Ian Lindley, Barry Williams, Barbara and Jim Needham, and Said Gallip for their help and support
- Yvonne Gosling, Julie Askin and Alison Wray, their patient typists
- Other colleagues, friends and members of their families who have offered advice and support
- Julian Thomas (Hodder Headline)

In addition, the authors and publishers would like to thank the following for permission to use material in this publication:

The Image Bank for Figures 1.1, 1.2, 3.9, 3.17, 3.18, 4.1, 4.2, 4.3, 7.10 and 7.17; The Telegraph plc for Figures 1.8 and 2.12; Associated Newspapers Ltd for Figures 3.1, 3.2, 8.5, 8.10, 8.18, 9.3 and 9.4 and Tables 3.1 and 9.7; Boots the Chemist for Figure 3.5; Hull City Council for Figure 3.6; Barclays Bank PLC for Figure 3.7; Allied-Domecq for Figure 3.8; Paul Salvidge and the Boothferry Ward Labour Party for Figure 3.10; the Heathrow Penta Hotel for Figure 3.14; Millward Brown International and The Market Research Society for Figure 3.15; the British Standards Institution for Figure 3.19; Alba plc for Figure 3.20; Crystal Fashions for Figures 3.21, 3.22 (parts 1, 2 and 3), 3.23, 3.24, 3.25 and 8.8; Omron Systems UK Limited for Figures 4.4a, 4.5a, 4.6a and 4.8a; Chris Davies for Figure 4.12; the Inland Revenue for Figures 5.17, 5.18 and 5.19; Acco-Rexel Limited for Figure 5.24; the Department of Social Security Contributions Agency for Table 5.1; the Department of Employment for Tables 1.3, 1.4 and 6.1; the Department of Employment and the Department of Economic Development, Northern Ireland for Table 1.5; Rex Features for Figure 7.1; Canon UK Limited for Figure 7.8; Hird's Jewellers for Figure 8.2; Brooks and Bentley Ltd for Figure 8.3; Littlewoods Home Shopping Group Limited for Figure 8.4; J Sainsbury plc for Figure 8.6; The Vehicle Builders and Repairers Association Limited for Figure 8.9; *The Grocer* for Figure 8.12; P&O Cruises Ltd for Figure 8.13; Times Newspapers Ltd for Figures 1.6 and 8.14; Anheuser-Busch European Trade Ltd for Figure 8.15; *Marketing* for Figures 3.11 and 8.16; Fiesta Travel (Humberside) Limited for Figure 8.17; PriceCostco for the photograph in Figure 8.18; John Kellett, author of *European Business*, Hodder & Stoughton, 1995, for Figure 9.1; the Office for Official Publications of the European Communities for Figures 9.5, 9.8, 9.11, 9.12, 9.13, 9.14, 9.15, 9.16, 9.17, 9.18, 9.19, 9.20 and 9.21 and Tables 9.1, 9.2, 9.3, 9.4, 9.5, 9.6, 9.8 and 9.9; Europay International SA for Figure 9.6; and The European Limited for Figure 9.10.

Figures 3.13, 5.20 and 5.22 and Tables 3.2 and 3.3 have been reproduced by the kind permission of the Controller of Her Majesty's Stationery Office HMSO.

Chapter

1

BUSINESS ORGANISATIONS AND EMPLOYMENT

This chapter should help you to understand about different types of business organisation, the reasons for their existence, their location and the way they operate. It will enable you to investigate types of employment and employment trends.

EXPLAIN THE PURPOSES AND TYPES OF BUSINESS ORGANISATION

PURPOSES OF BUSINESS ORGANISATIONS

The objectives (aims or purposes) of organisations vary between the public and private sector.

The **private sector** consists of organisations that are set up, funded and run privately by individuals or groups of people. Examples are: sole traders, partnerships, public limited companies and limited companies. Their objectives are:

■ to make a profit
■ to meet demand
■ to be a market leader
■ to expand
■ to develop operations abroad
■ to survive
■ to minimise costs
■ to provide customer service

The **public sector** consists of organisations that are owned by the state (or the public) and controlled by the government. They are mainly funded by the government and through public taxes. Examples are: central government departments, local government, public corporations (or nationalised industries). Their objectives are:

■ to supply essential services
■ to meet public needs
■ to be cost effective
■ to run efficiently
■ to provide customer service

COMPARING TYPES OF BUSINESS OWNERSHIP

The private sector

SOLE TRADERS

A sole trader organisation is one which is set up and funded by an individual. A sole trader provides all the capital (or money) to start up, takes all the profits and has full control of the running of the business. The sole trader may or may not employ other people (including a manager) and has no special legal status. The sole trader obtains funds from private sources including banks, overdrafts, personal loans, hire purchase, grants and mortgages. He or she is personally responsible for *all* the losses of the business, i.e. has 'unlimited liability'.

FIG. 1.1 SOLE TRADER ORGANISATIONS

1

Examples of possible sole trader organisations are: a newsagent, a corner shop, a builder and a plumber.

Advantages

1 The sole trader is independent.
2 The sole trader takes all the profit.
3 The business is easy to set up.
4 The sole trader can make decisions easily.
5 The sole trader owns the business.

Disadvantages

1 The sole trader pays all the losses.
2 The sole trader works long hours and has few holidays.
3 It is often hard to raise finance.
4 The business can fail if the sole trader falls ill or has an accident.
5 The sole trader need to be a 'jack of all trades', i.e. accountant, administrator, sales person, etc.

PARTNERSHIPS

A partnership involves two or more people setting up and funding a business organisation.

Partnerships are governed by the Partnership Acts (must have a minimum of two partners) and are limited to a maximum of 20 partners. A legal document called the Deed of Partnership is usually drafted which covers the following:

- the amount of money to be invested by each partner
- the voting rights of each partner
- details as to how profits and losses will be shared
- arrangements if the partnership is dissolved
- rules relating to admitting and expelling partners
- the role of any sleeping partners (see below)

A **sleeping** (or silent) **partner** is someone who invests money into the business but is not active in its day-to-day running.

FIG. 1.2 PARTNERSHIPS

Partnerships are popular with doctors, solicitors and accountants.

Advantages

1 Mutual support.
2 Chance to specialise.
3 Chance to raise more finance.

Disadvantages

1 Each partner is personally liable for all the debts of the business.
2 Disagreement can occur.

COMPANIES

There are two main forms of company: private limited companies and public limited companies.

A **private limited company** (Ltd) is a corporate organisation that in law is treated as a separate body from its shareholders and directors. It can sue and be sued, employ staff and own property. In a private limited company capital (or money) is raised through selling shares. All shareholders have limited liability, i.e. they are only liable for the company's debts in relation to the amount of their shareholding (the amount they have invested in the company), the company is run by a board of directors, and shareholders will normally have one vote per share.

Public limited companies (PLCs) are also corporate bodies. In a PLC capital is raised through issuing shares, which can be sold to the general public through trading on the stock exchange. The minimum share capital is £50,000, profit is distributed to the shareholders in the form of a 'dividend' and shareholders have limited liability. PLCs must make the accounts public and produce an annual company report.

All limited companies must present two important documents to the registrar of companies in order to receive a Certificate of Incorporation which enables them to start trading. The documents are:

1 *The Memorandum of Association* – this identifies the name and address of the company, states the objectives (aims) of the company, provides details of the capital of the company and explains the liability of members.
2 *The Articles of Association* – these outline relations between the company and its members and between members themselves. They identify the directors and the company secretary, explain the powers and responsibilities of the directors and outline how they will be appointed, explain the control of shareholders (and how shares are to be issued and transferred) and detail the organisation of company meetings.

Advantages

1 Money can be raised quite easily through issuing shares.
2 Shareholders have limited liability.
3 Treated in law as a separate legal body.
4 Economies of scale (see p.9).

Disadvantages

1 Companies are complicated to form.
2 Companies are costly to set up.
3 Diseconomies of scale (see p.10).
4 Decision-making can be time consuming and administration very complex.

CO-OPERATIVES

A co-operative is a 'self-help' organisation made up of independent groups of householders, workers and businesses who join together to share the profits of their products. **Consumer** or **retail co-operatives** are the most common form, operating from shops in the high street. In consumer co-operatives the members are also the customers who use the shops and purchase the shares. Shares may be purchased by anyone (usually in £1 denominations) and may be redeemed at their face value (purchase price) when required. Shareholders have only one vote regardless of the size of their investment in the co-operative; any number of shares may be issued. A proportion of the profits are ploughed back into the organisation and the remainder distributed to the members in proportion to the amount invested – this sometimes takes the form of 'dividend' or 'trading' stamps. The co-operatives have an elected board of directors or committee of management who will employ officials to oversee the day-to-day running of the organisations. Co-operatives are members of the CWS (Co-operative Wholesale Society) from whom they purchase the majority of their stock.

Worker co-operatives are organisations owned and run by the employees or workforce. They are less common than retail co-operatives. In worker co-operatives all employees are eligible to become members. The employees provide all the capital and take all the risks. Profits are shared among the members, each of whom has a single vote.

Producer co-operatives are a third type. Here people group together to produce goods or services.

Advantages

1 Open membership.
2 Democratic decision making i.e. all members only have one vote.
3 Profits are distributed fairly or ploughed back into the business.
4 Economies of scale (see p.9).

Disadvantages

1 Competition from larger organisations.
2 Members may lack business experience.

FRANCHISES

A franchise is an arrangement whereby the retailer enters into an agreement with the manufacturer to be the sole agent in a particular area for a product or service. The **franchisor** is the manufacturer or organisation in control of the particular product or service; the **franchisee** is the person who runs the business. The majority of the starting capital is raised by the franchisee, who will also pay an initial licensing fee to the franchisor. Examples of franchises are McDonalds and The Body Shop.

Advantages

1 Enables a person to run their own business with the security of an established business behind them.
2 There are fewer decisions to make.
3 Security.
4 Use of an established trade name.
5 The franchise is cheaper to establish than the franchisee's own business.

Disadvantages

1 Raising capital can be hard.
2 The franchisee only receives a share of the profits.
3 The franchisee cannot *own* the business.
4 The franchisee is restricted to the prices, products and regulations established by the franchisor.
5 Limited expansion possibilities.

The voluntary sector (charities)

Charities do not fit specifically into either the public or private sector. They are often referred to as being part of the voluntary sector. Most charities have trust status. This means that a person (a trustee) is responsible for the funds and assets which have been given to the charity. Charities do not aim to make a profit but to provide a service and help the under-priviledged or a particular cause.

TYPES OF CHARITY

1 *Registered charities* – an example is Oxfam.
2 *Charitable trusts* – these use money bequeathed in wills and endowments. Examples are schools and old people's homes.
3 *Companies limited by guarantee* – companies that do not aim to make a profit. Examples are schools, certain colleges and examination boards.

The public sector

CENTRAL GOVERNMENT

There are many reasons why we need a government:

- to make sure that there is law and order in society
- to help to defend the country
- to communicate with other countries
- to achieve growth in the economy
- to ensure that as many people as possible have jobs

The government can be divided into three sections:

1 *Legislature* – functions carried out by the legislature. i.e. Parliament.
2 *Administrative* – functions carried out by the executive, i.e. the government and the civil service.
3 *Judicial* – functions carried out by the judiciary, i.e. the courts.

Parliament can also be divided into three sections:

1 *The House of Commons* – members of Parliament (MPs) who are voted in by members of the public.
2 *The House of Lords* – non-elected representatives, i.e. Lords and Ladies, such as Lady Thatcher.
3 *The Monarch* – the Queen.

The two main functions of Parliament are: to act as a debating chamber to discuss government decisions and other important issues; and to provide a process to pass laws (or legislation).

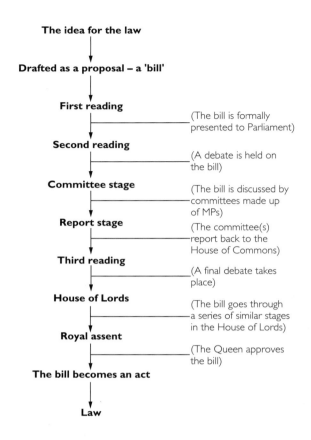

FIG.1.3 INTRODUCING A LAW

Most **legislation** is passed through government bills (proposals). For example, a bill could be introduced to propose that there should be a law to ban smoking. To become law a bill must pass through the House of Commons and House of Lords and receive royal assent. The procedure involves the stages shown in Figure 1.3.

In theory **the Queen** has wide powers. She can stop laws or dismiss a government. In practice, however, she is really only a nominal head of government (i.e. a figurehead) and rarely uses these powers.

The **prime minister** is the leader of the party with the majority in the House of Commons. The present prime minister is John Major who is the leader of the Conservative party.

The **cabinet** consists of between 20 and 25 ministers (mostly MPs and some members of the House of Lords). They meet at least once a week to discuss important government issues and to formulate policies.

Most **cabinet ministers** are responsible for a **government department**. They are supported by junior ministers. Some departments are headed by ministers who are not members of the cabinet. The following are government departments:

- The Ministry of Defence
- The Department of the Environment
- The Employment Department Group
- HM Treasury
- The Department of National Heritage
- The Home Office
- The Export Credits Guarantee Department
- The Department of Social Security
- The Department of Health
- The Foreign and Commonwealth Office
- The Board of Inland Revenue
- HM Customs and Excise
- The Department of Trade and Industry
- The Department of Transport
- The Ministry of Agriculture, Fisheries and Food

A C T I V I T Y

What sort of things do you think each of the government departments might be responsible for?

Members of the **civil service** are responsible for the public administration of the government of the country. It is their job to put government policies and ideas into practice. Civil servants are employed by central government departments and do not leave their jobs if a different political party comes into power.

Central government finance (the way the government raises its money) takes the following forms:

- direct taxes – taken directly from the public e.g. income tax
- indirect taxes – e.g. value added tax (VAT), a tax on spending
- government borrowing

LOCAL GOVERNMENT (LOCAL AUTHORITIES)

Local government is responsible for providing services to meet the needs of a local community. Some of the main areas of local government provision are as follows:

- housing
- education
- social services
- planning and development
- leisure and recreation
- public protection
- highways
- environmental health

County councils deal with services which need to be provided and administered over a wide area, for example education and the police. **District councils** (also called borough or city councils) provide services for a smaller area, for example housing.

The advantages of local government provision are that people who run local services can respond to local needs and attitudes; there can be close contact with the people who use the local services; and time and money can be saved in comparison to services being run by central government in London.

A C T I V I T Y

Can you think of any more advantages of local government provision?

Although local authorities run and make decisions about local services, central government still have ultimate **control** over them. This is to:

- ensure minimum standards across the country
- control spending in the interests of local people, i.e. protect them against wasteful expenditure
- make sure that local government is following the principles (or thinking) of central government
- ensure that services are being run efficiently

Local government finance (the way local government raises its money) takes the following forms:

- local taxes – the council tax
- business rates – the taxes paid by local business
- the revenue support grant and other central government grants
- profitable activities – for example the sale of council houses, charges for the use of leisure facilities, etc.

A C T I V I T Y

Look in your local telephone directory. What is the name of:

a the county council?
b The district, city or borough council?

Make a list of the services provided by each.

PUBLIC CORPORATIONS

Public corporations or nationalised industries are business organisations that are owned and controlled by the state. They are mainly financed by the state (or government) through public taxes. There are **no** shareholders and profits are ploughed back into the organisation. Public corporations are run by a board of management appointed by the government and must operate within guidelines laid down by Parliament. Examples of public corporations are British Rail, British Coal and the Post Office.

Privatisation

Since 1979 when the Conservative Government came into power they have carried out a massive programme of privatisation. This means that public corporations have been taken out of the public sector (and the control of government), sold to the private sector and become public limited companies (PLCs).

Below is a list of all the organisations which have been privatised since 1979.

Year	Organisation
1979	International Computers
1980	Ferranti Electronics
1981	British Aerospace British Sugar Corporation Cable and Wireless
1982	Amersham International National Freight Corporation
1983	Associated British Ports
1984	British Telecom Enterprise Oil Jaguar Cars Naval Shipbuilding Yards Sealink Ferries
1985	British Oil
1986	British Gas
1987	British Airways British Airport Authority Rolls Royce
1988	British Steel Bus Services
1989	Water Authorities
1990	Electricity (except nuclear power stations)
1994	British Coal

The British Rail track has now been privatised and is owned by Railtrack. The rolling stock is due to be privatised in 1996.

Look in a national newspaper and see if you can find an article about the privatisation of British Rail.

ADVANTAGES OF PRIVATISATION

- less control by the government
- more incentive to do well as the organisations aim to make a profit
- more efficient running
- cost effectiveness
- improved standards
- members of the public have the opportunity to buy shares
- encourages competition

DISADVANTAGES OF PRIVATISATION

- in many cases, there is no real competition
- the government loses valuable income
- the advantages of economies of scale may be lost (see p.9)

INDUSTRIAL SECTORS

Primary sector

The primary sector includes organisations which are involved in extracting raw materials. Examples are forestry, fishing, farming and the mining of raw materials which will then be used by the secondary sector.

Secondary sector

The secondary sector includes those organisations involved in manufacturing or processing the raw materials into finished products. Examples are car manufacturers, steel production, brewing and road construction.

Tertiary sector

The tertiary sector is not involved in the production process. It provides services which are essential in order for production to take place. There are two types of service: **personal** – involved in providing services to people, e.g. doctors, teachers, solicitors and firefighters; and **commercial** – involved in providing services for business, e.g. marketing, banking, accountancy and training.

Below is a list of occupations. Write down which sector of industry you think each belongs to:

- college lecturer
- shop assistant
- baker
- dentist
- farmer
- miner
- insurance broker
- furniture maker

Draw a map of your local town or city centre. Highlight all the business organisations and indicate which sector of industry they belong to.

Now see if you can find out some information about business organisations that operate on the outskirts of your town or city. To which sector of industry do they belong? How does this compare with businesses in the city/town centre?

DEVELOPMENTS IN INDUSTRIAL SECTORS

In the early part of the 20th century, Britain, along with most of western Europe and the USA, had very stong manufacturing industries which employed a large percentage of the countries' workforces. However, two significant factors have caused this to change over the last few decades:

- the increase of automation leading to greater efficiency, but resulting in the shedding of jobs
- the increase of employment within the service sector (now the largest employer of all three sectors) contributing up to seven out of ten jobs in the UK

The recessions of the 1970s and early 1980s affected UK manufacturing, making it more streamlined and less labour intensive. During the 1980s the service sector has increased as consumers with increased spending power now purchase many services, for example dry-cleaning, restaurant meals or leisure services. The primary sector employs a small percentage of the population: agriculture and farming in the UK are two examples of efficient industries which no longer require labour intensive methods. For the future it is difficult to expect anything other than continued growth for services, although a slight resurgence in manufacturing is possible, particularly in relation to export markets.

The increased use of technology has affected levels of employment in the different industrial sectors.

Write a paragraph to explain how you think it has affected each of the following:

- Primary sector – farming
- Secondary sector – car manufacturing
- Tertiary sector – a supermarket

THE SIZE OF AN ORGANISATION

Organisations can vary in size; they can be small, medium or large. A common abbreviation used is SME which means small- or medium-sized enterprise, normally one which employs fewer than 500 people. There are other factors to take into consideration when measuring the size of an organisation. These are outlined below.

Scale

The **scale** really means the size of an organisation. When measuring scale, a number of factors can be taken into account:

1 Market Share.
2 Turnover.
3 Number of people employed.
4 Number of branches/outlets.

Market share

Sometimes organisations will measure their performance by the size of their market share, that is, how much of the overall market their company's products account for. The example below illustrates how this works. Let us assume that in 1996, 10,000 widgets are sold in the UK. Each company which sells widgets will then calculate what percentage of the market their own widgets account for.

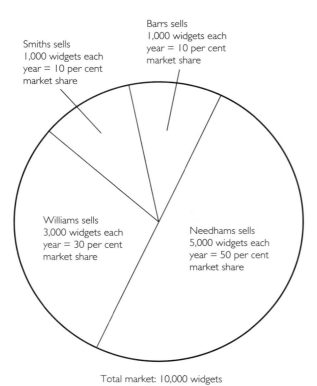

Smiths sells 1,000 widgets each year = 10 per cent market share

Barrs sells 1,000 widgets each year = 10 per cent market share

Williams sells 3,000 widgets each year = 30 per cent market share

Needhams sells 5,000 widgets each year = 50 per cent market share

Total market: 10,000 widgets

FIG. 1.4 UK MARKET SHARE OF WIDGETS 1996 BY VOLUME

In the example above, the market share is calculated by volume, i.e. the number of units sold. Sometimes, however, it is more relevant to measure the market share by value, i.e. the value of all sales made. This is calculated by multiplying the selling price of the widgets by the number of units sold.

	UNITS SOLD	SELLING PRICE PER UNIT (£)	TOTAL SALES VALUE(£)
Smiths	1,000	3	3,000
Barrs	1,000	2	2,000
Williams	3,000	15	45,000
Needhams	5,000	1	5,000
		Total market =	55,000

TABLE 1.1 UK MARKET SHARE OF WIDGETS 1996 BY VALUE

This shows quite a different picture from the one based on volume sales.

Generally, companies will wish to have a large market share so they can dominate the market. Sometimes however, a company will be quite content to have a small market share if they have a 'niche' or

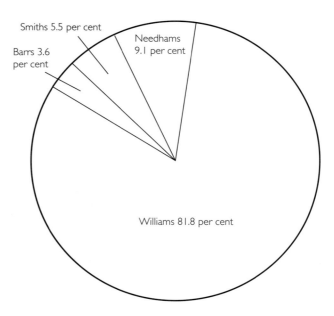

Smiths 5.5 per cent

Barrs 3.6 per cent

Needhams 9.1 per cent

Williams 81.8 per cent

FIG. 1.5 UK MARKET SHARE OF WIDGETS 1996 BY VALUE

specialised market. For example, Rolls Royce only has a small market share of the total car market, but would never expect to have one of the largest shares due to the expense of their product.

Some figures relating to the market share of food retailers are shown in Figure 1.6.

Turnover

This is the total amount of money a business receives from its sales in a year. A business with a large market share will have a high turnover.

Number of people employed

The number of people employed can be an indication of the size of a business. However, other factors should be taken into account, for example, how many hours the staff work, whether the staff are full or part time and whether the business uses new technology to a large extent (which will reduce its need for so many employees).

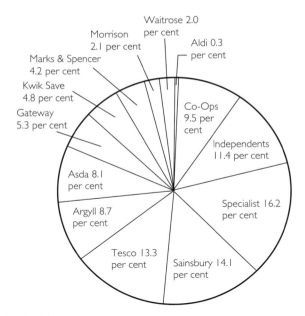

FIG. 1.6 FOOD RETAILERS' MARKET SHARE
SOURCE: THE SUNDAY TIMES 7/11/93

Pie chart labels:
Waitrose 2.0 per cent
Morrison 2.1 per cent
Aldi 0.3 per cent
Marks & Spencer 4.2 per cent
Kwik Save 4.8 per cent
Gateway 5.3 per cent
Co-Ops 9.5 per cent
Independents 11.4 per cent
Asda 8.1 per cent
Specialist 16.2 per cent
Argyll 8.7 per cent
Tesco 13.3 per cent
Sainsbury 14.1 per cent

Number of branches/outlets

A large number of branches or outlets can also be an indication of the size of a business. However, not all businesses need as many as others and may be able to operate in a very 'centralised' way. This will depend very much on the nature of the business.

The number of people employed and of branches/outlets can tell us about the size of an organisation. However, they are not an indication of the size of the market share or the amount of profit being made.

Comparisons

When looking at scale it is important to compare similar organisations. Two car manufacturing companies may use similar methods and be easy to compare. It could, however, be difficult to draw a comparison between a car manufacturer and a bank. A bank may be a large-scale organisation but may only employ a small number of staff due to extensive use of technology. It would be difficult to compare the market share of a producer of personal compact disc players with a crisps company: most people eat crisps but a much smaller number own personal CD players.

Scope

The scope of organisations is concerned with whether they operate on a local, national or international basis.
Multinationals are organisations which have branches or subsidiaries in more than one country.

Examples are IBM, Ford, Mobil and Esso. Multinationals aim to expand their operations on a worldwide basis and gain as large a market share as possible.

Economies of scale

Economies of scale are the benefits an organisation experiences as it grows in size.

INTERNAL ECONOMIES

- *commercial economies*:
  - being able to buy goods in bulk
  - advertising on television or in national newspapers
  - promotional activities, e.g. glamorous packaging, free gifts
- *technical economies* – being able to purchase up-to-date technology and machinery
- *financial economies* – easier to obtain finance, for example loans at low interest rates, issuing of shares
- *managerial economies* – being able to afford to employ skilled managers and specialists
- *research economies* – being able to afford to spend money on research into new products and techniques
- *welfare economies* – good working conditions and provision of facilities for staff, for example canteens, leisure facilities
- *risk bearing economies* – being able to risk bringing out new products, as they can be subsidised by successful products already on the market (even if the new product fails)
- *division of labour* (specialisation) – tasks can be divided up, for example an organisation can employ a marketing specialist and a finance manager

EXTERNAL ECONOMIES

These are the benefits experienced when a number of organisations group together in an area.

- labour – a number of suitably trained people will build up in the area, which assists recruitment and can therefore reduce training costs
- concentration – an area may become known for a particular product or service, for example, car sellers who often set up in the same area
- information – the organisations can combine resources and facilities, and carry out joint training

A C T I V I T Y

Can you think of any other benefits?

Diseconomies of scale

Diseconomies of scale are the disadvantages an organisation can experience as a result of its size. These include:

- *division of labour* – people feeling bored and isolated carrying out a specific or single job or task
- *personal contact* – this can be lost between staff and customers and also between managers and staff
- *lack of work* – staff might not work as hard, as they may see their work as insignificant due to the size of the organisation
- *administration* – this tends to become more complex and time consuming as the organisation grows

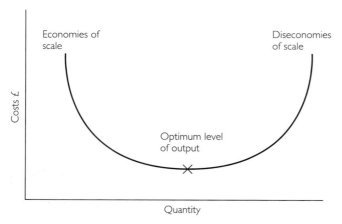

FIG. 1.7 ECONOMIES OF SCALE – THE OPTIMUM (OR BEST) LEVEL OF OUTPUT IS ACHIEVED WHERE UNIT COSTS ARE AT THEIR LOWEST FOR THE AMOUNT OF OUTPUT PRODUCED

Monopolies

A monopoly situation is where there is only one seller of a product or service. Tate and Lyle, for example, have a virtual monopoly over the sale of sugar in the UK. Monopolies are regulated by the Monopolies and Mergers Commission.

Oligopolies

An oligopoly situation is when there are only a few sellers of a product or service, for example high-street banks.

How do organisations grow?

Organisations can expand internally, i.e. grow themselves, or merge with or take over other organisations. Mergers or takeovers can take place in four different ways:

1 Horizontal integration.
2 Vertical integration.
3 Lateral integration.
4 Conglomeration.

HORIZONTAL INTEGRATION

This is the simplest type of merger. In this case two businesses producing the same product join together. An example of a horizontal merger is Clarke Foods with Lyons Maid.

VERTICAL INTEGRATION

This involves a business buying up other businesses involved in the same chain of production. For example, Brooke Bond has purchased a number of tea plantations.

A **sideways merger** is also a form of vertical integration. This is where an organisation takes over another which, although not directly associated with its particular product, will play a supporting role in the production process. For example, a shoe manufacturing company may take over a packaging company.

LATERAL INTEGRATION

This is where organisations which appear unrelated in terms of production join with one another (there is usually an underlying link). The market outlets, raw materials or products may be similar, as in the case of the merger between Cadbury and Schweppes.

CONGLOMERATION

This is where totally dissimilar firms merge with one another in order to spread the risk of their business activities. For example, the Imperial Tobacco Company owns Ross Frozen Foods.

BUSINESS OPERATION

Businesses can take many forms and operate in many different ways. As discussed on pp.1–10, they will have different purposes: they may be owned by private individuals or by the government and the public; they may make or sell a product, for example, hairdressing; and they can operate locally or nationally. A small business might have one branch in the north of England, a larger company may have 20 branches nationwide. All businesses will rely on the support of other businesses to survive, for example financial advisers and accountants will depend on office suppliers, sandwich delivery services and window cleaners to help the smooth running of their businesses.

C A S E   S T U D Y

Sainsbury's plc

J Sainsbury started out in the last century as a local supplier of provisions. Since then the business has flourished and now owns a chain of supermarkets nationwide. Although Sainsbury's sell products, food retailing is actually a service. Sainsbury's would count amongst its business objectives the need to make a profit, to provide good customer service and to maintain high levels of quality in terms of product and service. Sainsbury's is now a PLC which means it is owned by private shareholders. It has many links with other businesses: other food manufacturers sell their products to Sainsbury's; an advertising agency helps to promote them; and, in terms of the public sector, Sainsbury's must work with local government planners when seeking to develop new sites.

Manufacturing industries

A manufacturer produces products from raw materials. Some of the manufacturing industries in Britain are as follows:

- steel production and metal manufacture
- the ceramics industry
- glass production
- the chemical industry
- machinery
- computers
- the aerospace industry

Service industries

Service organisations are those which support and assist businesses, for example:

- banks
- shops
- insurance companies
- recruitment agencies
- wholesalers

They are *not* involved in the production of a product from raw materials.

A C T I V I T Y

Below is a list of business organisations. Which are manufacturing and which are service organisations?

- ICI
- Midland Bank
- British Telecom
- Halifax Building Society
- BP

Transport

Producers have to decide the most suitable method of transporting their goods to the consumer. The three main methods of transport are land, air and sea.

LAND

Rail transport is cheap and suitable for transporting bulky goods. Special containers are often used to pack the goods, which are sent to the nearest freight depot.

Road transport is flexible and allows an organisation to choose its own delivery times and routes. Goods can be transported from door to door and special refrigerated lorries can be used to transport perishable goods. However, delays can be caused by traffic jams and bad weather.

AIR

Air transport is expensive, so it tends to be used only for goods which require urgent transportation or for small, light or perishable goods. Goods are normally charged according to weight.

SEA

Transport by sea can be time consuming, but is suitable for bulky goods. Special containers, which can be stacked neatly on board, are used to pack the goods. They can be loaded onto the ship by lorry, and unloaded onto another lorry at the end of the journey.

Make a list of the advantages and disadvantages of transporting goods by:

- land
- air
- sea

Below is a list of terms associated with the transportation of goods. See if you can find out what each of them means:

- roll-on, roll-off
- haulage companies
- perishable goods
- freight agents

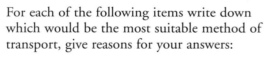

For each of the following items write down which would be the most suitable method of transport, give reasons for your answers:

- flowers
- jewellery
- frozen meat
- lawn mowers
- coal
- ice cream
- industrial machinery
- clothes

When making decisions about methods of transport, organisations will need to bear in mind the following factors:

- how quickly the goods need to be delivered
- the distance involved
- the costs involved

THE CHANNEL TUNNEL

A important development in terms of transport has been the opening of the Channel Tunnel (Eurotunnel) which provides an alternative for producers who would normally send goods from Britain to France by sea. Below is a diagram of the Tunnel.

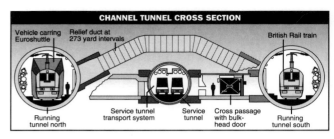

CHANNEL TUNNEL CROSS SECTION

Vehicle carring Euroshuttle — Relief duct at 273 yard intervals — British Rail train — Running tunnel north — Service tunnel transport system — Service tunnel — Cross passage with bulk-head door — Running tunnel south

FIG. 1.8 CHANNEL TUNNEL CROSS-SECTION
SOURCE: DAILY TELEGRAPH 11/12/93

Distribution

Distribution is the way the producer decides to bring the finished product to the consumer. The aim is to make the product more accessible (easier to buy) than that of the competition. Producers have a choice of a number of different channels of distribution (see Figure 1.9).

1 The product is sold directly to the consumer cutting out any 'middlemen'. For example, Freemans mail-order catalogue.
2 Many retailers, for example Sainsburys, now buy directly from producers. This cuts out the costs of dealing with wholesalers.
3 Products can be sold to a wholesaler for resale to customers in smaller quantities, for example at a cash and carry.
4 The manufacturer is responsible for delivering the goods to the customer. The agent does not hold any stock but sells the goods for the manufacturer and takes a commission for doing so.
5 Producers sometimes sell to specialists who will then sell on to the consumer. Examples are Billingsgate Fish Market, Smithfield Meat Market, and the Tea Auction Room at Plantation House which specialises in tea and coffee.

Trading (or buying) in the specialist markets is often carried out in unusual ways. Some of these are listed below, see if you can find out what they mean.

- auctions
- 'spot' markets
- ring trading
- 'sights' markets
- 'futures' markets

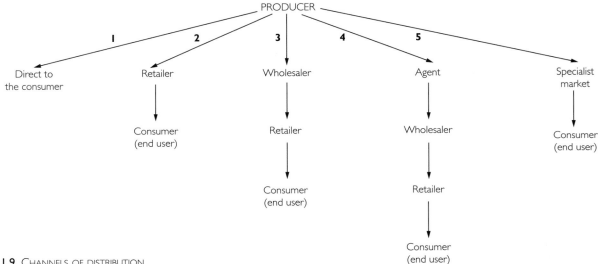

FIG. 1.9 CHANNELS OF DISTRIBUTION

Retail

Retailers are concerned with selling goods to customers. There are a number of different types of retailer:

1 *Supermarkets*, for example Sainsbury's, Tesco, Safeway. A relatively new, more cost effective form of supermarket is also emerging in this country: organisations such as Netto and Aldi are setting up large stores and keeping their prices low by cutting out glamorous packaging, fancy displays or selling well known brands.
2 *Department stores*, for example Debenhams, Marks & Spencer, British Home Stores.
3 *Independent Retailers* – these tend to be small and often sole traders, for example a local corner shop.
4 *Multiple stores* – these are groups of shops which specialise in particular types of products, for example Currys and Burtons.
5 *Co-operative retail societies* – see p.3.
6 *Franchise agents* – see p.3.
7 *Mail order (local commission agents)* – mail order companies act a bit like a department store, selling well known names. Sales are often helped by local commission agents who receive a percentage of the value of the sale for persuading or influencing a member of the public to make an order.
8 *Shopping centres*, for example Meadowhall and the Metro Centre.
9 *Hypermarkets* – these are very large supermarkets usually based away from the town with extensive parking facilities. They are self-service and sell a wide range of goods. An example is Asda.

Wholesale

The wholesalers act as a link between the producer and the retailer and have the following functions:

- they can hold stocks of different goods in one place – this means that the producer (or manufacturer) can deliver to one place rather than to lots of separate retailers
- the wholesalers split the goods into smaller quantities to sell on to retailers
- they advise retailers about the demand for products
- they can provide credit for the retailers

EXAMINE BUSINESS LOCATION, ENVIRONMENT, MARKETS AND PRODUCTS

REASONS FOR LOCATION

When a business organisation decides to set up, a number of factors will influence its location:

- *transport costs* – are local transport facilities cheap and nearby?
- *power supplies* – are the necessary power supplies accessible?
- *land* – is it cheap and suitable?
- *labour* – does the area contain people with the necessary skills?
- *economies of scale* – see p.9.
- *inertia* – are specific types of industry located in the area, e.g. steel in Sheffield, mining in South Yorkshire?
- *government grants* – is financial support available from the government or the European Union as an incentive to set up in the area?
- *proximity of local services/facilities* – are there enough of them and are they nearby?
- *access to customers* – are potential customers nearby?
- *special factors* – is the climate suitable? (e.g. tropical fruits can only be grown in a hot climate)
- *personal factors* – is everybody mobile i.e. are they able to move to a different part of the country to work?
- *proximity of other businesses* – where is the competition located and are suppliers accessible?

A C T I V I T Y

Below is a list of business organisations. Where do you think each is likely to locate and why?

- supermarket
- steelworks
- clothes manufacturer
- newsagent

INFLUENCES ON THE BUSINESS ENVIRONMENT

Competition

Businesses do not operate in isolation; very rarely will they be the only business producing a product for a particular market. In competitive markets a business needs to make sure that its product stands out from the rest in terms of its quality, style or value for money. It is essential for a business to be aware of the activities of competitors and to try and stay one step ahead of them.

Legislation

Legislation is an external influence which has to be taken into consideration. Laws which affect business can be either national or European and are constantly being updated. It is the duty of businesses to be aware of legislation and to implement it correctly. Areas of the law which affect businesses include health and safety, consumer protection, environmental protection and employees' rights.

A C T I V I T Y

Which areas of the law do you think might affect the following businesses?

- a toy manufacturer
- a large restaurant
- a hot-dog seller
- a pig farmer

Some specific laws are discussed in Chapter 2, 'People in Business Organisations' on pp.42–43, and in Chapter 3, 'Consumers and Customers' on pp.69–70.

Environmental influences and public pressure

In recent years concern for the natural environment has grown and businesses have had to respond to this concern. Pressure has come from consumers either individually or as members of groups: pressure groups such as Greenpeace. Pressure groups consist of individuals who join together in support of a common cause. An increasing number of environmental pressure groups have been created over recent years. They have put pressure on the government to introduce legislation, such as the creation of the Environmental

Protection Act, and on businesses to improve working practices. Businesses have addressed these concerns by reviewing and reducing their pollution levels, for example levels of waste or noise.

A C T I V I T Y

Greenpeace is an example of a pressure group. Do you know of any more pressure groups who support environmental issues? Make a list including details of specific areas in which they are interested.

MARKETS

A market consists of the individuals and organisation who are or may be (i.e. potential) customers for a product or service.

Types of markets

A single product or service may be purchased by many different people or organisations. The two major markets are:

1 *Consumer markets* – individuals or groups of individuals who buy products or services for their own personal use and satisfaction.
2 *User markets* – individuals or groups who buy products or services to use in the process of producing another product or service.

Taking baked beans as an example, the consumers buy them in small tins to eat as a snack or as an accompaniment to meals. The users consist of:

a café and restaurant, canteen and hotel owners, who buy beans in large containers to serve with meals; and
b shop owners who buy large quantities of beans to resell to the general public.

Domestic and international markets

It is important to remember that businesses might find markets outside the country in which they operate. We would call the UK our domestic market and any other country an international market, for example Germany or the USA.

Total market and market share

Today there are many competitive markets where a number of companies are selling the same type of goods to the small customers, for example if you wish to buy an iron you could choose from Morphy Richards, Tefal or Rowenta. If you were to add all the money from sales of all of the businesses selling irons together you would end up with the total market value for that product.

Market share is each company's sales in relation to the total market value, for example if Tefal's sales come to £40 million per year and the total market value for irons per year is £100,000 million, then Tefal has 40 per cent market share. Market share is discussed in more detail on pp.7 –8.

DEMAND

Needs and wants

Business organisations have to be aware of the important difference between the goods and services people need, i.e. those which are essential, and the ones they want, i.e. those which are non-essential.

The process organisations use to identify customers (or markets) and respond to their needs and wants is called marketing.

Many organisations will draw up a marketing plan which should include four key elements.

1 *Product.* What are existing products for? Who are the competitors? What products and services are planned for the future?
2 *Place.* Which distribution channel will be used both now and in the future?
3 *Promotion.* What methods will be used to communicate information about the products/services to the consumer?
4 *Price.* What will be the cost to the customer?

These four elements are also know as 'the four Ps'.

A C T I V I T Y

Think about your own life. Make a list of five things you need to live, in other words things that are essential to your existence. Compare your needs with those of your friends.

ACTIVITY

Below is a list of suppliers of goods and services. Decide whether each one caters for people's needs or wants.

- hospital
- social services
- leisure centre
- builder
- toy shop
- farmer
- department store

MARKET RESEARCH

This is the way businesses find out about:

- customer needs and wants
- opinions and attitudes towards products or services
- vital information for products developments
- 'gaps' in the market for new products to fill

The most common method of market research is the questionnaire.

Market research is discussed in more detail in Chapter 3 'Consumers and customers' on pp.72–5.

Factors affecting demand

Demand can only be created if certain conditions exist. People must not only wish to buy products they must have the ability to buy, for example a teenager may wish to have his or her own car, but may not be able to afford to buy one. In addition, the purchaser must also have the authority to buy the product. A 15-year-old may wish to buy a bottle of cider and have enough money to do so, but does not have the authority as is is illegal for anyone under the age of 16 to buy alcohol.

Demand is created by the purchasers of a product, the customers, or those who use the product, the consumers. For example, children may pester their parents to buy a certain brand of cereal or toy thus creating demand from consumers. Pressure from the 'green movement' has meant that many businesses have changed their products to make them more environmentally friendly. For example, many cosmetics companies no longer test their products on animals.

Trends and fashions can also influence demand: the popularity of the recent film, *The Lion King*, created a sudden demand for 'Lion King' merchandise.

ACTIVITY

Food health scares, for example salmonella in eggs, can severely affect demand. What would be the impact on demand for pork following an outbreak of pig disease in the south of England?

PRODUCTS

Consumables

These are the products that people buy on a regular basis and use fairly quickly. Examples are food, drink, newspapers, stationery and toilet paper.

Durables

These are products that people tend to buy less frequently and which will last for a longer period of time, for example CD players, cars, TVs and lawn mowers. They are usually more expensive than consumables.

ACTIVITY

Below is a list of products. Which are consumables and which are durables?

- pickled onions
- a lightshade
- long-life milk
- a bunch of flowers
- a textbook
- a chest of drawers
- a tube of toothpaste

Goods and services

People sometimes use the word 'product' to mean either a physical good or a service. A good is something tangible, something you can touch, hear, see, smell or taste, for example a can of baked beans. You can buy a good and use it later. Goods tend to be mass produced and each type of good is normally identical to another of the same type. A business can store goods to sell at any date. When a customer buys a good they then own it. With services you do not gain ownership following the delivery of a service, you normally buy and consume the service at the same time, for example having a haircut. You cannot see, taste, touch, smell or hear services. As services tend to involve staff delivering the service, the standard may differ each time.

Who buys products?

There are all sorts of purchasers, for example industrial consumers, governments and business organisations. Please refer to 'Characteristics and importance of consumers' on pp.56–60 of Chapter 3, 'Consumers and customers'.

Product development

Businesses need to undertake a number of different activities in order to assist with the development of their products. As discussed on p.56, they need to carry out market research. Other activities will include:

- *Design.* This will involve making sure the product meets customer requirements. It could involve the technical design or the look and image of the product, its style, packaging and brand.
- *Production.* This involves manufacturing the product to the specification of the designers, that it is durable, of a high quality and is produced cost effectively and efficiently.
- *Marketing communications.* Getting your message across to your customers is vital if your business is to be successful. There are a number of different ways of communicating with your customers, the most common being advertising (this could be TV, radio or press), sales promotion methods (special offers such as 'Buy one, get one free' or competitions), sponsorship, for example Walkers Crisps sponsor Leicester City, or sales literature such as brochures or leaflets. (Marketing communications are discussed in more detail in Chapter 8, 'Promotion, sales and the media'.)

- *Sales.* In competitive industries it is important for a business to gain a good sales advantage over competitors, and businesses often actively sell using sales representatives. Effective selling is essential for the product to reach the appropriate customer. Selling is most commonly seen in retail outlets, for example Debenhams or River Island.
- *After sales service.* This is very important as once a customer has bought a product, the business hopes the customer will purchase from them again. To ensure this businesses offer guarantees, good refund policies and feedback questionnaires.

New products

The sales of many products will eventually decline. Organisations need to be innovative and identify new products or services with which to replace them. They should also be responsive to the changing needs and wants of consumers and alter existing products or develop new products accordingly. For example, many items of clothing are fashionable for a short period of time, but after a while clothes manufacturers have to produce new designs as tastes and fashions change. Alternatively, a CD player manufacturer may have to adapt its product to cater for the changing demand for personal CD players.

A C T I V I T Y

Make a list of new products or services which may be provided as a result of the following factors:

- increasing concern for the environment
- fashion for 1960s clothing
- fashion for healthy eating

PRESENT RESULTS OF INVESTIGATION INTO EMPLOYMENT

TYPES OF EMPLOYMENT

Part-time employees

Part-timers tend to be employed to carry out tasks which require a limited number of hours to complete, for example, cleaners. They may be employed to cater for busy periods, for example in shops on a Saturday, and are attractive to employ as businesses do not normally pay them overtime rates. Some employers may offer part-time hours to valued staff who no longer wish to continue working on a full-time basis. Part-time employees are often flexible in terms of the hours they are prepared to work and some take part in 'job shares' where, for example, two part-time staff together work the equivalent of one full-time job. Many people prefer to work in this way as it increases their leisure time.

Full-time employees

Full-timers work regular hours and receive a wage or salary. They can claim unemployment benefit and statutory sick pay (if National Insurance contributions have been made). National Insurance and income tax is deducted by the employer. Full-time employees are protected under the Employment Protection (consolidation) Act and their jobs are often more secure than part-time work. However, full-timers work longer hours than part-time staff.

Temporary employees

These are staff employed on a temporary basis usually to cover for holidays or illness, or to deal with specialist or one-off tasks. For example, an administrator may be employed on a temporary basis to set up a new filing system in an office. Temporary employees are sometimes referred to as 'temps' and are normally provided by employment agencies. Seasonal workers are employed at certain times of the year. For example, extra staff are recruited to work in department stores over the Christmas period. Casual workers tend to be employed on a day-to-day basis subject to demand.

Permanent employees

A permanent employee has a commitment from his or her employer to continued employment. This gives the employee a sense of job security which will not be experienced by temporary/casual employees and often not by part-time workers either.

Self-employed workers

These are people who work for themselves. They often hire out their services to or are given work by companies, for example builders and window cleaners. Being self-employed can mean greater independence and flexibility, but there is a high risk involved as a self-employed person is responsible for all his or her debts. Self-employed people are usually unable to claim unemployment benefit or statutory sick pay and have no protection under the Employment Protection (Consolidation) Act.

Skilled workers

These are people who have trained for a particular craft, trade or occupation. In the past they may have served an apprenticeship, but today they are more likely to be working towards achieving a national vocational qualification through their work (this includes the Modern Apprentice Scheme). They will display a wide range of skills and competences. Examples of skilled workers are hairdressers, electricians and plumbers.

Unskilled workers

These workers tend to be involved in repetitive work and are often closely supervised. They will have had minimal training and are likely to have few responsibilities within the workplace. Examples include labourers and cleaning staff.

A C T I V I T Y

Draw up a chart to compare the following:

- employed
- self-employed
- part-time staff
- full-time staff
- permanent workers
- temporary workers
- skilled workers
- unskilled workers

Include the characteristics, advantages and disadvantages of each.

COMPARING WORKING CONDITIONS

Physical working conditions

Employees are more likely to be motivated and work hard if their working conditions are pleasant and safe. Physical conditions vary significantly between occupations, industries and sectors of industry:

A C T I V I T Y

Think of three more occupations and draw a similar table to the one below to compare them in terms of physical working conditions.

HOW CAN EMPLOYERS IMPROVE PHYSICAL WORKING CONDITIONS?

1 *Lighting.* Employees will benefit from natural daylight where possible. Avoidance of glare is essential if artificial light is used. Inadequate lighting can cause eyestrain and headaches.

2 *Heating.* Employers should be aware of the minimum acceptable temperatures laid down by law. Most organisations heat buildings between October and April. Maximum output and efficiency will not be achieved if staff are too hot or cold.

3 *Noise.* Measures should be taken to keep noise levels to a minimum. Old buildings may absorb some noise but newer ones tend to reflect it. Acoustic screens and absorbent floor and wall coverings can be used as required. Equipment and machinery should be fitted with soundproofing covers where appropriate and the positioning of machinery should be carefully thought through. Noise can damage health and cause fatigue and/or a lack of concentration.

4 *Ventilation.* There must be an adequate flow of air either through windows or an air-conditioning system. Lack of air can cause tiredness and a lack of concentration.

Training

Training is the passing on of information, knowledge and skills. The benefits of having trained staff are:

- less waste and spoiled work
- less need for close supervision
- increased job satisfaction if employees know what they are doing and feel that their employer is taking an interest in their development
- employees can do other people's jobs in times of absence

On-the-job training is when an employee learns a job by actually doing it. He or she will have close supervision from other members of staff. **Off-the-job training** is when an employee is trained to do a job away from the place of work, for example attending a day release course at a local college. **'Sitting next to Nellie'** is where an employee watches another member of staff doing the job and then has a go at it themselves (with the support of 'Nellie').

	OFFICE WORKER	BUILDER	CHEF
Weather	works indoors, usually warm	works outside in all types of weather	works indoors, often hot conditions
Equipment	modern equipment and technology	heavy equipment and machinery	often heavy-duty catering equipment
Safety	generally safe working conditions	unsafe	unsafe
Clothing	smart	casual/protective (often dirty)	Chef's whites (protective clothing)
Surroundings	pleasant	dirty	hot, at times smelly

TABLE 1.2 WORKING CONDITIONS

REASONS FOR TRAINING

Organisations may need to train their staff on very specific matters:

- the introduction of new technology
- new working methods/techniques
- new legislation affecting the organisation
- health and safety issues
- induction training for new employees
- the introduction of a new product or service

Training for new employees is known as *induction*.

DESIGNING A TRAINING PROGRAMME

Training for employees should be carefully planned and will involve a number of steps.

Step 1   *Decide the aims of the training.* What do you want to achieve as a result of the training programme? For example, to ensure that all reception staff can operate the new switchboard efficiently.

Step 2   *Choose the order.* Any training programme should follow a logical sequence. For example, it is no use telling someone how to use the switchboard until they know where it is located (the length of the programme will also need to be considered).

Step 3   *Choose the learning method.* How are the trainees going to be taught or instructed? A range of methods can be used, for example lectures, videos, role plays, discussions and practical activities.

Step 4   *Choose the instructors.* Who are the most appropriate people to carry out the training? Examples of possible instructors are existing staff, guest speakers and specialists, for example health and safety representatives.

Step 5   *Choose the location.* Where will the training take place? It may be carried out 'in-house', i.e. at the organisation itself, or at an outside location, perhaps a local college. A combination of the two may also be used.

Step 6   *Draw up the programme.* Finally, when steps 1–5 have been carefully thought through the programme can be drawn up and a copy given to all trainees in advance.

Qualifications

There are a wide range of qualifications available to meet the requirements of different organisations in both the public and private sector.

School pupils now study a National Curriculum. The traditional 'academic' route through the education system leads from GCSEs to A levels to HND or degree courses at universities or further education institutes.

Design a two-day induction programme for nine new employees who are going to be working as checkout assistants for a large supermarket chain. Your programme should include the following information:

- a detailed timetable (including coffee and lunch breaks)
- details of locations, instruction and methods of delivery at each stage
- an introduction for trainees and some sort of feedback session

Try to think through the needs of new employees carefully. Remember they will need to know how to do the job and also about broader issues such as health and safety and administrative procedures.

General National Vocational Qualifications (GNVQs) aim to test understanding in general vocational areas such as business, manufacturing and caring. There are three GNVQs: Foundation, Intermediate and Advanced.

National Vocational Qualifications (NVQs) are designed to assess competence in specific vocational areas, such as administration and selling. There are five NVQs, ranging from the assessment of basic skills at level 1 to the assessment of professional and managerial skills at level 5.

These are some of the most common qualifications. However, there are many more in specialist areas. Examples relating to business include:

- The Chartered Institute of Marketing Certificate and Diploma
- The Institute of Administrative Management Certificate and Diploma
- The Chartered Institute of Bankers' Banking Certificate
- The Association of Accounting Technicians accounts qualification

People do not necessarily have to follow a single route through the education system. A person may take GCSEs and then choose to study for a GNVQ. Alternatively, a student may pass an Intermediate GNVQ and then go on to take A levels.

Some organisations will want employees to have an academic qualification, others will prefer a good knowledge of the relevant vocational area and will want their employees to possess the specific skills required for the job in question.

A C T I V I T Y

Think about a job you would like to do in the future. Visit your local careers office and find out what qualifications you would need to be able to apply for the job.

Incentives at work

An incentive is something which drives you on or **motivates** you to do something.

A C T I V I T Y

Think about your personal life and make a list of five things which motivate you. Compare your list with those of the rest of your group.

Some of you may have listed money, family or friends.

A C T I V I T Y

Now think about people at work. Make a list of some of the things which you think gives them the incentive to go to work.

Some of the incentives you may have written down are:

- a safe working environment
- the desire to help people
- the opportunity for initiative and responsibility
- the opportunity for development/promotion
- working with experts
- money
- job security

It is important that organisations are aware of the factors which motivate people at work and do all they can to encourage them.

Some employers go one step further and offer their staff additional incentives. These are known as **fringe benefits**, for example:

- company cars
- a staff canteen
- recreational facilities
- a pleasant environment – carpets, comfortable chairs, attractive surroundings
- financial incentives – bonuses, profit-sharing schemes, expenses, pension schemes
- status symbols – personal offices
- staff discounts
- luncheon vouchers
- extra holidays

A C T I V I T Y

Below is a list of occupations.

1 What do you think are the motivating factors of each?
2 What do you think are the fringe benefits of each?

- farmer
- sales representative
- business executive
- nurse
- teacher
- footballer

Paying employees

Contracts of employment are covered in Chapter 2 'People in business organisations' on p.39.

WAGES AND SALARIES

Wages are paid weekly and are usually calculated on an hourly rate. **Salaries** are calculated on an annual basis and are paid monthly.

Piece rates are wages that are calculated in terms of output, for example factory work. The work must be measurable and require minimal supervision, and workers should be able to work at their own pace.

Performance related pay recognises the contribution of an individual to an organisation. The employee may be given a bonus or pay rise as a result.

NATIONAL INSURANCE

All employees must pay national insurance contributions. These enable them to claim state benefits such as unemployment benefit, the retirement pension and statutory maternity pay. National insurance is deducted by the employer on a weekly or monthly basis and details should be recorded on an employee's payslip.

Self-employed people must also pay national insurance. They receive a quarterly bill from the Department of Social Security (or they can pay on a monthly basis by direct debit).

INCOME TAX

Income tax is paid by both employed and self-employed people. Employed people normally have the income tax deducted by their employer, who then forwards it to the Inland Revenue. The employer uses tables supplied by the Inland Revenue to calculate the amount due. The amount is worked out on the basis of the amount earned by an employee during the financial year (6 April one year to 5 April of the next). This is called 'pay as you earn' (PAYE).

VOLUNTARY DEDUCTIONS

Income tax and National Insurance are both statutory deductions, i.e. they are required by law. **Voluntary deductions** are payments which an employee *chooses* to make. These can include donations to charities, subscriptions to clubs or societies, additional pension contributions or trade union subscriptions.

A C T I V I T Y

Employees will sometimes have the opportunity to earn extra money on top of their normal wage or salary. Below are some examples – see if you can find out what each means.

- commission
- bonus payments
- expenses
- profit sharing schemes

Travelling to work

A person's working day can be dramatically affected by the time taken to travel to work, the method of transport used and the costs involved. For example, a bank worker living in Kent having to commute into the City of London every day by rail would have to spend a couple of hours travelling each day, and have to bear the cost of an expensive rail pass. A bank worker living and working in a small market town, however, might be able to walk to work and would therefore spend less time travelling each day and incur no travelling expenses.

Hours of work

Working hours will vary from job to job. Normal office hours usually run from 9 am to 5 pm. However, some people may have to work shifts. For example, a factory worker may start work at 6 am and finish at 2 pm, or work from 2 until 10 pm. This means that the factory can continue production for 16 hours per day. Some businesses have introduced a scheme called 'flexi-time'. This means that workers can choose their working hours to a certain extent. For example, a council worker who is required to work an eight-hour day may be able to choose to start work between 8 and 9.30 am. He or she may also be able to choose to finish work between 5 and 6.30 pm as long as he or she works a minimum of eight hours. Sometimes workers are allowed to work extra hours to build up and take as time off at a later date.

TECHNOLOGY

Impact on employment

The increasing use of **computers** and more sophisticated machinery has meant that there has been a reduction in the number of employees required to make products or perform certain tasks. In other works, they have been replaced by technology. This has caused an increase in the number of people who are unemployed in the country. Lots of different types of organisations are affected in this way. For example, banks have introduced computers to perform many of the tasks traditionally carried out by employees.

Technology has also meant that some jobs have been created. For example, in the computer industry people are needed for research and development. Staff are now required to operate the technology, sort out technical problems and queries and train other members of staff.

For many people technology has meant that the nature of their jobs has changed significantly. Look at the case study below.

DE-SKILLING

Because technology has replaced many of the functions originally performed by humans many staff no longer

C A S E S T U D Y

Sally has worked as a bank clerk for 15 years. When she joined the bank she spent a large proportion of her time filling in forms and documents. These were then filed manually. Today she is able to enter most of the information onto a computer (instead of filling in forms). The information can be stored on the computer. The bank has cash machines which reduces Sally's workload as many customers do not even need to come into the bank. The machines produce instant balances and statements.

A C T I V I T Y

What do you think are the advantages and disadvantages for Sally of the introduction of new technology into the bank?

Can you think of any other jobs which may have been affected significantly by the introduction of new technology?

---

need to be trained to the same levels; instead they are simply required to operate and maintain the technology. For example, in the engineering industry many skilled people are no longer required as their jobs can largely be carried out by technology.

New technology

The advent of new technology has created new **demands and wants**. Examples are video games and home computers. Business organisations have to take note of this and develop production accordingly.

Robots have been developed to perform many tasks. They can carry out such tasks as welding and loading and jobs that are dangerous or dirty. Robots are time saving but they can also be costly.

Telecommunciations are covered in Chapter 6 Business communications' on p.142.

A C T I V I T Y

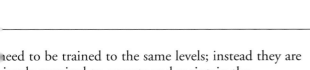

Make a list of:

1 The technology used at your school or college.
2 Any technology you have in your home.

Below is a list of terms associated with technology. See if you can find out what they mean:

- information processing
- CAD
- CIM
- CAM

REGIONAL DIFFERENCES

The number of people in employment varies in different parts of the country. Those people who are unable to obtain jobs are called unemployed. There are several types of unemployment:

1 *Frictional*. This includes people who are seeking their first job or who are between jobs.
2 *Seasonal*. This includes people who are unemployed because their skills are only required at certain times of the year, for example Father Christmases and ice-cream sellers.
3 *Structural*. This includes people who have become unemployed due to the long-term decline in a major industry in their area, for example the coal mines.
4 *Cyclical*. This is mass unemployment caused by a lack of demand in the economy and occurs in virtually every country.
5 *Technological*. This includes people who have become unemployed as a result of technological developments.

Regional policy and investment

This aims to reduce the difference between unemployment rates in different areas of the country. Regional policy can take a number of forms:

1 Taking the work to the workers. For example, the government can set up its own departments in areas of high unemployment.
2 The government can force firms to move to areas of high unemployment if they wish to expand by asking them to apply for an Industrial Development Certificate.

3 Incentives can be given to a firm to relocate or set up in areas of high unemployment, for example reducing a firm's costs by charging lower rents or offering tax concessions.

4 The Department of Trade and Industry offers some grants to encourage firms to set up in 'assisted' or urban-programme areas.

5 The Department of the Environment also offers some grants (particularly in inner-city areas).

6 The European Union tries to help regions through the Regional Development Fund and the European Social Fund.

7 Urban development agencies are organisations which have been set up by the governments to co-ordinate and administer the issuing of regional grants.

8 Local Training and Enterprise Councils (TECs) run the Enterprise Allowance scheme to encourage new small businesses to set up in an area.

9 Some local authorities offer their own small business or enterprise grants to encourage business development in an area.

Table 1.3 shows some statistics on regional unemployment by for the years 1992/93, produced by the Department of Employment.

Reasons for regional differences

Some areas of the country are more prosperous than others and can create more job opportunities. For example, London is a large city with many major industries and good access to airports.

	September 1993	% change from August 1993	% change fro September 199
South East	458,500	− 0.3	4.1
East Anglia	83,500	− 0.7	3.6
London	471,300	0	6.0
South West	215,500	− 0.6	− 0.3
West Midlands	280,600	− 0.6	1.9
East Midlands	183,600	− 0.1	3.1
Yorkshire and Humberside	243,400	− 0.7	1.4
North West	320,700	− 0.7	−1.8
Northern	170,800	− 0.2	7.4
Wales	131,800	− 0.5	1.8
Scotland	243,400	−1.0	0.3
Great Britain	**2,802,900**	**− 0.5**	**2.6**

SOURCE: DEPARTMENT OF EMPLOYMEN

TABLE 1.3 UNEMPLOYMENT BY REGION 1992/93

OCCUPATIONAL IMMOBILITY

This is the inability of labour to move from one job to another. This may be due to a lack of skills, training or confidence.

GEOGRAPHICAL IMMOBILITY

This is the inability of labour to move from one area to another. There may be unemployment in one area but jobs available in another. People may be unable or unwilling to move.

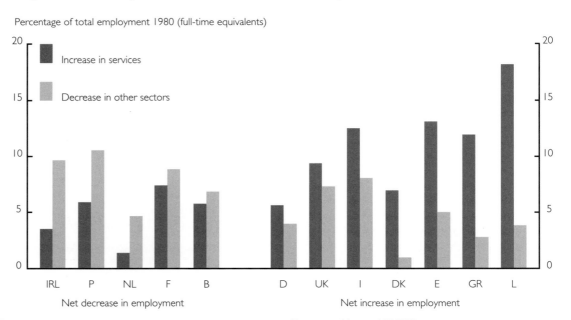

FIG. 1.10 CHANGES IN EMPLOYMENT IN SERVICES AND OTHER SECTORS IN THE EUROPEAN UNION 1980/89
NB FIGURES DO NOT INCLUDE 1995 ENTRANTS TO THE EU – FINLAND, AUSTRIA AND SWEDEN
SOURCE: EUROSTA

NATURAL RESOURCES

Employment in an area can be affected by the availability of natural resources which can create jobs. For example, the coal industry is traditionally associated with areas such as South Yorkshire. Grimsby is associated with the fishing industry.

ANALYSING EMPLOYMENT INFORMATION

There are a number of sources of statistical information about employment, for example *Social Trends*, published by the Central Statistical Office. General statistical information can be broken down to highlight specific employment patterns. Examples of current statistical information are shown in Fig. 1.10.

Recently, there has been a trend away from employment in the manufacturing sector and into the service sector. This is true for the UK and Europe as a whole. Fig. 1.10 illustrates this.

The chart in Table 1.4 gives a breakdown of the UK's active population (all individuals who are either working or seeking work). The chart also examines activity in terms of age, gender and ethnic group. For example, the statistics tell us that 67 per cent of white females aged 16–24 are either working or seeking work, compared to 35 per cent of Pakistani/Bangladeshi females of the same age.

The figures in Table 1.5 overleaf give a breakdown of employment in different regions of the country (including types of employment). For example, the statistics tell us that in the UK as a whole 17.3 per cent of the labour force are employed in manufacturing and

53.9 per cent work in the service sector. In comparison, the region of Greater London has only 9.5 per cent of its labour force employed in manufacturing, yet 60.7 per cent are employed in the service sector.

A C T I V I T Y

For Tables 1.4 and 1.5 represent one piece of information in a different format using a computer.

A C T I V I T Y

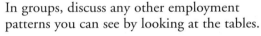

In groups, discuss any other employment patterns you can see by looking at the tables.

| | Males | | | Females | | Percentages |
	16–24	25–44	45–64	16–24	25–44	45–59
White	77	95	79	67	75	70
Black[1]	62	86	77	51	71	72
Indian	55	93	76	51	69	53
Pakistani/Bangladeshi	57	92	63	35	24	:
Other[2]	45	82	80	34	57	54
All ethnic groups[3]	75	94	79	65	74	70

1 Includes Caribbean, African and other Black people of non-mixed origin

2 Includes Chinese, other ethnic minority groups of non-mixed origin and people of mixed origin

3 Includes ethnic group not stated

SOURCE: EMPLOYMENT DEPARTMENT

TABLE 1.4 POPULATION OF WORKING AGE ECONOMIC ACTIVITY RATES IN GREAT BRITAIN; BY ETHNIC GROUP, GENDER AND AGE, SPRING 1994

	Manufacturing employees	Service employees	Other employees	Percentages Self employed
United Kingdom	17.3	53.9	5.9	11.3
North	17.0	52.3	8.5	8.7
Yorkshire & Humberside	20.9	50.9	6.5	10.0
East Midlands	24.8	48.9	5.9	10.2
East Anglia	16.9	53.3	7.0	13.1
South East	13.1	58.8	4.5	12.4
Greater London	9.5	60.7	3.4	12.1
Rest of South East	15.4	57.6	5.2	12.6
South West	15.2	54.5	5.2	14.9
West Midlands	24.2	47.1	5.2	10.5
North West	19.3	52.6	5.5	10.2
England	17.5	54.1	5.5	11.5
Wales	19.0	51.4	6.8	11.9
Scotland	15.6	54.3	9.5	8.9
Northern Ireland	15.2	52.0	5.7	11.2

SOURCE: LABOUR FORCE SURVEY, EMPLOYMENT DEPARTMENT; DEPARTMENT OF ECONOMIC DEVELOPMENT, NORTHERN IRELAND

TABLE 1.5 THE LABOUR FORCE, SPRING 1993

AVAILABILITY OF WORK

Searching for a job

The most common methods people use to look for work are as follows:

- job centres
- situations vacant columns in newspapers
- advertisements in local papers or journals

A C T I V I T Y

Visit your local job centre and find out what services it offers for people seeking employment. Prepare a leaflet about the services. Your leaflet should be produced using information technology.

- through personal contacts (i.e. word of mouth)
- letters and telephone calls to organisations
- private agencies

Changing patterns of employment

- The rise of the tertiary sector has meant that more and more people are being employed in service organisations.
- There has been a rise in the number of part-time workers.
- There are an increased number of women in the workforce. Women now have higher career expectations and often return to work shortly after having a child (or children).
- Many organisations have introduced flexible working hours or 'flexi-time' so that employees have an element of choice about the hours they work.
- Job sharing is becoming quite common in a number of occupational areas.
- Increased technology has altered the nature of many jobs.
- Some organisations close early on a Friday and ask employees to work longer hours on the other days of the week.

THE FUTURE

It is unlikely that there will be a dramatic increase in the number of jobs available in the future. It is likely therefore that the pattern of employment will change even more. There will be more part-time workers, an increased number of job shares and the possibility of a shorter working week (which would mean more leisure time for people and could create more jobs in the leisure industry).

CHAPTER ONE

Test Yourself!

1 State two advantages of being a sole trader.
2 State two disadvantages of a partnership.
3 True or false? A public corporation is part of the public sector.
4 What do the initials PLC stand for?
5 What is a multinational organisation?
6 List three services provided by local government?
7 What is meant by the term 'privatisation'?
8 Write an explanation for each of the following sectors of industry:
  ■ primary
  ■ secondary
  ■ tertiary
9 List three factors which may influence a business when deciding where to locate.

10 What is an SME?
11 True or false? A bank is an example of a service organisation.
12 What is a skilled worker?
13 Explain what is meant by the term flexi-time.
14 What is a market?
15 State three differences between full-time and part-time employees.
16 What is 'on-the-job' training?
17 What does NVQ stand for?
18 True or false? Wages are paid on a monthly basis.
19 What is meant by the term 'de-skilling'?
20 Explain two ways in which technology has affected levels of employment.

CHAPTER ONE

Evidence-Gathering Projects

1 Explain the purposes and types of business organisation.

  i Select seven organisations (some local and some national; at least one public sector organisation and at least one organisation from each of the primary, secondary and tertiary sectors of industry) and complete the chart on the following page (Table 1.6).

  ii On your chart you will have identified different types of business ownership. Make a list of three differences between each type of ownership and explain each point on the list.

  iii Pick one of the organisations on your chart and write a paragraph to explain each of the following:

  ■ the reasons for the type of ownership

  ■ the reasons for its location
  ■ details of its product
  ■ the links you think it might have with other businesses

  iv Select three organisations from your chart, one from the primary sector, one from the secondary sector and one from the tertiary sector. Find some statistics which show how employment has increased or decreased in each of the industrial sectors. Write a paragraph to describe how the changes might have affected each of the three organisations. *Social Trends* and *Regional Trends* are useful sources of information. Both are published by the Central Statistical Office.

2 Examine business location, environment, markets and products.

Select three business organisations and complete the following tasks:

i State the name, address, type of business and type of product manufactured by each organisation. State whether the product is consumable or durable.

ii For each organisation write a paragraph to explain the following:

  a the likely external influences on the business
  b reasons for location

iii Describe the different markets/customers the product of each organisation is likely to have.

iv Suggest a new product each of the three organisations could introduce to meet the needs of the identified markets/customers in iii) above.

v Suggests a change that could be made to an existing product to increase its demand.

vi Select one of the new products you have suggested and design a questionnaire which the organisation could ask potential customers to complete to find out whether or not there would be a demand for the product.

vii Write a paragraph to explain activities one of the businesses could undertake to improve its market position.

3 Investigate the UK employment market.

In groups of two or three prepare a 10-minute presentation to include the following:

i A description of different types of employment.

ii An outline of the features of employment.

iii A comparison of levels of employment locally and in another region, including possible reasons for differences between the regions. (You should include visual information in your comparison.)

iv An explanation of the effects of technology on physical working conditions and levels of employment.

TABLE 1.0

	ORGANISATION 1	ORGANISATION 2	ORGANISATION 3	ORGANISATION 4	ORGANISATION 5	ORGANISATION 6	ORGANISATION 7
Name							
Large, medium or small							
Public or private sector							
Type of business ownership, e.g. sole trader, partnership							
Sector of industry							
Explanation of purposes							
Details of location							

Chapter

2

PEOPLE IN BUSINESS ORGANISATIONS

> This chapter examines organisational structures and working arrangements. It investigates the rights and responsibilities of employers and employees, and gives you the opportunity to investigate different job roles and also to assess your own skills in preparation for employment or self-employment.

EXAMINE AND COMPARE STRUCTURES AND WORKING ARRANGEMENTS IN ORGANISATIONS

ORGANISATIONAL STRUCTURES

Organisations vary in their structure for a number of different reasons. Organisations produce different products and services. Some may be large with many staff, others may be much smaller. Some may perform a few different tasks while others may perform many. Some may operate 24 hours a day, others on a 9–5 basis.

A C T I V I T Y

Can you think of any more variations?

There are two main types of organisational structure.

Tall structure (hierarchical)

A tall structure is a hierarchical one which means that there are lots of different levels. People have clearly laid out responsibilities and there is little delegation (passing on of responsibilities from the top).

ADVANTAGES

- more opportunity for promotion, therefore morale can be high
- encourages close control and co-ordination of activities
- roles and responsibilities are clearly defined

DISADVANTAGES

- it can take time to pass on information (red tape and bureaucracy)

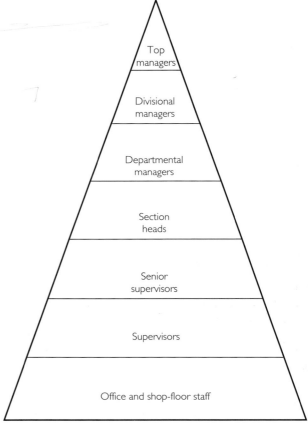

FIG. 2.1 A TALL STRUCTURE

- high costs
- there tends to be more rigid supervision and control, i.e. lots of rules and procedures
- decision-making can be slow
- communication often breaks down

Flat structure

This structure is less hierarchical so there are fewer levels. There tends to be more delegation. In other words, responsibilities are passed down from the top.

FIG. 2.2 A FLAT STRUCTURE

ADVANTAGES

- a quicker and easier passage of information
- less 'red tape'
- less rigid supervision and control
- more sharing of decisions
- better communication

DISADVANTAGES

- fewer career paths/opportunities for promotion therefore morale could be low
- people's roles and responsibilities are not always clear

Matrix structure

Within this structure individuals usually report to a manager in their own department. For example, someone working in market research might report to the market research manager or a person working in purchasing might report to the purchasing manager. Occasionally businesses will set up project teams under project leaders. The project teams will be made up of individuals from each department. For example, if a business needs a project team to develop and launch a new product the team might have an engineer, a marketing person, an accountant, a salesperson and a production worker. All of the team will report to the project manager, at the same time reporting to the managers in their own departments. Once the project is completed they will return to their normal jobs.

Common features

The structure of an organisation will be influenced by the function it performs, i.e. what it does. Because of this no two organisations will be the same. There are however, some common features between most structures:

- A hierarchy – different levels with a chain of command.
- A division into outlets, areas, departments or functions.
- Managers.
- Employees.
- A span of control – this means a number of people who are accountable or answerable to one person.
- Line relationships - these are the relationships which take place between a senior person and the person directly below them (their subordinate). This relationship can take place at any level of the organisation.
- Lateral relationships – these are the relationships which take place between members of staff working at the same level within the organisation. For example, the relationship between a production manager and sales manager.
- Functional relationships – these are between people holding specialist (or functional) positions and people with direct executive responsibilities.
- Staff relationships – an example here is the relationship between a manager and his or her personal assistant who will not have a direct working relationship with other employees or departments.
- Informal relationships – staff build up informal systems for communicating with one another and passing on information. An example here may be a discussion between a sales assistant and a production worker.

Types of organisation

Tall and flat organisations can be broken down further into different structures based around the type of organisation.

FUNCTIONALLY BASED ORGANISATIONS

In this case the organisation is structured around the different functions it requires to sell its product or service (see Figure 2.3 overleaf).

MARKET-BASED ORGANISATIONS

This sort of structure will apply to an organisation producing a range of products or services. The company will set up subsidiaries to cater for the relevant customers for each product (see Figure 2.4 overleaf).

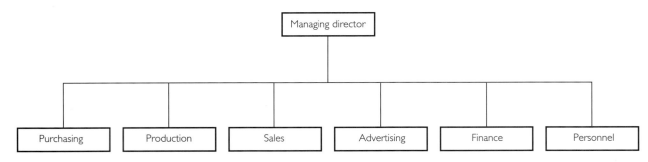

FIG. 2.3 FUNCTIONALLY BASED ORGANISATIONS

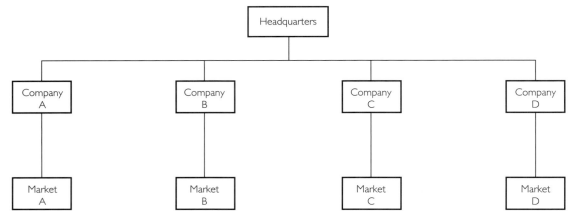

FIG. 2.4 MARKET-BASED ORGANISATIONS

GEOGRAPHICALLY BASED ORGANISATIONS

This is when an organisation has similar outlets in different parts of the country (see Figure 2.5).

PRODUCT-BASED ORGANISATIONS

Here the organisation is structured around the product being manufactured (as the company produces more than one product). Each company will have its own departmental functions, e.g. accounts and sales (see Figure 2.6 opposite).

Organisation charts

An organisation chart is the way the structure of a business can be shown visually.

Why do we need organisation charts?

- to show roles and responsibilities
- to show the chain of command i.e. who is responsible to whom

FIG. 2.5 GEOGRAPHICALLY BASED ORGANISATIONS

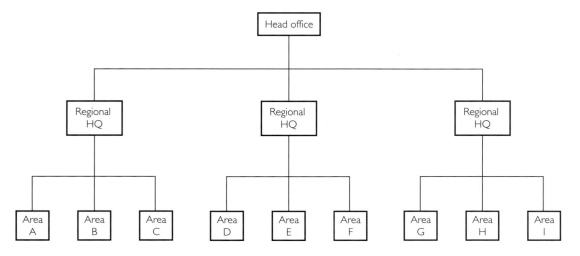

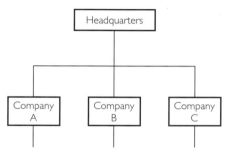

FIG. 2.6 PRODUCT-BASED ORGANISATIONS

- to indicate the span of control
- to provide an overview of the whole organisation

VERTICAL OR 'T' CHARTS

These are the most traditional method of presenting the structure of an organisation (see Figure 2.7).

HORIZONTAL CHARTS

These are charts which are read from left to right (see Figure 2.8).

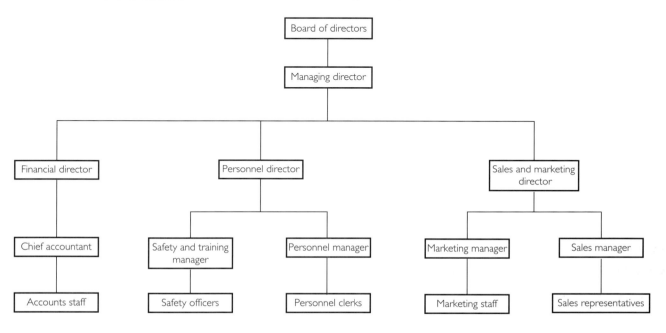

FIG. 2.7 A VERTICAL OR 'T' CHART

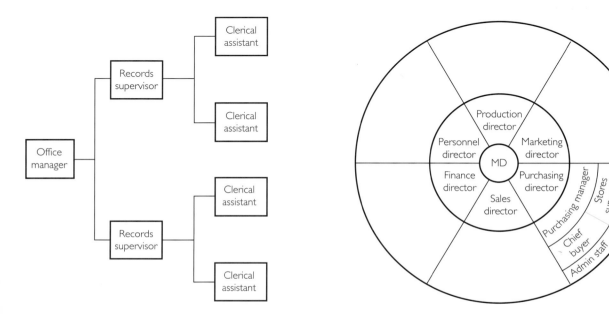

FIG. 2.8 A HORIZONTAL CHART

FIG. 2.9 A CONCENTRIC ORGANISATION CHART

CONCENTRIC CHARTS

These are circular charts which are read from the centre outwards. The most important positions within the organisation are placed close to the centre (see Figure 2.9 on the previous page).

HOW TO INTERPRET ORGANISATION CHARTS

———————— A continuous line shows formal relationships

– – – – – – – Broken lines indicate informal (functional) relationships (see Figure 2.10).

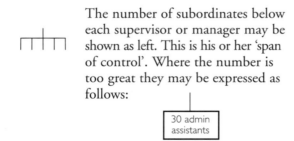

FIG. 2.10 ORGANISATION CHART SHOWING FUNCTIONAL RELATIONSHIPS

The number of subordinates below each supervisor or manager may be shown as left. This is his or her 'span of control'. Where the number is too great they may be expressed as follows:

30 admin assistants

Departments' functions or positions within an organisation are often expressed within a box.

Below is an example of a basic organisation chart. From the basic structure we can tell that:

- the organisation has a hierarchy
- there are two levels of management
- there are three functional areas, outlets or departments
- there are 19 employees, including four managers
- the span of control of each manager is five employees

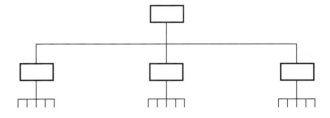

FIG. 2.11 A BASIC ORGANISATION CHART

A C T I V I T Y

Below is a second example of an organisation chart. Write down what it tells you about the business

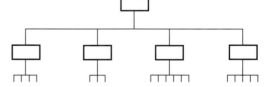

A C T I V I T Y

Mr and Mrs Hill buy an antiques shop in Birmingham. It takes some time to get the business off the ground but after a while they find they are doing really well and decide to take on two sales assistants, Janice and Paul.

Task 1   Draw a horizontal chart to show the structure of the organisation once the sales assistants have been taken on.

After 18 months the business is doing really well and the Hills decide to open three additional shops in Manchester, Leeds and Liverpool. They employ someone to manage each shop, two sales assistants to run the Leeds and Liverpool shops and three for the Manchester shop (one full-time and two part-time operating on a job-share scheme).

Task 2 Draw horizontal charts to show:

1 The whole business.
2 The individual structure of each shop.

Create your own organisation. Explain how it develops over a number of years, drawing organisation charts as you go along.

Below is an article about the changing structure of some business organisations. Read it carefully and then answer the following questions:

1 Why have some companies cut down on the number of middle managers they employ?
2 Why are there now fewer chances for promotion in these organisations?
3 Explain what is meant by 'flatter company structures' referred to in the article.

Shrinking role of the middle ranks

By Hugh Muir

DOWNSIZING is the process haunting middle managers today. As companies have responded to recession and taken advantage of technology, traditional middle managers have seen their prospects fade, perks eroded and roles marginalised.

Middle managers have learned that, when strategists talk of "flatter company structures", the tier of authority threatened is usually theirs.

Increasingly, they see the power and responsibility they once wielded handed down to teams of junior employees, who largely monitor themselves in accordance with targets set by senior managers.

It seems an inexorable slide. As the middle manager's role diminishes, so does their value and the need for cost-conscious firms to cosset them with perks.

The executive dining room may not be extinct but sightings are now rare and, with changes in taxation, the company car has lost its shine.

Thousands of middle managers have lost their jobs, a tragedy not only for them but also for colleagues who have to work harder to fill the gaps.

Fewer layers of authority means less chance for promotion. Indeed, one leading industrialist has predicted that,

for many middle managers, the chance of advancement may only occur once in a decade.

Mr Andrew Forrest, human resources director for The Industrial Society, said "Middle managers often feel they have been sold down the river. They were told by glossy recruiting brochures that their prospects were terrific but this has not turned out to be the case."

"Things middle managers once decided are being pushed down the line and they are left wondering what is left for them to decide about."

Dr Paul Sparrow, a lecturer in human resource strategy at the Manchester Business School, added: "The people who keep their jobs after downsizing often suffer a degree of guilt. Their attitudes also change.

"They say 'well if that's your attitude, if you are taking away what I thought was my career, I will make sure I screw everything out of you that I can'."

However, Mr Forrest believes there is hope for middle managers.

"If they develop a real team approach instead of the old style middle manager approach, it could, in time, be an exciting thing to see."

Fig. 2.12
Source: Daily Telegraph 19/2/94

DEPARTMENTS

Organisations are normally divided into sections or functions according to their products or services, size and requirements. Some typical departments or sections are as follows:

Personnel (human resources)

- organisation of human resources i.e. employees
- recruitment and selection of staff – advertisements, interviews
- promotion of staff
- termination of employment
- dealing with health and safety issues
- keeping employee records – pensions, sickness, superannuation payments
- work with trade unions
- confidential counselling and advice for staff

Finance (accounting)

- keeping the books
- dealing with cash
- cash flow
- cost accounting – keeping a check on the costs involved in running the organisation
- management accounting – providing information on the financial performance of the organisation
- credit control
- wages

Production

- planning production – the layout and use of the plant and machinery
- scheduling – deciding timetable and priorities for work
- manufacturing products
- checking progress of work
- allocation of work to employees
- setting and meeting production targets
- quality control
- work study – monitoring work
- using relevant computer programs
- designing tools to assist with production
- monitoring trends in production techniques
- monitoring wastage levels

Research and development (R&D)

R & D carries out the work needed to turn an idea into something that can be produced/manufactured to make a profit.

Administration

- provision of an administrative service for management and departments
- reprographics
- word processing
- typing
- desktop publishing

Management information systems (MIS)/Computer services (IT)

A computer-based department to:

- provide information about the organisation to management
- provide computer training
- purchase equipment and software
- keep computer records
- write computer programs
- provide maintenance

Marketing

- provides the organisation with information about the products and services the market wants and the prices people are prepared to pay
- conducts market research
- plans advertising and promotion
- works with research and development and production departments in the design and development of products or services (image)
- studies local and national trends
- provides advice about the life cycle of existing products and the potential of new ones

Sales

- prepares an annual sales plan, target sales for production, target profits, targets for regions, districts and individual representatives
- oversees all sales staff

- works with marketing to supply point-of-sale material and advice to customers
- monitors the competition

Public relations (PR)

- works to establish a suitable public image
- writes press releases
- attends exhibitions
- obtains sponsorship
- develops literature about the organisation
- makes regular contact with consumers

Distribution (logistics)

- works to ensure that the manufactured product reaches the consumer
- transports goods
- arranges deliveries
- often responsible for depots and warehouses

Purchasing

- orders stock and materials
- buys stock and materials
- buys services for the organisation
- negotiates with suppliers
- chases deliveries of goods

A C T I V I T Y

Some other departments or sections you may come across in organisations are as follows:

- stores
- legal
- import/export
- purchasing

See if you can find out what sort of task each may be responsible for.

Customer services

- provides information to customers
- deals with customer queries and complaints
- makes sure that customers are dealt with politely and efficiently
- trains staff in customer care
- obtains feedback from customers

Cleaning

Cleaners ensure an adequate standard of hygiene and cleanliness.

Security

- safeguards personnel, buildings, equipment and vehicles
- monitors personnel entering and leaving the building

DIFFERENCES IN WORKING ARRANGEMENTS

Teamwork

Although the majority of people have their own tasks to complete in the work place there will be occasions when most will be involved in teamwork of some kind.

A C T I V I T Y

Think about your own life. In which situations are you involved in teamwork (or group work)?

An effective team member should:

- be co-operative
- have the ability to listen to other people's ideas and points of view
- have the ability to adapt their own ideas to assist the decision-making process
- be able to work to deadlines
- be prepared to have their own thoughts or ideas rejected
- be able to communicate with and be supportive of other team members
- be able to take responsibility for group decisions and their outcomes
- be flexible

Some instances where an employee may be asked to work as part of a team are as follows:

- the introduction of a new product or service
- a special project
- interviewing potential employees

A C T I V I T Y

How many more can you think of?

Centralisation

Centralisation is a way of organising a particular function or service which is required by many different departments in a business. For example all departments will require the use of photocopying facilities, therefore a central reprographics (photocopying) section may be set up within a business to serve the needs of each of the departments.

Centralisation can also refer to the way decisions are made in a business, where major decisions are made by a few individuals.

Decentralisation

Decentralisation occurs where departments in a business are responsible for their own functions or services such as filing or photocopying.

Decentralisation in decision-making means that, where possible, departments are responsible for making their own decisions.

A C T I V I T Y

Make a list of the advantages and disadvantages of centralisation and decentralisation.

Flexibility

Further information about flexibility of working hours, such as shift work and flexi-time, can be found on p.22 in 'Hours of work'.

Contracts

Further information regarding contracts of employment can be found on p.39 of Chapter 2, 'People in business organisations', and on p.18 of Chapter 1 'Business organisations and employment'.

Workbases

The actual place where people work will vary from job to job. The working environment will affect the physical conditions discussed on p.19. Examples of different working environments include a secretary working in an office, an engineer working in a factory, a pharmacist working in a shop (chemist), a farmer working outdoors, a hairdresser working from home and a librarian working from a mobile van.

A C T I V I T Y

Identify the likely workbase for the following occupations:

- an optician
- a bank manager
- a fitter
- a builder

REASONS FOR CHANGE IN WORKING ARRANGEMENTS

Sometimes businesses have to make alterations to the ways in which they work. Reasons for this may include:

- *Productivity.* A business might want to increase the amount of goods it produces whilst keeping its costs the same. In order to do this it may review the structure of the organisation, the way in which people work and the numbers and types of employees.
- *Quality assurance and competition.* As business becomes more and more competitive, customers seek higher levels of quality and customer service. Therefore, individual businesses need to adapt working practices to ensure that their product is better than that of the competition, and that their reputation for customer care is constantly being improved.

A C T I V I T Y

Make a list of changes a business could make to improve customer care.

Technology

On p.22 of Chapter 1, 'Business organisations and employment', we discussed the impact of technology on levels of employment. Technology may also affect working practices. Examples are as follows:

- a business could use a computer package to process staff wages instead of calculating them manually
- a computer could be used in the design of a product (this is known as computer-aided design or CAD)
- robots could be introduced in factories to make production more efficient

A C T I V I T Y

Can you think of any other examples where the introduction of technology may affect working practices?

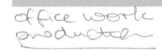

office work
production

INVESTIGATE EMPLOYEE AND EMPLOYER RESPONSIBILITIES AND RIGHTS

Employee participation and consultation

Most organisations today recognise the benefit of seeking the views of employees and involving them in the decision-making process.

BENEFITS FOR THE EMPLOYER

- staff feel valued and therefore may work harder, more efficiently and with greater motivation
- staff are more likely to be co-operative and committed if they feel they have been consulted
- the business will have a greater chance of survival if employer and employee work together

WAYS OF INVOLVING EMPLOYEES

- Holding regular meetings with managers, supervisors and employees.
- Worker councils – these consist of worker representatives and mainly give advice and assistance to the organisation.
- Worker directors – in some cases a member of the workforce becomes a director of the business.
- Joint consultative committees – these consist of trade-union and management representatives. The committees discuss management decisions and negotiate industrial relations issues.

EMPLOYEE RIGHTS

- guaranteed daily pay for five days in a three-month period when there is no work available

- sickness payment
- maternity leave and a right to return to work within 29 weeks of giving birth
- paid leave to fulfil certain trade union and public duties
- an itemised pay statement showing details of gross and net pay
- a written statement giving reasons for dismissal
- employer compliance with the terms of the employment contract
- equal opportunities at work
- health and safety at work
- legal representation

A C T I V I T Y

You are a trade-union representative of a medium-sized sweet factory. Write a memorandum to the managing director advising him or her of the benefits of employee consultation and participation.

EMPLOYEE RESPONSIBILITIES

- to obey his or her employer within the scope of the contract of employment
- to use reasonable care and skill at work
- to act reasonably, i.e. not dishonestly or incompetently
- to act in good faith – an employee's own interests should not conflict with those of the organisation, for example the disclosure of confidential information to someone outside the organisation
- to stick to agreements on wages and hours
- to do the work they are being paid for
- to meet the objectives of the business
- to meet health and safety regulations
- to meet customers' needs
- to maintain quality standards

EMPLOYER RESPONSIBILITIES

- to explain business objectives
- to provide work
- to pay wages (see p.21)
- to comply with health and safety regulations
- to take care of employees at work

- to consult employees regarding changes which will affect their conditions of employment
- to ensure equal opportunities

In addition employees and employers will have certain expectations of one another.

EMPLOYER RIGHTS AND EXPECTATIONS OF EMPLOYEES

- loyalty
- commitment
- consistency
- honesty
- good time-keeping
- adaptibility/flexibility
- co-operation
- the ability to follow instructions
- the ability to seek clarification on matters which are unclear
- employees' compliance with the terms of the contract
- employees' compliance with health and safety regulations
- the right to take disciplinary action
- legal representation

EMPLOYEES' EXPECTATIONS OF EMPLOYERS

- remuneration, i.e. payment
- safe working conditions
- trade-union membership
- employee consultation
- equal opportunities

The contract of employment

The contract of employment comes into existence when the offer of a job is made and accepted. A contract does not have to be written down: what a person is actually *told* about the job and what the law says counts as much as any piece of paper. Everything a person is told at their interview is part of their contract so it is important that they remember to write down the details.

A written statement showing details of the job must be given to an employee within 13 weeks after their employment has commenced. It will normally include the following information:

- the grade and title of the job
- the date employment started
- the rate of pay (and method of calculation)
- details as to whether payment is to be made weekly or monthly
- hours of work
- holiday entitlement
- details of sickness benefit
- employee rights concerning trade union membership

- the organisation's disciplinary procedure
- the amount of notice required
- details as to whom applications for redress/grievance should be made

TIPS FOR EMPLOYEES

1 If you are ill phone your supervisor or personnel manager immediately.

2 *Timekeeping* – make sure that you arrive at work on time, check the times of tea breaks and lunch breaks, and be sure that you know the correct procedures for overtime.

3 *Time off* – ask your personnel manager or supervisor for permission, give plenty of warning, be polite, and ask at the interview about the holiday entitlement (this information may be included in the written statement).

REMUNERATION

Look at Chapter 1 'Business organisations and employment' at the Section 'Paying employees' on pp.21–2 and then complete the following task.

ACTIVITY

Design a leaflet which could be used as a general guide for new employees. It should be called 'Getting paid'. Your leaflet should be produced using information technology

RESOLVING DISAGREEMENTS

Trade unions

Trade unions are organisations of workers that aim to control or influence the relationship between employers and employees. They play a key role in resolving disagreements.

TYPES OF TRADE UNION

Craft unions normally represent skilled crafts and trades and were the earliest type of union. An example is the United Patternmakers Association (UPA).

General unions were developed in the nineteenth century by comparatively unskilled groups of workers not catered for by craft unions.

Industrial unions aimed to bring workers in one industry under a single union, for example mineworkers and dockers.

White-collar unions are unions made up of clerical, supervisory and professional workers, for example the National Union of Teachers.

FUNCTIONS OF TRADE UNIONS

- social – provision of clubs and recreational facilities, for example staff outings
- welfare – legal advice and assistance, strike pay
- political – influencing the decisions of the government to ensure that national policies are favourable to members (some unions are linked to political parties)
- collective bargaining – negotiating (or bargaining) with employers about issues such as wages and salaries, breaks, hours and conditions of work
- co-operation with employers – working with employers to solve problems, for example efficiency and the organisation of jobs
- advice – advising members how to deal with problems, for example unfair dismissal

TRADE UNION TERMS/ACTIONS

Strike action – a refusal by employees to work.

Official strike – a strike backed by the union.

Unofficial strike – members striking without the support of the union.

Token strike – a one-day strike (or less), planned in advance and designed to draw attention to a particular grievance.

Lightning strike – a short, sharp strike taken without any warning.

Sympathy strike – workers come out on strike in support of workers outside their union.

Solidarity – the loyalty and support of workers to the cause.

Picketing – where trade union members gather outside an organisation to try to discourage other workers from entering.

Blackleg – people who ignore the call to strike and go to work.

Working to rule – working strictly to the rules and regulations of the organisation.

Go slow – where workers deliberately slow down at work.

ACTIVITY

Below are three more terms associated with trade unions. See if you can find out what they mean.

- peaceful picketing
- secondary picketing
- closed shop

TUC (TRADES UNION CONGRESS)

This is the umbrella organisation of all the trade unions. It holds a conference at which union delegates meet to discuss and vote on union policy. The TUC represents the collective point of view of the unions and puts this forward to the government and other organisations.

Employers' associations

Employers form associations to protect their own interests (often against trade unions) in the same way that employees join trade unions. The **CBI (Confederation of British Industry)** is the main employers' association. It helps British industry decide on policies and acts as a representative for organisations seeking the views of industry. The CBI encourages British Industry to be competitive and efficient.

Advisory Conciliation and Arbitration Service (ACAS)

If employers and trade unions fail to reach agreement on employment issues ACAS may be able to help. ACAS normally takes the role of a mediator (go-between), talking to the employer and employees separately, to establish areas of agreement. ACAS will then try to help the two parties come to an agreement.

The European Court of Justice

This court consists of a number of judges who come from the member states of the European Union. The court acts to settle disputes which have arisen from conflicts in European Union law. Individuals and businesses (both public and private sector) can use the court to resolve disputes between employer and employee which cannot be settled within the British legal system.

Disciplinary procedures and dismissal of employees

If an employee's conduct breaks the contract of employment an employer must:

1 Give the employee a *verbal warning* (first warning) and make a note on his or her file.
2 Give a *formal warning*. This may be verbal but is more likely to be in writing and will probably contain targets for the employee to achieve. The consequence of failing to meet the targets should be pointed out. One copy of the warning should be included in the employee's file and one copy sent to management.
3 Give a *final warning*. This will normally be verbal and written and will be given for a persistent offence or when an employee has ignored previous warnings and/or failed to meet targets.
4 Dismissal – if all forms of warning have failed an employee may be dismissed. Notice should be given as required in the contract of employment.
5 Summary dismissal – in serious circumstances, for example theft, an employee can be dismissed immediately.

REDUNDANCY

An employee can be made redundant if an employer discontinues or intends to discontinue their business or because the requirements of the business have altered or diminished (or are likely to diminish).

An organisation planning to make people redundant will contact a recognised trade union as soon as possible. It must also give its employees notice that they are going to be made redundant. They should also issue employees with a letter showing how redundancy payments have been calculated. The Employment Protection (Consolidation) Act 1978 controls the payment of compensation to employees who have been made redundant. No redundancy payment will be made if an employee rejects an offer of suitable alternative employment made by the employer. An employee must have been in continuous employment for two years or more to be entitled to a redundancy payment.

UNFAIR DISMISSAL

To be *fair*, dismissal must relate to:

- an employee's capability
- qualifications
- conduct
- redundancy

Some reasons for dismissal are considered to be automatically *unfair*:

- dismissal for joining a trade union
- dismissal because of pregnancy

If an employee feels he or she has been unfairly dismissed he/she can take his/her case to an **industrial tribunal**. If the industrial tribunal feels that there has been a case of unfair dismissal the employer may have to pay compensation to the former employee or reinstate him/her.

A C T I V I T Y

Below are a number of instances where employees have been dismissed. Decide which of them have been dismissed fairly.

1 John Drinkwater is caught stealing from the paint factory where he works and is sacked on the spot.
2 Paula Carey is dismissed by her employer when she joins a trade union.
3 Elizabeth Brown, a factory employee, is asked to leave after notifying her boss that she is pregnant.
4 Peter Naylor, a worker at an engineering plant, is dismissed after making a number of serious mistakes that have cost his employer thousands of pounds.

LEGISLATION

Health and safety at work

All employees will expect to work in a safe environment and there are a number of laws relating to health and safety at work. The **Health and Safety at Work Act** (HASAWA) **1974** is the major piece of health and safety legislation and is concerned with safe working conditions. Under the terms of the Act employers have the following responsibilities to employees:

- the provision and maintenance of a safe plant and safe systems of work
- safe use, storage, handling and transport of goods or substances
- proper safety information, supervision and training
- safe and adequate points of entry and exit to and from buildings

Employees must:

- take reasonable care for the safety of themselves and others at work

- co-operate with the employers to act safely and comply with the duties given
- not interfere with anything provided in the interest of health, safety and welfare

The **Office Shops and Railway Premises Act 1963** is concerned with the physical conditions within which employees work, for example premises which are unsuitable because of inadequate heating.

The **Employers Liability (Compulsory Insurance) Act 1969** is concerned with the insurance of employees at work.

The **Fire Precautions Act 1971** deals with the protection of employees against fire.

The **Control of Substances Hazardous to Health Regulations** (COSHH) lays down procedures for the way hazardous substances i.e. dangerous chemicals, are controlled and how people are protected against them in the workplace.

THE HEALTH AND SAFETY COMMISSION

This is a body appointed by the government to oversee the health, safety and welfare of employees at work. It has wide powers including the conduct of investigations or enquiries into particular issues. The Commission has set up a number of advisory committees to help with specialised advice and information, for example on nuclear safety.

THE HEALTH AND SAFETY EXECUTIVE (HSE)

This body's main duty is to ensure that organisations comply with health and safety legislation. Some of its main branches include:

- the Factory Inspectorate
- the Explosives Inspectorate
- the Mines and Quarries Inspectorate
- the Nuclear Installations Inspectorate
- the Alkaline and Clear Air Inspectorate
- the Agriculture Health and Safety Inspectorate

The HSE carries out inspections, gathers evidence, issues enforcement notices and prosecutes offenders where appropriate.

SAFETY OFFICERS

Many organisations have their own safety officers. Their duties will include the following:

- safety policies
- ensuring a safe working environment and systems of work
- overseeing the inspection, testing and maintenance of machinery and equipment

- control over storage and use of hazardous substances
- supervision of the provision of safety equipment and clothing
- training staff on health and safety issues
- compliance with relevant legislation
- providing information
- keeping records
- investigations into health and safety issues
- budgets
- communication with employees and management
- keeping up-to-date with health and safety information

HEALTH AND SAFETY DANGERS

Below is a list of things which could be a health and safety risk in the work place.

- loose wires
- spillages
- food lying around
- broken equipment
- out-of-date fire extinguishers
- insufficient light or heat
- people smoking whilst working with food

A C T I V I T Y

Make a list of possible health and safety risks in the following working environments:

- a restaurant kitchen
- a factory
- an office
- a farm

Discrimination in employment

All employees have the right to be free from discrimination at their place of work. This means that they should not be treated differently on the grounds of factors such as sex, age, disability or race.

THERE ARE A NUMBER OF IMPORTANT LAWS RELATING TO DISCRIMINATION AT WORK

The **Sex Discrimination Act 1975** and **1986** makes it illegal to discriminate against people at work on the grounds of their sex, for example not appointing a woman because she has young children.

The **Race Relations Act 1978** makes it illegal to discriminate against people at work on the grounds of their colour or ethnic origin. An example would be

turning a person down for promotion because they are black.

The **Disabled Persons (Employment) Act 1958** makes it illegal to discriminate against people who are disabled. If a person's disability would not prevent them doing a job as efficiently as an able-bodied person, then it should not prevent them from being given the job. For example, there may be three applicants for the position of a computer operator in a business organisation, two able-bodied and one disabled. The disabled person has more experience and qualifications than the other two applicants and the person's disability would not hinder his or her ability to do the job. In this case, if the disabled person has not been appointed it could be argued that he or she had been discriminated against on the grounds of disability.

The **Equal Pay Act 1970** aims to provide women with the same pay as men for similar or equal work.

The **Rehabilitation of Offenders Act 1978** makes it illegal to discriminate against an ex-offender whose crime is considered to be spent (after a certain amount of time has elapsed since the crime was committed).

EQUAL OPPORTUNITIES

Many organisations now have their own equal opportunities policy or statement, which outlines ideas and procedures relating to discrimination.

A C T I V I T Y

Obtain an equal opportunities policy from your college or a local business. See how it compares with the policies collected by other members of the group.

DIRECT DISCRIMINATION

This is where a person is treated less favourably on the grounds of race, sex, age etc. Examples would be segregating black workers or selecting a married female worker for redundancy.

INDIRECT DISCRIMINATION

This is where a person is asked to meet a condition which as a result of sex, race etc. is hard to satisfy. For example, asking job applicants to have been educated in the United Kingdom or to have blond hair.

VICTIMISATION

This is where people are treated less favourably because they have claimed they have been discriminated against. For example, a female secretary who has made a complaint about sexual discrimination could claim that she has been victimised as a result of her complaint if she is moved to a different, less well-paid job.

GENUINE OCCUPATIONAL QUALIFICATION

This occurs when it is either desirable or essential that a person of a specific age or sex be given a job. Examples are:

■ a part in a play
■ an attendant in a male toilet
■ a job involving people of a single sex

A C T I V I T Y

Hold a discussion with other members of the group about the following issues relating to discrimination.

1 What you would do if a member of your group was being picked on because they were black?
2 How might a female at work deal with a male colleague who is always patting her bottom and making suggestive comments?
3 Why do you think that more men achieve senior positions at work than women?

JOB ADVERTISEMENTS

A job advertisement should not break any of the laws relating to discrimination in employment. Many organisations state that they are 'an equal opportunities employer' on their advertisements.

A C T I V I T Y

Below is an advertisement for a telephonist/receptionist. Rewrite it so that it could not be considered to be discriminatory.

```
        Allpus Electronics
        Require a Female
      Telephonist/Receptionist

     Must be: Attractive and
   hardworking, aged 17-21 and
   have NVQ Level 2 in Business
          Administration.

   Telephone: John on 72539 for
           further details.
```

A C T I V I T Y

Below are some examples of discrimination. Decide whether each is:

a direct discrimination
b indirect discrimination
c victimisation

1 A black worker who is given lower wages than other employees doing the same job.
2 Peter Smith, an Asian office manager, has made a complaint that he has been discriminated against and overlooked for promotion on the grounds of his race. Following the complaint his manager has moved him out of his office to one he has to share with three other members of staff.
3 John Bulman applies for the position of secretary for a large furniture supplies company. He is turned down because the job advertisement asked for a female.

PRESENT RESULTS OF INVESTIGATION INTO JOB ROLES

JOB ROLES

For a discussion of job **functions** see p.35.

As well as the division of organisations into sections or departments there are a number of individuals (or in some cases, groups of individuals) with specific roles or responsibilities.

Managing director (MD)

The MD is the executive head of a private-sector business and has authority over all of the staff within the organisation. He or she will be a member of the board of directors and will have responsibility to ensure that decisions and policies laid down by the board of directors are put in place.

Director

All private-sector organisations must have at least one director. A director will be responsible for managing the day-to-day operations of a function, for example a marketing director will oversee the running of the marketing department. In addition, he or she will be responsible for developing the long-term strategy for the business along with the other directors.

Company secretary

A secretary is answerable to the managing director and will normally be responsible for the following:

- ensuring that the affairs of the company are conducted in accordance with legal requirements
  carrying out administrative tasks including:
  - administration of company meetings
  - typing/word processing
  - dealing with correspondence relating to the company
  - dealing with confidential material and legal documentation

SKILLS REQUIRED:

- ability to act on own initiative
- organisational capabilities
- trustworthiness and efficiency
- expertise at dealing with people (both individually and as a member of a team)
- ability to cope under pressure
- good communication skills
- discretion

Departmental manager

The departmental manager is responsible for the work of a single department within the organisation, for example sales or production. He or she will direct the work carried out by staff in the department in line with company policy. Specific responsibilities will include:

- appointing staff to the department
- acquiring physical resources
- managing a budget
- ensuring that departmental targets are met

The departmental manger is answerable to the managing director.

Supervisor

A supervisor is answerable to the departmental manager and is responsible for the work within a specific section or unit of the department. For example, a sales department may be split into:

- UK sales
- European sales
- worldwide sales

Each section may have a supervisor to oversee the work. The section supervisor will review work with the departmental manager on a regular basis to ensure that targets are being met. He or she will be responsible for staff working in the section.

Production operative

This is a member of staff whose main job involves actually producing a good or service. For example, a car production line worker or a kitchen hand in a restaurant.

A C T I V I T Y

Make a list of the qualities which you think may be required for the following job roles:

- managing director
- departmental manager
- section supervisor

Support staff

These are staff who work in a supporting role to others within an organisation. For example, for a college to achieve its objective of delivering a high quality education, the teaching staff and managers will require the assistance of people such as secretaries, computer technicians, library staff, cleaners and caretakers.

Levels and responsibilities of managers

Senior managers, for example the MD, set policies and rules, and decide the mission statement (see below right). **Middle managers**, for example departmental managers, implement the rules and policies, and liaise with senior managers and supervisors. **Junior managers**, for example section supervisors, oversee the day-to-day activities in a part of the organisation.

Levels of activity

On p.35 we discussed different departments/functions within organisations. Within each of these functions there will be staff operating at different levels. For example, within a biscuit factory the production department may have:

- production operatives actually making the biscuits
- a section supervisor to oversee each production line
- a production manager who oversees total production within the factory

A C T I V I T Y

The biscuit factory will also have marketing and finance amongst its functions. For each of these, outline the different job roles and levels which are likely to exist.

ROUTINE TASKS

Routine tasks include those which are carried out by members of staff at different levels on an on-going basis. They will include the following:

Planning

Planning is the process businesses use to decide in advance what they want to achieve, how, by when and what resources will be required.

Setting and achieving targets

The **objectives** are the specific aims of an organisation, which tend to be broad and long term. Examples would be: to maximise profits, to become market leaders, to survive and to be cost-effective. The **targets** are very specific objectives to be achieved within a stated period of time (normally short term). The **policies** are courses of action decided by organisations to help achieve their objectives.

Below is a case study which should help to clarify some of these terms.

C A S E   S T U D Y

Mitchells is a chain of shoe shops based in Solihull. The main **objective** of the company is to maximise profits. A **target** is to increase sales by 1 per cent over the next two months. A **policy** within the business is that all new employees should be given the opportunity to attend a day-release course at the local college.

A C T I V I T Y

1 State three objectives a bank might have.
2 Explain a policy a car-manufacturing company might introduce.

MISSION STATEMENTS

A mission statement is a document which lays down the objectives of an organisation. It tells us:

- what an organisation is
- why it exists
- the contribution it can make to society

Here is a mission statement for Chubby's Chocolates. The example is simplified. The mission statement of an actual organisation would be written in greater detail.

**CHUBBY'S CHOCOLATES
MISSION STATEMENT**

What business are we in?
The provision of a range of high quality confectionery for our customers.

Why do we exist?
To develop our production techniques in the United Kingdom and abroad in order to meet the requirements of the market.

What unique contribution can we make to society?
● to make a fitting contribution to the local community in which we operate
● to use environmentally friendly production techniques

Objectives:
● growth
● increased profits
● improved production techniques
● increased work force
● development of new lines
● modernisation

Decision-making in the organisation

Decisions are made about lots of different issues at all levels of an organisation. A person's position within the hierarchy will often influence the level of importance of decision-making he or she is involved in.

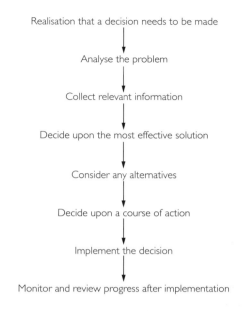

Realisation that a decision needs to be made
↓
Analyse the problem
↓
Collect relevant information
↓
Decide upon the most effective solution
↓
Consider any alternatives
↓
Decide upon a course of action
↓
Implement the decision
↓
Monitor and review progress after implementation

FIG. 2.13 STEPS IN THE DECISION-MAKING PROCESS

Strategic or long-term decisions tend to be made by senior managers and will relate to an organisation's overall objectives. Examples would be decisions about major investments or a switch to a new product.
Tactical or medium-term decisions are often made by middle managers and relate to ensuring that the organisation achieves its overall objectives. An example would be decisions about the use of resources.
Operational or short-term decisions are day-to-day decisions about the running of an organisation. An example would be deciding the rota for operating the switchboard.

C A S E   S T U D Y

Mary Gosling is a supervisor at a bakery in Eastbourne. There have been disagreements amongst the staff at the bakery about the times at which lunch breaks are to be taken (most prefer to have lunch from 1–2 pm but the company requires an equal number to take the 12–1 pm break to maximise output).

1 Mary realises that she will have to make a decision about how to tackle the problem.
2 She notes that most people prefer the 1–2 pm lunch break as it makes the time worked in the afternoon much shorter.
3 She collects details about the times of lunch breaks taken by staff over the past months and speaks to all

staff about their preferences.
4 Mary decides that the most effective solution would be to ask staff to alternate their lunch breaks 12–1 pm one week and 1–2 pm the next.
5 An alternative is staff alternating their lunch breaks on a daily basis but this could be complicated to work out and may cause confusion.
6 Mary writes a memo to inform staff of her decision and then draws up a rota.
7 The rota commences the following Monday.
8 After one month Mary holds a staff meeting to discuss any problems. The majority of staff appear to be happy with the decision.

Below is a series of decisions to be made in Bodens Department Store. Decide whether you think each should be made by:

- a senior manager
- a departmental manager
- a shop-floor supervisor

1 Whether or not to have a sale in October.
2 The rota for tea breaks in the furniture section.
3 The quantity of ladies' coats to display in the clothing department.
4 The number of temporary employees to be taken on over the Christmas period.

Solving problems

It is inevitable that in any organisation problems will arise from time to time. Solving them is closely linked to the decision-making process discussed earlier. Things to consider are:

- Is the problem large or small?
- Why is it a problem?
- Does the problem require an immediate solution?
- Is the problem complex?
- Who needs to be involved in trying to solve the problem?

When the problem has been solved and any necessary action taken, a review should be carried out in order to decide whether the solution has proved to be effective.

NON-ROUTINE TASKS

Non-routine tasks are the aspects of people's jobs which are difficult to predict and may only occur from time to time. Examples may include dealing with accidents or emergencies, undertaking disciplinary procedures or responding to an unexpected deadline.

Benefits of team membership

Although members of staff will have specific job roles, they may be able to carry these out more effectively either by working with or having the support of other members of staff. For example, a market researcher may survey a number of shoppers in the high street him or herself. However, after the research has been carried out he or she may work as part of a team to collate and interpret the results.

Some general benefits of team membership at work include the following:

- it is sometimes easier to achieve objectives and targets if everyone in a team pulls together
- working as part of a team helps to raise awareness of the needs of other functions and/or staff
- if people can see how their jobs fit in with the rest of the organisation (through teamwork), they are more likely to have a greater level of commitment to the job

PREPARE FOR EMPLOYMENT OR SELF-EMPLOYMENT

Types of employment

Paid workers (in the public and private sector) work for an organisation, will normally have regular hours and a set wage or salary. They will have a contract of employment and some may work on a temporary or part-time basis.

Voluntary workers give up their services and time free of charge and usually work for charity organisations such as Oxfam or Save the Children.

People running their own businesses, or **self-employed workers**, may be sole traders, members of a partnership, own a franchise or be part of a family-run business (possibly a limited company).

Types of employment are discussed in greater detail in Chapter 1, 'Business organisations and employment'.

Information sources

Finding a job or becoming self-employed can often be a pretty daunting prospect. Fortunately, support agencies are available to help with the process.

THE CAREERS SERVICE

Local authorities have set up careers offices which provide details about local job vacancies in most towns and cities. Specialist careers staff are trained to give information and advice to those seeking employment. Careers offices also provide general information about jobs and details about colleges and universities (including how to apply for courses). Schools and colleges usually have their own careers section or officer who can help leavers get in touch with personnel officers in appropriate organisations.

EMPLOYMENT AGENCIES

These are privately run organisations which assist businesses with the recruitment of workers, often temporary staff. They tend to deal with specialist areas, for example, administrative, secretarial or managerial positions. Potential workers sign up with the agency and business organisations register with the agency. As work is required the agency matches up the workers with the business. The wages are paid directly to the agency who deduct their fee and then pay the worker. People often sign up with a recritment agency as a short-term measure while they are seeking full-time or permanent employment.

JOB CENTRES

Job Centres are run by the Department of Employment and are found in most towns and cities. They display cards with details of job vacancies in an area. If a person is interested in a job (and has the relevant experience and/or qualifications) the job centre will make an appointment for an interview or provide information about how to apply for the job.

BUSINESS START-UP AND ENTERPRISE SCHEMES

There are a number of different organisations which have set up schemes to help people start their own businesses. These operate on both a local and a national level. Examples include:

- *The Business Expansion Scheme.* This is a government-run scheme which gives tax incentives to people or businesses who invest in new small enterprises.
- *The Loan Guarantee Scheme.* This is where the government encourages bank lending to new small businesses by guaranteeing a loan.
- *The Enterprise Allowance Scheme.* This is a government scheme which encourages the unemployed to set up their own businesses. The applicant must be prepared to put down some of his or her own money to start the business and the government in turn will pay a weekly grant for six months.
- *Local authorities.* Most local authorities have a limited amount of finance available for grants for prospective businesses. This will often take the form of loans or grants to people wishing to start businesses.
- *Banks.* Most of the major banks have their own business start-up schemes. For example, the opportunity to negotiate loan repayments may be given to a person seeking a loan to start a small business.

THE MEDIA

The media are an important source of information when seeking employment. Local and national newspapers include job advertisements on a regular basis, often on a particular day of the week. Many local radio stations include regular bulletins where information

A C T I V I T Y

Visit three local banks and find out about any business start-up packages they offer.

about local job opportunities is broadcast. Independent television channels also provide information about jobs. For example, 'Jobfinder', on ITV's Teletext gives details of jobs, locations, wages, hours, experience and qualifications required. Channel 4's Teletext provides information on appointments, advice for career and work problems and for setting up businesses.

FEDERATION OF SELF-EMPLOYED

This is a pressure group which aims to help and support small businesses and the self-employed. The organisation represents the needs and views of its membership by talking to MPs and local authorities. It charges a membership fee which varies from between £60 and £100 plus depending on the number of employees. In return for the fee, the member receives a number of benefits including different types of insurance. The Federation has a number of contacts and offices which deal with most general business concerns, for example import/export regulations.

BANKS

Banks are a valuable source of information and advice for people wishing to set up a business and/or become self-employed.

TRAINING AND ENTERPRISE COUNCILS (TECS)

TECs are independent local bodies which have been set up to develop training and enterprise schemes/initiatives appropriate to local needs. Money is provided by central Government to help them set up. However, they operate as limited companies and are expected to finance themselves through local businesses. TECs oversee the new Training Credits which are replacing Youth Training.

CHARITABLE ORGANISATIONS

There are a number of charities which may assist people wishing to set up in business. These include:

- *The Prince's Youth Business Trust.* The trust provides grants for young unemployed people (between the ages of 18 and 25 and up to 30 years of age for disabled people). For individuals grants are available for up to £1,500, for groups the figure is up to £3,000. There are restrictions as to how the money can be spent.
- *Livewire.* This is a scheme sponsored by Shell which encourages 16–25-year-olds to plan and develop their own businesses.
- *Instant Muscle.* This charity helps people who may experience difficulty obtaining employment to set up their own businesses. Examples include the disabled and ethnic minorities.

Employment opportunities – location

The possibilities for employment are endless. People may work:

- locally, for example a school leaver obtaining employment in a local department store
- nationally, for example, the same school leaver moves to another part of the country to gain promotion at a different branch of the organisation
- internationally, for example, the same school leaver moving abroad to take up a position within an overseas branch of the same organisation

The same pattern can be true for the self-employed. For example, a builder might work on local sites, move to a part of the country where there is a shortage of builders or move abroad to work on an overseas building development.

Analysing employment skills

WORKING WITH OTHERS

If a person works alone this skill will not be essential. However, as a business grows and staff are employed the workers will all need to pull together so that the business can survive and prosper. This skill is extremely important if working for an organisation as this normally involves a significant amount of team work.

WORKING INDEPENDENTLY

This is extrememly important if a person works alone. He or she will need to be self-disciplined and able to complete all aspects of the job, often without the support of other people. Working for an organisation will sometimes involve an employee completing a job or task individually. However, there will normally be other people available to provide assistance or advice as required.

TIME MANAGEMENT

Time management is important in any job. Working for yourself requires excellent time management skills. It involves setting (and meeting) your own targets and deadlines. In organisations, employers will often set targets and deadlines to work to. It is then up to the employees to manage their time in order to achieve targets and meet deadlines.

DECISION-MAKING

A person working for him or herself will be responsible for all decision-making. Being part of a partnership, franchise or family-run business will mean that all decisions are made by just a small number of people. In an organisation staff at different levels will be involved in varying degrees of decision-making.

PROBLEM SOLVING

In a small business, problems may have to be solved by a single person or small group of people as they arise. Alternatively, the services of specialists may have to be bought in to help them out, for example, an accountant. In an organisation, problem solving is a skill which may be required of any one of a number of people with relevant expertise at different levels, depending on the nature of the problem.

PLANNING

Planning skills will be particularly significant for a person setting up his or her own business. Lack of planning can prevent the success or even survival of a business. In an organisation, planning skills will be required particularly by people employed as managers at different levels.

INFORMATION SEEKING

Good information is vital for the success of any business. Self-employed workers will normally have to gather all relevant information themselves to help the business. In an organisation, the requirement for information seeking skills will depend on the nature of the job. Businesses sometimes choose to buy in specialists to assist with information gathering.

EVALUATING

Self-employed workers will have to review and reflect on the business and its progress on an on-going basis. In an organisation, the ability to evaluate is a skill more likely to be required by a manager.

COMMUNICATION

Good communication skills are vital for a person running his or her own business. All business communication and customer contact is likely to be carried out by one person or a small number of people. In an organisation, the degree of communication skills required will depend on the nature of a person's job. For example, the job of a production operative will require fewer communication skills than that of a sales representative.

APPLICATION OF NUMBER

Self-employed workers will need to understand the overall financial position of the business. However, they may choose to employ or buy in the services of specialists to carry out financial functions. In organisations, most employers will expect their staff to have a basic level of numeracy. Some jobs will focus heavily on these skills, for example, an accounts clerk, others less so, for example, a cleaner.

INFORMATION TECHNOLOGY

Whilst not an essential skill, the ability to use IT is becoming increasingly important to any business. IT skills may help to give a new business a head start. In an organisation there will probably be a number of IT experts, but most employees will be affected by IT to some degree and will therefore be expected to have at least a basic level of IT skills.

OCCUPATIONAL SKILLS

Self-employed workers may decide to set up their own businesses because of particular occupational skills they possess, but they will also need to develop a broader range of skills to get the business up and running. For example, a painter and decorater may also have to act as the accountant, salesperson and administrator. In an organisation, staff are normally taken on to work in specific sections because of the skills they possess, for example, a computer programmer. They will not be required to develop a whole range of skills across the organisation.

The next activity shows that a broad range of skills is important in both employment and self-employment. To help you in your search for employment GNVQ courses are designed to encourage you to develop your skills (core skills) – communication, application of number and information technology, and the grading of the qualification concentrates on skills such as planning, information seeking/handling and evaluation.

ACTIVITY

Collect 10 job advertisements from a local or national newspaper. Which of the skills in the chart are included in the advertisements?

ACTIVITY

For each of the employment skills listed below give yourself a rating between 1 and 5 (1 = excellent, 2 = good, 3 = average, 4 = poor, 5 = very poor).

- working with others
- working independently
- time management
- decision-making
- problem solving
- planning
- information seeking
- evaluating
- communication
- application of number
- information technology
- occupational skills

ACTIVITY

Keeping in mind your strengths and weaknesses from the skills analysis in the previous activity, write a short report to include the following:

- your ideal job
- reasons why you think you would be good at it
- skills you might need to develop in order to do the job effectively

Developing and improving skills

Whether an employee or self-employed, a person will always need to review existing skills and be prepared to develop new skills in order to respond to changes in the working environment, the nature of the job or to gain promotion. Ways of improving and developing skills include:

- taking a college course
- attending a training session at work
- observing another employee with a higher skill level

A C T I V I T Y

Draw up a list of five other ways of developing and improving skills.

Preparing for a job interview

- carefully read through any information you have been sent about the job
- try to find out some background information about the organisation who have advertised the job

---

C A S E   S T U D Y

Peter is 18 years old. He has been working as a sales assistant in a specialist computer shop since leaving school at 16. He has four GCSEs (English, maths, history and geography). He has recently decided that he would like to become a computer technician. He asks himself the questions shown in the table below.

- think about some of the questions that you might be asked and draft out some possible answers
- ask a friend or member of your family to ask you some of the questions so that you can actually practice for the interview
- think about some questions you might want to ask the interviewers

Some common questions asked at interviews are:

- Why have you applied for the job?
- What qualifications do you have?
- Do you have any relevant experience?
- Why do you think you would be good at the job?
- What are your interests/hobbies?
- Are you able to work as a member of a team?
- Are you good at managing your own time?

Avoid simply answering 'yes' or 'no' to questions. Try to expand your answers where possible (without waffling!). At the interview:

- make sure that you are dressed appropriately
- arrive in good time
- keep calm
- smile
- speak up and talk clearly
- think about your body language – don't fidget!
- think carefully before you answer each question

A C T I V I T Y

Think about a job you might like to do in the future. What questions do you think you need to ask yourself?

Question	Answer
1 Do I have the right qualifications?	My GCSEs (particularly English and maths) will give me a good grounding but I will need to take a specialist computing qualification.
2 Who should I see to find out more about the job and the qualifications required?	The careers office and my local library.
3 Can I afford to give up work to study full time?	No. However, I am prepared to take an evening course at college for a couple of years in order to achieve the relevant qualifications.
4 How will I pay for the qualifications?	I have some savings and some money from my 18th birthday. I would like to spend this money on my future.
5 Do I need to do anything else?	Yes. I shall write to appropriate businesses to find out whether anyone would be prepared to take me on and give me day release to complete my training

CHAPTER TWO

Test Yourself!

1 What is a matrix structure?
2 Explain the difference between tall and flat organisation structures.
3 List three functions of the personnel department.
4 List three rights of employees.
5 List three duties of employers.
6 What is an industrial trade union?
7 True or false? An official strike is a strike backed by a union.
8 What do the initials CBI stand for?
9 What are two possible duties of a safety officer?
10 Which law prevents employees from being discriminated against because of their sex?
11 Explain what is meant by a genuine occupational qualification.
12 What do the initials ACAS stand for?
13 True or false? Dealing with an emergency is an example of a non-routine task at work.
14 True or false? Decisions are made at all levels of an organisation.
15 List three functions of the personnel department.
16 List three functions of the finance department.
17 State two differences between an employed and a self-employed worker.
18 State two qualities of an effective team member.
19 What do the initials TEC stand for?
20 Make a list of eight skills needed for employment.

CHAPTER TWO

Evidence-Gathering Projects

1 Examine and compare structures and working arrangements in organisations.

Identify two local business organisations and complete the following tasks:

i Draw an organisation chart for each organisation and explain whether the structure is tall or flat.
ii List the advantages and disadvantages of tall and flat structures and explain how decision-making takes place in each type.
iii List the different departments included in each of the organisations and outline what each is responsible for, and how they work with the other departments.
iv Write a short report highlighting the differences in working arrangements between the two organisations. Identify changes in working arrangements in one of the organisations and explain why you think the changes have been made.

2 Explain rights and responsibilities of employees and employers.

Design a leaflet which could be given to employees when they start a new job. It should include the following information:

i Details about the rights and responsibilities of employees.
ii An explanation of the rights and responsibilities of employers.
iii An outline of relevant legislation which applies to employers and employees.
iv An explanation of the benefits of employer and employee co-operation.
v A description of ways to resolve disagreements between employers and employees.
Your leaflet should be attractive to look at, clearly written and easy to understand.

3 Present results of investigation into job roles.

Arrange a visit to one or two business organisations and make an appointment to interview two of the following:

- a director
- a manager
- a team member

i Prepare a list of questions in advance to find out the following information:

   a their role within the organisation
   b the different tasks their job involves
   c any work they carry out with other departments/sections in the organisation

ii Write a summary about each of the people you interviewed.

You may wish to carry out your interviews in groups of two to save the valuable time of the business organisation.

Your interview could be taped and included in your portfolio as evidence.

iii Write a short report to explain the benefits of team membership in performing job roles.

4 Prepare for employment or self-employment.

i Interview three people in three different types of employment and complete the chart on the following page.

ii Collect 12 job advertisements from newspapers. Identify which are local, national and international job opportunities (and include at least one of each).

iii Select two other sources of employment information from the following list and gather further details about local, national and international job opportunities.
   – Job Centre
   – television
   – radio
   – Careers Office
   – employment agencies

iv Hold a discussion with three or four other members of the group to discuss your own strengths and weaknesses with relation to skills for employment or self-employment. Your teacher/lecturer will observe the discussion.

Name	Job title	Type of employment	Description of main tasks/ responsibilities of the job	Analysis of skills required for the job

Chapter
3

CONSUMERS AND CUSTOMERS

This chapter explains why consumers and customers are important to businesses and how businesses respond to consumer needs and wants. It describes promotional activities and will enable you to plan, design and produce promotional materials. It highlights the importance of customer service and the need for continual improvement in this area.

EXPLAIN THE IMPORTANCE OF CONSUMERS AND CUSTOMERS

CHARACTERISTICS AND IMPORTANCE OF CONSUMERS

Businesses depend on customers for their prosperity or even survival. If a business does not satisfy its customers' needs it is unlikely to thrive and develop. It is vital therefore that both businesses and customers realise that they depend on each other and that they can both benefit from their interlinked relationship. The customer receives the good or service and its benefits from the business, and the business receives its revenue (i.e. money) and ultimately its profit from the customers' spending power.

Businesses need customers so that:

- the business can grow and expand
- the business can receive revenue
- the business can receive feedback and information from its customers
- customers become loyal and return to purchase again

There are different names for different types of customers. The general public or individuals who buy goods for their own personal consumption and do not aim to sell them on are called **consumers**. You can be *a* consumer of a product and yet not be *the* customer who bought them. For example, you might consume food bought by your parents.

People who are not aware of the term 'consumer' sometimes call anyone who purchases goods a customer. For the purposes of this text we sometimes use the term 'customer' to cover both businesses and individuals, but wherever possible we will highlight who the consumers are if appropriate.

A business may have customers who are not consumers. For example, a company like Heinz will sell goods to:

- catering customers, such as restaurants
- local councils, for distribution to schools and hospitals
- retailers like Sainsbury's, who then sell on the goods to consumers in their stores

A business will also have internal customers, for example a cleaner with a query about wages will be a customer of the finance department. External customers are those customers outside the organisation and will include members of the public and other businesses.

Consumers and customers come in many different forms and it is important that businesses can identify them accurately. Imagine you are running a Ford dealership. Describe the typical consumers and customers you think will buy the following range of cars:

- Fiesta
- Escort
- Mondeo
- Granada
- Cosworth

How can consumers be classified?

Businesses need to identify clearly different types of consumers so that they can provide the different goods each category of consumer requires. The most common ways of identifying consumers are as follows:

AGE

The age groups used to classify consumers are 16–24, 25–34, 35–44, 45–54, 55–64, and 65+. Companies and advertising agencies like to use these age groups, as people within these bands often have similar lifestyles. In addition, if all businesses use the same age groups, statistical information can be easily compared. There may be times when businesses use different age groups, for example if they look at all teenagers, they will use a 13–19 age group.

CHECK-OUT LIST

SMART SHOPPERS

Fresh carton soup, pistachio nuts, garlic bread, Ciabatta loaf, rye bread, Pont l'Evaque, Vignotte and Rocquefort cheeses, Milano salami, pastrami, Parma ham, crab claws, fresh-made garlic dressing, thick-cut bacon, duck, venison and game birds, Bart Simpson cake, custard-style and Greek-style yoghurt, French country and New World wine, fruit sorbets, continental ice cream, fromage frais, grissini, fresh blood orange juice, flavoured vodkas, designer lagers, frisee lettuce, cherry tomatoes, loose tea, obscure mineral waters, baby vegetables.

ASPIRATIONAL FOODS

Earl Grey tea bags, frozen Pavlova, mix-your-own Muesli, low-fat milk, spicy jumbalaya, Hellman's mayonnaise, bottled carbonated spring water, Bulgarian wine, brie, camembert, wheatmeal cheese biscuits, macedonia nuts, chocolate mint creams, maple-cured ham, frozen spare ribs, decaffeinated coffee beans, fillet steak, unsliced wholemeal bread, ready-made canapes, crudites with individual dips, taramasalata, pitta bread, chilled vegetarian cannelloni, chilled Peking duck, chicken satay, fresh orange juice, avocado, kiwi fruit.

COUNTRY CACHET

Mixed dried fruit, local dairy yoghurt, English and French wine, butcher's best sausages, Stilton, Farmhouse cheddar, Bath Olivers, mixed-grain bread, instant coffee granules, double cream, brown sugar, chocolate ginger biscuits, fresh topside of beef, root vegetables, Dundee fruit cake, free-range eggs, whisky, gin, tonic water, dry ginger ale, Horlicks, Heinz tomato soup, Gentleman's Relish, Loseley ice-cream, ham on the bone, strong tea bags, local variety mustards.

G. 3.1   SOURCE: DAILY MAIL 12/10/91

A C T I V I T Y

Read the article entitled 'Check-out list' below. Do you agree that consumers can be categorised according to their food purchases? If you had to invent a group name like 'smart shoppers' for students, what would the name be and what would the group's typical shopping basket include?

GENDER

Companies often need to identify whether their consumers are male or female. For example, Philips makes men's and women's shavers and Seiko makes different styles of watches for the different sexes.

TASTE

Individuals have different tastes and preferences. Some people are more adventurous than others and are willing to try new and different things, like exotic foods or new entertainment experiences. Your taste might dictate what sort of products you buy and which brands you select. Taste can cover food, fashion, travel, the arts and entertainment. Sometimes taste is dictated by spending power.

LIFESTYLE/LIFE CYCLE

Lifestyle is discussed in some detail in Chapter 8 'Promotion and Sales' in the section on audience targeting on pp.207–12. Life cycles are also a good way of identifying consumers. The recognised stages are as follows:

- bachelor stage – young single people not living at home

- newly married – young couple, no children

- full nest 1 – youngest child under 6

- empty nest 2 – older married couple, no children living with them, main wage earner retired

- full nest 2 – youngest child over 6

- solitary survivor in employment

- solitary survivor retired

- full nest 3 – older married couple with dependent children

GEOGRAPHIC DIFFERENCES

There are often geographic differences amongst customers. People's needs and wants will differ if they live in a city or the countryside. They may also lead a different type of life depending on the region or even the country they live in.

ACTIVITY

Read the article entitled 'Families going rapidly out of fashion' on the next page. Choose the role of marketing manager for a house-building company or a drinks or cigarette manufacturer. How would the factors mentioned in the article affect your plans for your company's products for the year 2000?

- empty nest 1 – older married couple, no children living with them, main wage earner working

FIG. 3.2 (OPPOSIT
SOURCE: DAILY MAIL 5/1/9

ONE IN SIX HOMES NOW HAVE SINGLE PARENTS

By JACKI DAVIS, Consumer Affairs Correspondent

RECORD numbers of women are raising children single-handedly as the breakdown in British family life gathers pace.

Only a quarter of households now comprise the traditional family group of a couple with dependent children, although 42 per cent of people still live in such housholds, says a Government report.

The number of families headed by one parent – normally a single or divorced woman – doubled from one in 12 in 1971 to one in six by 1988 with the numbers increasing sharply over the last five years.

The latest evidence of the decline of the traditional family emerges from a survey of more than 10,000 homes across the country by the Office of Population, Censuses & Surveys.

The number of couples living together has more than doubled over the last decade, according to the survey based on interviews with nearly 20,000 adults.

Impact

About one in five non-married women between 18 and 49 were cohabiting in 1988, compared with one in ten in 1979.

There has also been a sharp increase in trial marriages – up from just 4 per cent in the late 60s to 37 per cent by the early 80s. Births outside marriages rose from 7 per cent in 1968 to 23 per cent in 1987.

The statistics also highlight the impact on family life of rising divorce rates. By 1988, one in seven women and one in nine men had gone through a divorce.

And they show that divorced women are much more likely to go for younger men if they embark on marriage again. Only 14 per cent of first-time brides have younger husbands, compared to 33 per cent of those women who remarry.

The average age of women starting a family was 24 in 1988,

Families going rapidly out of fashion

with those in white collar groups having their first baby later than others.

And despite the fight for more equality, traditional divisions between the sexes persist in terms of educational qualifications.

Nearly two-thirds of men had some sort of qualification, compared with just over half of women. Men were twice as likely to have a degree or equivalent qualification.

The survey shows that average household sizes continued to decrease in 1988 with more people living alone and fewer homes including children.

The average household dropped from 2.91 people in 1977 to 2.48 in 1988. Most of the population had no children living with them in 1988 and the proportion of people living alone rose from 17 to 26 per cent over the 17-year period. Britain also has more old and sick than ever before.

Those with a long-standing illness have risen over the last two decades from 21 per cent in 1972 to 33 per cent in 1988.

In 1988, 5 per cent of men and 8 per cent of women were aged over 75 compared with 3 per cent and 6 per cent in 1977.

Smoking out the nicotine addicts

HEALTH campaigners are winning the battle to persuade more smokers to kick the habit.

One in three men and 30 per cent of women over 16 smoked cigarettes in 1988, compared with 52 per cent of men and 41 per cent of women in 1972. But the men who still smoke are getting through more cigarettes – 120 a week on average in 1988 compared with 115 in 1986. The figure for women was unchanged at 99.

The report adds that more than half of those who are still smoking now buy low to middle tar brands.

WOMAN'S WORK ...

TWO out of three married women now work compared with just over half in 1973.

The report shows that the number of working mothers with dependent children also rose steadily between then and 1988 – from 47 per cent to 50 per cent.

The figure jumped by another 3 per cent in 1989.

The career girls driven to drink

CAREER women drink more than those in semi-skilled or unskilled jobs.

But researchers found no clear link between men's work and the amount they drink.

One in ten women exceeded the recommended weekly 14 units – 14 glasses of wine, measures of spirits or halves of beer. But among the professional women the figure was one in seven, compared with one in 12 of unskilled women. One in four men exceeded their recommended 21 units. Overall, excessive drinking rose only slightly between 1984 and 1988.

Analyse the chart below and answer the following questions.

1 Why are housing costs highest in the South-East?

2 If Scotland spends a lot on alcohol and tobacco, what are the implications for the Scottish health service?

3 What do the leisure services spending levels tell us?

If you are an international company and sell electric coffee makers, you may find that the market in the UK is small, as most people drink either instant coffee or tea, but the market will be large in France and Italy, where ground coffee is the traditional drink. It is important that businesses recognise that consumers in different countries may have different tastes. This is not a hard and fast rule of course. You may be able to identify a common consumer in many countries across

Europe, for example in a youth market for a particular band's concert tickets or latest CD.

WHAT INFORMATION WILL HELP TO IDENTIFY DEMAND FOR GOODS AND SERVICES?

Before deciding on which products to sell to consumers, all companies need accurate information to identify the exact needs of consumers. Information is available from market research agencies and you can also carry out your own surveys by asking consumers, but this can be a very expensive process. The UK government is a very good source of information about the general public and how they spend their money, as they gather statistics on this every year. The Central Statistical Office gathers figures on a regular basis and publishes them. Most good public reference libraries will hold some of these statistics. The major sources are:

1 *General Household Survey* The General Household Survey is published by the government statistical service. It has been running since 1971 and focuses each year on the lives of a sample of the general population who are resident in private households in Great Britain. It looks at different aspects of people's lives – health, housing and

PROPORTION OF HOUSEHOLDS WITH EACH ITEM (%)		REGIONAL BREAKDOWN OF WEEKLY SPENDING, 1990 (£)						
		YORKSHIRE & HUMBERSIDE	NORTH WEST	WEST MIDLANDS	SOUTH EAST	SOUTH WEST	SCOTLAND	UK
One car/van	43.9	Housing	34.36	41.05	45.57	54.52	48.50	31.99	44.42
Two cars/vans	19.1	Fuel light & power	11.33	10.92	10.54	10.85	10.87	11.82	11.11
Three or more cars/vans	3.8	Food	41.59	42.71	43.50	48.92	42.88	44.32	44.81
All with cars/vans	66.8	Alcohol	9.92	11.62	8.91	10.16	9.12	10.50	10.01
Central heating	79.3	Tobacco	5.56	5.76	4.42	4.19	3.47	6.58	4.82
Washing machine	86.3	Clothing & footwear	14.16	16.23	15.72	17.48	14.28	17.58	16.03
Fridge or fridge/freezer	98.1	Household goods	18.53	19.81	20.02	22.65	18.49	18.94	20.00
Freezer or fridge/freezer	80.1	Household services	10.69	11.24	11.35	15.18	12.87	10.37	12.28
Television	98.1	Personal goods & services	8.63	8.44	8.14	10.95	11.05	8.49	9.47
Telephone	87.4	Motoring	27.65	39.63	38.93	33.89	39.63	27.07	33.83
Video recorder	61.2	Fares & other travel costs	5.22	5.33	4.61	8.81	4.30	5.98	6.19
Home computer	16.8	Leisure goods	9.89	10.26	9.37	13.68	11.60	9.86	11.28
Second dwelling	2.9	Leisure services	18.66	21.30	16.76	27.50	21.96	18.72	21.54
		Miscellaneous	1.15	1.07	1.10	1.88	0.99	1.06	1.37
		WEEKLY SPENDING	217.34	245.37	238.94	280.66	250.01	223.28	247.16

TABLE 3.1 WHO HAS GOT WHAT? REGIONAL BREAKDOWN OF WEEKLY SPENDING, 1990
SOURCE: DAILY MAIL 6/12/91

employment for example, and helps the government to formulate social policy.

2 *Key data* This covers a wide variety of subjects such as population trends, employment, income and leisure patterns.

3 *Social Trends* This covers similar subjects to the *General Household Survey*.

4 *Family Spending* and the *Family Expenditure Survey* This covers how people spend their money.

All of the above will give you an idea of how lifestyles and spending patterns are changing over time. Businesses are very keen to discover information about the market. By this they mean the number of actual and potential buyers for their product or service. Market information can be very valuable, as companies will try to forecast demand for their product by analysing the buying habits of the customers who make up their particular market. The type of information businesses use and which they might need to establish will include:

- how big the market is
- whether it is growing or declining
- what type of products people are buying
- how much they spend
- when they spend and how frequently
- how much they earn

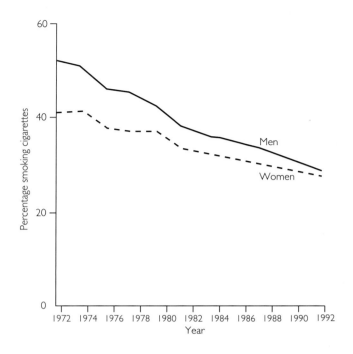

FIG. 3.3 CIGARETTE SMOKING BY SEX: GREAT BRITAIN, 1972–92
SOURCE: GENERAL HOUSEHOLD SURVEY, 1992

ACTIVITY

Review the statistics in the next column on smoking habits in the UK between 1972 and 1992. If you were a cigarette manufacturer how would you react to these figures? Are there any other products you might consider selling?

ACTIVITY

If you analyse the table below you can see that household expenditure on food and alcohol seems to be decreasing. Can you explain these figures? Are we all eating less? Could prices have any impact on these figures?

	1977		1982		1987	
	£m	%	£m	%	£m	%
Household expenditure on food	16,047	18.5	25,649	15.2	33,643	13.0
Expenditure on meals out	3,690	4.2	6,619	3.9	12,348	4.8
Total expenditure on food	19,737	22.7	32,268	19.1	45,991	17.8
Alcoholic drink	6,545	7.5	12,003	7.1	17,309	6.7
Total food and drink	26,282	30.2	44,271	26.2	63,300	24.5
Total consumers' expenditure	86,887	100.0	168,545	100.0	258,431	100.0

TABLE 3.2 CONSUMERS' EXPENDITURE IN THE UNITED KINGDOM
SOURCE: NATIONAL FOOD SURVEY, 1987

Demand for products will inevitably also depend on how much money people have. This can also be affected by the amount of credit that is available. The table on p.63 shows the change in attitude by consumers towards buying on credit between the years 1976 and 1991. It shows that people have not only changed where they get credit from, but also how willing they are to take credit on. Credit lending has increased enormously. Clearly, the more easily available the credit is, the more it increases the potential for consumer demand.

A C T I V I T Y

Analyse the graph below. What changes have taken place in society between 1964 and 1991 to allow the ownership of consumer durables to increase in this manner?

WHY DOES DEMAND CHANGE?

Some change in demand is often a result of a corresponding change in tastes and fashions. Consumers are used to seeing products from all over the world. With such a wide choice, consumers often seek new and different products and can tire of existing ones quickly.

Other changes come about for more practical reasons, for example if someone has been promoted or found a new job they will probably feel relatively well off. If someone has savings, a secure job, or a high wage and low out-goings (rent, bills, etc.) they will probably feel confident and secure enough to spend their money freely. People will also spend freely if they feel that the cost of living is low or not rising. This means that prices in the shops are not increasing, that mortgage rates are low or falling, and that people's income will cover their expenses fairly well. It may even mean that people have money left over to spend or save as they wish.

Higher wage earners will probably have more money to spend and therefore more choice of what they buy. Advertising will also influence demand. For example, advertisements for overseas holidays appear frequently after Christmas to encourage people to book trips to exotic destinations while the weather is still wintry at home.

In a recession other factors apply. If someone loses their job, they will cut down on their expenditure. They may stop spending on certain items, for example luxuries, and they may decrease their spending on essentials by switching to cheaper brands. Even those still in employment may worry about the prospect of redundancy and alter their spending patterns accordingly.

Remember that needs and wants change over time. In the 1950s a meal out would have meant either a traditional English meal or possibly French food in a restaurant or a café. By the 1990s this need could be satisfied by any number of ethnic restaurants, by themed restaurants, for example the Hard Rock Café, by pubs serving food or by wine bars, bistros and so on.

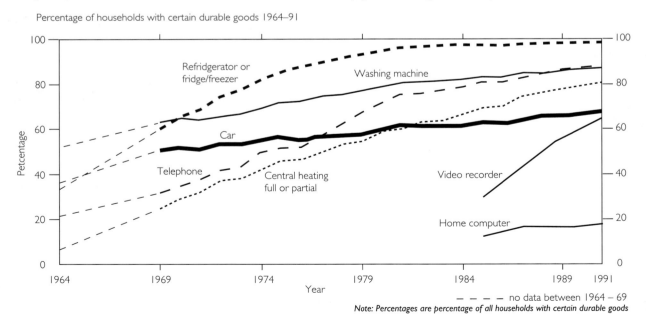

Percentage of households with certain durable goods 1964–91

Refridgerator or fridge/freezer

Washing machine

Car

Telephone

Central heating full or partial

Video recorder

Home computer

Percentage

Year

— — — — no data between 1964 – 69

Note: Percentages are percentage of all households with certain durable goods

Fig. 3.4 Consumer durables

Source: Key Data, 199

Effect of consumers on sales of goods and services

Consumers can play a vital role in creating demand for a product (a good or service). Individually one consumer's needs will have little effect, but when grouped together the needs and wants of consumers can strongly influence demand. This pattern can often be seen just before Christmas when parents are buying the latest toys or fashions as presents for their children. Over recent years we have seen very strong demand pre-Christmas for Cabbage Patch Dolls, Ninja Turtles toys, Transformer Robots and Power Ranger merchandise, often resulting in shortages of these products. Once the toy or television programme falls out of favour with children, parents no longer rush to buy them and demand falls, becoming much weaker.

Buying habits of consumers

Different consumers have different buying habits. Buying habits simply describe what people buy, when they buy it, how much they spend, where they shop and how often they shop. Consumers buy both goods, for example food, clothes, toiletries, and services, for example, hairdressing, transport (buses and trains) and dry cleaning. The type of good and service bought will depend on consumers' lifestyles and spending power. They will also have different levels of buying for different goods and services. For example, a consumer might buy bread and milk every day and spend a small amount of money on these goods. He or she might also have his or her hair cut once every six weeks and spend a moderate amount of money. The same person might buy a car once every six years and spend a large amount of money. These buying habits also show the frequency of purchase.

Trends in consumer demand

As people's tastes and lifestyles change they will create demand for new and different products. Sixty years ago consumers' major needs would be for basic products: food, clothes, entertainment, housing. There was limited choice in terms of consumer goods. Few families had cars, people took holidays locally, entertainment was limited to the cinema, dancehalls and the pub. By the 1970s and 1980s, trends in demand had changed. Many families would own cars and other consumer goods, for example TVs, washing machines, fridges and stereos. Overseas holidays were common and entertainment could be at sports and leisure facilities, different restaurants, pubs and clubs, bowling alleys or entertainment at home with videos and computer games. Inevitably, over time, demand for certain products will decrease or increase. For example, few people now buy typewriters, instead they buy personal computers with word processing packages. Fewer record players are sold as CDs are now generally preferred. Demand increases when new products are seen as either better or cheaper. For example, more people now buy free range eggs and environmentally friendly toiletries. Demand has also increased for new consumer goods such as satellite dishes, TVs and video recorders as people generally have more money to spend.

Fashions also change over time. With the youth market different young people can ge grouped by their tastes in fashion and/or music, for example, 'grunge', heavy metal, punk, rock or rap.

Great Britain							Percentages
	1976	1981	1984	1989	1990	1991	1992
All payments							
Cash[1]	93	88	86	80	78	78	76
Non-cash	7	12	14	20	22	22	24
Non-cash payments							
Cheque	68	68	64	55	52	50	46
Standing Order/Direct Debit	21	20	22	23	23	24	25
All plastic payment cards	7	9	13	18	20	23	25
of which:							
Credit/charge card	6	8	12	15	15	14	14
Retailer card	–	1	–	1	1	1	1
Debit card	0	0	0	2	4	8	11
Other[2]	2	2	1	4	4	3	4

1 Cash payments under 50 pence in 1976 and £1 from 1981 onwards are excluded
2 Includes deductions made directly from wages and salaries and payments made by Postal Order

TABLE 3.3 CONSUMER PAYMENT: BY METHOD   SOURCE: RESEARCH SURVEYS OF GREAT BRITAIN LTD FOR ASSOCIATION FOR PAYMENT CLEARING SERVICES

PLAN, DESIGN AND PRODUCE PROMOTIONAL MATERIAL

PURPOSE OF PROMOTIONAL MATERIAL

Depending on their own objectives, businesses will use promotion for different reasons:

- to create awareness of and inform people about a company, its products and its services
- to let customers know about a new product or service
- to create, improve or maintain the image of a business
- to influence consumer perceptions
- to stimulate sales growth and demand
- to counter the competition

Policy on the Environment

❝ Our **commitment** is to strive continuously to minimise adverse effects on the **environment** without compromising the high standards **customers** associate with our name ❞

FIG. 3.5 BOOTS' POLICY STATEMENT

Promotion is all about how businesses *communicate* with their customers and how they make them aware of the goods and services they offer. All types of businesses therefore need to use some of the different types of promotion that are available.

Local authorities like your city or county council may use local newspapers to inform of their services or direct mail to their customers.

FIG. 3.6 HULL CITY COUNCIL GUIDE

Service industries sometimes use the direct mail approach, sending leaflets directly to potential customers through the post. Larger service industries might use national advertising.

FIG. 3.7 BARCLAYCARD MASTERLOAN LEAFLET

Major businesses in the private sector often use the mass media such as TV or the press to promote their products or services.

FIG. **3.8** TV ADVERTISING

Business-to-business promotions often take the form of personal selling.

FIG **3.9** A SALES REPRESENTATIVE

Political parties often promote their candidates in elections using direct mail.

LABOUR PARTY NEWS

In this edition:

- ◆ Labour's Conservation Strategy. How it Affects You

- ◆ Liberal Plans to Divert Traffic on to Anlaby, Pickering Road and Boothferry Road

- ◆ Labour Fights Crime.

- ◆ Safer Roads Plans for Your Area.

ACTIVE IN YOUR AREA
LABOUR
ALL YEAR ROUND

Paul Salvidge has been selected as Labour's candidate for the local elections on May 5th.

Paul is a 29 year old Law graduate. He works as a Projects Controller with a successful local company. Paul has also worked at British Aerospace and then as a Law lecturer. He is a Governor at Eastfield School and Chairman of the local Labour Party.

FIG 3.10

TYPES OF PROMOTION

There are many different ways to promote. Businesses will choose whichever methods are most appropriate for them. They will also consider how much money they have available to spend on promotion (their budget) and what they are trying to achieve by promoting (their objectives).

Advertising

This can be used on TV and radio, in newspapers and magazines, and on billboards. It uses these 'mass media' to communicate a simple message to a large audience. It can be very expensive.

ACTIVITY

Collect your favourite advertisements from magazines and bring them to class to discuss what makes the best ones work well.

Sales promotion

This is an often-used technique that creates special offers. These include competitions, offers like 'buy two, get one free', free products and prizes, special events and so on. These can all be used to create a short-term boost to sales.

ACTIVITY

Collect the leaflets for as many consumer competitions as you can find. What are they trying to achieve? Create your own competition in groups.

Direct mail

This is sent directly to consumers and can bypass the retailer. It often requires a response from the consumer. Businesses buy mailing lists of names and addresses to target specific customers.

ACTIVITY

Collect one month's worth of direct mail that has arrived through your letter box. Which are the most effective leaflets? For which products does direct mail work best?

Sponsorship

A business sponsors a team, person or programme by providing funds. In return the sponsor has its name linked and promoted with the team.

ACTIVITY

List as many sponsors as you can and try to establish the link between the sponsor and the team sponsored.

ACTIVITY

On your next visit to the cinema list the advertisements you see there. What types of products or services do you think can be promoted most effectively at the cinema? Give your reasons for choosing these.

In its simplest form promotion can be seen as the design on shop fronts and signs, plastic bags carrying business names and logos, sandwich boards, display materials and packaging.

ACTIVITY

From the list below decide which method(s) of promotion would be the most effective.

- a regional car dealer has a limited number of cars to sell and is offering interest-free credit for a limited period
- an international confectionery business launches a new chocolate bar
- the local council wishes to advise householders of a change in collection day for their bins
- a computer company wants to launch a new business mini-computer
- a retailer wants to provide an end-of-season sale

Point of sale (POS)

This uses material available in retail or wholesale outlets where a product is sold. It is intended to stimulate sales of the product. It usually takes the form of leaflets, brochures, posters, showcards and display stands.

Choosing the right method

Promotion can be expensive so it is important that a business knows it is spending its promotional money wisely and getting good results from it. It makes sense for a company to try and measure how effective its promotion has been. There are different ways of doing this:

- measuring sales to see if they have increased during the promotional period
- asking customers via market research for their opinion of the promotion and their response to it
- monitoring spontaneous feedback from customers on the promotion, for example letters received
- monitoring general awareness of the company and promotion in the media

The performance of the promotion needs to be measured against any targets that were set when the promotion was created. Promotions can cause problems if they are not fully researched or monitored. Sometimes it is difficult to assess the performance of a promotion, as uncontrollable factors might affect it. For example, your competitors might introduce some discounts on their products at the same time your promotion is running.

PLANNING RESOURCES FOR PROMOTIONS

Like most other business functions, there are some key resources required in order to develop promotional materials.

Time

Time is required to develop materials effectively. Rushed materials that have not been checked efficiently may contain factual or spelling errors. Long planning cycles are required to make sure the end result has the right message attractively presented and correctly executed.

Human

Promotional material is a specialised area and you may need experts to help you develop them. These could be advertising agencies, sales promotions agencies, designers, photographers, printers and so on.

Physical

The same experts listed above will also have access to specialised physical resources. These could include film and photographic studios, print machinery, computer software such as graphics packages, as well as consumables such as stationery and film.

Financial

Time and human and physical resources all require the extra vital resource of finance. Promotional materials can be expensive so it is vital that an appropriate amount of money is allocated to them (see Chapter 8 'Promotion, sales and the media' for budgeting methods).

MEDIA USED TO PRODUCE PROMOTIONAL MATERIAL

The most common type of promotional material is **paper based**. This includes leaflets, showcards, posters or brochures. **Lens-based** material could include photographs. If you did not want to employ expensive experts and agencies and your company had its own computer experts, you could produce excellent **computer-based** promotional material using desktop publishing computer packages such as Aldus Pagemaker or QuarkXpress.

A C T I V I T Y

If you have IT facilities within your college ask one of your IT lecturers to demonstrate a desktop publishing package. As a group, with his or her help, produce a leaflet for a student social event.

The article below, entitled 'ASA consults trade bodies over code', lists several different bodies who are responsible for ensuring that businesses adhere to promotional codes of practice. Can you find out who the authorities are and what they do?

CONSTRAINTS ON PROMOTIONAL MATERIALS

Standards

Businesses do not have a totally free hand in producing promotional material. They have to ensure that they are not attempting to mislead consumers in any way. There are certain authorities who exist to make sure that businesses promote honestly and ethically. Broadcast advertising, for example on TV or on the radio, is regulated by a different system of rules to print advertising. The Broadcasting Act of 1981, using the control of the Independent Broadcasting Authority, aims to ensure that:

- advertising is not misleading
- an agreed code of practice is drawn up and reviewed
- all advertisers stick to the agreed code of practice

All non-broadcast media, for example the press, posters and direct mail, are controlled using the British Code of Advertising Practice and the British Code of Sales Promotion Practice. The requirements are that advertisements:

- are legal, decent, honest and truthful
- demonstrate a responsibility towards the consumer and society overall
- allow fair competition amongst businesses

In addition to the points above there are special rules for advertising health-care and medical products, advertising aimed at children, advertising using price cuts, and advertising featuring cigarettes, alcohol, slimming products and hair-care products. Can you find out what the special rules are? Why should these products require special rules?

FIG. 3.11
SOURCE: MARKETING, 1993

ADVERTISING REGULATION

ASA consults trade bodies over code

By Alyson Cook

The Advertising Standards Authority begins a review of the British Code of Advertising and Sales Promotion Practice this week – the first time guidelines have been scrutinised since 1988.

Normally, the 21 self-regulating advertising and marketing bodies which comprise the Committee of Advertising Practice review the codes alone. But this time, the ASA which administers them, is asking over 100 organisations, including trade and professional bodies, to participate in the review.

"As well as asking CAP committee members such as ISBA for their input, we will be asking other self-regulating bodies like the British Standards Institute, Government bodies such as the Broadcasting Complaints Commission, ABTA, the Food and Drink Federation, the Law Society, consumer bodies, as well as others who have expressed interest, such as political parties, "says the ASA's director general Matti Alderson.

Alderson denies there is anything "fundamentally wrong with the system devised by CAP", but hopes the new approach will lead to greater enthusiasm for the revised codes.

"It does seem to me that if everyone is going to have to use it, and they are, they should have a say in what it does, how it looks and how it's constructed."

"I think the earlier you can get people to feel they are buying into the system the more commitment they are going to have to following those rules when they eventually come into force – it's only human nature," says Alderson.

Organisations will be consulted at two stages this year – "first when looking at what we're doing with the code and second when changes are made when they will have an opportunity to comment", she says.

PROTECTION

Legal rights of customers

The law says that when a customer buys something they have certain rights. There are three rules:

1 Goods must be of merchantable quality. This means the goods should be fit to sell, i.e. they should be free from fault and not damaged or broken.
2 Goods must be fit to be used for their designated purpose. For example, if a shop says that a pair of scissors will cut paper, they must do so.
3 Goods must be as described. For example, if a customer buys a colour television set and takes it home, only to find out that it is black and white, then the set is not as described.

The law that deals with the buying of goods is the **Sale of Goods Act 1979**. The law that deals with services or goods that are provided as part of a service is the **Supply of Goods and Services Act 1982**.

The **Trades Descriptions Act 1968** says that sellers cannot make false descriptions and statements about goods and services. It also stops them using false or misleading prices. **The Consumer Protection Act 1987** aims to ensure that all goods bought are safe and that there is a remedy if goods are not safe.

Contracts

When customers buy goods or services, they make a contract with the seller. This is a voluntary agreement that is enforced by law. There are two main types of contract:

1 Formal contracts. These are in a written form, for example a contract for the sale of land or a house.
2 Informal contracts, for example buying a packet of crisps at the newsagents.

A C T I V I T Y

List five contracts you have made in the past two weeks. Were the contracts formal or informal?

There are three parts that make up a contract (whether formal or informal):

1 Offer and acceptance. One party must have offered something and the other party must have accepted it before the contract is valid.
2 Consideration. This is where something is given or received in return for the promise of payment. For example, Ian may have promised to give Barry one of his golf clubs, but fails to do so. In this case Barry can do nothing. However, if they made an agreement that Ian would sell Barry the clubs for £20 and Ian then fails to do so, Barry can sue Ian. There must be consideration for the contract to be valid.
3 Intention to create a legal partnership. For the contract to be valid both the buyer and seller must intend to stick to the agreement and the terms involved, for example, when somebody buys an item from a shop. Social agreements, such as going out for a meal with a friend, do not constitute a contract.

A C T I V I T Y

'Invitation to treat' is another important term to understand when learning about contracts. See if you can find out what it means and then write a paragraph about it.

A C T I V I T Y

Look at the following situations and decide whether or not the contracts are valid. Give reasons for your answers.

1 Roland agrees to buy Glenn's stereo for £200. At the last minute he decides to buy a stereo from a local store instead. Can Glenn take action against Roland?
2 Ralph promises Dave his computer as he has just bought a new one. Dave does not receive the computer. Can he take action against Ralph?

The Citizen's Charter

The Citizen's Charter was introduced by the Conservative Government in 1991. It deals with the rights of consumers in the following areas:

- Public sector
  - central government departments
  - local government departments
  - the National Health Service
- Private sector
  - key utilities, for example water, gas, electricity, telecommunications

Because the public pay for the above services either directly or indirectly (through taxes), they have the right to expect high-quality provision. Under the Charter the organisations concerned have to offer a certain standard of service to their customers. In addition, the organisations should be responsive to and prepared to cater for the needs of their customers.

The aims of the charter are as follows:

- to improve the quality of service offered
- to provide a better choice for consumers
- to improve standards
- to make organisations accountable (answerable) for their operations

Guarantees

See p.80 of Chapter 8 'Promotion, sales and the media'.

Consumer Associations

The following organisations seek to represent the interests of consumers.

CITIZENS ADVICE BUREAUX (CAB)

The CAB is funded by central government. It is a confidential service that aims to assist people with problems or concerns. The CAB:

- publishes booklets on consumer problems and other issues
- provides a free appointment service for members of the public needing help or advice
- helps people to obtain legal aid
- offers advice
- assists with letter writing, form filling and negotiations with organisations
- arbitrates in disputes between consumers and businesses

Areas dealt with by the CAB include: family and personal issues; housing, property and land; and consumer, trade and business.

THE OFFICE OF FAIR TRADING

This is a government organisation that:

- publishes information about consumer rights
- encourages organisations to establish codes of practice
- enforces the Consumer Credit Act
- makes recommendations to the government about consumer laws
- takes action against unfair traders
- deals with monopolies and mergers

THE CONSUMERS' ASSOCIATION

The Consumers' Association tests products to check their quality and standard, and publishes the results in its magazine *Which?* The organisation is independent and has quite a significant influence on business and consumers.

LOCAL CONSUMER GROUPS

These are set up locally and are encouraged by the Consumers' Association. Their aim is to encourage members of the public to take an interest in consumer issues and to campaign for improvements to local businesses and/or their products and services.

ACTIVITY

When you buy something, lots of tags or labels show symbols that give useful information about quality, content of products and so on. See if you can find the symbols listed below and explain what they mean.

- BSI safety mark
- BSI Kite mark
- the hand-in-tub symbol
- toy safety symbols

THE BRITISH STANDARDS INSTITUTION (BSI)

This is a national organisation that is run independently. It draws up specifications against which it tests products (and sometimes services). A product approved by the BSI is entitled to carry the BSI Kite mark.

The Department of Environmental Health

This is part of local government and is involved with the administration of legislation dealing with food, drink and hygiene.

The ombudsman

An ombudsman is responsible for dealing with complaints about the operations of certain organisations.

The first ombudsman, created in 1967, was the parliamentary commissioner for administration. He or she deals with complaints about central government departments, for example social security. The local commissioner for administration deals with complaints about local government departments, for example housing and social services.

The ombudsman scheme has grown over the years and there are now ombudsmen in the following areas: The National Health Service, insurance, banking, legal services, estate agents, pensions and building societies.

Consumers will go through a similar process when complaining to the ombudsman in other areas. NB There are some areas of complaint that the ombudsman cannot investigate.

Other relevant issues are covered under the heading 'Legal and ethical constraints on businesses' in Chapter 8, 'Promotion, sales and the media'.

Evaluating promotional materials

There is a wide range of promotional material available for businesses and it is sometimes difficult to choose the right promotional method. The business needs to be clear about what the promotion is supposed to achieve. Is it to increase sales or simply to give customers a message? Could it be to influence customers' perceptions? Once the purpose has been decided, businesses will then be able to assess which method is the most suitable. For each method, businesses will want to ask:

- Will it effectively communicate with the chosen audience?
- Will the promotion help to make and/or increase sales of the product?
- Will it positively influence consumers, leaving them with an improved perception of the product and/or company?
- Can the promotion get the right information over to the customer?

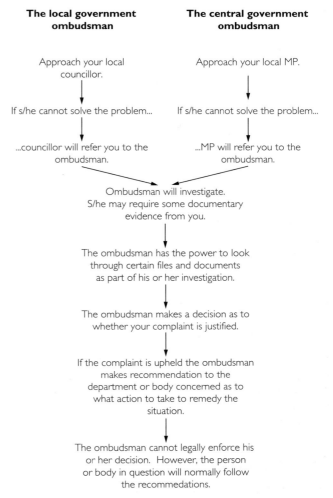

The local government ombudsman

Approach your local councillor.

If s/he cannot solve the problem...

...councillor will refer you to the ombudsman.

The central government ombudsman

Approach your local MP.

If s/he cannot solve the problem...

...MP will refer you to the ombudsman.

Ombudsman will investigate. S/he may require some documentary evidence from you.

The ombudsman has the power to look through certain files and documents as part of his or her investigation.

The ombudsman makes a decision as to whether your complaint is justified.

If the complaint is upheld the ombudsman makes recommendation to the department or body concerned as to what action to take to remedy the situation.

The ombudsman cannot legally enforce his or her decision. However, the person or body in question will normally follow the recommedations.

FIG. 3.12 MAKING A COMPLAINT

See pp.216–18 of Chapter 8, 'Promotion, sales and the media', for a detailed evaluation of the main methods of promotion and promotional materials.

Some customers will have special or different needs. For example, a vegetarian customer in a restaurant or a disabled customer in a department store, and this may affect the type of promotion chosen by an organisation.

PROVIDING CUSTOMER SERVICE

MEETING CUSTOMER NEEDS AND WANTS

Generally speaking, all customers need the following from businesses:

- the opportunity to purchase
- help, advice and information
- guarantees
- efficient after-sales service
- service over and above the minimum requirements in law
- a helpful exchange and refund policy
- complaints to be dealt with swiftly and fairly
- a fair pricing policy
- to be treated fairly and honestly

For more information on these services see Chapter 8 'Promotion, sales and the media'.

It is important that businesses are aware of the requirements of their customers so that:

- they can provide the right product or service at the right price and quality
- standards of service can be improved
- staff and customers will be content
- their business performance will improve

Finding out what customers want

As businesses depend on their customers it is important they find out exactly what customers want.

As customers and consumers have lots of different decisions to make when they buy, businesses try to find out as much as possible about what their customers want. Once they know this they can try to provide goods and services that meet the customers' wants exactly. They find out customers' wants by carrying out market research.

MARKET RESEARCH

There are several types of market research. One type is **primary** research. This is new research being done for the first time and it usually takes the form of a **survey**. Surveys use questionnaires that ask customers for their views, knowledge and opinions.

Where shall I buy it from?

Will I buy it now or wait until I get paid?

How much shall I spend?

Will I make this a regular purchase?

FIG. 3.13

Businesses can also use **secondary** research. This is information that has already been gathered and processed. Secondary research can be done without interviewing people and is sometimes called **desk** research. The information can be found in directories, company reports, newspapers, magazines and books.

ACTIVITY

Go to your local library and look for the titles listed below. They may be found in the reference or business section. These publications could be used for secondary research. List the type of information you can extract from these publications. What type of customer do they provide information about? How could you use this information to build up a profile of your customers?

- *Kompass Directory*, published by Reed Information Services in association with the CBI
- *Who Owns Whom?*, published by Dun and Bradstreet, eds Fiona Brodie, Paul Locke and Michael Wood
- the latest government census
- *Thomson Local Directory*
- the electoral register
- Mintel reports

Heathrow Penta Hotel

	excellent	good	fair	poor
Room reservation	☐	☐	☐	☐
Reception/Lobby				
Furnishings/atmosphere	☐	☐	☐	☐
Reception service	☐	☐	☐	☐
Cash desk service	☐	☐	☐	☐
Telephone service	☐	☐	☐	☐
Porterage service	☐	☐	☐	☐
Room				
Furnishings/atmosphere	☐	☐	☐	☐
Cleanliness	☐	☐	☐	☐
Maid service	☐	☐	☐	☐
Breakfast				
Furnishings/atmosphere	☐	☐	☐	☐
Quality of food/drink	☐	☐	☐	☐
Service	☐	☐	☐	☐
London Chop House				
Furnishings/atmosphere	☐	☐	☐	☐
Quality of food/drink	☐	☐	☐	☐
Service	☐	☐	☐	☐
Meridian Coffee Shop				
Furnishings/atmosphere	☐	☐	☐	☐
Quality of food/drink	☐	☐	☐	☐
Service	☐	☐	☐	☐
Bar				
Furnishings/atmosphere	☐	☐	☐	☐
Quality of food/drink	☐	☐	☐	☐
Service	☐	☐	☐	☐
Room service				
Promptness	☐	☐	☐	☐
Quality of food/drink	☐	☐	☐	☐
Service	☐	☐	☐	☐
Conference and Banqueting facilities				
Atmosphere	☐	☐	☐	☐
Technical conference facilities	☐	☐	☐	☐
Quality of food/drink	☐	☐	☐	☐
Service	☐	☐	☐	☐
Fitness area				
Furnishings/atmosphere	☐	☐	☐	☐
Cleanliness	☐	☐	☐	☐
Service	☐	☐	☐	☐
Other hotel facilities or services				
_____	☐	☐	☐	☐
_____	☐	☐	☐	☐

Remarks

FIG. 3.14

A C T I V I T Y

Collect as many questionnaires from businesses as you can. You can find them in magazines, on product guarantee forms and in retail outlets. Compare them. What do you think the business was trying to find out? Which of the questionnaires do you think works best? Why?

A C T I V I T Y

Look at the questionnaire printed opposite. Try and fill in the gaps with questions that you think are appropriate. What else do you think the business would want to know?

A survey is a fairly complicated operation to run effectively. It needs to be planned properly and thought about before the research can be carried out.

The chart on p.75 lists the steps you need to go through to carry out a survey. The left-hand column shows the planning steps you need to take into account; the right-hand column shows the questions you might ask yourself or the decisions you might take in response to each of the planning steps.

The Market Research Society MRS

MARKET RESEARCH
Your Opinion Counts

Thank You **For giving your time**

This interview was carried out by INT No. O33600___
For
Millward Brown International
Olympus Avenue, Tachbrook Park, Warwick CV34 6RJ
Tel Warwick 0926 452233   Fax 0926 315570

Millward Brown
International
Market and Social Research

Millward Brown International
are members of

(A) (M)
(S) (O)

c / o The Secretary,
Martin Hamblin Resear
36 Smith Square

If you wish to verify th
MRS Cod

market research

■ Why is market research important?

Market research is your opportunity to give your opinion on things that may affect you and your family. Manufacturers, retailers, service companies, political parties and the Government can only succeed if they please you, the customer, so they need to find out what you need and what you want. Your opinion can influence a wide range of products from pension plans to washing powder and also have a bearing on issues that affect the quality of your life.

It is the job of market researchers to ask questions - to find out what you, and people like you, think.

■ Why were you chosen?

For most research projects it is necessary to talk to a cross-section of the public-people from all walks of life and all ages. You have been asked to give your opinion as a representative of the population.

■ Why is it necessary to ask personal questions?

To make sure that we do achieve a cross-section of the population we do need to ask personal questions which may include details on occupation, income and age. This information is given in total confidence and is only asked to ensure that we have a representative sample of the population.

■ The replies are confidential so why do we ask for your name and address?

This is a safety mechanism mainly for your benefit. To check that this interview has been carried out fairly, and that the correct cross-section has been contacted, the Supervisor of the fieldwork company may contact you to confirm the accuracy of the interview. Nobody outside the fieldwork company will gain access to your name and address.

■ About The Market Research Society

The Market Research Society (MRS) is the professional body for market researchers, all MRS members have to operate under a Code of Conduct which includes certain guarantees for you, the interviewee. These guarantees state that you are entitled to remain anonymous if you wish, that you will suffer no adverse effects from being interviewed and that you may withdraw from the interview at any stage.

Answering questionnaires, in face-to-face interviews, via the post or on the telephone, gives you the opportunity to speak directly to those who can make the changes you want. As a safeguard for the public, the MRS has developed three schemes to check that you have been approached by authentic researchers and not by somebody trying to sell to you.

■ Interviewer Identity Card

Carried by up to 65,000 interviewers across the country, giving the interviewer's name, photograph and the company they work for.

■ Market Research Mark

For
na
to

s, sent out by post-this guarantees that the question-
oses only and that your name is not being added

Society

a week, 9am-
Mar-

The Market Research Society (MRS), the professional body for market researchers, has developed three schemes that help identify market researchers:

✓ INTERVIEWER IDENTITY CARD
for face-to-face interviews

✓ MARKET RESEARCH MARK
for postal surveys

✓ FREEFONE MARKET RESEARCH SOCIETY
for telephone interviews.

✓ Remember

Genuine market research, whether through the post, on the telephone or in the street

✓ is always confidential
✗ never tries to sell you anything
✗ never requests money
✗ never asks you to make an appointment with a salesperson.

■ Data Protection Act

Members of The Market Research Society operate within the Data Protection Act, which means that any personal data supplied will only be used for statistical and research purposes.

■ Code of Conduct

In addition to the Data Protection Act, all Market Research Society members abide by a strict Code of Conduct. This ensures that all research is carried out to the highest ethical and professional standards. It also means that it is possible to withdraw from the interview at any stage.

The Market Research Society MRS

15 Northburgh Street, LONDON EC1V 0AH
Tel: 071-490 4911 Fax: 071 490 0608

FIG. 3.15 EXAMPLES OF MARKET RESEARCH DOCUMENTATION

Planning steps	Questions/decisions
Decide what you want to find out. What is the business problem you need to solve?	Would my customers buy edible paper plates?
Decide if you will carry out the survey or use a market research agency to do it for you.	An agency is expensive, but more expert in research. I'll pay them to do it.
How will you collect this information?	In the street, as I don't want to use the phone or post my questionnaire.
How many people will you interview? How will you find them? What type of people should you interview?	I need to speak to busy families and young singles. I must speak to at least 1 per cent of all of them in the UK. The agency will select a sample of these people to interview.
Design your questionnaire, carefully checking the questions.	• Don't make the questionnaire too long or short • Arrange the questions in a logical order • Ask for personal details at the end of the questionnaire – people will be more likely to give details at this stage • Try and have a mixture of yes/no and open questions • Avoid ambiguous or misleading questions • Don't ask two questions in one • Always test your questionnaire on someone to iron out problems
Carry out your survey.	Hard work!
Process the information.	Where's the computer?
Analyse the information.	Most people wouldn't buy them.

FIG. 3.16 HOW TO CARRY OUT A SURVEY

Customer and business expectations

When customers buy a good or service, there will be certain things they expect:

- a good quality good or service
- value for money
- to be treated fairly

In turn the organisation will expect certain things from its customers:

- commitment to contracts
- fair dealing

Imagine that you go into a local store to buy a new CD player. When entering the store what would you expect:

a in the way you are treated by the staff in the shop
b in terms of the product you are buying
c with regard to the price of the product

Write a couple of sentences to answer each question and then discuss the questions in groups of two or three.

Write a list of other expectations a business organisation may have of its customers. Compare your list with those of others in the class. What are the most common expectations?

COMMUNICATION

Good communication is essential for any organisation dealing with customers. This is particularly important in the following areas:

- verbal communication
- non-verbal communication
- face-to-face communication
- use of the telephone

Have a look through the relevant sections in Chapter 6 'Business communications' to find out more about each of the above.

CUSTOMERS

When customers want to purchase products how they are treated may influence whether or not they decide to buy. If they are treated well they may choose to return to the organisation or tell their friends about it.

Tips for dealing with customers

1. Smile.
2. Greet the customer politely.
3. Show an interest in the customer's needs.
4. Give the customer time to explain what they want or need.
5. Listen.
6. Ask questions to check points or to find out additional information.
7. Be honest.
8. Use precise language, for example avoid using words such as 'er' or 'like'.
9. Be pleasant.
10. Be patient even if the customer isn't.
11. Avoid losing your temper.
12. Be smart.

TIPS FOR DEALING WITH CUSTOMERS ON THE TELEPHONE

1. Greet the customer properly. Some organisations may require that you use their standard greeting, for example 'Good morning, Smith's Superstore, how may I help you?'
2. Ask for the name of the caller and use this if possible (this will make the caller feel important).
3. Listen carefully.
4. Speak clearly.
5. Ask questions to check points or to find out additional information.
6. Make notes for reference.
7. Run through what has been said to avoid mistakes or confusion.
8. Thank the caller.

FIG. 3.17

FIG. 3.18

R O L E P L A Y

For the activity below one or two people should play the part of sales assistants and the other members of the group should play the part of the customers listed. It might be an idea to set up a shop counter with a telephone to make the situation more realistic. The organisation in question is Priestman's, a large, city-centre stationery chain.

The aim of the activity is to learn how to deal with customers. At the end of each roleplay discuss with the group and/or the lecturer or teacher how well the sales assistants dealt with each customer and what, if anything, could have been done differently.

1. A young man who is looking for a birthday present for his wife.
2. A disabled customer who cannot reach a notepad on one of the higher shelves in the store and needs some help from one of the sales assistants.
3. A young couple who wish to look at samples of wedding invitations printed by the store.
4. An angry customer making a complaint about a ruler purchased last week which has now snapped in half.
5. A teenager enquiring about whether there are any Saturday jobs in the shop.
6. A pushy salesperson working for a firm supplying pens and pencils.
7. A reporter from a local paper who is interested in writing an article on local businesses.
8. A lost lorry driver requiring directions to a nearby furniture shop.
9. An elderly gentleman who is taken ill in the store.
10. A small child in tears as s/he has lost his/her parents.

Try to act out the roleplay situations more than once if possible in order to give everyone a chance at playing the part of the sales assistants.

In pairs try to write some roleplay situations of your own and then carry them out with the rest of the group.

Customer complaints

There are four main areas of customer complaint:

1 Complaints about goods, for example faulty or damaged goods.
2 Complaints about services offered, for example delivery or credit.
3 Complaints about shops' fixtures and equipment, for example being dirty and unhygienic, causing damage to the customer.
4 Complaints about the staff, for example being rude or incompetent.

Most organisations will have a policy for dealing with complaints. Complaints should always be treated as genuine until proved otherwise.

Design a complaints form that could be used by a business organisation of your choice. When you have finished the form ask one of your friends to fill it in to see if it is easy to complete.

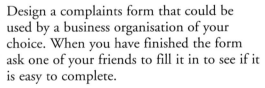

Customer complaints are dealt with in more detail on pp.194–6 of Chapter 8 'Promotion, sales and the media'.

Product knowledge

When buying a product it is important for the customer to feel that the seller is competent and efficient and above all has full knowledge of what he or she is selling, i.e.:

- how the product works
- what a service involves
- the costs
- details about guarantees
- methods of payment

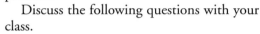

Kim visits Jutsum's electrical store to buy a personal stereo. She sees one she likes and approaches a sales assistant for further details. The assistant is unhelpful and demonstrates little knowledge of the product.

Discuss the following questions with your class.

1 How would Kim feel? Would she return to the store? Would she recommend it in future to her friends?
2 Had you been in the sales assistant's shoes, what would you have done?

Business communications

Chapter 6, 'Business communication', looks at the variety of methods of business communication in detail. Some are particularly relevant to customer needs. Outlined below are some common methods and their relevance to customer needs.

- *Oral (face to face)*. Most customers are dealt with on a one-to-one basis and require personal attention. Appropriate body language is important.
- *Oral (telephone)*. This is most relevant when dealing with queries and complaints. A good telephone manner is important as there will not be the benefit of face-to-face contact.
- *Written (letter)*. Customer letters will normally be written formally. They should be clear, polite and accurate.
- *Written (memo)*. These will be particularly important when communicating with internal customers. They should be clear, polite and accurate.
- *Customer/product information (statement of account)*. This will help to give the customer a clear and up-to-date picture of money spent and money owing.
- *Prices*. Customers should always be able to access information about up-to-date prices.
- *Guarantees*. Customers should be given details of a guarantee. This will normally be in written form such as a leaflet.
- *Safety notices*. Safety notices should be displayed clearly and prominently for both internal and external customers.

LEGAL REQUIREMENTS

Health and safety

It is important that business organisations are aware of the health and safety laws they must abide by. There are many legal areas a business has to be aware of, particularly in relation to their customers.

Safety is something that is often taken for granted by consumers. The Consumer Protection Act 1987 helps to ensure that goods being sold are safe and that there is a remedy if they're not; in other words, something the consumer can do if the goods are not safe.

It is a criminal offence to sell certain goods that do not meet safety standards laid down in the regulations of the Consumer Protection Act (and some laid down in certain other Acts). If goods appear on the market that might be dangerous the government can act swiftly to prevent their sale. Goods being sold must meet the 'general safety requirement'. The Consumer Protection Act of 1987 created a new general safety duty. This requires all suppliers of consumer goods to achieve an acceptable standard of safety where reasonable. It is a criminal offence to supply consumer goods which fail to comply to the general safety standard.

There are also a number of voluntary safety standards. The British Standards Institution has drawn up many of these and has its own specialist committees to prepare them. Other bodies also draw up standards. There are a growing number of world and European Community standards.

A C T I V I T Y

Earlier we mentioned the 'general safety requirement'. Have a look through some consumer legislation books to see if you can find out more about it. Prepare a leaflet about it for consumers to read.

FIG. 3.19 THIS SYMBOL INDICATES THAT A PRODUCT HAS BEEN CHECKED FOR SAFETY TO BSI STANDARDS

A C T I V I T Y

Draw the layout of a shop of your choice. Label the fire exits and write a paragraph to explain why you placed them where you did.

RESTRICTED SALES

Some goods that could be dangerous have restrictions on who is able to sell them and to whom. For example, many medicines can only be sold if a pharmacist is present; cigarettes cannot be sold to people under 16 years of age.

CONSUMER SAFETY IN SHOPS

Under the Occupiers' Liability Act 1957 the law says that when customers enter a shop the shopkeeper has a duty of care not to expose them to any hazard.

Let's take an example: Mr Hampson goes into a hardware store. Whilst waiting to be served a hammer falls off a shelf and hits him on the head. Mr Hampson could claim compensation as the store is at fault for not putting the hammer in a safe place.

There must be fire exits in shops. These should be marked clearly and not obstructed.

Other legislation to protect customers includes:

- The Trades Descriptions Act
- The Sale of Goods Act
- The Consumer Protection Act

These are discussed earlier in the chapter on p.69.

Honesty

The law says that businesses must be honest when dealing with customers. For more detail on this see p.70.

PRESENT PROPOSALS FOR IMPROVEMENT TO CUSTOMER SERVICE

THE IMPORTANCE OF CUSTOMER SERVICE

Customer service can help a business to become more competitive and more attractive to a customer. When a customer is reassured by the help and service he or she receives, he or she is more likely to go back to that business and buy again. Satisfied customers are likely to recommend the business to friends and family and, in doing so, improve the organisation's image. Positive 'word of mouth' recommendation can act as free advertising for the business.

BUSINESS ORGANISATIONS

Private sector

These are organisations set up and run by private individuals with the aim of making a profit. They need customers in order to be able to do it.

Public sector

These businesses may not be trying to raise money or make profits from their customers, but they still need customers and are becoming more customer orientated or 'user friendly'. This type of organisation needs customers so that:

- the business can provide a good or service to the community
- the business can provide services and receive support from the local public

The customers may not pay for the service directly as they would when buying a can of beans from a shop. For example, you do not pay the refuse collector who empties your bin every week. Householders do pay for local services indirectly, however, through their council tax. A local council is an example of a public-sector business that depends on its customers for its custom and existence. The customers could be householders, local businesses or other public services that no longer

form part of the public sector.

For more details about public- and private-sector organisations see pp.1–7 of Chapter 1, 'Business organisations and employment'.

SATISFYING CUSTOMERS

There are many ways businesses can satisfy customers. They can:

- provide help, advice and information
- give guarantees
- provide efficient after-sales service
- give customer service over and above the minimum requirements in law
- promote a helpful exchange and refund policy
- deal swiftly and fairly with complaints
- offer a fair pricing policy

For further information on these services refer to Chapter 8 'Promotion, sales and the media'.

ACTIVITY

Do your own mini-survey in your high street.

1 How many retailers have customer service desks?
2 What customer care services are available to customers?
3 Which retailers have clear statements about refunds and exchanges? What do they say?
4 Are there any retailers displaying signs that do not comply with the law?

Some companies who sell or install technical equipment to their customers have help desks or helplines so that customers can ring up for help if they have a problem. Most help desks have a 'charter' that guarantees a range of services to customers. If you were responsible for a help desk for a business that installs photocopiers:

1 What promises would you make to your customers in your 'charter'?

2 List the type of problem a typical day's calls to the helpline might throw up.

How businesses monitor customer satisfaction

There are several ways customers can demonstrate their feelings to a business.

Sales figures can indicate whether customers are happy with a company or product, particularly if customers are loyal and go back to the same business to buy the same product again and again. If sales are down it is possible that customers are dissatisfied with the goods or services.

The most obvious way is for customers to give **direct feedback** to the business concerned. This could be a letter of complaint or praise, or even a telephone call. The aim of businesses will be to keep complaints to a minimum.

Businesses sometimes ask for **guarantee cards** to be sent back to them for registration when you buy a product. These often include extra questions on the card to gather more feedback from their customers. Alternatively, businesses will conduct **market research** (see p.72) to receive the feedback.

Businesses can also ask their customers for feedback directly by asking them to take part in discussion groups. These groups are often used by businesses to test new products or packaging before they are launched onto the market.

Review the *Which?* magazines in your library. They often outline customer complaints and their solutions. How did the businesses you read about react to complaints? What would you have done if it had been your business?

There are now many programmes in the media that allow individuals to air their grievances against businesses they feel have acted unfairly. The most famous of these are programmes such as *Watchdog*, *That's Life* and *The Cook Report*. In groups prepare a script for one of these programmes and videotape the programme. Make sure each point of view is fairly represented and that your group provides a solution to the problem that is acceptable to all the parties concerned.

Fig. 3.20

ALBA | **CERTIFICATE OF REGISTRATION** | **IMPORTANT**

REGISTERING YOUR NEW ALBA PRODUCT

To register your product for its 12 month guarantee please complete and return the section below.

MR
MRS
MS SURNAME   INITIALS

NUMBER/HOUSE NAME/STREET

TOWN

COUNTY   POSTCODE

PRODUCT DETAILS

MODEL No.   SERIAL No.   DATE OF PURCHASE

PRODUCT DESCRIPTION   PRODUCT VALUE

NAME OF RETAILER

On the expiry of the manufacturer's guarantee you will be sent details of our annual insurance plan but if you have already bought an extended warranty for this product from your retailer please tick box ☐

The information provided will be held on computer by the Alba Registration Department of Domestic & General Insurance Co. Ltd for the provision of warranty insurance or product related purposes. This information will not be disclosed to third parties, should you prefer not to receive such details write to Domestic & General Insurance Co. Ltd, on the address overleaf.

YOUR 1ST YEAR MANUFACTURER'S GUARANTEE

Please keep this with your purchase receipt, which will be required if service is needed on this product during the guarantee period.

KEEP THIS SECTION FOR FUTURE REFERENCE

MODEL No.

SERIAL No.

DATE OF PURCHASE

Customer service

Examples of customer service include:

- the way staff deal with customers
- the level of product knowledge that staff have
- the time customers have to wait to be served
- the treatment customers receive on the telephone
- the company's returns and refund policies
- the method of dealing with complaints and problems
- the availability of customer helpdesks
- the range of customer facilities, for example, baby-changing areas

Improvements to customer service

CASE STUDY

Daniels is a small, family-run department store which has been established since 1926. The business has a good reputation in terms of the way it treats its customers. However, Mr Daniels, the manager, has realised that competitors offer more modern methods of customer care and that Daniels should be offering the best possible customer service. He has decided to introduce the following measures:

- a written statement which outlines the policy for exchanges or refunds
- a new lift and wider entrances and exits to assist wheelchair users and customers with pushchairs
- a guarantee to customers that all ordered goods will be delivered within two days
- the review and introduction of a wider range of products available to customers
- to send all staff on a one-day customer care training course to ensure reliable and friendly service
- to employ extra cleaning staff to ensure a rubbish-free, cleaner store
- to organise a health and safety inspection to be carried out to ensure customer safety
- to introduce a customer care section within the store
- to introduce a new uniform and name badges so that customers can clearly identify members of staff

CHAPTER THREE

Test Yourself!

1 State two reasons why businesses need customers.
2 List three ways to improve customer service.
3 What is primary research?
4 What is secondary research?
5 List three ways in which a business can satisfy the needs of its customers.
6 State two reasons why businesses use promotions.
7 Explain one way in which businesses might promote their products.
8 When a customer buys something, the law has three rules. What are they?
9 List three ways of classifying consumers.
10 Outline two causes of change to consumer demand.
11 List five important things to remember when dealing with customers.
12 What is point-of-sale material?
14 How does sponsorship work?
15 Why is product knowledge important?
16 What resources are required for promotions?
17 Name two constraints on producing promotional materials.
18 List four types of business communication.
19 Identify two pieces of consumer legislation.
20 List three ways of monitoring customer satisfaction.

CHAPTER THREE

Evidence-Gathering Projects

CASE STUDY

Crystal Fashions is a successful company that markets costume jewellery all over the world. Established in 1929 the company has a multi-million pound turnover and sells its product in quality retail outlets in the UK, particularly in department stores. The jewellery is sold under three different brand names: Trifari, Monet and Marvella. The business has customers in many different European countries and therefore has to deal in many languages and currencies. It has become expert at satisfying not only the needs of the consumers who buy and wear the jewellery, but also the needs of its direct customers, for example the department stores who sell the jewellery to the general public. This requires a great deal of research and good planning.

Fig. 3.21

You have just been appointed the European marketing manager after your previous job as marketing manager with a cosmetics company.

1 Explain the importance of consumers and customers.

You need to find out about the organisation's customers as quickly as possible.

i Using the press releases provided (Figure 3.22, parts 1, 2 and 3), identify the consumers Crystal Fashions are currently aiming at. Explain differences in buying habits between the consumers you have identified.

ii Write a short report to describe the effect of consumers on Crystal Fashion's sales and explain possible causes of a recent increase in sales.

iii Identify trends in the fashion industry (past, present and future) which might affect the style of jewellery Crystal Fashions sell. For example, silver jewellery becoming popular.

iv Design an item of jewellery which could be introduced in response to one of the trends identified in iii above. The jewellery can be designed manually or by using a computer package.

v You are considering the possibility of introducing a telephone ordering service at Crystal Fashions. Explain how you think this will affect:

- consumer demand
- the types of consumer purchasing the jewellery
- changes in consumer buying habits

vi Prepare a short presentation for the sales staff to explain the importance of customers to Crystal Fashions.

2 Plan, design and produce promotional material.

i Prepare a new promotional campaign together with proposed promotional materials. You must state what you expect to achieve, any constraints on the content of your material and the resources you will require. Examples of existing materials are shown in Figure 3.21.

ii Write a memo to the Marketing Director, informing her of your new campaign and evaluating its likely success. In the memo, identify other types of promotions Crystal Fashions may use in the future.

3 Providing customer service.

i Prepare a staff handbook for new sales assistants to include:

- details of Crystal Fashion's customers and their needs
- details of Crystal Fashion's customer service
- samples of business communications which meet customer needs (written, customer/product information)
- the procedure for dealing with customers (face to face or on the telephone)
- details of consumer legislation of which your staff should be aware

4 Present proposals for improvement to customer service.

Produce a company newsletter to help maintain and improve the level of customer service provided by your company. All employees will receive this on a regular basis. Your first issue should include:

- an explanation of why customer service is important at Crystal Fashions
- an outline of the methods Crystal Fashions currently uses to monitor customer satisfaction
- details of any recent improvements to customer service
- proposals for improvements to customer service in Crystal Fashions

T R I F A R I

FOR IMMEDIATE RELEASE

NOVEMBER 1991

SPRING/SUMMER 1992

SPRING BOUQUETS

Trifari launches a whole new Spring Collection using the season's hottest motif - flowers. Daisies, Morning Glories, Pansies, Dogwood are all in full bloom in the SUNFLOWER Collection. The flowers are moulded in textured semi bright gold to achieve a true floral dimension.

SUNFLOWER COLLECTION (Model)

Sunflower Necklace	£75.50
Sunflower Bracelet	£40.50
Sunflower Earrings	£22.50

The essence of Tulips is interpreted into a dramatic graduated collar with matching ensemble in the TIGER LILY Collection. The fluid link-on-link design provides the mechanics for an extremely flexible necklace and bracelet.

TIGER LILY COLLECTION (Still Life)

Tiger Lily Necklace	£55.50
Tiger Lily Bracelet	£35.00
Tiger Lily Earrings	£20.00

All Trifari jewellery is 22 carat gold plated.

For further information, or colour transparencies please contact :

Simonetta Dickinson/Aly Dracup
Crystal Fashions Press Office
18 Queen Anne's Gate
London
SW1H 9AA

Tel No : 071 222 9002

Hélène Rabilloud	Liliana Capovilla	Dagmar Köster	Jarka Plevier	Regine Gobin
3 Rue de Nancy	Piazza Belgiojoso, 2	Rosenstrasse 35	Scandinavia/Benelux	Felix Boix 18
75010 Paris	20121 Milano	4000 Dusseldorf 30	De Steiger 206	28036 Madrid
France	Italy	Germany	1351 AW Almere-Haven	Spain
Tel: (33) 14 200 9264	Tel: (39) 02 7600 2213	Tel: (49) 211 498 2560	Holland	Tel: (34) 1250 6905
			Tel: (31) 32 4012 864	

FIG. 3.22 PART I

FOR IMMEDIATE RELEASE

NOVEMBER 1991

SPRING/SUMMER 1992

LUXURIOUS MOMENTS

This season "classic" design is the key - simplicity is the look. For a more feminine approach to softer daytime dressing Monet launches the MOHAIR Collection: bunched chains of textured gold. Beautifully finished collars, bracelets and earrings.

MOHAIR COLLECTION (Model)

Mohair Necklace	£53.00
Mohair Bracelet	£31.00
Mohair Earrings	£22.00

For the dynamic woman Monet presents the BUCKSKIN Collection. A bold design of interlocking links with polished elements to create a sharper dramatic look.

BUCKSKIN COLLECTION (Still Life)

Buckskin Necklace	£53.00
Buckskin Bracelet	£31.00
Buckskin Earrings	£19.50

All Monet jewellery is triple-plated in 22 carat gold.

For further information, or colour transparencies please contact :

Simonetta Dickinson/Aly Dracup
Crystal Fashions Press Office
18 Queen Anne's Gate
London
SW1H 9AA

Tel No : 071 222 9002

Hélène Rabilloud	Liliana Capovilla	Dagmar Köster	Jarka Plevier	Regine Gobin
3 Rue de Nancy	Piazza Belgiojoso, 2	Rosenstrasse 35	Scandinavia/Benelux	Felix Boix 18
75010 Paris	20121 Milano	4000 Dusseldorf 30	De Steiger 206	28036 Madrid
France	Italy	Germany	1351 AW Almere-Haven	Spain
Tel: (33) 14 200 9264	Tel: (39) 02 7600 2213	Tel: (49) 211 498 2560	Holland	Tel: (34) 1250 6905
			Tel: (31) 32 4012 864	

FIG. 3.22 PART 2

marvella

FOR IMMEDIATE RELEASE
NOVEMBER 1991

SPRING/SUMMER 1992

A PALETTE OF PEARLS

Marvella launches into Spring with two new and innovative colour combinations of pearl - a jazzy black and white theme and a delightful melange of frosted pink, mocha and vanilla. The BLACK AND WHITE Collection is the perfect match for the current graphic trend of polka dots and stripes. Dynamic combinations for day or night.

BLACK AND WHITE COLLECTION (Still Life)

Black and White Necklace	£30.50
Black and White Bracelet	£36.00
Black and White Earrings	£15.50

Rose and Taupe pearls also available.

Large or small, baroque or freshwater, twisted or single stranded, Marvella pearls offer an unlimited variety for every occasion.

CLASSIC PEARL COLLECTION (Model)

Graduated Necklace	£18.50
Bracelet	£37.00
Drop Earrings	£18.50

Marvella pearl strands are hand-knotted and all Marvella clasps are 22 carat gold plated.

For further information, or colour transparencies please contact :

Simonetta Dickinson/Aly Dracup
Crystal Fashions Press Office
18 Queen Anne's Gate
London
SW1H 9AA

Tel No : 071 222 9002

Hélène Rabilloud	Liliana Capovilla	Dagmar Köster	Jarka Plevier	Regine Gobin
3 Rue de Nancy	Piazza Belgiojoso, 2	Rosenstrasse 35	Scandinavia/Benelux	Felix Boix 18
75010 Paris	20121 Milano	4000 Dusseldorf 30	De Steiger 206	28036 Madrid
France	Italy	Germany	1351 AW Almere-Haven	Spain
Tel: (33) 14 200 9264	Tel: (39) 02 7600 2213	Tel: (49) 211 498 2560	Holland	Tel: (34) 1250 6905
			Tel: (31) 32 4012 864	

FIG. 3.22 PART 3

FIG. 3.23

FIG. 3.24

G. 3.25

Chapter
4

FINANCIAL AND ADMINISTRATIVE SUPPORT

This chapter enables you to understand different financial transactions and other business documents. It will help you to develop the skills to complete the documents.

IDENTIFY, EXPLAIN AND COMPLETE FINANCIAL TRANSACTIONS AND DOCUMENTS AND EXPLAIN FINANCIAL RECORDING

WHY DO ORGANISATIONS NEED TO RECORD FINANCIAL TRANSACTIONS?

In most organisations a number of financial transactions will take place every day. It is important to record (or document) each stage of the buying and selling process. This will mean that:

- the organisation can keep customer accounts up-to-date
- the organisation will have an accurate and up-to-date picture of its current financial position
- it will be able to produce a set of accounts at the end of the financial year
- the organisation can take security measures
- the information recorded can be used to monitor business performance, i.e. whether or not the organisation is doing well

ACTIVITY

1 Find out what the Inland Revenue and Customs and Excise are responsible for.
2 What sort of information do you think a business organisation may have to supply them with?

- there will be a permanent record which can be checked if necessary
- other organisations can be supplied with information, for example: the Inland Revenue, Customs and Excise or external auditors
- the organisation can monitor income and expenditure

Examples of financial information produced by businesses include internal accounts, external annual accounts and budgets.

INFORMATION TECHNOLOGY

Information technology is becoming important for financial recording within businesses. It is often more common for businesses to use accounting software packages and/or speadsheets rather than manual methods.

FINANCIAL TRANSACTIONS

Outward transactions

These are financial transactions which take money out of the business to cover costs such as wages, materials and overheads.

Inward transactions

These are financial transactions which bring money into the business, for example, payments from customers or bank loans.

PURCHASES

Organisations have to buy or *purchase* a number of different things as part of their business operations.

Materials are the items used in the manufacturing process to produce the finished goods which will then be sold by the organisation, for example wood to make furniture. They are usually referred to as raw materials.

FIG. 4.1 MATERIALS (WOOD)

Capital equipment is the major equipment used in the business which normally requires a large amount of capital (or money) to purchase, for example buildings, furniture and machinery.

FIG. 4.2 CAPITAL EQUIPMENT (BUILDING)

Consumables are the products used in the day-to-day running of the business, for example stationery.

Businesses will require other organisations to provide **services** to assist them, for example painting and decorating, maintenance, sandwich delivery.

In a way, when an organisation takes on its staff, it is purchasing their service or labour. The cost involved will be the payment of their **wages/salaries** plus National Insurance and pension contributions.

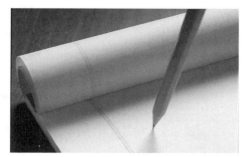

FIG. 4.3 CONSUMABLES (PEN AND PAPER)

A C T I V I T Y

1 Make a list of as many different services you think a business organisation might use.
2 Make a list of as many different consumables you think a business organisation might use.

Purchasing documents

There are a number of documents involved in the purchasing process.

ORDER FORM

An organisation will normally have their own pre-printed order form. The form will provide clear details about the type and quantity of goods required. Sometimes a request for a specific delivery date may be included. The total price is not shown on the order form. Also included on the form will be a reference number. At least one copy of the document should be kept for reference purposes. An example of an order used by a real business organisation, Omron Systems UK Limited, is shown on p.90.

Once an order has been made, the seller will sometimes write to the buyer to confirm that the order has been received. At this stage the seller may check that the buyer is 'credit worthy', i.e. whether it conducts its financial affairs in a proper manner. The buyer will be asked for some form of reference, possibly from the bank.

ADVICE NOTE

This is the document sent by the seller that tells the buyer the goods have been despatched. This gives the buyer the chance to check for any mistakes and to prepare for the arrival of the goods.

CARTERS LTD
7 Cooke Street Cardiff Wales CD1 1AX

ORDER

Tel: (01222) 127352

VAT Reg No.: 187/4295/21
Date: 19/11/19_ _
Order No.: 173/24

To: Billabong Stationery Supplies
       Beed Road
       BRADFORD
       BD1 7HQ

DESCRIPTION	QUANTITY	REF NO.	UNIT PRICE	TOTAL
Boxes of A4 plain paper	10	P4	£6.50	£65.00
Ink pens	6	I3	£5.00	£30.00
				£95.00

GOODS WILL ONLY BE ACCEPTED ON PRODUCTION OF AN OFFICIAL ORDER NUMBER

Signed   ....

Designation   ....

FIG. 4.4 AN ORDER FORM

OMRON SYSTEMS U.K. LIMITED
Victory House, Cox Lane, Chessington, Surrey KT9 1SG
Tel: 081-974 2166   Customer Service: 081-974 1556
Fax: 081-974 1864

OMRON

PURCHASE ORDER

No.   S 07529

TO:

Date of Order	Date Required	Your Reference:	For Queries Contact:

Item	Quantity	Description	Unit Price	Price

PLEASE QUOTE ORDER NO. ON DELIVERY ADVICE NOTE AND INVOICE.	Name in Capitals	Authorised Signature for OMRON SYSTEMS

PRF/003-1

FIG. 4.4A AN ORDER USED BY A REAL BUSINESS
ORGANISATION, OMRON SYSTEMS UK LIMITED

GOODS RECEIVED NOTE

This is a record of the goods actually delivered. It is completed by the person who checks the delivery. All the items are checked against the delivery note that should accompany the goods. A goods received note used by a real business organisation, Omron Systems UK Limited, is shown on p.92

PURCHASE INVOICE

A purchase invoice is received by an organisation purchasing goods. It may be sent in advance, with the goods or after they have been delivered. This document shows in detail the quantity and type of goods that have been sent. It also contains a detailed breakdown of the cost of each item plus additional information such as cash discounts (normally shown as 'Terms'). The total price of the goods will be included. The invoice can be checked against the order form to check that the information on the invoice is correct. The goods received will also be checked against the invoice.

VAT stands for value-added tax and is added to most things you buy (except children's clothes, essential foods and some services). See Figure 4.6.

FIG. 4.5 GOODS RECEIVED NOTE

ACTIVITY

Look at pp.117–18 in Chapter 5 'Financial recording', and carry out the activities relating to the calculation of VAT.

SALES TRANSACTIONS

Business organisations rely on customers purchasing their goods or services (i.e. making sales) to survive. It is important to remember that customers buy *both* goods and services. Sales might come from other businesses or members of the public.

Sales documents

When a sale is made it is important that details of the transaction are accurately recorded. Every time a customer makes a purchase the business makes a sale. For this reason, sales documents tend to be closely linked to purchase documents.

CARTERS LTD

GOODS RECEIVED NOTE

GRN No.: 1734
Date: 20 June 19_ _
Delivery Note No.: 12/321

Supplier:
    Billabong Stationery Supplies
    Beed Road
    BRADFORD
    BD1 7HQ

ORDER NO.	QUANTITY	DESCRIPTION	REF NO.
173/24	10	Boxes of A4 plain paper	P4
	6	Ink pens	I3

Received by ....

GOODS RECEIVED NOTE

OMRON

No: 6764

Date Received:	Advice No:	Invoice number:	Omron purchase order No:	Ordered by:	Site:

Supplier:	Carrier:	Goods taken in by:	Stock card entry:		Property of:	
			Yes	No	Omron	Supplier

Comments:	Customer	Other
	For repair:	
	Yes	No

Omron part No:	Description	Quantity: Advised:	Received	Counted: Yes	No	Serial No: (or identifying marks)

Now located in:	G.R.N Completed By:	Handed over to:	Signature:

WHF/005 - 2

FIG. 4.5A A GOODS RECEIVED NOTE USED BY OMRON SYSTEMS UK LIMITED

FIG. 4.6 PURCHASE INVOICE

Billabong Stationery Supplies
Beed Road
Bradford
BD1 7HQ

Tel: (01274) 127341

VAT Reg No.: 173/1096/67

Invoice

Order No.: 173/24
Invoice No.: 1235
Despatch Date: 24 June 19_ _

To: Carters Ltd
      7 Cooke Street
      Cardiff
      Wales
      CD1 1AX

QUANTITY	DESCRIPTION	UNIT PRICE	TOTAL PRICE
10	Boxes of A4 plain paper	£6.50	£65.00
6	Ink pens	£5.00	£30.00
	Goods total		£95.00
	Plus VAT at 17.5%		£16.60
	INVOICE TOTAL		£111.60

Terms of payment: 28 days
E&OE

ORDERS RECEIVED

On p.89 order forms were discussed. When an order form is received it should be carefully checked to ensure that the information on it is correct. Any problems should be resolved as soon as possible.

DELIVERY NOTE

A delivery note usually accompanies the goods sent to the buyer. When the buyer is happy that the goods received are the ones ordered he or she signs the note. A copy will be kept by both the supplier and the customer.

SALES INVOICE

On p.92 we looked at an example of a purchase invoice. In the same way, organisations issue sales invoices to their customers when they make a sale. In many cases a sales invoice is not necessary. For example, if people call in to an organisation to make a purchase it is likely that they will be paying for the goods immediately. An invoice only needs to be issued when payment is to be made after the goods have been delivered or the service carried out.

STATEMENT OF ACCOUNT

This is usually sent by the seller to the buyer and includes the following information:

- a summary of all transactions made during the month (individual items are *not* indicated)
- money outstanding from the previous statement
- details of the total amount of money due on each invoice
- information as to whether or not payment has been received on credit notes issued
- the amount of money to be paid (the balance shown at the end of the statement)

An example of a statement used by a real business organisation, Omron Systems UK Limited is shown on p.95.

REMITTANCE ADVICE

A remittance advice often accompanies a statement. The advice slip will be returned with a cheque when the purchaser pays for the goods. It includes the account number, invoice details, date of payment and total payment due. The remittance advice helps the supplier to accurately process the payment when it is received. An example of a remittance slip is included alongside the statement in Figure 4.8A on p.95.

FIG. 4.6A AN INVOICE USED BY OMRON SYSTEMS UK LIMITED

OMRON SYSTEMS U.K. LIMITED
Victory House, Cox Lane, Chessington, Surrey KT9 1SG
Tel: 0181-974 2166 Customer Services 0181-974 1556
Fax: 0181-974 1864

OMRON

VAT. No. 317 9391 35

SALES INVOICE

INVOICE No:
DATE
ACCOUNT No:
DELIVERY NOTE No:
ORDER REF:
SALESMAN No:

Invoice Address:

Delivery Address:

CUSTOMER ORDER No.

PRODUCT CODE	DESCRIPTION	SERIAL No.	ORD	SUPP	DISCOUNT	UNIT PRICE	VAT RATE	TOTAL

VAT RATE	GOODS	VAT

Non delivery or any delivery discrepancy must be reported, in writing, to the above address within 21 days of invoice otherwise no claim maybe entertained for loss in transit.

GOODS TOTAL
VAT TOTAL
INVOICE TOTAL

E. & O. E.
REF SAF 015-2

TERMS 30 DAYS

CARTERS LTD
7 Cooke Street Cardiff Wales CD1 1AX

INVOICE

Tel: (01222) 127352

VAT Reg No.: 187/4295/21

Deliver to: B. Smithson

To: Hills Hardware
      High Street
      HUTTON
      HU3 1ET

Invoice Date/ Tax point	Invoice No.	Despatch Date	Order No.
13/7/19_ _	B92/137	15/7/19_ _	113/907

DESCRIPTION	QUANTITY	UNIT PRICE	TOTAL
Boxes of 3 inch nails	25	£1.80	£45.00
Screwdrivers	3	£14.99	£44.97
		GOODS TOTAL	£89.97
		PLUS VAT @ 17.5%	£15.70
		TOTAL OF INVOICE	£105.67

TERMS: E&OE

FIG. 4.7 SALES INVOICE

FIG. 4.8 STATEMENT OF ACCOUNT

Billabong Stationery Supplies
Beed Road
Bradford
BD1 7HQ

Statement

Tel: (01274) 127341

VAT Reg No.: 173/1096/67

To: Carters Ltd
      7 Cooke Street
      Cardiff
      Wales
      CD1 1AX

Date: 22 June 19_ _

Account No.: 1735

DATE	DETAILS	DEBIT	CREDIT	BALANCE
1 June	Goods supplied on Invoice No. 1235	£95.00	NIL	NIL
	VAT 17.5%	£16.60		
				£111.60

TERMS: E&OE

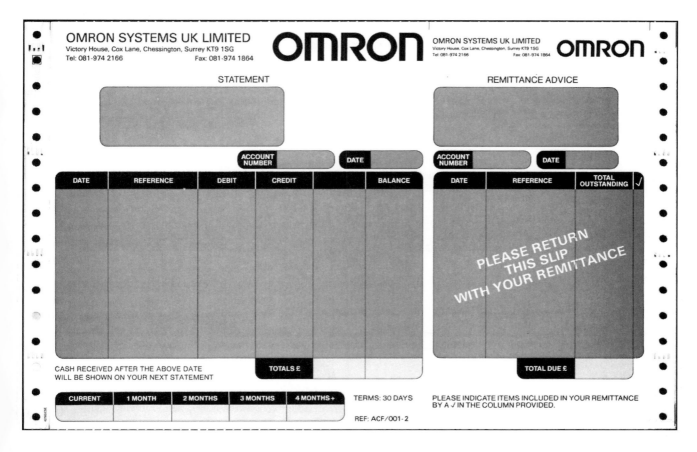

FIG. 4.8A A STATEMENT USED BY OMRON SYSTEMS UK LIMITED

Discounts

Sellers will often offer discounts to attract custom.

TRADE DISCOUNT

This is normally given to buyers who purchase in large quantities. They will usually be told that orders over a certain amount will receive a discount of X per cent.

CASH DISCOUNT

This is given to encourage a buyer to pay quickly. For example, a buyer may be given a 3 per cent discount for paying cash within a time limit of, say, one month. Details of the discount will appear on the invoice and statement, for example 'Terms: 3% one month'.

CREDIT NOTE

Imagine that you have bought a new pair of shoes from a shop in your local high street. When you return home and put them on you discover a split in the sole of one of the shoes. You would be entitled to return the shoes to the shop and ask for a refund. Alternatively, you could choose to accept a credit note. This would entitle you to return to the shop at some point in the future and exchange the note for goods of the same value. Many companies do not have separate credit note forms, but use an invoice (such as the one on p.93) to credit customers. In large organisations which have computerised systems, this will be done by programming the computer to print the words 'credit' or 'credit note' on the invoice when being used as a credit.

Debit Note

A debit note is really the opposite of a credit note. It is sent to the business which has bought the goods when the amount paid is less than the total value of the goods. In other words, the buyer still owes some money and has been undercharged as in the example below.

If 'E & OE' is printed on the invoice, the seller has the right to issue a debit note. 'E & OE' means 'Errors and Omissions Excepted'. This entitles the seller to charge an additional amount at a later date for items that were delivered but that were left off the original invoice.

CREDIT NOTE

Tel: 01567 102359

Shipton's Shoes Plc
Shirewell
Shropshire
SH3 7WJ

To: B Smithson
      1 Hopewell Street
      Shirewell
      Shropshire
      SH5 0WY

Credit Note: CN71/137
Invoice No.: K82/498

Date: 18 March 19_ _

QUANTITY	DESCRIPTION	UNIT PRICE	TOTAL PRICE
1	Pair of blue suede shoes	£20.00	£20.00
	VAT		£3.50
	Total price		£23.50

FIG. 4.9 CREDIT NOTE

SECURITY

It is essential that financial transactions are recorded clearly and accurately for security reasons. The transactions have to go through many different processes and are looked at by countless people, and unclear figures can easily lead to mistakes. Security checks are important to prevent fraud and theft and to ensure high standards of honesty.

FIG. 4.10 DEBIT NOTE

Authorisation of orders

If an order is sent to a supplier, the purchasing organisation must be sure that they require the goods, and are committed to paying for them. There will be certain people within an organisation who are able to 'authorise' an order. Senior members of staff will normally be responsible for authorising large amounts of money. Generally speaking, people will only be allowed to authorise orders for work or goods appropriate to them.

DEBIT NOTE

Tel: 01567 102359

Shipton's Shoes Plc
Shirewell
Shropshire
SH3 7WJ

Deliver to: Petersons Ltd
             Long Lane
             Shirewell
             Shropshire
             SH4 9OL

Date: 24 March 19_ _

24 April 19_ _
         For goods on invoice no. K82/123

£5.80

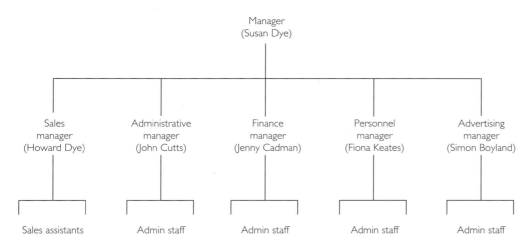

Manager
(Susan Dye)

| Sales manager (Howard Dye) | Administrative manager (John Cutts) | Finance manager (Jenny Cadman) | Personnel manager (Fiona Keates) | Advertising manager (Simon Boyland) |

| Sales assistants | Admin staff | Admin staff | Admin staff | Admin staff |

FIG. 4.11 DYE'S DECOR ORGANISATION CHART

For example, Dye's Decor is a large organisation selling a range of painting and decorating supplies (see Fig. 4.11). Susan Dye is the overall manager and can authorise large amounts of spending, such as on a new retail outlet. In addition, each manager is responsible for a budget. This is an agreed amount of money available to his or her department.

METHODS OF PAYMENT

When dealing with customers it is important to be aware and have knowledge of the different ways in which they can pay for goods and services.

Cash

Cash is the most common method of payment and comes in the form of coins or banknotes. It is important to be aware of the different notes and coins currently in circulation. For example, the five-pence piece has recently been replaced by a smaller version. It is often wise to check notes to see if they are genuine and not copies or forgeries.

Cheques

A cheque is an instruction by the person writing the cheque to their bank to pay money to the person or company named on the cheque.

A **cheque card** is a guarantee by the bank that it will pay anyone who accepts a cheque signed by the card holder (up to a fixed amount of £50 or £100).

Credit cards

Credit cards can be used to make payment for goods or services from organisations which accept the cards, as an alternative to cheques or cash. They can be used at

home or abroad. The holder of the card hands it to the seller who issues a pre-printed or computerised transaction voucher. The voucher is signed by the customer and he or she is given a copy. The seller sends a copy of the voucher to the organisation who issued the card. This organisation will send a statement to the card holder to tell them what is owed.

The statement is received some time after the transaction. This allows the card holder a period of free time before payment is due.

Debit cards

A debit card works like a cheque book and cheque card combined. The debit card is usually combined with a customer's cheque guarantee card. Instead of writing a cheque the customer hands the card to the sales assistant. He or she then issues a computerised transaction voucher. This is signed by the customer, who receives a copy. The money is debited from the customer's bank. Examples of debit cards are Switch, Delta and Connect.

Debit cards can only be used at organisations which are linked to the EFTPOS (Electronic Funds Transfer at Point of Sale) system.

FIG. 4.12 A SWITCH DEBIT CARD

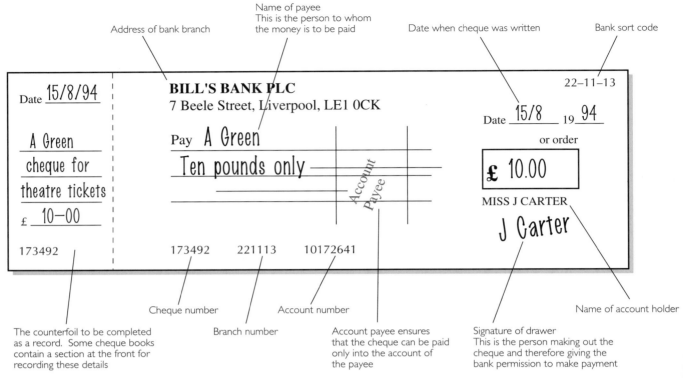

Address of bank branch

Name of payee
This is the person to whom the money is to be paid

Date when cheque was written

Bank sort code

Date 15/8/94

A Green cheque for theatre tickets

£ 10—00

173492

BILL'S BANK PLC
7 Beele Street, Liverpool, LE1 0CK

Pay A Green

Ten pounds only

Account Payee

22–11–13

Date 15/8 19 94

or order

£ 10.00

MISS J CARTER

J Carter

173492   221113   10172641

The counterfoil to be completed as a record. Some cheque books contain a section at the front for recording these details

Cheque number

Branch number

Account number

Account payee ensures that the cheque can be paid only into the account of the payee

Signature of drawer
This is the person making out the cheque and therefore giving the bank permission to make payment

Name of account holder

FIG. 4.13 A CHEQUE

Hire purchase

Hire purchase (HP) is a method offered to customers who want to pay for something by instalments rather than all at once. The finance company actually purchases the goods and hires them to the customer. Here is an example.

Mr and Mrs Griffin want to buy a washing machine. They visit a local store and see one they like for £300. They decide to pay by HP. They put down a deposit of £30 (10 per cent of the asking price in this case) and take the machine home. After this they will pay 11 monthly instalments of £25.78. This includes 5 per cent interest (on the remaining £270) which is paid to the finance company. The Griffins will not actually own the washing machine until the final payment has been made.

Bankers Automated Clearing Service (BACS)

BACS is a system used for making payments electronically, for example, payments of direct debits, standing orders and salaries. The system reduces the need to send vast amounts of paper between organisations. It uses magnetic tapes carrying the relevant information and makes the transfers using telecommunications.

Electronic Data Interchange (EDI)

EDI makes use of data communication technology so that organisations can exchange bills, orders and banking information. Through EDI, organisations are able to electronically exchange specially formulated business documents. An example of its use would be for a business to order new supplies. The computer within the business will transfer the data directly instead of people having to send forms through the post. With the addition of Electronic Funds Transfer (EFT) a business would also be able to pay its bills electronically. EDI leads to:

- less paperwork
- fewer data entry forms
- more efficient management of data
- cost savings for an organisation in the long term

Checking documentation

When an invoice is received someone in authority should check it against orders and goods received notes before payment is authorised. If possible, more than one person should carry out the checks.

ACTIVITY

WORDSEARCH

Hidden in the grid are words relating to methods of payment when buying goods or services. See if you can find them.

Words to find:

Bank

Branch

Cash

Cheque

Credit Card

Drawer

Hire Purchase

Instalments

Money

Payee

A	S	T	Y	O	P	B	C	E	A	P	D
B	C	L	U	W	A	C	W	P	R	G	
Q											
F	C	A	M	P	Y	R	B	N	V	A	
U											
A	N	Y	S	D	E	H	Y	O	H	R	D
E	C	F	A	H	E	K	N	A	B	W	
Q											
S	U	P	L	H	B	M	B	U	D	N	
N											
R	B	K	R	O	U	Y	L	K	V	X	L
C	R	E	D	I	T	C	A	R	D	S	O
N	A	R	B	M	C	F	Y	J	I	Z	E
U	N	U	J	D	C	U	L	I	B	S	U
I	C	O	O	Y	M	N	F	C	A	T	
M											
L	H	M	H	O	F	Y	P	H	X	N	
N											
M	W	X	N	O	N	I	C	E	G	E	
G											

ACTIVITY

Make contact with a local shop. Ask them if you can carry out a survey about the methods of payment used by their customers. You may like to use a form like the one below to record the information you have gathered.

When you have gathered the information, record it on a bar chart and compare it with those charts drawn up by other members of your group.

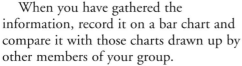

DATE	CUSTOMER NO	METHOD OF PAYMENT (E.G. CHEQUE, CASH)
	1	
	2	
	3	
	4	
	5	
	6	
	7	
	8	
	9	
	10	

ACTIVITY

Below is a list of items to be purchased by Dye's Decor. With reference to Figure 4.11, who do you think should authorise each order?

- a new computer system to be installed in *all* offices
- some display boards to be used for promotional activities
- three sets of sales manuals
- filing cabinets for finance and administrative staff
- a new desk for the personnel manager

Inaccurate financial information can cause all sorts of problems for an organisation. Therefore, all financial documents should be checked carefully to ensure that the information recorded on them is accurate, and where possible documents should be checked by more than one person. Documents should be filled in neatly – or better still typed or word processed where possible. This way the information is less likely to be misread.

Finally, it is essential that the data included is reliable as copies of many of the documents are supplied to a number of different people.

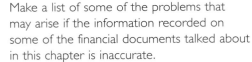

ACTIVITY

1 Make a list of some of the problems that may arise if the information recorded on some of the financial documents talked about in this chapter is inaccurate.

2 What measures can businesses take to try to prevent inaccurate recording of financial information?

Authorised cheque signatories

Cheques from an account held in a sole name can only be signed by that person. Most cheques from joint accounts can be signed by one of the two parties unless an agreement has been made stating otherwise.

For larger organisations, such as charities, more than one signature will usually be required for security purposes. For example, two authorised signatures may be required out of a list of four held by the bank.

Petty cash vouchers

Petty cash is a small amount of money kept aside to pay for minor items at short notice, for example postage, fares and office supplies. A certain amount of money is put into petty cash. The money is usually kept in a metal cash box that is locked. This is usually a round amount, for example £20. This money is called the 'float'. The float is fixed to cover an agreed amount of time – maybe one or two weeks. At the end of the agreed period the person in charge of petty cash will 'top up' the balance to restore it to its original amount. For example, if the original float was £20 and £16 petty cash was spent during the agreed period there would be £4 left in petty cash and £16 would have to be added to restore the £20 float.

When someone wants to use some of the money in petty cash, they need to complete a petty cash voucher. The voucher should include the following information:

- the date
- details as to what the money is to be spent on
- the amount
- the signature of the person spending the money
- the signature of the person who issues the petty cash

PETTY CASH VOUCHER

Received by:	Authorised by:	Department:	
DATE	DETAILS OF EXPENDITURE	REF NO.	AMOUNT
		VAT	
		TOTAL £	

FIG. 4.14 A PETTY CASH VOUCHER

COMPLETING A PETTY CASH VOUCHER

VAT (see pp.117–8) should always be shown on a petty cash voucher. At times it will have already been calculated and shown as a separate item on the receipts you were given when you made your purchases (see opposite). Sometimes, however, it will be up to you to extract the VAT from the total amount.

PETTY CASH BOOK

The petty cash book is used to record all petty cash payments and is split into a series of columns known as 'analysis columns'. The headings of these columns are the most common types of expenditure, for example postage, travel expenses and stationery.

ACTIVITY

Draw out two blank petty cash vouchers using Figure 4.14 as a model. Enter the information from the receipts in Figure 4.15 onto the vouchers. Ask your teacher or lecturer to check that you have completed the vouchers correctly.

JEAN'S GROCERS
6 Hill Street, Hull

RECEIPT

Date.......... 13/2/94

Goods

Mixed groceries

£ 8.00

TOTAL £ 8.00

Prices include VAT at 17.5%

Signature.......... Jean Smith

GINGO GARAGES
6 Green Street, Greenwich, GN17 0AU
VAT No: 177 9773 14

27-4-94   1702/   1   04

PUMP PRODUCT   LITRES   VALUE (£)

                30.98   17.15

07 DERV   £17.15

                         £17.15

CASH SALES

VAT included

THANK YOU

FIG. 4.15

Because the headings are usually self-explanatory, it is quite easy to work out which expenditure should be entered in which column. Every column should be totalled at the end of each week or month.

Look at Figure 4.16 which shows an example of a filled-in petty cash book. At the *start* of each agreed period, the imprest or float is recorded in the book.

At the *end* of the agreed period all the petty cash vouchers in the petty cash box are recorded in the book. Each column is then totalled up. The total amount of money paid out should then be taken away from the imprest or float. The 'balance' is the amount of money left. This can be checked by counting the money in the cash box. Once this has been done the imprest can be restored.

RECEIPTS

When a cheque is paid into a bank, the cheque itself is proof of payment and a receipt is not required. When payment is made by cash, some form of proof of the transaction is necessary, i.e. a receipt. The **payer** (remitter) will require a receipt as written proof of payment for their purchase. A receipt will also provide information about VAT paid. The **payee** issues a receipt

FIG. 4.16 FILLED-IN PAGE OF A PETTY CASH BOOK

	PETTY CASH BOOK											
	RECEIPTS					PAYMENTS						
£	P	FOLIO	DATE 19_ _	DETAILS	VOUCHER NO.	TOTAL PAID OUT	TRAVEL	POSTAGE	CLEANING	STATIONERY	SUNDRIES	VAT
30	00		15 8	Cash received								
			16 8	Petrol	8	10.00	10.00					
			19 8	Envelopes	9	1.50				1.50		
			23 8	Stamps	10	0.75		0.75				
			25 8	Taxi	11	3.95	3.95					
			25 8	Petrol	12	6.00	6.00					
			29 8	Stamps	13	1.50		1.50				
6	30		29 8	Balance b/d Cash Recvd	£	23.70 6.30	19.95	2.25		1.50		
23	70											
30	00				£	30.00						

Float or imprest

Petty cash vouchers

Balance

when accepting cash for goods or services. A copy of the receipt will be kept for the records. It will also provide evidence of VAT for recording purposes.

A receipt should include the following information:

- date
- receipt number (when a business issues receipts they are usually numbered consecutively)
- name of remitter
- description of the goods sold
- amount paid (including the portion relating to VAT)

Other types of receipt are:

- till receipts
- cheques
- bank statements
- bank paying-in slips

A C T I V I T Y

Draw up a page of a petty cash book, enter the information from the petty cash vouchers below and then total up each column. Ask your teacher or lecturer to check your work.

FIG. 4.17 PETTY CASH VOUCHERS

PETTY CASH VOUCHER

Received by	Authorised by	Department
P Lowson	N Smith	Sales

Date	Details	FO	Amount
12/8	Tea and biscuits		1 87
		VAT	
TOTAL			1 87

PETTY CASH VOUCHER

Received by	Authorised by	Department
R Latus	R Jones	Finance

Date	Details	FO	Amount
13/8	Stamps		1 50
		VAT	
TOTAL			1 50

PETTY CASH VOUCHER

Received by	Authorised by	Department
L Peters	N Smith	Sales

Date	Details	FO	Amount
13/8	Pens		1 35
		VAT	
TOTAL			1 35

PETTY CASH VOUCHER

Received by	Authorised by	Department
P Jackson	N Smith	Personnel

Date	Details	FO	Amount
17/8	Paper		2 35
		VAT	
TOTAL			2 35

PETTY CASH VOUCHER

Received by	Authorised by	Department
R Latus	N Smith	Marketing

Date	Details	FO	Amount
21/8	Stamps		1 00
		VAT	
TOTAL			1 00

PETTY CASH VOUCHER

Received by	Authorised by	Department
L Brown	R Jones	Production

Date	Details	FO	Amount
23/8	Polish		0 79
		VAT	
TOTAL			0 79

CASH RECIEPT	**CATH'S CLOTHES** 6 Cloud Street Cambridge CD1 0BC	Date 5/9/94		No.120
DESCRIPTION		£		
1 Jumper		9		95
VAT @ 17.5 %		1		74
TOTAL		£	11	69
RECEIVED WITH THANKS				
FROM: P Latus				
CASHIER R Smith		VAT Reg No 127/4173/22		

FIG. 4.18 A RECEIPT

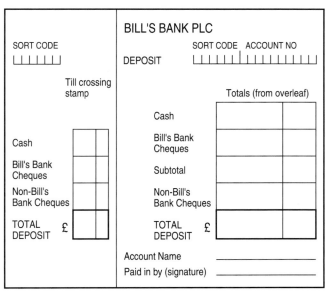

FIG. 4.19 PAYING-IN SLIP (FRONT)

Draw up some blank receipt forms for Cath's Clothes and enter the following information:

Date	Details	Purchaser	Price before VAT
6/9	Man's cardigan	R Andrews	£15.99 each
7/9	6 wool scarves	P Long	£6.99 each
9/9	10 blouses	R Cawdwell	£8.00 each
12/9	2 hats	B Smithes	£4.99 each

Paying-in slip

When money is paid into a bank account a paying-in slip must be completed. This slip usually has a detachable counterfoil attached to it. This is stamped by the bank and given to the person or organisation paying in the money.

The slips will vary from bank to bank but the basic information they contain will be the same.

Bank giro credits

This is a form that enables customers to make payments to businesses who have accounts either at their own bank or at other banks. Customers who do not have a bank account can also use the forms to pay cash over the counter.

CASH		BILL'S BANK CHEQUES		NON-BILL'S BANK CHEQUES	
£50					
£20					
£10					
£5					
£1					
50p					
Silver					
Bronze					
POs					
TOTALS £					
Enter all totals overleaf					

FIG. 4.20 PAYING-IN SLIP (BACK)

Gas, electricity and water bills are often paid using bank giro credits. In these cases the forms are preprinted with details of the bank, branch and account number of the organisation. All the customer has to do is fill in the amount to be paid and sign the form.

Bank statements

From time to time a bank issues all its customers with a statement. Both personal and business customers will receive statements. **Deposits** are amounts of money paid *into* the account. **Withdrawals** are amounts of money taken *out* of the account. The numbers in the particulars column are the serial numbers of the cheques that have been paid.

ACTIVITY

Draw up some paying-in slips and complete them for each of the deposits listed below. You should sign the slips in your own name.

These are your bank details:
Account No.: 10172641
Sort code: 22-37-19
BILL'S BANK PLC
BOOTLE BRANCH

1 5 May

Cheques	P Fewings	£126.72
Cash	B Lewis	£93.45
		£151.19

2 10 May

Cheques	L Stubbs	£19.72
	W Bridges	£111.11
Postal order	P Fielder	£91.72

3 15 May

Cash	£300.00

4 21 May

Cheques	D Andrews	£96.23
	R Taylor	£222.41

5 28 May

Cheques	E Cheyne	£721.51
	S Heath	£401.03
Postal order	R Wilson	£307.57
Cash		£333.33

BANK GIRO CREDIT   BILL'S BANK PLC

SORT CODE [– –]
BANK _____
BRANCH _____

FEE	NO. OF CHEQUES

CREDIT _____
ACCOUNT NO. _____
PAID IN BY _____
ADDRESS _____
_____
_____

Notes		
£50		
£20		
£10		
£5		
50p		
20p		
SILVER		
BRONZE		
POs		
Total Cash		
Cheques, POs, etc.		
£		

FIG. 4.21 A BLANK BANK GIRO CREDIT

ACTIVITY

See if you can find out some information about the following:

- direct debits
- standing orders

FIG. 4.22 A BUSINESS CUSTOMER'S BANK STATEMENT

BILL'S BANK PLC

7 Beele Street
Bootle
Liverpool
LE1 0CK

Tel (0151) 927342
CONFIDENTIAL

Current Account Carters Ltd
A/c No. 1723471123
Date of Statement 28/9/19_ _
Sheet No. 84

DATE	PARTICULARS	WITHDRAWALS	DEPOSITS	BALANCE
	Balance brought forward			1,115.07
2 Sep	British Gas Plc DD	119.72		
7 Sep	00825	73.52		
8 Sep	00826	15.15		
12 Sep	City Office Liverpool CM	30.00		
14 Sep	00828	51.00		
17 Sep	00827	19.87		
21 Sep	Lunns Ins SO	21.12		
				784.70

KEY	DD	Direct Debit	SO	Standing Order	CH	Charge	CC	Cash/Cheques	OD	Overdrawn
	VIS	Visa	TR	Transfer	CM	Cash Machine	BGC	Bank Giro Credit		

PRODUCE, EVALUATE AND STORE BUSINESS DOCUMENTS

Letters, memoranda, invitations, notices and messages are all types of business documentation. They may be hand written, typed, word processed, printed or photocopied and are used by people in business to communicate with customers, colleagues and other businesses. Documents can also vary in terms of appearance, for example, memoranda and letters can be written in different styles or formats, and language, for example, a letter may be formal or informal.

All business documents should be checked for spelling and grammatical errors before being issued.

You will find further information about business documents on pp.147–51 in Chapter 6, 'Business communication'.

Comparing and evaluating business documents

LETTERS

If word processed, letters are highly legible and can be produced quickly. Any alterations can also be made easily. They can, however, sometimes be expensive to send. They are normally stored on computer disk or hard copies (paper copies as opposed to those on disk) are kept and filed.

MEMORANDA

As with letters, memoranda produced on a word processor have good legibility, can be produced quickly and corrected easily. They are also relatively cheap as they are sent internally. They can be filed on disk or as paper files.

INVITATIONS

The legibility of invitations is good and they are often attractively designed. They can be expensive to produce if printed professionally, and high postage costs may be involved if there are a large number to be sent at any one time. Also, if they are professionally printed the time required for design and production may be lengthy and it may be more difficult to make alterations. Again, they can be stored on disk or as paper files.

NOTICES

The legibility of notices is good as they are usually written in bold and capitals. They can be produced fairly quickly and cheaply as limited numbers of copies are normally produced, and they can be hand written if necessary. Notices are unlikely to be stored.

MESSAGES

The legibility of messages can be poor as they are often hand written or scribbled. They are quick to produce and minimal costs are incurred. Changes can be made very easily and, as messages are usually dealt with immediately, they are not normally stored.

Referencing, storing and sending business documents

Good communication practice requires that documents are referenced accurately, stored securely and sent in the most effective way possible. The different methods for referencing, storing and sending documents are all discussed in detail in Chapter 7, 'Operating administrative systems'.

CHAPTER FOUR
Test Yourself!

1 What is capital equipment?
2 What is an advice note?
3 True or false? GRN stands for goods returned note.
4 True or false? A delivery note usually accompanies goods sent to the buyer.
5 Write down two pieces of information normally included on a statement of account.
6 Explain the difference between a cash and a trade discount.
7 What is a credit note?

8 Who will normally be responsible for authorising large payments?
9 Give two reasons why it is important to complete financial documents accurately.
10 Explain what is meant by the term 'imprest'.
11 Write down two pieces of information normally included on a petty cash voucher.
12 What does VAT stand for?
13 What is a cheque?
14 What is a debit card?
15 What does HP stand for?

CHAPTER FOUR

Evidence-Gathering Projects

1 Identify and explain financial transactions and documents.

i Make a list of reasons of why financial recording in business organisations is necessary and explain the importance of each.

ii Collect examples of the following financial documents:

- an order
- a goods received note
- an invoice
- a statement of account
- a receipt

Write a short note to explain the function of each document

iii Design a notice to be displayed in the offices of a business organisation, outlining the security checks which should take place for payment documents.

2 Complete financial documents and explain financial recording.

Croziers is a large company that manufactures carpet tiles.

i Design an order form to be used by Croziers.

ii Transfer the following information to the order form: An order to Steele's Toiletry Supplies for 12 boxes of industrial hand towels at £6 a box (dated 16 August). You can make up your own reference numbers and addresses.

iii Design a goods received note to be used by Croziers.

iv Transfer the information relating to the order onto the goods received note.

v Design an invoice to be used by Steele's Toiletry Supplies.

vi Complete the invoice with the correct information relating to Croziers' order.

vii Design a statement of account to be sent by Steele's Toiletry Supplies.

viii Complete the statement of account with the correct information relating to Croziers' order – you may wish to create information about previous orders at this stage.

ix Draw up a blank cheque and complete it for the payment due to Steeles for the hand towels.

x Design a pay slip to be used by Croziers. Complete a sample slip for one of their employees.

xi Croziers keep £30 available for petty cash. Money taken out of petty cash in August was as follows:

2 August	£2.00	Taxi
3 August	£1.25	Stamps
5 August	0.68p	Bus fare
10 August	£2.00	Taxi
15 August	£6.00	Stationery
19 August	£3.30	Stationery
24 August	£1.99	Cleaning fluid
26 August	£1.65	Coffee

Prepare a petty cash book for August. Total it up at the end of the month and restore the imprest.

xii On 28 August a member of Croziers' finance department is asked to visit the bank to pay in some cash and cheques. Draw up a blank paying-in slip and then fill in the details as follows:

Cheques	R Lindholme	£113.69
	B Slattery	£ 97.53
	L Ludlow	£ 17.27
Cash		£82.50

xiii Draw up a blank receipt form and complete it for the following sales made by Croziers:

5 August	1 box of blue carpet tiles sold to P Lewis	£16.99 (including VAT)
7 August	10 boxes of luxury tiles (assorted colours) sold to Smithsons Ltd	£315.72 (excluding VAT)
21 August	7 boxes of black heavy duty tiles sold to N Withers	£165.53 (including VAT)

xiv Prepare a memorandum to explain the importance of the recording of financial information – to be sent from the finance manager to all the staff.

xv Visit a local retail outlet specialising in computer software for businesses and collect information about packages available to help businesses record and monitor financial information.

3 Produce, evaluate and store business documents.

i Prepare a short presentation to:
- explain the purpose of routine business documents
- compare the methods of processing business documents

Your presentation should be no longer than 10 minutes and must include some sample business documents as visual aids.

ii You work in the marketing department of Thomas Ltd who produce children's toys. The company is about to launch its new Christmas range of toys. You need to:

- Write a letter to a retail buyer in a local department store who wishes to stock your range. The letter should confirm details of a forthcoming meeting (date, time, content, people to attend).
- Write a memorandum to the sales department informing them of the date when toys will be available for sale.
- Design an invitation to be sent to journalists inviting them to a party to launch the product range.
- Prepare a notice to be displayed on the staff noticeboard informing them of staff discounts on the toys.
- Write a message to a colleague in the marketing department with details of a telephone call received from the caterers for the party, asking for confirmation of the number of people attending the party.

iii Working with another member of the group exchange the documents you have produced. Write comments on the appearance (style, format) and language (spelling, grammar) for each document.
(Your teacher/lecturer will also make comments on the above when assessing the documents.)

iv Over a period of two weeks, complete an index card for each member of your group. Each card should contain the following details:

- date card completed
- surname
- first name
- date of birth
- address
- favourite subject at college
- a reference number

Your teacher/lecturer will then observe you filing the cards in the following ways:

- alphabetically
- by subject
- numerically (by age)
- in date order
- numerically (by reference number)

Your teacher/lecturer will also ask you to retrieve documents as part of the excercise. He or she will provide you with a feedback sheet about your performance.

v Make a list of different ways of sending and storing business documents. Describe the advantages and disadvantages of each one.

Chapter
5

FINANCIAL RECORDING

RECORD AND CALCULATE SIMPLE FINANCIAL TRANSACTIONS

BOOKS AND PROCEDURES

In Chapter 4 we looked at financial transactions. All financial transactions generate documents. These documents are known as prime documents which act as a basis for book-keeping. Examples of prime documents are sales invoices, purchase invoices and cheque counterfoils.

A C T I V I T Y

Collect as many different examples of prime documents as you can. Which documents will be used in the accounts of a business?

Businesses need to keep books:

- for tax reasons
- to provide their accountants with up to date information
- to provide a clear picture of the performance of the business
- to show whether a profit or loss has been made

The cash book

This is the book used to record the income and expenditure of a business, i.e. money coming in and going out. It should include as detailed a record as possible – separate columns are used for cash transactions and those made through the bank (i.e. by cheque). Any money received from customers is credited to their account in the ledger (see later). Any payments made to suppliers are debited from their

accounts in the ledger. We will use the accounts of Carters, a do-it-yourself supplies company, as an example of a cash book (see Figure 5.1).

The cash book is divided into two sections. On the left-hand side are the receipts, i.e. money coming into the organisation, and on the right-hand side are the payments, i.e. money leaving the organisation.

DISCOUNT ALLOWED

This is the amount which a business allows its customers (debtors) to deduct from the total payment, provided that they pay within the given time period.

DISCOUNT RECEIVED

This is the amount that a business is allowed to deduct when settling the creditor's (supplier's) account. An agreement will have been made to accept less money in settlement of debts paid within a given time period.

Discount allowed and discount received are both recorded in the cash book and in appropriate ledger accounts.

DEBITS

A debtor is someone who has received goods and owes money for them. Debits are shown on the left-hand side of the cash book and the ledger (receipts side), and are shown as DR.

CREDITS

A creditor is someone who has parted with goods and is owed money for them. Credits are shown on the right-hand side of the cash book and the ledger (payments side), and are shown as CR.

CARTERS

CASH BOOK CB1

DR	RECEIPTS						PAYMENTS				CR
Date 19__	Details	FO	Discount Allowed	Cash £	Bank £	Date 19__	Details	FO	Discount Received	Cash £	Bank £
Oct						Oct					
1	Balances	b/d		150.00	4000.00	2	Rent	N12		50.00	
3	Bank	C		50.00		3	Cash	C			50.00
5	B Robinson	R1	10.00		400.00	3	J Bloggs Supplies	B1			300.00
6	Sales	SA1		40.00		4	Heat/Light	H1		70.00	
						6	P Port Supp	P1	30.00		500.00
						6	Balance	c/d		120.00	3550.00
		£	10.00	240.00	4400.00			£	30.00	240.00	4400.00
Nov1	Balance	b/d		120.00	3550.00						

Fig. 5.1 An example of a cash book

BALANCE

This is the difference between the debit and credit sides of an account. It is also the name of the method used to make the totals of each side add up to the same amount.

FOLIO

This is the reference used to trace an entry from one section of the accounts to another, and is shown as FO.

CONTRA ENTRY

A contra entry is used when the same amount of money appears on both sides of the cash book. For example, money from the bank (payments side) may be transferred to petty cash (receipts side). The letter C is shown (under FO) on both sides of the cash book and no entry is required in the ledger.

A SUMMARY OF CARTERS' CASH TRANSACTIONS

On 1 October the amount in the bank was £4000 and the amount held in cash £150.

On 2 October a cash payment of £50 was made for rent.

On 3 October £50 was drawn from the bank and put into petty cash (contra entry). Also on 3 October a supplier, J Bloggs, was given a cheque for £300.

On 4 October £70 was paid in cash for gas to heat the boiler.

On 5 October Carters received a cheque for £400 from B Robinson in settlement of his account.

On 6 October £40 was received for cash sales. Also on 6 October a cheque for £500 was paid to P Port Supplies.

BALANCING THE CASH BOOK

Look at Carters' entries in each of the cash columns (on the payments and receipts sides).

The total receipts are	£150.00
	+ £50.00
	+ £40.00
	= £240.00

The total payments are	£50.00
	+ £70.00
	= £120.00

So the total amount of cash received is £240. Subtract the total amount of cash paid (£120) and enter the difference as the balance on the side with the smallest total (in this case, the payments side).

	£240.00
	− £120.00
	= £120.00

The total for cash on both the receipts and payment side will be £240.

A similar exercise is worked through for the bank column:

First add up the bank column on the receipts side.

	£4000.00
+	£400.00
=	£4400.00

Then add up the bank column on the payments side.

	£50.00
+	£300.00
+	£500.00
=	£850.00

The total cheque receipts are:	£4400.00
Subtract the total cheque payments	£850.00
The amount is the balance of the bank account:	£3550.00

The balance of £3550 is recorded on the side with the smallest total (in this case, the payments side). The total for the bank on both the receipts and payments side will be £4400. The entries for October are now complete. November's entries are shown by bringing down (balance b/d) the balance on the receipts side at the bottom of the cash book. The term balance c/d (carried down) is written here.

BALANCES CARRIED DOWN AND BROUGHT DOWN

At the end of a trading period (the last day of the month of the financial year) the accounts are balanced.

The total on one side of the cash book will normally be greater than the other. The 'balance' is inserted in order to make both the totals equal. This balance is entered on the opposite side of the same account, but beneath the totals (underlined). This completes the double entry (see below).

The balance is really the amount of money left over to take into the next trading period.

The balance carried down will be dated on the last day of the trading period. The balance brought down is the date of the first day of the next trading period.

Double-entry book-keeping

Traditionally, accounts were always kept in large volumes known as ledgers. Today, many organisations have their own computerised accounting systems. Whether manual or computerised, ledger accounts are usually kept through a system of double-entry book-keeping. This means that every transaction is recorded twice (in the ledger accounts) for:

- each person
- each firm

A C T I V I T Y

Prepare the cash book for Carters from the following information for March and balance the cash book at the end of the month.

1 March	£450 cash, £4000 in the bank
2 March	Paid £100 rent in cash
3 March	Bought a second-hand filing cabinet for £75 cash
6 March	Cash sales £90
10 March	Received a cheque from R Davis in payment for 2 drills £80
13 March	Paid a cheque for telephone bill £60
21 March	Received a cheque from J Howlett for £78.50
24 March	Purchased goods by cheque £20
28 March	Paid wages by cheque £300

- each liability
- each expense

When a debit entry is made it is matched by a credit entry.

The ledger

The ledger contains details of all the financial transactions within an organisation. The ledger is made up of lots of separate accounts, each with a debit and a credit side. An account will be created for each person, organisation, liability or expense.

POSTING THE CASH BOOK TO THE LEDGER FOR OCTOBER

The figures in the entries of the cash book are posted (recorded) or transferred to separate accounts in the ledger as in Figure 5.2. The ledger entries for October are now complete.

NB In the actual ledger a separate page would be used for each account.

Purchases day book

Carters will buy a range of goods and services from different suppliers. Each of these will send an invoice (see Chapter 4 'Financial transactions' p.91). Each

CARTERS DR						LEDGER					CR
Date 19__		Details	FO	£	p	Date 19__		Details	FO	£	p
						CASHBANK A/C CB1					
Oct	1	Cash	CB1	150	00						
Oct	1	Bank	CB1	4000	00						
						SALES A/C SA1					
Oct	6	Cash	CB1	40	00						
						B ROBINSON A/C R1					
Oct	5	Bank		400	00						
						P PORT A/C P1					
						Oct	6	Bank		500	00
						J BLOGGS A/C B1					
						Oct	3	Bank		300	00
						RENT A/C R2					
						Oct	2	Cash		50	00
						HEAT AND LIGHT A/C H1					
						Oct	4	Cash		70	00

FIG. 5.2 POSTING THE CASH BOOK TO THE LEDGER

invoice should be checked carefully to ensure that it is accurate and that the price charged is correct. The invoices are then recorded in the purchases day book before being filed in alphabetical order. The purchases day book provides information about the money the business owes. Before filing each invoice, the invoice number from the purchases day book will be recorded on it to enable easy location.

Figure 5.3 shows examples of entries in the purchases day book for invoices Carters received in December.

TRADE AND CASH DISCOUNT

Cash discount is money deducted when a bill is paid promptly, i.e. on time. Trade discount is a reduction on the price of goods bought and is provided by the manufacturer to the trader (in this case Carters) to help them make more money.

A C T I V I T Y

Figure 5.4 is Carters' cash book for April. Transfer the information on it to the ledger. Make sure that you show the folio references.

POSTING THE PURCHASES DAY BOOK TO THE LEDGER

An account will be opened for each of Carters' suppliers. These are their creditors, i.e. Carters will pay them money. The information is therefore recorded on the credit (payments) side of the ledger.

To complete the double entry, the receipts side of the ledger is debited with the total value that Carters have received from their suppliers during December.

CARTERS									
		PURCHASES DAY BOOK PDB1							CR
Date 19__		Details	Inv No	FO	£	p	£	p	
Dec	5	Billabong Stationery Supplies Goods	1	B2	15	50			
		Less trade discount				50	15	00	
✓	7	F Forte Ltd Goods	2	F1			30	00	
✓	12	Curlys Caterers Ltd Goods	3	C1	50	00			
		Less trade discount			5	00	45	00	
✓	18	Billabong Stationery Supplies Goods	4	B2	31	00			
		Less trade discount			1	00	30	00	
✓	31	Total purchases for the month		PA1		£	120	00	

FIG. 5.3 PURCHASES DAY BOOK FOR DECEMBER

CARTERS					CASH BOOK CB1						

DR			RECEIPTS			PAYMENTS					CR
Date 19__	Details	FO	Discount Allowed	Cash £	Bank £	Date 19__	Details	FO	Discount Received	Cash £	Bank £
April											
1	Balance	b/d		80.00	1800.00	2	Rent			100.00	
2	Sales			60.00		4	P Mead		15.00		150.00
5	R Hope			45.00		6	Wages				200.00
9	Thomes plc		25.00		250.00	7	Advertising			50.00	
17	M Notts				21.00	22	Coopers Ltd				25.00
21	Sales				27.00						
23	Sales				51.00						
						30	Balance	c/d		35.00	1774.00
		£	25.00	185.00	2149.00			£	15.00	185.00	2149.00
May 1	Balance	b/d		35.00	1774.00						

FIG. 5.4 CARTERS' CASH BOOK FOR APRIL

Sales day book

Some customers will buy goods from Carters on credit, i.e. they will be given time to pay for the goods. In these cases Carters will send the customers invoices and keep copies for their records. They will record the information from the invoices in the sales day book, as in Figure 5.6. The invoice number from the sales day book will be written on the invoice before it is filed.

CARTERS DR							LEDGER				CR
Date 19__		Details	FO	£	p	Date 19__		Details	FO	£	p
						BILLABONG A/C B2					
						Dec	5	Purchases	PDB 1/1	15	00
						✓	18	✓	PDB 1/4	30	00
						F FORTE LTD A/C F1					
						Dec	7	Purchases	PDB 1/2	30	00
						CURLYS CATERERS LTD A/C C1					
						Dec	12	Purchases	PDB 1/3	45	00
						PURCHASES A/C PA1					
Dec	31	Total for the month	PDB1	120	00						

FIG. 5.5 POSTING THE PURCHASES DAY BOOK TO THE LEDGER

A C T I V I T Y

Carters receive the invoices shown here for May. Enter them in the purchases day book using the column headings as shown on p.111.

Then add up the total purchases for the month and post the entries to the ledger.

1 May	Purchased from Billabong Stationery Supplies:	
	2 dozen manila envelopes	£4.50
	200 ballpoint pens	£20.00
15 May	Purchased from Fallows Farms:	
	20 bags of manure	£20.00
21 May	Purchased from Billabong Stationery Supplies:	
	15 boxes of computer paper	£80.00

POSTING THE SALES DAY BOOK TO THE LEDGER

An account will be opened in the ledger for each of Carters' customers. These customers are Carters' debtors because they owe them money (for the receipt of goods). The information is therefore recorded on the debit (receipts) side of the ledger. **NB** Each account would be recorded on a separate page.

To complete the double entry, the payments side of the ledger is credited with the total value of goods that Carters have given out during January.

CARTERS

		SALES DAY BOOK PDB1				CR
Date		Details	Invoice Number	FO	£	p
Jan	3	Beadles Ltd	I	B3	21	90
		Goods				
Jan	7	B Long	2	L1	160	00
		Goods				
Jan	20	Medicis Ltd	4	M1	28	50
		Goods				
Jan	31	Total sales for the month		SA2	305	40

FIG. 5.6 SALES DAY BOOK

FIG. 5.7 POSTING THE SALES DAY BOOK TO THE LEDGER

CARTERS
DR LEDGER **CR**

Date 19__		Details	FO	£	p	Date 19__		Details	FO	£	p
			BEADLES LTD A/C B3								
Jan	3	Sales	SDB 1/1	21	90						
			B LONG A/C L1								
Jan	7	Sales	SDB 1/2	160	00						
			STUTTARDS A/C S1								
Jan	10	Sales	SDB 1/3	95	00						
			MEDICIS LTD A/C M1								
Jan	20	Sales	SDB 1/4	28	50						
			SALES A/C SA2								
						Jan	31	Total sales for the month	SDB 1	305	40

ACTIVITY

Here is a list of invoices sent out by Carters in June.

Head up the columns of the sales day book, enter the invoices and post them to the ledger. Post the total sales for June to the sales account.

Dec 3	Sent an invoice to Peter's Paints Ltd for 10 tins of white paint	£89.50
Jan 10	Jenson's Plc, 2 lawnmowers, Doncaster	£310.00
Jan 16	Hogwash Supplies, 1 lawnmower, Manchester	£155.00
Jan 22	K Smithey, 4 large plant pots, Hull	£16.72

The returns book

CREDIT NOTES

Credit notes are issued when goods have to be returned for some reason. Carters will have goods returned from time to time and will issue their own credit notes as in Figure 5.8.

CREDIT NOTE			Tel: (01222) 127352
CARTERS LTD			
7 Cooke Street, Cardiff, Wales CD1 1AX			
To: Stuttards 17 South Street Southampton SE17 0PQ		Credit Note CN14/289 Invoice No. K73/127 Date 9 July 19__	
QUANTITY	DESCRIPTION	UNIT PRICE	TOTAL PRICE
50	Plant Pots (cracked)	0.50p	£25.00
			£25.00

FIG. 5.8 CREDIT NOTE

RETURNS INWARDS BOOK (SALES)

This is the book in which credit notes are recorded. It is called this because the goods are being *returned* to the organisation.

RETURNS INWARDS BOOK SR2						
Date 19__		Details	Credit note	FO	£	p
July	9	Stuttards 50 plant pots (cracked)	1	S1	25	00
	31	Total returns (sales) inward for the month		SR2	25	00

FIG. 5.9 THE CREDIT NOTE IS RECORDED IN CARTERS' RETURNS INWARDS BOOK

POSTING THE RETURNS INWARDS TO THE LEDGER

If we look back to Carters' ledger in Figure 5.7 we can see Stuttards' account as show in Figure 5.10.

The credit note for £25 is now recorded on the credit side of Stuttards account as shown in Figure 5.11.

FIG. 5.10 STUTTARDS' ACCOUNT IN CARTERS' LEDGER

CARTERS DR						LEDGER					CR
Date 19__		Details	FO	£	p	Date 19__		Details	FO	£	p
						STUTTARDS A/C S1					
Jul	10	Sales	SDB 1/3	95	00						

CARTERS DR						LEDGER				CR
Date 19__		Details	FO	£	p	Date 19__	Details	FO	£	p
					STUTTARDS A/C S1					
Jul	10	Sales	SDB 1/3	95	00	Jul 9	Credit note	SR 2	25	00
					RETURNS INWARDS A/C R14					
Jul	31	Total returns for the month	SR2	25	00					

FIG. 5.11 POSTING THE RETURNS INWARDS TO THE LEDGER

In order to complete the double entry, the total goods returned will be shown in the ledger as in Figure 5.11.

A C T I V I T Y

On 19 August Carters sold Stuttards a lawnmower for £190. Stuttards returned it on 21 August as it didn't work.

1 Draw up a credit note for Stuttards.
2 Show the entries for Stuttards' account in the ledger.

RETURNS OUTWARD BOOK (PURCHASES)

Sometimes Carters may have to return goods to *their* suppliers. They will therefore be issued with credit notes. These are recorded in the returns inwards book.

Figure 5.12 is a credit note to Carters who returned 100 sheets of headed paper to Billabong Stationery Supplies as they were incorrectly printed.
The details would be recorded in the returns outward book as in Figure 5.13.

POSTING THE RETURNS OUTWARD BOOK TO THE LEDGER

If we look at Carter's ledger in Figure 5.15 we can see Billabong's account as shown in Figure 5.14.

We now record the details of the returned goods as in Figure 5.15.

To complete the double entry the total amount of goods that Carters have returned during the month will be shown in the ledger, as in Figure 5.16.

CREDIT NOTE

Billabong Stationery Supplies
Beed Road, Bradford, BD1 7HQ   Tel: (01274) 127341

To: Carters Ltd   Credit Note   CN71/023
      7 Cooke Street   Invoice No.   LP2/135
      Cardiff
      Wales
      CD1 1AX

Date 12 December 19_

100 sheets headed note paper
@ £8.00 per 100
(incorrectly printed)   £8.00

FIG. 5.12 CREDIT NOTE TO CARTERS

CARTERS						
		RETURNS OUTWARD BOOK PRB1				CR
Date 19__		Details	Credit note	FO	£	p
July	12	Billabong Stationery Supplies				
		100 sheets headed notepaper (incorrectly printed)	1	B2	8	00
	31	Total returns outward for the month		PR1	8	00

FIG. 5.13 RETURNS OUTWARD BOOK

CARTERS

DR			FO	£	p			LEDGER	FO	£	p	CR
Date 19__		Details	FO	£	p	Date 19__		Details	FO	£	p	
								BILLABONG A/C B2				
						Dec	5	Purchases	PDB 1/1	15	00	
			✓				18	✓	PDB 1/4	30	00	

Fig. 5.14 Billabong's account in the ledger

CARTERS

DR			FO	£	p			LEDGER	FO	£	p	CR
Date 19__		Details	FO	£	p	Date 19__		Details	FO	£	p	
								BILLABONG A/C B2				
Jul	12	Credit note	PRB1	8	00	Dec	5	Purchases	PDB 1/1	15	00	
						✓	18	✓	PDB 1/4	30	00	

Fig. 5.15 Posting the returns outward book to the ledger

Fig. 5.16 Posting the returns outward book to the ledger — completing the double entry

CARTERS

DR			FO	£	p			LEDGER	FO	£	p	CR
Date 19__		Details	FO	£	p	Date 19__		Details	FO	£	p	
								BILLABONG A/C B2				
						Dec	5	Purchases	PDB 1/1	15	00	
			✓				18	✓	PDB 1/4	30	00	
								RETURNS OUTWARDS A/C PRB1				
						Dec	31	Total returns for the month		8	00	

A C T I V I T Y

Carters purchased two dozen staplers from Billabong Stationery Supplies on 15 August. They had to return them on 21 August as they didn't work.

1 Issue a credit note to Carters from Billabong.
2 Show the entries in:
   a the returns outward book
   b Billabong's account in the ledger
   c the returns outward account in the ledger

FINANCIAL CALCULATIONS

Percentages

FINDING THE PERCENTAGE OF A NUMBER

Example: What is 12 as a percentage of 200?

To calculate the percentage manually, the smaller number (12) should be divided by the larger number (200) and multiplied by 100.

$$\frac{12 \times 100}{200} = 6 \text{ per cent}$$

To work out the percentage using a calculator, the smaller number (12) should be entered, followed by pressing ÷ and the larger number (200), and then by pressing %.

FINDING THE NUMBER AFTER BEING GIVEN THE PERCENTAGE

Example: What is 6 per cent of 170?

To calculate this manually the two numbers should be multiplied together and divided by 100.

$$\frac{6 \times 170}{100} = 10.2$$

To work it out on the calculator, the two numbers should be entered as a multiplication (170 × 6) and the % key then pressed.

A C T I V I T Y

Practise your percentages! Work out the following (you may use a calculator if you wish):

1. 10 per cent of 25
2. 22 per cent of 1670
3. 60 per cent of £93.75
4. 16 per cent of 95
5. 12.5 per cent of 365
6. 19 as a percentage of 35
7. 20 as a percentage of 1572
8. 2 as a percentage of 10
9. 12.5 as a percentage of 100
10. 0.13 as a percentage of 7

VAT

It is essential to be able to calculate percentages in order to work out VAT (value added tax) which currently stands at 17.5 per cent.

CALCULATING VAT WITHOUT A CALCULATOR

Example: How much VAT would be paid on £180?

$$\frac{17.5 \times 180}{100} = £31.50$$

A C T I V I T Y

Quickly work out the VAT on the following (you may use a calculator if you wish):

1. £10
2. £71
3. £193
4. £2025
5. £11
6. £28.50
7. £111
8. £895.75
9. £1021.57
10. £0.75

CALCULATING VAT FROM INCLUSIVE AMOUNTS

Sometimes the amount paid already includes VAT, for example petrol. If someone submits an expense claim the amount of VAT will have to be calculated in order that it can be recorded separately. The following equation shows how to work out the amount of VAT.

$$\frac{\text{VAT rate}}{\text{VAT rate} + 100} \times \text{amount spent} = \text{amount of VAT}$$

Example: The amount spent is £44. The current rate of VAT is 17.5 per cent. How much VAT does the amount include?

$$\frac{17.5}{17.5 + 100} = \frac{17.5}{117.5} \times £44 = £6.55$$

CALCULATING THE EXCLUSIVE PRICE

This can be done by subtracting the amount of VAT calculated from the total paid.

Example: The amount spent is £44. The current rate of VAT is 17.5 per cent. What is the price exclusive of VAT?

$$£44 - £6.55 = £37.45$$

Calculate the VAT and the exclusive price for each of the following amounts:

1 £67.52
2 £21.75
3 £10.93
4 £11.73
5 £19.75

CHANGING VAT RATES

The calculations above will remain the same even if VAT rates change. For example, VAT used to be 15 per cent but is currently 17.5 per cent. All you need to do is substitute different figures.

Example: How much VAT would be paid on £180?

VAT at 15 per cent $\quad = \dfrac{15 \times 180}{100} \quad = £27.00$

VAT at 17.5 per cent $\quad = \dfrac{17.5 \times 180}{100} \quad = £31.50$

For the previous exercise, assume that VAT now stands at 19 per cent. Recalculate your figures.

Discounts

As discussed in Chapter 4 'Financial transactions' p.95, traders will often give discounts to attract custom. Discounts will normally be calculated in terms of percentages.

Calculating totals

When you are adding up:

- make sure that all numbers are copied down clearly and accurately
- use a ruler to keep your place with a long list of numbers
- make sure that numbers are carefully lined up, i.e. hundreds under hundreds, tens under tens and so on

Exley Enterprises manufacture kitchen and bathroom units. They give trade discounts for buyers purchasing large quantities and cash discounts to people paying in cash.

Calculate the discounts for the following customers:

1 Mr Christie, a builder, purchases 18 fitted kitchens at £3500 each. He is given a 5 per cent discount.
2 Mr and Mrs Burridge pay cash for a new bathroom suite costing £4000. They are given a 4 per cent discount.

Below are some activities to carry out to practise calculating totals.

Transfer the following numbers into a neat list and then add them up.

15034
66713
2345   7026
1371
54
73   702

Change the following into numerical form and then have a go at adding them up.

seven hundred and fifty two
six thousand, three hundred and nine
twenty seven
eight hundred and twenty four
three million

CALCULATE WAGES AND SALARIES

PAYING STAFF

All types of organisations need to have clear systems for paying their staff and there are standard procedures and documents for businesses to use. Payroll systems should be easy for staff working in the payroll section to use and administer and also easy to understand, so that employees are clear about their pay and the deductions that have been made.

Types of pay

Employees usually earn a fixed amount of money each week or month: this is called their **wages** (**salary** is the term used to describe the annual earnings of an employee). For example, a sales assistant might earn £150 per week. Sometimes earnings can be increased by commission. The sales assistant might receive a percentage commission on everything he or she sells. For example, if the sales assistant sells goods to the retail value of £320 one Saturday and receives 5 per cent commission on all sales, he or she will earn an extra £16 in addition to the £150 he or she already earns.

A C T I V I T Y

List as many occupations as possible where the employees can earn commission.

1 What are the advantages and disadvantages of this system of payment to the employer and employee?
2 In your opinion is this a good method of motivating staff?

Staff may also increase their earnings by receiving **bonuses.** The usual way for this to happen is for the company to set a target that either an individual or the company has to meet. The target could run over any period: it could be monthly, quarterly, six-monthly or yearly. The target could be fixed in terms of profit (e.g. the aim is to make £1 million profit this year), sales revenue, or growth (e.g. the company plans to increase its sales by 10 per cent more than last year). If the

company hits the target it may then pay a bonus to the staff that is very often a percentage of their salary, usually 1–10 per cent. A bonus scheme need not be this complicated. A bonus may simply be any payment over the agreed hourly rate to an employee.

Overtime is another common way of increasing earnings. Employees are normally contracted to work a number of hours a week, say 37 hours. In some industries, if the employee is asked to work more than the contracted number of hours, he or she will receive payment at a higher rate, often called 'time and a half' or 'double time'. This means if the employee normally receives £5 per hour, the overtime rate will be either £7.50 or £10 per hour respectively. Overtime rates may be set at any level that the employer chooses.

Common payroll terms

With the many different ways of earning money it is clear, therefore, that there needs to be an efficient way of dealing with this. There are some standard terms which all organisations use:

WAGES

An employee earns wages when he or she is paid on an hourly basis. Wages are therefore calculated by the hour. Traditionally these wages were paid weekly and in cash. This is now changing, both for security and for efficiency reasons.

SALARY

An employee is said to be salaried when his or her earnings are calculated on a yearly basis. For example, an engineer might earn £15 000 p.a. (per annum, meaning each year). An employee paid in this way receives payment each month. It is now common for the salary to be paid directly into the employee's bank account.

TIME RATE

This is where an employee's earnings are calculated by the amount of time worked, rather than the amount of output (as in 'Piece rate' below). For example, an employee is paid £x per hour for an agreed number of hours per week.

119

OVERTIME

This is where someone works in excess of the stipulated number of hours per week. He or she may be paid extra for this, for example time and a half (the normal hourly rate plus 50 per cent) or double time (twice the hourly rate).

PIECE RATE

This is sometimes called piecework. An employee in this case is paid according to their output. For example, in a clothing factory a machinist may be paid per item of clothing produced. The more productive the worker, the higher the earnings. This method is sometimes called payment by results.

BONUS RATE

This is a rate that is higher than the normal hourly rate of pay.

ANNUAL RATE

This is the calculation of an employee's earnings over one year.

COMMISSION

Often calculated on a percentage basis, this can be paid on levels of sales or orders. Commission is a common form of earnings amongst sales people.

GROSS PAY

This is the total amount of earnings an employee has before anything is deducted, for example income tax. It could include basic salary plus any commission, bonus or overtime payable.

NET PAY

This is the amount of money the employee actually receives once deductions have been made. It is sometimes called 'take-home pay'.

DEDUCTIONS

All earnings have to be reviewed to see if the employee is liable to pay income tax and national insurance, which the vast majority of employees are. The tax and national insurance contributions each employee has to pay are deducted from the gross pay, leaving the employee with the net pay.

Which documents will help?

In order to pay staff correctly the payroll department needs to use a number of documents. One of the key

ACTIVITY

Which methods of payment are best suited to the following occupations? Give your reasons why.

- firefighter
- teacher
- skilled worker in car factory
- packer on a production line
- potato picker
- nurse
- office supervisor

areas that needs checking is staff attendance, and man organisations collect information to maintain attendance records.

ACTIVITY

How many ways can you list of monitoring staff attendance? What are the advantages and disadvantages of each one?

ACTIVITY

Design your own attendance record card for a small business with 11 employees.

In addition to this the payroll section also needs to us national insurance and tax tables (see p.121). These w help them to calculate the wages and salaries.

STANDARD FORMS USED IN THE TAX SYSTEM

There are several standard forms used by both the Inland Revenue and business organisations to communicate details about the tax situation of individual employees.

P45 is given to an employee who is leaving a job. It will contain all the details of their earnings and tax paid to date. It should be given to a new employer immediately the employee starts a new job. This will enable the Inland Revenue to allocate an appropriate tax code to the new employee.

Inland Revenue

P45 part 1
Details of employee leaving work

District number Reference number

1 PAYE Reference

2 Employee's National Insurance number

(Mr Mrs Miss Ms)

3 Surname
(in capitals)

First name(s)
(in capitals)

Day Month Year

4 Leaving date (in figures)   19

Code   Week 1 or Month 1

5 Tax Code at leaving date. If week 1 or Month 1 basis
applies, write 'X' in the box marked Week 1 or Month 1

Week   Month

6 Last entries on   Week or month number
Deductions
Working Sheet (P11).
Make no entry
here if Week 1 or   Total pay to date   £   p
Month 1 basis
applies. Go to item 7   Total tax to date   £   p

7 If Week 1 or
Month 1 basis   Total pay in this employment £   p
applies
Total tax in this employment £   p

8 Works number/   9 Department or
Payroll number   branch if any

10 Employee's
private
address and
Postcode

11 I certify that the details entered above in items 1 to 9 are correct
Employer
Address and
Postcode

Date

To the employer   For Tax Office use
• Complete this form following the 'Employee leaving' instructions in the
Employer's Basic Guide to PAYE (P8). Make sure the details are clear on
all three parts of this form.
• Detach part 1 and send it to your Tax Office immediately.
• Hand parts 2 and 3 (unseparated) to your employee when he or
she leaves
• If the employee has died, write 'D' in this box and send all three
parts of this form (unseparated) to your Tax Office immediately.
P45

Fig. 5.17

P46 is given to an employee who has no previous tax details.

A **P2(T)** (notification of coding) tells an employee how he or she will be taxed over the next year. It will list any allowances that can be claimed against tax. For example, for the tax year 1994/95 the married person's allowance is £1720. This means that £1720 of your income will not be taxed if you are married. The form also lists deductions in tax that are subtracted from your allowances. For example, if you have a company car the Inland Revenue will tax you on this perk. A **P9** is sent to the employer, informing them of the employee's tax code (see Figure 5.18).

At the end of each tax year (on 5 April) each employee receives a **P60** which gives details of all earnings and tax paid for that year.

Inland Revenue

Employer's PAYE reference

District date stamp

Notice to employer of employee's tax code

Employee's name

National Insurance number

Works/Payroll no, Branch etc

Code:
The code of this employee is

To be used for the
tax year to 5 April

Instructions to employer
1. Keep this form as your authority.
2. Please make sure that you put the employee's National Insurance number on
• your payroll records **and**
• the end of year documents that you send in with your annual return after 5 April.
If the National Insurance number already on your records is different from the number shown above please tell your Tax Office.
3. If the employee has left your employment please destroy this form. **Do not send it back to your Tax Office.**

P9   CCO 7/94

Fig. 5.18

A **P14** is the document that the employer sends to the Inland Revenue. It contains the same information as the P60.

The **P35** is an annual statement made by the employer to the Inland Revenue.

The **P11** is a deductions working sheet. Each employee has one completed by their employer. It contains the national insurance number and contributions and tax details on a monthly basis.

The **P30** is a payslip booklet. Payslips are sent to the Inland Revenue each month detailing national insurance contributions and tax deducted in the previous month.

Calculating payroll

Information required before calculating payroll

There are several reference documents you will need before you are able to calculate payroll. The Employer's Starter Pack, which is published by the Inland Revenue, contains all the necessary documentation. Your school or college will need to have access to one of these packs for use as a central reference source to allow you to complete some of the calculation activities within the payroll section.

Small businesses will probably have a simple form of recording salaries and use a wages book. There are slightly more sophisticated manual methods, one of which is the 3-in-1 system. This is where the payroll, a pay advice slip and a tax and earnings record are produced at one time manually. Larger organisations may well use a computer.

A C T I V I T Y

List as many advantages as possible of a computerised payroll system over a manual system. Does the computerised system have any disadvantages?

BASIC STEPS

In order to avoid mistakes, wages staff need to follow the procedure laid down below.

1 Check whether the employee is paid weekly or monthly.
2 Check the rate of pay.
3 Check employee's attendance record.
4 Calculate employee's gross pay.
5 Calculate statutory deductions.
6 Establish net amount payable.
7 Complete payroll.
8 Fill in payslip.
9 Select appropriate method of payment and pay wages.

If the employee is paid a salary, the annual amount will need dividing up (normally into 12 monthly periods). If the employee is paid wages, then the calculation may involve different hourly rates for overtime and so on.

Attendance may be checked from time sheets. Often in manufacturing industries, employees have to 'clock in' and 'clock out', using a card that is punched in a time clock to provide a record of attendance.

The following are examples of how to calculate **gross pay:**

1 Sarah Smith's annual salary is £14 400 p.a. She is paid monthly.
   Her monthly gross pay = $\frac{£14\ 400}{12}$ = £1200 per month.

2 Mark McDermott's annual salary is £11 440. He is paid on a four weekly basis.
   His four-weekly gross pay = $\frac{£11\ 440}{52}$

   = £220 per week × 4 = £880 per four-week period.

3 Elaine Briggs is paid hourly at £5 per hour. She works a 35-hour week.
   Her weekly gross pay = 35 hours @ £5 per hour
   = £175 gross pay.

4 Tim Smith is paid hourly at £2.40 per hour. He works a 35-hour week. He has worked four hours overtime at double time.
   35 hours @ £2.40 per hour = £84.00
   4 hours @ £4.80 per hour = £19.20
   Weekly gross pay = £103.20

A C T I V I T Y

Now try calculating the gross pay for the following salaries/wages.

1 Annual salary – paid monthly:
   a £12 000
   b £4500
   c £6900
2 Annual salary – paid 4 weekly:
   a £7214
   b £11 500
   c £9200
   d £6600

3 Paid hourly:
   a 35 hours @ £3.50 per hour
   b 40 hours @ £5.50 per hour
   c 37 hours @ £9 per hour
   d 40 hours @ £2.20 per hour
4 Paid hourly:
   a 37 hours @ £4.50 per hour + 2 hours overtime @ time and a half
   b 40 hours @ £4 per hour + 7 hours overtime @ time and a half
   c 40 hours @ £3.70 per hour + 6 hours overtime @ double time
   d 30 hours @ £2.50 per hour + 5 hours overtime @ double time

Statutory deductions have to be deducted from gross pay. The normal deductions are made up of income tax, under the pay-as-you-earn scheme (PAYE), and national insurance contributions.

In order to calculate deductions you will need:

- a PAYE code
- tax tables (see Employer's Starter Pack)
- deduction working sheets (P11) (as above)

PAYE CODES

All employees should have one of these. They indicate how much an employee can earn before any tax is deducted. Because of this the PAYE code is often call

Inland Revenue
PAYE–Notice of Coding

*Please keep this notice for future reference
and let me know of any change
in your address. Form P3(T) enclosed
(or previously sent) explains the entries.*

Issued by
H.M. Inspector of Taxes
CROYDON 2
13/15 DINGWALL ROAD
CROYDON
SURREY

CR9 2XR

201

MRS M WILLIAMS
20 LABURNUM AVENUE
HAYES
MIDDLESEX

Please use both lines of this reference if you
write or call – it will help to avoid delay.

221/H591

| YZ | 45 | 36 | 75 | C |

Date 06.05.95

This notice cancels any previous notice of coding for the year shown below. It shows the allowances which make up your code.
Your employer or paying officer will use this code to deduct or refund the right amount of tax under PAYE during the year shown
below.
Please check this notice. If you think it is wrong please return it to me and give your reasons. If we cannot agree you have the right
of appeal.
Please let me know at once about any change in your personal circumstances which may alter your allowances and coding.
By law you are required to tell me of any income that is not fully taxed, even if you are not sent a Tax Return.

See Note	Allowances	£	See Note	Less Deductions	£
17	PERSONAL ALLOWANCE	3445			
				Less total deductions	
	Total allowances	3445		Allowances set against pay etc. £	

Your code for the year to 5 April 1995 is 344L Please see Part B overleaf

P2 (T)

FIG. 5.19 ILLUSTRATION OF TAX CODING

---

tax allowance. The code is made up of numbers and a
letter.
  Mrs William's tax code is 344L. This means she will
be taxed on any earnings over £3445. New codes are
introduced every year in the budget by the chancellor
of the exchequer.
  The list below shows what the letters in the tax code
mean and what the most common allowances are for.

Gives the basic personal allowance.
The basic personal allowance plus the basic married
couple's allowance, or the basic personal allowance plus
additional personal allowance.
The personal allowance for anyone between 65 and 74.
The personal allowance for those aged 65–74 plus the
married couple's allowance for those aged 65–74.
This may cover different sets of circumstances:

- if the tax payer gets an allowance for being aged 75 or
  over
- if the tax payer does not receive the full higher, age-
  related allowance because his or her total income
  comes to more than £14 200
- if a wife receives some or all of the married couple's
  allowance

There are some other, less common codes:

BR Tax is deducted at the basic rate because no allowances
have been given.
OT Where no allowances have been given or none remain
after all other adjustments have been made. Tax is
deducted at lower, basic then higher rates depending on
income.
D This is usually followed by a number. Tax will be
deducted at a higher rate.
K Also followed by a number. Where deductions are
greater than total allowances. This results in a negative
tax code. For example:

Note	Allowances	
17	Personal Allowance	3445
	Reductions	
25	Benefits (car - new)	4428
25	Medical health	174
	Mobile phone	200
		4802
	Net allowances	(1357)
	Code	(135)K

NT No tax will be deducted.

Tax tables and deductions

The Inland Revenue calculates how much tax each employee should pay and lists these amounts in published tax tables. There are a number of different tables, the most common of which are **Tables A** (free pay tables) and Tables **LR + B–D** (taxable pay tables).

National insurance

All employees have to pay national insurance contributions. Contributions are of two kinds:

1 The employee's contribution, which is deducted from their gross pay.
2 The employer's contribution.

The employee's contributions are deducted at source (i.e. taken out of a salary by the employer before payin an employee) in much the same way as tax is. Nationa insurance payments help to provide social protection benefits such as the state old-age pension and contribut towards the running of the National Health Service. Employers also contribute to the national insurance scheme. A percentage of salary (up to 9 per cent currently) is deducted from salary up to a limit of £21 06

A C T I V I T Y

For the next activity you will need the following documents:

- a P2 notice of coding
- tax tables A and LR + B–D (available via an employer's starter pack)
- a deduction working sheet P11

Study the P11 form in Figure 5.20. Weeks 1 and 2 have already been completed. The steps below explain how this was done.

Week 1

1 Gross pay (£110) is entered in column 2.
2 Total pay is entered in column 3. This is the same as column 2 as it is the first week. It will change in subsequent weeks.
3 Check the tax code (344L).

4 Now use Table A and refer to Week 1. Find the tax code (344). This is printed in bold. Next to the code you will find another figure (66.33). This figure is the amount of tax-free pay allowed to date. This figure should be entered into column 4a. Mary will not pay tax on the first £66.33 she earns. **NB** If the employee has a K code there is a different process to follow.

5 Take gross pay   110.00
   Subtract free pay to date   – 66.33
   Total taxable pay to date   = 43.67
   £43.67 should be entered in column 5.

6 Now refer to Table B. Take your taxable pay (£43.67) and round it down to the next pound (£43). Find the figure 43 printed in bold. The figure next to it (£10.75) is the total tax due to date at the 25 per cent tax band. To establish the correct amount of tax relief due on this amount you must refer to lower-rate relief tables (20 per cent tax

band) in Table B. Refer to Week 1: the amount to subtract is £2.89.
   Total tax due if tax paid at 25 per cent   10.75
   Subtract to allow for tax payable at 20 per cent – 2.89
   Total tax payable to date   = 7.86
   Enter this figure into column 6.

7 As this is Week 1, Mary has not paid any tax yet in this tax year. This means the tax due this week is the same the total tax due to date. This figure should be entered into column 7.

Week 2

1 Gross pay is entered in column 2 (£110).
2 Total pay to date should be entered in column 3 (Wee 1 at £110 and Week 2 at £110 = £220).
3 Check the tax code (344L)
4 Using Table A, find Week 2. Refer to tax code 344 printed in bold. Next to it is the total of tax-free pay allowed to date (£132.66). This is entered in column 4a
5 Total gross pay to date   220.00
   Subtract total free pay to date   – 132.66
   Total taxable pay to date   = 87.34
   £87.34 should be entered in column 5.
6 Round down the taxable pay to £87 and then refer to Table B. Find £87 in bold on Table B. Take the figure ne to it (£21.75) Then refer to the lower-rate relief subtraction tables and find the figure next to Week 2 (£5.77).
                                        21.75
                                       – 5.77
                                      = 15.98
   £15.98 is the total tax due to date. This figure should b inserted into column 6.
7 Calculate total tax due to date   15.98
   Less tax paid up to last week   – 7.86
   Tax due   = 8.12
   £8.12 should be entered in column 7.

Contributions are calculated on gross pay as is income tax. Payment of national insurance contributions will help to determine if someone is eligible for state pensions for retirement, widowhood and invalidity.

If someone belongs to an approved pension scheme, they can **contract out** of one part of the state scheme. This means they and their employers will pay a lower contribution into the state scheme. Those **not contracted out** will pay a larger amount into the state scheme, as will their employers.

ACTIVITY

Now continue calculating Mary's deductions for Weeks 3–5. Note her change in earnings.

Week 3	=	£120
Week 4	=	£115
Week 5	=	£110

Employee's surname *in CAPITALS* WILLIAMS		First two forenames MARY				
National Insurance no. YZ, 45, 35, 75, C	Date of birth *in figures* Day 15, Month 06, Year 54	Works no. etc 299			Date of leaving *in figures* Day Month Year	
Tax code † 344L	Amended code† Wk/Mth in which applied					

PAYE Income Tax

	Pay in the week or month including Statutory Sick Pay/Statutory Maternity Pay 2	Total pay to date 3	Total free pay to date (Table A) 4a	K codes only Total "additional pay" to date (Table A) 4b	Total taxable pay to date i.e. column 3 minus column 4a **or** column 3 plus column 4b 5	Total tax due to date as shown by Taxable Pay Tables 6	K codes only Tax due at end of current period. Mark refunds 'R' 6a	Regulatory limit i.e. 50% of column 2 entry 6b	Tax deducted or refunded in the week or month. Mark refunds 'R' 7	K codes only Tax not deducted owing to the Regulatory limit 8	For employer's use
1	110 £ 00	110 00	66 £ 33	£	43 £ 67	7 £ 86	£	£	7 £ 86	£	
2	110 00	220 00	132 66		87 34	15 98			8 12		
3											
4											
5											
6											
7											

SPECIMEN

* You must enter the NI contribution table letter overleaf beside the NI totals box - *see the note shown there.*

† If amended cross out previous code.

Ø If any week/month the amount in column 4a is more than the amount in column 3, leave column 5 blank.

FIG. 5.20

HOW TO CALCULATE NATIONAL INSURANCE DEDUCTIONS

The Department of Social Security prints two sets of tables for employers to calculate national insurance contributions.

Table 1 covers not-contracted-out contributions, which is the most common system. Table 1a covers contracted-out contributions.

A C T I V I T Y

Figure 5.22 is the left-hand side of a P11 deductions working sheet covering standard rate national insurance contributions. Use Table 1 to complete the P11.

1 In column 1a enter gross pay for that week, for example Week 1 earnings are £110.

2 Look at Table 1 and find gross pay. If the table does not include the exact figure you're looking for, you should use the next lowest figure.

3 Enter the total of employee's and employer's contributions in column 1b.

4 Employee's contributions should be noted in column 1c.

A C T I V I T Y

Using the example of the P11 printed in Figure 5.22, calculate the national insurance contributions for Weeks 2–5 using Table 1.

How to calculate statutory sick pay

Employers are required to pay statutory sick pay (SSP) for anyone absent for up to eight weeks each year due to illness. Some people may be excluded from receiving SSP.

To understand how the system works there are several terms you need to become familiar with:

1 *Period of incapacity for work.* The employee is ill for four consecutive days and then becomes eligible for sick pay. This can include weekends and bank holidays.

2 *Qualifying days.* SSP is paid for those days of absence when the employee would have normally worked.

3 *Waiting days.* The first three qualifying days are unpaid.

After the waiting days SSP will be paid for the remaining qualifying days for up to eight weeks. If someone is ill for two periods in quick succession, these periods of illness may be linked together. They have to occur within 14 days so that the SSP can be paid from the first qualifying day in the second period of illness.

For example, Louise became ill on Sunday and needed a week off work to recover. She was entitled to two days SSP in that week (see Figure 5.22).

FIG. 5.21 EXAMPLE OF SSP CALCULATION

HOW MUCH SSP SHOULD AN EMPLOYER PAY?

SSP is paid according to the rates set out by the Department of Social Security. The rates from the 6th April 1995 are shown in Table 5.1 on p.128. All employees are paid SSP according to these rates.

Look again at Figure 5.21. In Louise's case Monday–Wednesday count as waiting days where SSP is not payable. Louise will therefore only receive SSP for Thursday and Friday of that week.

Using the Table find the number 5 in the column marked 'No. of QDs in Week'. (Figure 5.21 shows that there are five qualifying days in Louise's case, Monday–Friday.)

Louise is entitled to two days SSP so find the box in the column headed '2' which meets the five qualifying-days line. The amount of SSP payable is the figure in this box, therefore £21.

Note that PAYE and NI contributions are payable on SSP.

SSP will be treated like any other pay and entered on the P11 as other earnings would be.

Procedures

Every period (this may be weekly or monthly) the employer must complete the payroll including details of employees' earnings and deductions.

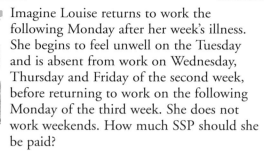

A C T I V I T Y

Imagine Louise returns to work the following Monday after her week's illness. She begins to feel unwell on the Tuesday and is absent from work on Wednesday, Thursday and Friday of the second week, before returning to work on the following Monday of the third week. She does not work weekends. How much SSP should she be paid?

HOW TO COMPLETE THE PAYROLL

1 Transfer all earnings and deductions from form P11 for all employees.
2 Check the employee's personal records for any agreement to voluntary contributions. This could be a trade-union or sports-club subscription.
3 Make sure all voluntary and statutory deductions are added and entered into the 'Total net deductions' column.
4 Net pay can then be calculated as follows:
Gross pay − total net deductions = net pay

Deductions Working Sheet P11   Year to 5 April 19 ____

Employer's name

Tax District and reference

Complete only for occupational pension sche
newly contracted-out since 1 January 1986.
Scheme contracted-out number

| S | 4 | | | | |

National Insurance contributions

For employer's use	Earnings on which employee's contributions payable 1a	Total of employee's and employer's contributions payable 1b	Employee's contributions payable 1c	Earnings on which employee's contributions at contracted-out rate payable included in column 1a 1d	Employee's contributions at contracted-out rate included in column 1c 1e	Statutory Sick Pay in the week or month included in column 2 1f	Statutory Sick Pay recovered. Only complete this column if you are claiming Small Employer's Relief 1g	Statutory Maternity Pay in the week or month included in column 2 1h	Month no
	Bt £ fwd	Bt £ fwd	Bt £ fwd	Bt £ fwd	Bt £ fwd	Bt £ fwd	Bt £ fwd	Bt £ fwd	Bt fwd Mth 7
	110 00	13 31	6 02						6 Nov to 5 Dec **8**
	110 00								
	125 00								6 Dec to 5 Jan **9**
	105 22								
	107 91								6 Jan to 5 Feb **10**
									6 Feb to 5 Mar **11**
									6 Mar to 5 April **12**
					▲ SSP total		▲ SMP total	

‡ NI Letter - When you make the first entry on the sheet, or when there is a change of table, enter letter showing contribution table you have used.

NI Totals - Enter in columns 1a to 1e separate totals for each table used

P11(1993)   Please keep this form for at least 3 years after the end of the year to which it relates, or longer if yo

Printed in the UK for HMSO 12/92 D.FAL 0101735 C50,000, 36925

(watermark: SPECIMEN)

FIG. 5.22

Statutory Sick Pay daily rates table

Unrounded daily rates	No of QDs in week	1	2	3	4	5	6	7
£		£	£	£	£	£	£	£
7.5000	7	7.50	15.00	22.50	30.00	37.50	45.00	52.50
8.7500	6	8.75	17.50	26.25	35.00	43.75	52.50	
10.5000	5	10.50	21.00	31.50	42.00	52.50		
13.1250	4	13.13	26.25	39.38	52.50			
17.5000	3	17.50	35.00	52.50				
26.2500	2	26.25	52.50					
52.5000	1	52.50						

Unrounded rates are included for employers with computerised payroll systems

TABLE 5.1

5 The payroll should be balanced. To do this you need to add up each column. Make sure the total of the gross pay minus the totals of all the deductions agrees with the total net pay.

A C T I V I T Y

You will need five completed P11s and details of voluntary deductions for the five employees whose P11s you are using. Draw out a blank payroll as in Figure 5.23, and complete and balance it for Week 1.

COMPLETING A PAY ADVICE

All employees have the right to an itemised pay advice. It has to include:

- gross pay
- deductions made
- net pay
- method of payment

ARRANGING PAYMENT

This can be done in several ways:

1 In cash (tends to be weekly wages).
2 By cheque (tends to be monthly salaries).
3 By credit transfer (tends to be monthly salaries).

Cash payments need careful planning. Each firm will need to ensure it has adequate money and the right proportion of notes and coins to pay its employees. To

FIG. 5.23 A BLANK PAYROLL

PAYROLL		PERIOD ENDING				PAYDAY		TAX WEEK/ MONTH					
WORKS NO.	NAME	EARNINGS				GROSS PAY	DEDUCTIONS				TOTAL NET DEDUCTIONS	NET PAY	EMPLOYERS NI
		HOURLY PAY	BONUS	SSP	OTHER		PAYE	NI	SAVINGS	SUBS			

Twinlock Payemaster Individual Payslip Ref. PM5/87	Code 11-73923	
© Twinlock 1987		
4 - 9 0		

Earnings period	No.	Date
WEEK 2		18.9.93
1		
2		
3		
4		
5		
6 P.I.W. (days) for period		
S.M.P. for period		
Basic pay for period	110	00
Bonus/overtime for period		
S.S.P. for period		
Gross earnings for period	110	00
Pension		
Pay for period less Pension		
Cum. pay to date less Pension	220	00
Total free pay to date	132	66
Total taxable pay to date	87	34
Total tax due to date	15	98
Tax refund this period		
Income tax this period	8	12
NI contribution	6	02
A		
B		
C Total fixed deductions		
TOTAL DEDUCTIONS	14	54
NET PAY	95	46
7		
8		
TOTAL AMOUNT PAYABLE	95	46
Name		
M. WILLIAM		

help wages staff to do this, the firm may draw up a **wages cash analysis**. Each net wage on the payroll will be analysed and broken down to check the notes and coins required. Then the totals for each note and coin will be checked and added up to ensure they agree with the total net payroll (see Figure 5.25).

Each employee will the receive a pay packet, with the cash and pay advice enclosed.

Payment by cheque is a safe way of handling money, and cheques are drawn up in the usual way. The cheque will be accompanied by a pay advice.

Payment by credit transfer is becoming more and more popular. It means that payment is made directly into the employee's bank or building society account. It is useful for the company as it does not have to handle large amounts of cash or cheques. The company will require bank details from each employee. It then simply draws up a list of the employees to be paid and the amount each is to receive (see Figure 5.26) and sends it to the bank with a cheque. This is more efficient in terms of time and effort.

A bank giro credit slip is sent from the employer's bank to the employee's bank simply to transfer money from the employer's bank account into the employee's account. It is a method of paying salaries.

This is a convenient and easy-to-use method of payment. The employee will receive a pay advice direct from the company.

Wages Cash Analysis													
Works No.	Name	Wage	£50	£20	£10	£5	£1	50p	20p	10p	5p	2p	1p
22	R Smith	62.30		2	2		2		1	1			
37	D Pearce	79.50	1		2	1	4	1					
2	J Brown	100.29	1	2	1				1		1	2	
11	B Halpern	42.60		1	2		2	1		1			
		284.69	2	5	7	1	8	2	2	2	1	2	—

FIG. 5.25 WAGES CASH ANALYSIS

FIG. 5.26 BANK SUMMARY FORM AND CREDIT SLIP

BANK SUMMARY FORM

Date: 28.1.19___

To: Lloyds Bank Ltd, Smithson Street, Harrow Branch
Please distribute the credit slips attached as arranged
with the recipients.
Our cheque for £2404.08 is enclosed.

Bank Sort Code No.	Bank & Branch	Account Holder	Account No.	Net Amount
23 21 06	Midland, Harrow	B Hook	449271	£989.32
02 35 96	NatWest, Pinner	T Smith	332911	£625.01
43 71 02	NatWest, Eastcote	J Brown	704329	£789.75

BANK GIRO CREDIT SLIP

From: Lloyds Bank Plc
        Smithson Street
        Harrow Branch   Date: 28.1.19___

Code No.	Bank and Branch Title	Account	Amount
23 21 06	Midland Harrow	B Hook	£989.32
By order of Touche-à-tout Knitwear		Ref 2140	

RECORD AND MONITOR STOCK MOVEMENTS

An area of business that is increasing in importance is that of stock control. When businesses have invested large amounts of money in their stock they need to monitor stock movements in and out of the business and also to create and maintain accurate stock records.

The key to an efficient stock-control system is to have accurate and up-to-date information. Previously businesses tended to have manual systems, where stock records were updated by employees filling in stock record-cards. It is more usual these days to find computerised systems in large organisations, however. In order to monitor any stock it needs to be clearly identified. To do this coding systems are frequently used. Bar-codes, for example, are often used these days for retail products. This code is on a label that can be read by a scanner to record a product's sale in the shop's central computer. The computer may also be linked to the stock-control system, which will register that

A C T I V I T Y

What are the advantages of a computerised stock system over a manual one? Has the manual system any benefits a computer cannot offer?

another product has been sold and automatically re-order it if stock falls below a certain level. The bar-code may contain information such as the country of manufacture (denoted by a number), a product code and other modifications. Besides the bar-code, companies often have an internal system of coding a product. This code can contain any combination of the following data:

- a description of the product
- the number of products contained in a packing/shipping case
- a product code or reference
- the location of the stock, which may be a particular warehouse or even a city

On a computer print-out for each item you would probably find the information shown on Figure 5.27. The 'Rejects/Return' figure shows products that have been sold, but then returned to the factory. This may have been because of a quality fault, in which case the factory would hold the stock before deciding whether to re-work (make good) the product or destroy it.

How can stock be controlled?

There are a number of steps and procedures involved in maintaining a good stock system:

1 *Raise order (requisition)*. The order can be raised manually or logged onto a computer. It could be an internal order: for example a mechanic working for a large car dealer would raise an order for two spark plugs from his own dealership stores. Alternatively an order might be raised by an external customer: for example a supermarket might send in an order to a food manufacturer for 100 cartons of baked beans. The order should contain the date, quantity required, reference, description and name of the person who raised the order together with the appropriate authorisation.

2 *Issue goods*. The order should be checked for quantities, dates, delivery conditions and so on. The correct stock should then be issued and logged out accordingly.

3 *Receive goods*. When stock is delivered to a customer, it should be accompanied by the appropriate paperwork. When the stock is delivered, the customer will normally be expected to sign a goods-received note after checking that the goods received correspond with the documents. The company delivering then has evidence of delivery and the customer has an accurate record of goods received.

There may be different ways of monitoring stock, depending on the goods involved. Stock can be categorised as **consumable** or **non-consumable**. Consumables are goods that are used up in an operation, but do not become part of a finished product. For example, a car manufacturer will need photocopier paper to use in its offices, but the paper does not form any part of the end product, which is the car. Consumables are often bought frequently and in large quantities from several suppliers.

Their movement needs to be strictly controlled to avoid stock loss. Consumables are frequently monitored using stock record cards or books (see Figure 5.28).

Non-consumables are goods which are not used up during the company's operation – computers, desks, filing cabinets are examples of non-consumables.

Stock and security

Stock checks or stock counts (also called stock takes) are carried out periodically to check if the stock accounted for on paper corresponds to the physical stock that can be actually counted in the warehouse.

Code	52901								
Description	Pretty Pink Lipstick								

Date	Opening stock	Number per pack	Deliveries		Sales Out	Rejects/ Returns	Stock held in Luton Warehouse	Stock held in Hull Warehouse	Total units of stock held
			Luton	Hull					
29.1	432	12					432		432
2.2			72	72			504	72	576
6.2			36	–			540	72	612
14.2					288		252	72	324
14.2						36 (L)	288	72	360
26.2						72 (H)	288	144	432
	432		108	72	288	108	288	144	432

FIG. 5.27 COMPUTER PRINT-OUT FOR STOCK

STOCK RECORD CARD

Item   Re-order Quantity:
Suppliers:

Date	Received	Issued	Balance

FIG. 5.28 A STOCK RECORD CARD

This is sometimes called an **inventory check**. Inventory is an accounting term that includes the cost of any stock being used or processed in a company. The inventory includes raw materials, work in progress and finished goods. An inventory control system uses sales forecasting and production planning to achieve the best levels of stock in a company. Normally, this is a low enough level of stock to minimise cash tied up in stock, but high enough to be able to supply customers when necessary.

It is vital for any stock to be kept secure. Businesses will obviously want to avoid both theft of and accidents with their stock. Hazardous stock should be kept very carefully and there should be strictly defined procedures for accessing the stock. This is also true of high-value stock. It is worthwhile in some cases restricting access to stockholdings. It may be appropriate for a business to nominate a number of responsible employees as being able to authorise the withdrawal of stock. This means in practice that they are required to sign a requisition or order to confirm approved stock movement.

MONITOR TRANSACTIONS AGAINST GIVEN BUDGET

Careful utilisation of resources is a key objective in any business. Just as an individual has to balance money received (income) against outgoings (expenditure), so do companies. Overspending budgets can have serious repercussions for any organisation. Most businesses will have limited resources or money to spend each year and a number of potential projects to spend them on. The business has to decide which is the most effective way of using their resources for the good of the business. The budget is simply a plan of how a business intends to spend its resources. It is always expressed in financial terms. This written document will help the business track its progress throughout the year against targets.

Budgets are normally planned over a year and cover expected revenue and costs. It is obviously difficult to draw up a budget that will be appropriate for the whole business. It is much easier for each department to draw up a budget, as each department will know what it has to achieve to hit its target and how much it may have to spend. The departmental budget can be split down even further so that a section or even an individual has a target. It is the manager's role to check that targets are being met, probably on a weekly or monthly basis.

ACTIVITY

Examine the sales budget here.

The revenue figures are calculated by multiplying the actual sales by the selling price. What would the revenue have been if the budget figures had been achieved? Has this business performed well in your opinion?

SALES BUDGET FOR 1995

PRODUCT	BUDGETED SALES	ACTUAL SALES	SELLING PRICE £	REVENUE	+/− SALES
A	50	72	3	216	+22
B	10	50	1	50	+40
C	100	99	28	2272	−1
D	100	97	35	3395	−3

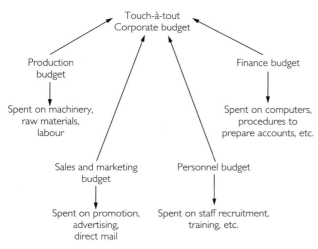

FIG. 5.29 DEPARTMENTAL BUDGETS

	INCOME		EXPENDITURE	
	Planned	Actual	Planned	Actual
Week 1				
Item 1				
2				
3				
4				
5				
6				
7				
Week 2				
Item 1				
2				
3				
4				
5				
6				
7				
Week 3				
Item 1				
2				
3				
4				
5				
6				
7				
Week 4				
Item 1				
2				
3				
4				
5				
6				
7				

It is also important to make sure that income and expenditure are allocated to the correct budget so that a true picture of activities and performance can be achieved.

All of these departmental budgets, if reviewed regularly, will give an up-to-date idea of how the business is performing. For example, in a clothing manufacturers the production department's *expenditure* on machinery, raw materials and labour can be contrasted with the number of sweaters they are *producing*. Has the department met their production targets and yet stayed within expenditure limits?

A C T I V I T Y

Look at the table in the next column and try and draw up a budget for your own personal use over the next month. This is a particularly useful exercise before Christmas!

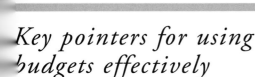

Key pointers for using budgets effectively

Timescales must always be attached to budgets: for example targets to be achieved in six months or expenditure to cover the period 1.1.96–31.12.96, and so on.

2 Budgets must be reviewed regularly!

3 Any significant variation from the plan must be reported and acted on immediately!

4 Any budget that is underused, i.e. where the funds are not being spent, should be cut and the funds used elsewhere.

5 If a business is underperforming against budget, figures must be verified and reported to the responsible

managers, who must plan to take effective action to improve this underperformance.

6 If a business is overperforming against budget, figures must be verified and reported to the responsible managers, who must check that the business is able to function and continue at this level. The budget needs to be amended and note taken of the miscalculation to avoid the same problem again.

A C T I V I T Y

In the activity on p.133, you may have found that you underestimated your expenditure. What would this mean for a business if it did this?

A C T I V I T Y

Draw up a report on the budget below. Calculate totals for proposed and actual budget for each year. What is the difference between proposed budget for this year and actual budget for this year? Which items in particular account for this variance? Was there any data from last year which might have allowed better planning for this year's budget? Make your comments on whether or not you think this year's budget was realistic.

CENTRAL ADMIN BUDGET

ITEM	PROPOSED BUDGET LAST YEAR	ACTUAL EXPENDITURE LAST YEAR	PROPOSED BUDGET THIS YEAR	ACTUAL EXPENDITURE THIS YEAR	VARIANCE + / −
Departmental Costs					
Materials	2000	1700	2000	1900	
Labour					
Management & supervisory	46 000	47 000	49 000	54 000	
Clerical	21 000	20 000	23 000	20 000	
Other Expenses					
Premises	20 000	20 000	22 000	22 000	
Office equipment	6000	8000	8000	12 000	
Consumables	4500	4500	5000	7500	
Telephone	1900	1800	2000	2500	
Postage	750	750	1000	800	
Travel and entertainment	750	1000	1000	2000	

CHAPTER FIVE

Test Yourself!

1 What is the cash book used for?
2 What does FO stand for and what does it mean?
3 What is a contra entry?
4 True or false? The ledger contains details of all the financial transactions within an organisation.
5 Explain the difference between trade and cash discount.
6 When is a credit note issued?
7 What is recorded in the returns inwards book?
8 True or false? 12 per cent of 200 = 25.
9 What does VAT stand for?
10 What is the current rate of VAT?
11 What is the difference between commission and bonus payments?
12 What is the difference between gross and net pay?
13 What is a P45?
14 What is a P11?
15 What are national insurance contributions used for?
16 What are the nine basic steps in the correct procedure for paying staff?
17 What are statutory deductions and who deducts them?
18 How many waiting days are there before statutory sick pay is payable?
19 What is a wages cash analysis?
20 What are the three basic steps involved in maintaining a good stock system?
21 Why do companies need to budget?
22 In what terms are budgets expressed?
23 Give three key pointers for using budgets effectively.

Chapter
6

BUSINESS COMMUNICATION

IDENTIFY THE COMMUNICATION SYSTEMS OF AN ORGANISATION

Good communication is essential within business organisations if they wish to succeed. The larger the organisation the more likely it is that communication will break down. It is vital therefore that an organisation has suitable systems to ensure that effective communication can take place.

At work people need to be able to:

- work alone – this involves people assessing situations and making their own decisions
- work with other members of staff
- deal with people outside the organisation

All of the above show that it is important for individual employees within an organisation to have good communication skills.

INTERNAL AND EXTERNAL COMMUNICATION

External communication

Business organisations need to communicate effectively with the world outside them. They need to inform the public about the service they provide for the community, i.e. providing goods and employment. They need to create an image (or impression) to which the public can relate.

WHO DO ORGANISATIONS NEED TO COMMUNICATE WITH?

- consumers and customers – i.e. the people who may wish to buy their product or service

- the government – government laws and policies affect the ways a business can be run, for example health and safety, wages, prices, protection of the environment, taxation and so on
- the European Union – Britain is now a member of the European Union (see Chapter 9 'Business in Europe'). This means that businesses are also affected by the laws and policies laid down by the Union
- financial institutions – these are organisations such as banks, building societies and so on that may help to fund the business
- the world of education – it is important that pupils/students have an accurate picture of the business world and its operations
- the media – for example newspapers, radio and television, who will be involved in advertising and publicity for business organisations

ACTIVITY

Below is a list of well-known retail outlets. Also listed are words which sum up the retail outlet's image. See if you can match the words to the shops.

- Marks & Spencer
- Poundstretcher
- Intersport
- McDonalds

- fun
- sporty
- cheap and cheerful
- quality

Now make a list of some more organisations and write down the word or words that you think sum up their image.

HOW DO ORGANISATIONS COMMUNICATE WITH THE ABOVE?

The **mass media** is probably the most effective way a business can promote its image and influence people. Use of the mass media can include the following:

- advertisements
- articles
- TV/press coverage of business events
- press releases
- photographs

FIG. 6.1 EXTERNAL COMMUNICATION

Communications with the media are normally handled in a large organisations by a public relations department. Smaller organisations tend to use the service of public relations specialists.

Exhibitions and conferences are a good source of information for customers. Exhibitions allow businesses to communicate with their customers, both consumers and trade customers. For example, the Boat Show and the Ideal Home Exhibition. Conferences are often used to improve internal communication within companies. They are very effective in launching new products and campaigns to salespeople and/or general employees.

Company annual reports are used to communicate with those who have a direct interest in the organisation, i.e. shareholders (current and potential). Copies of the reports are sent to the media.

Company newspapers contain general information about an organisation and are sent to employees, employees' families, the media and so on.

Sponsorship is where a business organisation invests money to support an event or activity. In return the organisation receives publicity. For example, Benson and Hedges are sponsors of golf and snooker competitions.

Direct advertising is where the organisation spends money to advertise its product or service. For example, advertisements in newspapers, TV, magazines and so on. With **indirect advertising** a business organisation may place a job advertisement in a newspaper or magazine. If the advert is well presented (i.e. clearly laid out, including a logo, etc.) it can act as a good form of publicity.

Business organisations may participate in **local events and activities** in order to enhance their image and promote themselves. Examples are donations of prizes at a local fete, offering free gifts to local schools, entering sports teams in a local sports league and so on.

In order to keep themselves up to date with government policies and legislation (and also to build a good relationship with government representatives), businesses should keep in **contact with central and local government**. As well as MPs and local councillors this should also include MEPs (Members of the European Parliament).

Visits to schools and colleges in the form of talks to students/pupils and their teachers/lecturers can help to improve the public's understanding of the business world, as well as acting as a good source of publicity.

Internal communication

Before an organisation can hope to communicate with the outside world it needs to ensure that communication *within* the organisation is effective and appropriate.

WRITTEN COMMUNICATION

Communication that may need to be used more than once or referred to should be kept in a written form. An example of a written communication is a memorandum.

NOTICE BOARDS

These are a good way of communicating with a large number of employees fairly quickly. Examples of information on a notice board would be general notices, health and safety information and details of social events.

IN-HOUSE MAGAZINES AND NEWSLETTERS

These provide up-to-date information about the organisation, staff, events and so on.

HANDBOOKS AND MANUALS

These can include staff handbooks (particularly aimed at new staff) and instruction manuals.

TELEPHONES

Business organisations normally have an internal telephone system so that employees can contact one another.

MEETINGS

Meetings take many different forms. They range from an informal discussion between two people to a large, formal board meeting.

COMPUTERS

Technological developments have meant that information can now be transmitted from one computer to another.

COMMUNICATION BETWEEN BRANCHES

If an organisation has more than one branch it needs to develop effective systems so that the different branches can communicate with each other. They may use the following methods:

- letters
- telexes
- facsimile transmissions (faxes)
- internal mail (i.e. a driver will transport the mail from branch to branch)
- computers
- telephones

A C T I V I T Y

Now that we have discussed the difference between internal and external communication you should be able to complete the following exercise.

Below are examples of business communications. Decide whether you think they are internal or external.

1 Websters, a large garden centre, places an advertisement in a local newspaper.
2 The managing director of Marshall's Meat Supplies Plc calls a meeting of the company's branch managers.
3 A poster is displayed on Smiths the Stationers' noticeboard to inform staff of the forthcoming Christmas party.

Face-to-face communication

This is where people choose to communicate with one another in person rather than by telephone, letter, memo and so on. This has many advantages in that it can:

- be quick
- be direct
- allow people to interpret body language and facial gestures
- allow people to seek clarification and ask questions

A C T I V I T Y

Can you think of any disadvantages of face to face communication?

Verbal communication

This is communication that takes place orally, for example a discussion, a meeting or a telephone conversation. This is closely linked with face-to-face communication. Verbal communication has the following advantages:

- it can be quick
- it is direct
- it tends to be less formal than non-verbal communication (see below)
- the receiver can seek clarification and provide instant feedback
- if the communication is being carried out on a face-to-face basis, body language and facial gestures can be interpreted
- tone of voice can add to the meaning of the communication

A C T I V I T Y

Can you think of any disadvantages of verbal communication?

Written communication

This is communication in a written form, for example letters, notices and memoranda. The advantages are that it:

- tends to be more appropriate for formal communication
- provides a permanent record that can be referred to
- is effective when communicating with a large number of people
- is clear and easy to understand

CORRESPONDENCE

Correspondence is a form of written communication that takes place between members of an organisation and also with people outside it. Examples are letters and memoranda.

The advantages are that it:

- can be thought through in advance (and checked) to avoid errors or confusion
- is clear and concise
- avoids unnecessary discussion
- can reach a large number of people fairly quickly

The disadvantages are that:

- it takes time if a response is required
- it can cause difficulties if clarity is required
- it has none of the advantages of personal contact, for example body language or facial expression

We will be looking at letters and memoranda in more detail later in the chapter on pp.147–50.

Non-verbal communication

Whenever verbal communication takes place it is accompanied and affected by non-verbal communication, for example body language, facial expressions, posture, gestures, tone of voice, space and time.

BODY LANGUAGE, FACIAL EXPRESSIONS AND POSTURE

The way people stand, position their head and hands and the expression on their faces can tell us a great deal. Generally speaking, people are unaware of their body language. Look at the examples below.

GESTURES

We use a variety of gestures to enhance our communication. Look at the examples on pp.140–1.

TONE OF VOICE

We can use our voices to emphasise words or points whilst speaking. The sound of our voice can also be an indication for feelings, for example anger or pleasure.

FIG. 6.2 THE POSITION THIS MAN IS SITTING IN INDICATES THAT HE IS IN DEFENSIVE MOOD

FIG. 6.3 THE POSITION OF THIS WOMAN INDICATES THAT HER MOOD IS VERY RELAXED

FIG. 6.4 THIS MAN IS OBVIOUSLY IN AN INTOLERANT, ANGRY MOOD

FIG. 6.6 IMPATIENCE

ACTIVITY

Observe some of your family and friends. What do you notice about their body language? Does it alter when they are talking to different people?

FIG. 6.5 NERVOUSNESS

FIG. 6.7 ATTRACTING ATTENTION

FIG. 6.8 APPROVAL/AGREEMENT

FIG. 6.9 ACCENTUATING A CONVERSATION

A C T I V I T Y

Now observe some more people you know. Which gestures do they use? What do these tell you?

SPACE

We all have 'spatial relationships' with one another. This means the gap or space we choose to keep between ourselves and other people. When we have a closer relationship with a person then we tend to feel less need to keep him or her at a distance.

Other factors also affect our spatial relationships:

- the country in which we have been brought up – some nationalities choose to move close to new acquaintances to show warmth and friendship, whilst others keep their distance until they have built up a relationship
- how well we know the person
- the event in question: for example at a business meeting people may keep their distance but at a party some of the barriers may be broken down

TIME

The time we take to listen to people during a conversation can give a person confidence, a sense of importance and may improve the communication.

Visual communication

This usually takes the form of posters or pictures. A good example is the use of road signs. The advantages of visual communication are that:

- it can be used for people who cannot read or hear
- people often remember images better than words
- it can reach a wide audience
- it can overcome any language difficulties

A C T I V I T Y

Can you think of any disadvantages of visual communication?

Computer-aided communication

Recent technological developments mean that businesses have access to a wider range of communications.

ELECTRONIC TYPEWRITERS AND WORD PROCESSORS

These have made the production of written communication quicker, better presented, easier to alter and more flexible (for example a range of different packages can be used on a word processor).

COMPUTERS

Mainframe computers are computers with a large memory capacity. They are used to undertake large-scale data-processing operations. They are quite expensive to run and usually operate for 24 hours a day for cost effectiveness.

Micro computers deal with smaller amounts of information. Micro computers are becoming faster and more powerful all the time.

Computers are extremely flexible. Different packages can be purchased to perform the required communication functions, for example database and spreadsheet software.

CALCULATORS

These are now an essential part of everyday life and assist in the communication of numerical information.

A C T I V I T Y

See if you can find out what a dictaphone is used for. Make a list of people who might use a dictaphone at work.

Telecommunications

Telecommunications is the word used to describe the way information is carried electronically through the atmosphere.

Examples of telecommunication equipment are:

- Television sets.
- Radios.
- Answering machines – people can now pick up messages left for them from a distance.
- Facsimile (fax machines).
- Bleepers and pagers.
- Mobile telephones.
- Video conferencing – this is where organisations can hold meetings without having to travel very far. There are special studios that can be linked together so that people can see the people in the other studios on a large screen and can also speak to them. An example of this is a service called confravision offered by British Telecom, which links together studios in some cities across Britain.
- Videophones – a recent development where you can

actually see the person you are speaking to on the telephone.

- Telex machines – these work in a similar way to a telephone but instead of the spoken work they send written messages. The message is typed on a machine called a teleprinter. A special number is dialled so that the message can be sent to the recipient through the public telex network where it is printed on another teleprinter at the recipient's destination.
- On-line databases – these are electronic information systems to which companies can subscribe for information external to their businesses. It may include general business information and news or specific legal and business information. Ceefax and Oracle are examples of basic systems which provide a one-way flow of information. Compusave is an example of a two-way system. The user can leave information on the system as well as obtaining information from it. A simple example would be ordering an office supplies catalogue through the system.
- Electronic mail – this is a method by which messages are sent electronically. Instead of sending letters, messages can be sent using computer links as follows:

1 The message is typed into the computer.
2 The message is stored in the memory of the computer.
3 The recipient accesses the computer in order to receive the message.

The advantages of electronic mail are that it is fast and allows for the storage of and access to information.

A C T I V I T Y

In groups of three or four find out about and prepare a presentation on one of the following:

- video conferencing
- computers
- electronic mail

Purposes of communication systems

1 A means of handling information.
2 An aid to decision making.
3 A method of informing people.

Purposes of communication systems

Below is a list of types of information being communicated. Decide which of the previous categories each one fits into.

- a poster displayed on all staff notice boards to let them know about the forthcoming Christmas party
- a memorandum from the managing director asking staff to express their views about the need for a new computer system
- a series of bar charts summarising a set of statistics collected for a business
- a management meeting to discuss staff pay
- a letter to customers telling them about a new product or service

---

USE INFORMATION SYSTEMS

RECORDING INFORMATION

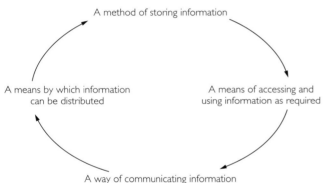

FIG. 6.10 PURPOSES OF INFORMATION SYSTEMS

1 Letter of enquiry

2 Catalogues, price lists, quotations

3 Orders

4 Invoice

5 Goods received note

6 Statement of account

7 Payment

8 Receipt

FIG. 6.11 DOCUMENTATION FOR THE BUYING AND SELLING PROCESS

Manual records

Chapter 4 'Financial transactions' looks at a range of different documents that businesses use to record information. These include orders, goods received notes, invoices, statements and receipts.

These documents are normally pre-printed to save time. They differ in design from organisation to organisation but generally speaking contain the same information.

In any business organisation documentation will be necessary at each stage of the buying and selling process as shown in Figure 6.11.

RECEIPTS

A receipt is a document that confirms the amount of money that has been paid. It may take the form of:

- a printed till receipt
- a handwritten receipt
- a bank paying-in slip
- a bank statement

On the next page is an example of a receipt that includes all the necessary information.

Collect as many different examples of receipts as you can. Do they all contain the same information?

Maria's Bakery, 7 Seven Street, Sevenoaks, Kent, SE77 777

Receipt No. 77
Received from: B Williams
the sum of: Fifty pounds   £50.00
as payment for: one birthday cake

Received by: Rhona Watts
Date: 16 April 1994

FIG. 6.12 A RECEIPT

A C T I V I T Y

Maria's Bakery has received payment from customers for a number of different items. Prepare receipts for each one. Make sure that you include all the information in the example.

1 £35 received from J Smith for a christening cake (17 April 1994).
2 £9 received from S Marshall for 90 bread buns (19 April 1994).
3 £4.50 received from S Gilliland for 9 mini Swiss rolls (20 April 1994).
4 £90 received from Mrs Cooper for a wedding cake (21 April 1994).
5 £6 received from Mrs Jones for 10 loaves of bread (21 April 1994).

FORM DESIGN

In certain circumstances there may not be any appropriate documentation available for use in the organisation. This may result in the design of a new form or document. When designing a form there are a series of questions you will need to ask.

1   What is the reason for the form?
2   What information do you need to gather?
3   Does the form include clear instructions for completion?
4   Are the questions clear and relevant?
5   Are there too many or too few questions?
6   Are there any irrelevant questions?
7   Is the form easy to complete? For example, there could be boxes to tick rather than spaces for written answers.
8   Is the order logical?
9   Is the form divided into appropriate sections?
10 Is there sufficient space for completion?
11 Does the form need a reference or code to link it to other documents?

12 Will the information on the form be input onto a computer (if so the design should take account of this)?
13 Is the paper strong enough?
14 Is the appearance of the form appropriate?
15 Is there any standard information to be indicated on the form, for example company letterhead?

A C T I V I T Y

1 Below is an example of a receipt that contains some errors. Make a list of the errors and re-write the receipt correctly.
2 Write a set of instructions to explain how to complete receipts correctly.

Maria's Bakery, 7 Seven Street, Sevenoaks, Kent, SE77 777

Receipt No.
Received from: John
the sum of: £27.50   £27.50
as payment for: Cake

Received by: Jane
Date: 18 April

A C T I V I T Y

Imagine that you work in the personnel department of a large stationery supplier. You have been asked to design a form to record personal details about employees.

The form should include the following information: name, age, date of birth, address, education, work experience, hobbies, plus any other relevant information.

When you have finished, ask another student to fill in the form to see how easy it is to complete.

CONTROL OF FORMS AND DOCUMENTATION

In any organisation there should be a system in place to oversee the design and use of forms to prevent people simply designing them as they think fit. Forms should be reviewed on a regular basis to check their purpose and whether or not they are still necessary. Alterations to existing forms or documents should be made as appropriate, and new ones designed after consultation. It is useful to keep a forms file containing examples of all forms. This should be kept in a central place for reference purposes.

ACCIDENT REPORT FORMS

An accident report form is an example of a form used in most organisations. The majority of businesses will have their own pre-printed forms. All employees should be shown a copy of the form in case they ever need to complete one.

A C T I V I T Y

In groups of three or four discuss what information you think should be included on an accident report form. When you have come up with a list have a go at designing one.

FILING, INDEXING AND MANAGEMENT OF MANUAL RECORDS

Read pp.163–6 in Chapter 7 'Operating administrative systems'.

A C T I V I T Y

Answer the following questions to check you have understood the text.

1 What is geographical filing?
2 What is alphabetical filing?
3 State three reasons for filing.
4 True or false? Chronological filing is filing in date order.
5 What is meant by 'electronic filing'?

Electronic records

MICROFILM AND MICROFICHE

With microfilm a photograph is produced on a continuous strip of film in miniature. Microfiche is a photographic image on a small sheet of film. A magnifier or 'reader' then shows the images on a screen. The two systems allow for a large amount of data to be stored in a relatively small space. However, they can be quite costly initially.

COMPUTERS

Detailed information can now be stored on computers. Packages can be purchased that are relevant to the particular information to be stored. Examples are databases and spreadsheets.

A C T I V I T Y

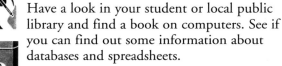

Have a look in your student or local public library and find a book on computers. See if you can find out some information about databases and spreadsheets.

SAFETY AND SECURITY

Safety

When businesses are communicating, a range of equipment may be used. Health and safety issues should always be a prime consideration.

FILING EQUIPMENT

The drawers of modern filing cabinets only open one at a time to prevent people bumping into them. The filing cabinets themselves are normally fire proof. Users should take care when reaching up to high shelves and avoid carrying too many files at a time – this should *prevent* accidents from happening.

COMPUTERS

It is believed that working with computers for long periods of time can cause harm to certain people, for example pregnant women and epileptics.

The glare of the machines should be kept to a minimum. Special screens can be purchased to reduce the glare and the brightness can be reduced using a special 'brightness control' switch. The computers themselves should be regularly checked and maintained.

Operators should be provided with adjustable chairs and desks at a suitable height. They should also be given regular breaks ('screen breaks'). Computer operators in some organisations now have their spectacles paid for by their employers if they are able to prove that their eyesight has suffered as a result of their working with computers, that is looking at a VDU (visual display unit, i.e. monitor).

Acoustic hoods can be added to printers to reduce noise.

REPROGRAPHICS (PHOTOCOPYING)

Photocopiers should not be pushed against a wall as it is important that they have a flow of air around them. Toner on the hands or face should be washed off immediately. Operators should not 'fiddle' with the machine unless they know what they are doing.

A C T I V I T Y

Below is a list of some other equipment that may be used in the communication process. Make a list of the safety issues your think are important for each one.

- stapler
- guillotine
- hole punch
- scissors

Security

Security is also very important as it prevents theft within or from an organisation and ensures that only relevant people have access to certain information.

COMPUTERS

Certain information kept on computer is confidential, for example details of personal accounts, salaries and criminal records. Only a few people in an organisation may have access to this sort of information. They will be given a 'password' to enter the relevant computer program.

Different members of staff may have different passwords. Different passwords may allow varying degrees of access. For example an office supervisor may have access to salary details while the manager may have access to *all* personal details.

Passwords should be altered on a regular basis and should *not* be written down. They should not be too

obvious (easy) for other staff to work out, for example the telephone number of the organisation.

THE DATA PROTECTION ACT 1984

This is the law that controls what information an organisation can keep on a computer. The Act ensures that:

- organisations who hold data on a computer are registered with the data protection registrar
- information kept is legal
- information is accurate and only used for specific purposes
- information is up to date and not kept for longer than is necessary
- there is limited access to the information held and that adequate security measures are in place to ensure this

FACE-TO-FACE COMMUNICATION

When an organisation is communicating with members of the public it is important that strict security measures are undertaken.

Some organisations ask visitors to wear a visitor's badge and sign a visitor's book. Large organisations often have a 'gatehouse' where visitors are checked in as they arrive and checked out as they leave. The main entrance to an organisation is normally clearly marked to prevent people from wandering about, and they often escort visitors between different buildings or sites.

Many organisations employ their own security staff.

Date	Name	Company	Time of arrival	Time of departure
Reason for visit				
Additional information				
Date	Name	Company	Time of arrival	Time of departure
Reason for visit				

FIG. 6.13 EXAMPLE OF A VISITOR'S BOOK

ACTIVITY

Design a visitor's badge to be used in a large organisation. Your badge should include the organisation's logo.

ACTIVITY

Now design your own visitor's book for the same organisation. Ask some of your friends to make entries in the book to see if it is easy to use.

PRODUCE BUSINESS DOCUMENTS

TYPES OF DOCUMENT

Memoranda

Memoranda (or memos) are similar to the letters an organisation sends to the people outside it. The difference is that memos are a means of communicating *internally* (inside the organisation).

Memos are normally used to send notes or brief messages to colleagues. They make a large contribution to the impression a person gives, so care should be taken when composing them. Memos are normally written or typed on pre-printed paper, often A5 size (quite small). When a memo is to be sent to a number of different people all of their names should appear on it, so that each person is aware of who else has received the memo. Sometimes memos are displayed on a noticeboard.

The format of memos varies depending upon the organisation in question. Below are some examples of different formats.

FIG. 6.14 DIFFERENT FORMATS OF MEMOS

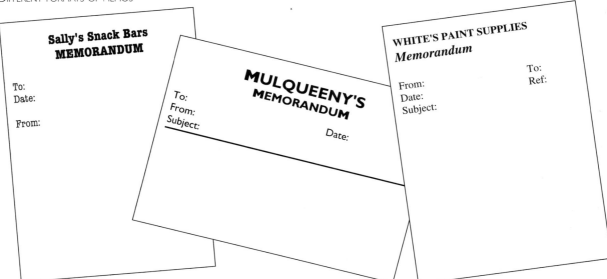

TIPS FOR WRITING

Memos should be clearly written, accurate and precise. Messages should be as brief as possible yet include all the relevant information, which should be well presented. Some memos may be confidential (in which case the words 'personal' or 'confidential' should be included and the memo placed in an envelope).

BURRIDGE'S BALLOONS
MEMORANDUM

To: Gillian Turner (marketing manager)
From: Tim Burridge
Date: 1 February 1994
Ref: TB/3

Summer Collection

Following your request for details of the forthcoming balloons for the summer collection there will be a total of five new designs as follows:

1   Yellow, featuring ducks in a pond

2   Green, featuring children playing on swings

3   White, featuring ice-cream design

4   Pink, featuring girl playing with a ball

5   Blue, featuring beach scene

The actual designs will be forwarded to you as soon as they have been completed.

TB

FIG. 6.15 EXAMPLE OF A WRITTEN MEMO

A C T I V I T Y

Write a memorandum from Gillian Turner thanking Tim Burridge for the information and asking for details about prices.

Business letters

There are two main types of layout currently in use in business organisations. The older style is the semi-blocked letter, and the most common today is the fully blocked letter, which is open or unpunctuated.

SEMI-BLOCKED

---

6 Swan Lane
Chine Street
NOTTINGHAM
DN11 0PO
25th April 1994

B J Needham Curtains Ltd
7 Duck Street
NOTTINGHAM
DN27 1PX

Dear Sirs,

I should be grateful if you would send me a catalogue showing your current designs.

I am particularly interested in your Austrian blinds.

Yours faithfully,

Alison Wray

A Wray (Miss)

FIG. 6.16 LAYOUT OF A SEMI-BLOCKED LETTER

The above is a letter which has been sent from a private address to a business organisation (on unheaded paper).

The sender's address is indented in the top right hand corner (her name is not included here). If necessary a telephone number or reference number could be included opposite the sender's address. The date appears directly below the address.

The recipient's (business organisation's) name and address is indented on the left-hand side slightly lower down, being in line with the left-hand margin rather than being indented.

The start of each paragraph is indented.

The complimentary close, i.e. 'yours faithfully' is written in the centre of the page and the signature included directly below (the person's name is then printed below the signature to avoid any confusion).

FULLY BLOCKED LETTER

The fully blocked letter is an example of correspondence between two business organisations.

The letter is typed on headed paper. All typing begins on the left-hand margin (this saves time when typing). The style is open punctuation. This omits all

GREEN GRASS COSMETICS Ltd

Tilton   West Sussex   TE5 1XY
Tel: (0553) 57304

Our Ref: PG/KL/3329

Your Ref: DJN/73

23 February 1994

I E Crump
Crump Cosmetics Ltd
Downham Market
NORFOLK
NE21 0PZ

Dear Mrs Crump

Thank you for your letter of 19 February 1994, enclosing detailed plans for our proposed merger.

I have arranged a board meeting for 3 March 1994, to discuss the plans in detail. I hope that you will be able to attend.

The plans look extremely promising, I expect that the board will feel the same way.

Yours sincerely,

D Neave

D J Neave
Managing Director

FIG. 6.17 LAYOUT OF A FULLY BLOCKED LETTER

non-essential punctuation in documents such as letters and memoranda. However, the body of the document is punctuated in line with conventional English language.

WRITING THE LETTER

The **designation** is the title of the person you are sending the letter to, for example purchasing manager or managing director.

The **salutation** is the greeting used in the letter. You may wish to use the name of the recipient if you know it, for example Mr Smith. Otherwise you can use Sir or Madam.

The **complimentary close** is the way you end the letter and it should always match the salutation. If you begin with 'Dear Sir (or Madam)' close with 'Yours faithfully'. If you begin with 'Dear Mr Smith' close with 'Yours sincerely'.

Your letter should always include an **opening paragraph** to introduce the subject matter. If you are

replying to a letter write: 'Thank you for your letter of [date] regarding...' Avoid starting with 'I am writing'. Examples of other opening statements are: 'Further to our recent conversation ...' or 'Following our recent telephone conversation'.

The **main body of the letter** will include additional paragraphs (as necessary) containing further information.

The **closing paragraph** is the paragraph that brings the letter to a close. There are a number of different ways to conclude a letter, for example 'We look forward to hearing from you ...'; 'Please let me know if I can be of further assistance'; or 'Don't hesitate to contact us if you require additional information'.

Other points to remember:

- your letter should be clear, concise and politely written
- it is useful to 'draft' out the letter in advance, so that it can be checked before the final version is typed and/or sent
- make sure the format of the letter is correct and that it follows a logical order
- checks should be made for errors in punctuation and spelling

DIFFERENT TYPES OF LETTER

- Letters of confirmation, for example to confirm a business meeting
- Letters of enquiry, for example an enquiry about a company's products
- Letters containing information, for example responses to enquiries
- Job applications, for example an application for a new secretarial position in an organisation

A C T I V I T Y

Can you think of any other types of business letter that an organisation may send or receive?

You are the sales manager of a large clothes manufacturing company based in Sheffield. Below is a series of letters for you to write.

1 A letter of complaint to a supplier regarding the poor quality of a stock of denim recently delivered.

2 A letter confirming a meeting with a clothing designer.

3 A letter providing information about the range of clothes offered by the company. This is to be sent to a prospective customer who has sent a letter of enquiry.

4 A letter to a local newspaper to arrange a meeting about future publicity for the company.

5 A letter of apology to a local clothes store who have received the wrong delivery.

Messages

Messages are an important form of communication. They may be taken face-to-face or by telephone, and can be passed on verbally or in a written form.

TELEPHONE MESSAGES

When taking a message by telephone it is essential that the information recorded is correct.

■ the caller's name should be recorded – he or she should be asked to spell it out if necessary, for example 'A for apple', 'B for balloon' and so on

■ the caller's telephone number should also be recorded and checked back

■ the caller's message should be carefully written down

■ a note should be made as to whom the message is for and who took the call

FACE-TO-FACE MESSAGES

When taking a message directly from a person, the above points all still apply. Alternatively, the person may wish to write down the message themselves. If this is the case it may need to be checked to ensure that all essential information (e.g. a contact number) has been recorded.

FACE-TO-FACE AND TELEPHONE MESSAGE FORMS

In both it is important to ensure that the message reaches the person for whom it is intended.

Many organisations have designed their own forms on which messages can be recorded. This saves time and prevents errors, or vital information being omitted. Below is an example of a message form.

F and M Lindley
Specialist Sports Cars

Date: Time:
For:
From:

Message:

Additional Information:

Message taken by:

FIG. 6.18 A MESSAGE FORM

Choose a well-known business organisation and design a message pad for their use. Ask a friend on your course to have a go at using the pad.

INVITATIONS

Businesses often send and receive invitations. Sometimes the invitations are printed by the business itself. However, when large quantities are required a specialist organisation will be paid to produce the invitations professionally. A business invitation will normally include the following information:

■ the name and address of the business sending the invitation

- details of the type of event
- date of the event
- time of the event
- RSVP (répondez s'il vous plaît) which means that the invitation requires a reply
- any other details, for example special dress requirements

Below is an example of a business invitation.

Leighton's Lingerie
12 Granby Road Leeds

Invite you to a Spring Fashion Show
Date: 12th March 199_
Time: 8 pm

Venue: Leeds Conference Centre
RSVP   Admits 2

A C T I V I T Y

Make a list of the different reasons why you think businesses may need to send out invitations.

A C T I V I T Y

Select a well known organisation and design an invitation for each of the following:

- an office party
- a trade fair
- a business conference

NSTRUCTIONS

nstructions can either be oral (spoken) or written.

A few tips

instructions should be clear
instructions should be concise
written instructions should include all necessary information – the person following them may not be in a position to check their meaning with anyone
oral instructions should be given clearly and audibly (so that the person can hear you)
if you are following written instructions make sure that you read through them *carefully* before taking any action

- if you are following oral instructions make sure that you listen very carefully and clarify any points you do not understand

A C T I V I T Y

Write a set of clear and simple instructions to enable a friend who is sitting on a chair to get up and leave the room, shutting the door behind them. When you have written the instructions, ask the friend to follow them. Were they able to? Did you miss out any vital steps such as turning the door handle?

A C T I V I T Y

See how good you are at following a simple set of instructions.

Instructions

Read all the questions and instructions carefully before completing them:

1 Write down your name.
2 Write down your address.
3 Write down your telephone number.
4 List three of your favourite foods.
5 What did you do last night?
6 Who is sitting next to you?
7 Write their surname backwards.
8 Draw a circle with a triangle in the middle of it.
9 Name two famous people.
10 Clap your hands three times.
11 Do you play football?
12 Draw three small squares in a row.
13 Scratch your nose.
14 Complete the following sum:
$1 + 2 + 3 + 4 = ?$
15 Write down the names of two of your friends.
16 Write down two names beginning with 'A'.
17 List three animals.
18 Write down today's date.
19 How many letters are there in your name?
20 Only complete numbers one to four of this test!!!

How did you do?!!!!

Giving directions

Within any business organisation it may be necessary at times to give people directions, for example directions around the building, directions to another site or building, or directions to a nearby organisation.

When giving directions it is useful to remember the following points:

- listen carefully to where the person needs to go
- think through the directions before passing on the information
- speak slowly and clearly
- point the way a person needs to go if appropriate but avoid waving your arms about too much (gesticulating), as this can cause confusion
- repeat the directions if necessary
- if the directions are complicated, it may be useful to write them down or draw a simple map
- if possible take the person to where they need to go
- most importantly, be patient and polite – the way you treat the persons requiring directions will add to the overall impression they have of the organisation

ROLE PLAY

Below are some role plays you can carry out in groups to practise giving directions. As a group make up a simple map of the local area around the business in the activity, before you carry out the role play. When you have completed the activity discuss in your groups how well you feel each of the situations was dealt with.

The organisation in question is Taylors Electronics, a large engineering company.

1 A lorry driver arrives at the reception desk. He has a delivery to make to the stores section.

2 A school teacher has brought a group of pupils to Taylors for a guided tour. He is at the reception desk and requires directions to the training office.

3 A visitor to the organisation asks one of the secretaries for directions to the toilet.

4 A junior employee has been asked by his supervisor to buy some stamps from the local post office but does not know where it is.

5 A sales representative asks the receptionist for directions to the sale manager's office.

6 A disabled customer asks a member of staff for directions to the nearest lift.

PRESENTATION

Earlier in the chapter we discussed visual communication on p.141. A simple diagram can often convey (put across) a piece of information or a message more effectively than written words. It is believed that we remember more of the things we see than the things we read.

Information can be presented visually in a number of different ways. For example:

- pie charts
- organisation charts
- bar charts
- pictograms
- tables
- diagrams
- maps

Pie charts

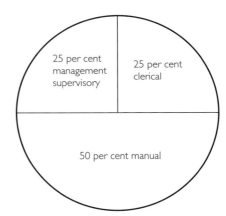

FIG. 6.19 PIE CHART TO SHOW AREAS OF WORK OF STAFF AT TAYLOR'S ELECTRONICS

A pie chart is a good way of simplifying information and is attractive to look at. It will often be used to convey information to a person who has little or no knowledge of the subject matter. The disadvantage of pie charts is that information tends to be generalised.

CALCULATION

The original figures for the number of staff at Taylor's Electronics shown in the pie chart in Figure 6.19 were as follows:

Management/Supervisory	50
Clerical	50
Manual	100
Total	200

To turn the figures into a pie chart we must first remember that a circle has 360 degrees. These 360 degrees will represent the total (200) number of employees. We can then work out the slice of the pie that represents manual staff as follows:

Total manual staff
Total no. of employees
$$\frac{100}{200} \times 360 = 50 \text{ per cent}$$

A C T I V I T Y

Following the same formula, calculate the percentages for clerical and management/supervisory staff. Make sure you show how you worked out your calculations.

A C T I V I T Y

Below are some figures about the age range of employees at Taylor's Electronics. Convert the figures into percentages and draw them up in the form of a pie chart.

16–21	20
22–30	37
31–40	59
41–50	61
51–65	23
Total	200

Make sure your pie chart has a suitable heading. Use different colours for each section of the pie chart to add to the visual impact.

Organisation charts

These are used to show the structure of an organisation and the levels of responsibility and authority. See the example in Figure 6.20. They are discussed in more detail in Chapter 2 'People in business organisations' on p.30–5.

Bar charts

Bar charts are a common form of presentation as they have a high visual impact, i.e. they are easy to understand at a simple glance.

FIG. 6.20 EXAMPLE OF AN ORGANISATION CHART

The bar chart for Cawoods in Figure 6.21 is a vertical bar chart that has been divided into two sections to show the numbers of males and females. A key has been included to indicate clearly how each has been represented. The chart also includes details as to what information is represented on each axis of the chart, i.e. number of employees/years.

Information can also be represented horizontally as in Figure 6.22.

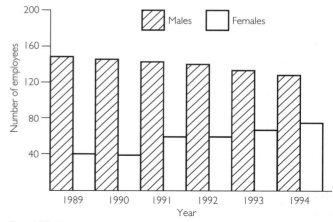

FIG. 6.21 EXAMPLE OF A BAR CHART SHOWING GENDER BREAKDOWN OF CAWOODS' EMPLOYEES, 1989-1994

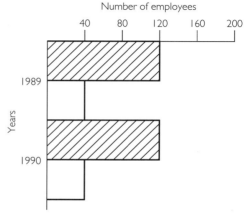

FIG. 6.22 HORIZONTAL BAR CHART

Information can also be represented by using a single bar to represent both sexes instead of a separate one for each as in Figure 6.23.

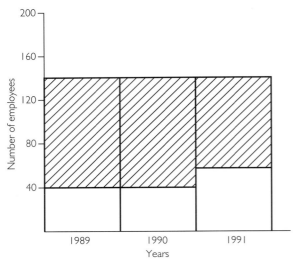

FIG. 6.23 SINGLE-BAR REPRESENTATION OF SEXES

Pictograms

A pictogram is used to represent figures in a visual form. As in the case of pie charts, pictograms are unable to provide detailed information. However, they can help to show trends and they have a good visual impact.

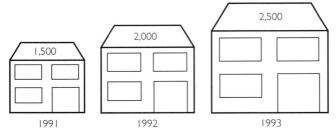

FIG. 6.24 PICTOGRAM OF NUMBER OF HOUSES BUILT BY HOYLANDS, 1992–1993

Tables

Tables may not be very interesting to look at but they can be a valuable way of presenting complicated information. If appropriate, specific data can be extracted from a table and then presented in a more user-friendly form.

Tables should always include:

- a title
- headings for columns and rows
- units of measurement, for example number of people
- any relevant explanatory comments
- the source of the data

Table 6.1 on p.155 is an example of a table of information that gives detailed information about unemployment statistics in West Midlands.

Diagrams

A diagram is often an effective way to help people understand how something works. For example, when you buy a new kettle or camera you will usually find that included with the instructions will be a diagram as to where everything is.

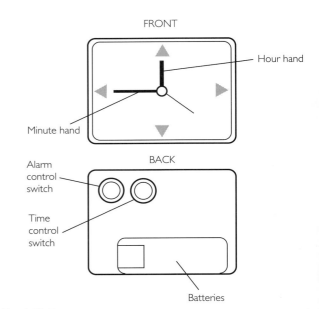

FIG. 6.25 DIAGRAM OF A TRAVEL ALARM CLOCK

A C T I V I T Y

Choose an item from your own home. Draw a simple diagram of it and include clear labels.

Maps

As we discussed earlier in the chapter it can often be quite confusing if we try to explain directions to people. A visual explanation in the form of a map can be much more effective. Figure 6.26 on p.156 demonstrates how a map can be effective in showing where an office is.

TABLE 6.1 UNEMPLOYMENT IN THE WEST MIDLANDS AT 8 JULY 1993

	MALE	FEMALE	ALL	RATE +	
				PER CENT EMPLOYEES AND UNEMPLOYED	PER CENT WORKFORCE
WEST MIDLANDS					
Hereford and Worcester	**20,623**	**7,212**	**27,835**	10.6	8.9
Bromsgrove	2,738	991	3,729		
Hereford	1,864	683	2,547		
Leominster	1,015	371	1,386		
Malvern Hills	2,210	770	2,980		
Redditch	2,840	995	3,835		
South Herefordshire	1,188	514	1,702		
Worcester	3,174	947	4,121		
Wychavon	2,384	896	3,280		
Wyre Forest	3,210	1,045	4,255		
Shropshire	**11,866**	**4,163**	**16,029**	9.9	8.4
Bridgnorth	1,221	485	1,706		
North Shropshire	1,193	464	1,657		
Oswestry	1,023	435	1,458		
Shrewsbury and Atcham	2,495	858	3,353		
South Shropshire	874	308	1,182		
The Wrekin	5,060	1,613	6,673		
Staffordshire	**33,780**	**10,938**	**44,718**	11.2	9.8
Cannock Chase	3,297	1,116	4,413		
East Staffordshire	3,317	1,070	4,387		
Lichfield	2,565	954	3,519		
Newcastle-under-Lyme	3,704	1,215	4,919		
South Staffordshire	3,251	1,161	4,412		
Stafford	3,116	1,066	4,182		
Staffordshire Moorlands	1,932	732	2,664		
Stoke-on-Trent	9,647	2,609	12,256		
Tamworth	2,951	1,015	3,966		
Warwickshire	**14,995**	**5,412**	**20,407**	10.1	8.7
North Warwickshire	1,972	667	2,639		
Nuneaton and Bedworth	4,609	1,508	6,117		
Rugby	2,612	1,092	3,704		
Stratford-on-Avon	2,382	944	3,326		
Warwick	3,420	1,201	4,621		
West Midlands	**135,136**	**40,034**	**175,170**	14.3	12.9
Birmingham	59,117	17,166	76,283		
Coventry	15,466	4,644	20,110		
Dudley	11,909	3,816	15,725		
Sandwell	15,898	4,657	20,555		
Solihull	6,995	2,430	9,425		
Walsall	12,328	3,399	15,727		
Wolverhampton	13,423	3,922	17,345		

SOURCE: *EMPLOYMENT GAZETTE*, SEPTEMBER 1993, PRODUCED BY THE DEPARTMENT OF EMPLOYMENT

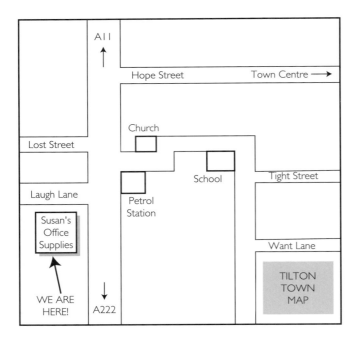

FIG. 6.26 LOCATION OF SUSAN'S OFFICE SUPPLIES

Draw a clear map to show a visitor how to find your school or college. Make sure that all the streets and roads are carefully labelled.

We have looked at a few different methods of visual presentation or communication; however, there are many more. Below are some of them. See if you can discover what each involves and find some examples if possible.

- line graphs
- flow charts
- symbols
- supply and demand curves
- breakeven charts
- histograms
- Gantt charts
- scatter diagrams
- cartograms

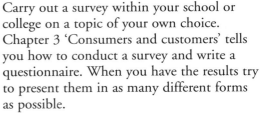

Carry out a survey within your school or college on a topic of your own choice. Chapter 3 'Consumers and customers' tells you how to conduct a survey and write a questionnaire. When you have the results try to present them in as many different forms as possible.

House style

House style is an organisation's own particular way of doing things. It helps the public to build up a distinctive image of the organisation. House style can include:

- the uniform worn by staff – for example members of the army all wear green
- the decor (i.e. furniture and the way the buildings are decorated) – for example branches of Marks & Spencer are all decorated in a similar way
- the way customers are treated – many organisations have a standard way of dealing with customers, for example McDonalds' 'Good afternoon, how may I help you?' or 'Have a nice day'; organisations may also have a set procedure (or policy for dealing with complaints)
- the way stationery and materials are presented – many organisations have their own logo (symbol) that is included on memos, letters (letterheads), reports and so on, for example the logo of Lloyds Bank is a black horse
- the colour scheme – many businesses will use a colour scheme that its customers will associate with the organisation, for example BP uses green and yellow

See if you can find out which logos are used by the following organisations:

- TSB
- Kelloggs (on Cornflakes)
- McDonalds
- Halifax Building Society

CHAPTER SIX

Test Yourself!

1 Why is good communication essential in a business organisation?
2 What is external communication?
3 What is internal communication?
4 Give two examples of written communication?
5 True or false? Body language is a form of non-verbal communication.
6 State two advantages of visual communication.
7 What is meant by the term 'telecommunications'?
8 List three different ways in which information can be filed.
9 Which Act controls what information an organisation can keep on a computer?
10 True or false? Fully blocked letters are normally used by business organisations.
11 What is a receipt?
12 List three things to think about when giving instructions.
13 Draw an example of a bar chart.
14 Draw an example of a pictogram.
15 What is an organisation chart?
16 What is meant by the term 'house style'?
17 True or false? A message should always be written down.
18 What is a logo?
19 What is meant by the term the 'mass media'?
20 State two advantages of face-to-face communication.

Chapter

7

OPERATING ADMINISTRATIVE SYSTEMS

IDENTIFY OFFICE SYSTEMS AND EQUIPMENT USED IN THEIR OPERATION

MAIL

Incoming mail

Mail received by an organisation should be dealt with as quickly and efficiently as possible. This will ensure that:

- urgent mail can be dealt with promptly
- queries can be followed up
- staff can organise their workload more easily

Many organisations have their own mailroom to receive and sort all incoming mail. Smaller organisations often have a specific member of staff, for example a supervisor or secretary, who is responsible for opening the mail.

FIG. 7.1

EQUIPMENT

Small organisations often use a **paper knife** to open the mail. A **letter-opening machine** is a machine that takes off a strip from the top of the envelope. It avoids damaging the contents of the envelope yet saves a great deal of time in opening it. A **date stamp** is used to mark the 'date received' on the incoming mail. Sometimes the time of receipt may also be recorded.

PROCEDURES IN THE MAILROOM

Procedures in the mailroom vary from organisations to organisation. In some cases mailroom staff will be responsible for actually opening much of the mail. In other cases their main responsibility will be to distribute the mail to the correct people.

ACTIVITY

You work in the mailroom of a large company. You have received a letter addressed to the sales manager marked 'confidential'. However, it is also marked 'urgent'. What do you think you should do?

OPENING THE MAIL

- if you are using a letter-opening machine, tap down the contents so that the machine does not damage anything (it slices a very narrow strip of paper off the envelope)
- make sure that *all* of the contents are removed from the envelope
- attach all enclosures to the document (a document with an enclosure should be marked 'enc.' at the bottom)

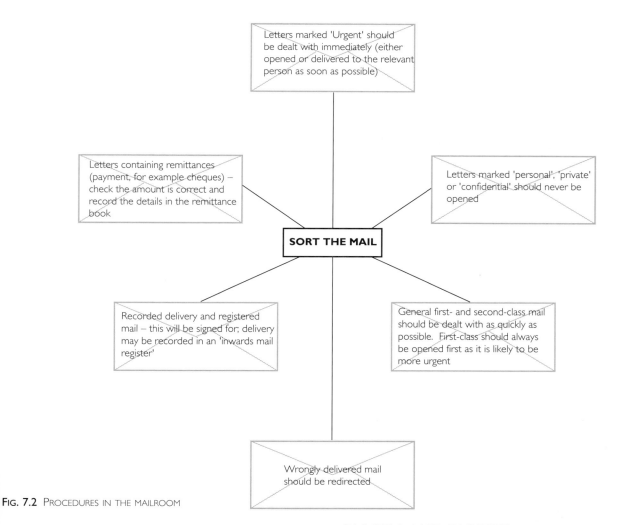

FIG. 7.2 PROCEDURES IN THE MAILROOM

- if a letter has the 'enc.' mark but the enclosures are missing mark the letter 'not enclosed' and initial the letter to show that you have dealt with it
- some organisations keep a record of all incoming mail, which you may be required to complete

PARCELS AND PACKETS

When a parcel or packet is delivered to an organisation it should be signed for (normally by mailroom staff). Depending on the organisation mailroom staff may be required to open the parcel or packet as well to check

A C T I V I T Y

You work in the mailroom of Worthingtons Ltd, a medium-sized wool supplies company. It has the following departments: finance, personnel, sales and marketing, production, management and administration.

When the incoming mail is received each morning it is your job to ensure that the mail is distributed to the correct departments. Below is a list of the letters received by the organisation one morning:

1 A letter enquiring about job vacancies
2 A letter containing a wool order

3 A request for a catalogue
4 A letter confirming a meeting with the managing director
5 A cheque from a customer
6 A note from a sales representative requesting a supply of leaflets
7 A letter complaining about the quality of some wool recently purchased
8 The bill for some building work recently carried out

Make a list of each department in the organisation. Under each department identify which of the letters you think it should receive.

the contents. Unopened parcels should be signed 'contents not checked'.

If a parcel is damaged it should not be signed for and should be returned to the sender if possible, *or* signed for as 'damaged on delivery'.

CIRCULATING THE MAIL

Mail may be received by the organisation that needs to be seen by a number of people. In many cases the mailroom staff will be responsible for ensuring that the mail is circulated correctly.

In this case a distribution list should be written neatly at the top of the original letter. Sufficient copies of the letter must be made and the appropriate name on each copy should be ticked or highlighted. For example, the distribution list at the top of the original letter might look like this:

c/c   G Stephenson
      S Baines
      L Corrigan
      S Williams
      J Thomason

On the copy to be sent to G Stephenson you would tick or highlight the name at the top of the copy. The person to whom the letter was originally addressed (the addressee) should receive the actual letter itself.

Some documents may be bulky or difficult to photocopy. However, a number of staff may still need to see them. If this is the case a **circulation or routing slip** will be attached. Figure 7.3 shows two examples.

CIRCULATION SLIP

Name:	Date received:	Date passed on:

G Stephenson
S Baines
L Corrigan
S Williams
J Thomason

Please return to G Stephenson after circulation.

CIRCULATION SLIP

G Stephenson   16/10/94
S Baines   17/10/94
L Corrigan
S Williams   15/10/94
J Thomason
Return to: G Stephenson

FIG. 7.3 TWO EXAMPLES OF CIRCULATION SLIPS

A **remittance book** is a written record of money received in the mail. Look at the example in Figure 7.4.

Date	Name	Payment method	Amount £	P	Account No. ref.	Notes
10 Jan	P Smith	Cash	33	00	1179	
	Teal Brothers	PO	71	50	1902	
	R Johnson	Cheque	102	75		Cheque not signed
	D Hill	Cheque	5	00	1367	
	Wilsons Ltd	Cheque	7	00		

Signed .... Date ...10 January 1994...

FIG. 7.4 A REMITTANCE BOOK

Outgoing mail

The size of the organisation will affect the procedures used for dealing with outgoing mail. Any outgoing mail should be dealt with as quickly as possible in order to meet postal deadlines.

POST OFFICE SERVICES

It is important that mailroom staff are aware of the mail services offered by the Post Office so that all mail is sent in the correct way.

Inland mail applies to letters and parcels that are posted within the UK. They can be sent first or second class (called the 'two-tier' system). First-class post will normally be delivered within 24 hours.

Recorded delivery is a method often used when sending important documents through the post, for example passports and birth certificates. The person posting the letter is given a receipt by the post office. When the letter is delivered the postman or woman asks the recipient to sign a book as proof that the letter has been received. If a letter or package goes missing the post office will pay compensation (this tends to be only a small amount so valuable items should not be sent by recorded delivery).

Valuable items (up to a certain weight and size) should be sent by **registered post**. A receipt is issued by the post office to the person sending the letter or parcel and the postman or woman will require a signature from the recipient. In the case of registered post the Post Office uses special security measures to ensure safe delivery. Again compensation is available for mail that goes missing.

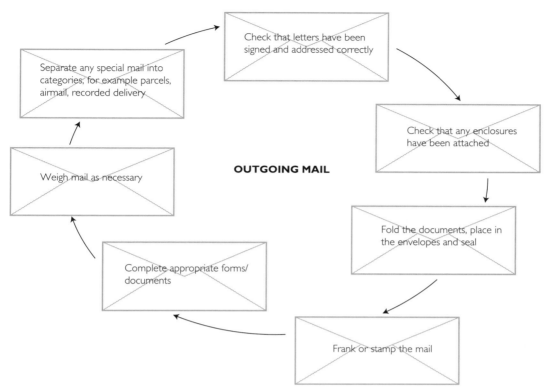

OUTGOING MAIL

FIG. 7.5 PROCEDURE IN THE MAILROOM

If a letter is important the post office will issue a **certificate of posting**. This is proof that a letter was posted. The service is free of charge. However, letters must be handed over the post office counter and not simply posted in a letter-box.

If you have sent a letter or parcel by registered post or recorded delivery you can complete an **advice of delivery** form so that the post office (for a small fee) can notify you when it has arrived safely.

A **business reply service** is provided by the Post Office for organisations who want their customers to reply to them without having to spend any money. The organisation has to pay a fee in advance as well as obtaining a licence from the Post Office. The reply forms take the form of envelopes, postcards or labels. They may be first or second class (this will be printed on the forms in advance), so the customer can send them back free of charge.

An organisation can buy or lease a franking machine from an approved company once it has obtained permission from the local head post office. The cost of the postage is covered through lump sums paid to the post office in advance. The machine stamps the value of the postage (first or second class) on the mail as well as a postmark.

A C T I V I T Y

Other services offered by the Post Office are:

- parcel post
- compensation fee
- airmail
- surface mail
- international business reply service
- airstream

Visit your local post office to see if you can find out what each involves.

SENDING PARCELS AND PACKAGES

When wrapping parcels and packages you need to make sure that:

- parcels and packages are wrapped securely so that the contents are not damaged or lost
- items that may bend are placed between pieces of card for protection
- space in the parcel is filled with packing material to avoid damage
- items are placed in a secure box if possible
- all edges and flaps are sealed well
- the parcel is clearly labelled and the sender's address

included at right angles to the delivery address as shown below.

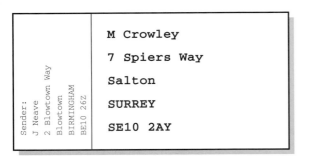

Sender:
J Neave
2 Blowtown Way
Blowtown
BIRMINGHAM
BE10 2GZ

M Crowley

7 Spiers Way

Salton

SURREY

SE10 2AY

FIG. 7.6 A PARCEL LABEL

The following are some of the materials needed for wrapping:

- strong boxes (available from post offices)
- crushed newspaper
- shredded paper
- Jiffy (padded) bags available from post offices and stationers
- corrugated paper
- bubble wrap
- polystyrene chips
- Sellotape or strong, brown packing tape
- brown paper
- strong cardboard
- scissors

Breakable items must be packed extremely carefully. The works 'Fragile – Handle with care' can be written on the parcel. If an item should not be folded or bent the words 'Do not bend' should be written on the parcel.

A C T I V I T Y

Have a go at wrapping a parcel of your own. Did you find it easy?

Once a parcel has been carefully packaged it should be weighed and the cost of postage calculated (the Post Office issues various leaflets detailing postage rates). The cost should be marked in the right-hand corner, ready for stamping or franking.

ADDRESSING ENVELOPES

When sending mail out of the organisation it is vital that it is addressed correctly. Figure 7.7 shows a correctly addressed envelope.

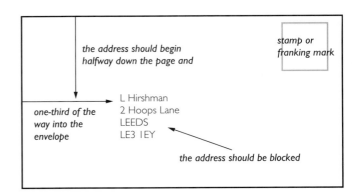

the address should begin halfway down the page and

stamp or franking mark

one-third of the way into the envelope

L Hirshman
2 Hoops Lane
LEEDS
LE3 1EY

the address should be blocked

FIG. 7.7 A CORRECTLY ADDRESSED ENVELOPE

SENDING MAIL OVERSEAS

When sending mail overseas parcels need to be clearly labelled and include the senders name on the outside and inside. The country should be shown clearly.

Letters and parcels can be sent by airmail. Special airmail envelopes can be purchased or, alternatively, a blue airmail sticker can be affixed to the envelope.

Packets on parcels must have a **declaration label**. This describes the contents and will be checked by Customs officers in the destination country (this saves them from having to open the packet).

DATAPOST

This service can be used for letters, packets and parcels which are urgent. Delivery is *guaranteed* within the UK and a speedy delivery overseas is also guaranteed. This type of mail travels separately from other mail and is often accompanied by Post Office staff.

SWIFTAIR

This is an extremely fast service for letters and papers that are being sent internationally. The post must be handed over the counter at a post office or collected from the organisation by the post office. Post must have a red Swiftair label attached.

POSTAGE RATES

Mailroom staff should be aware of current postage rates. The Post Office publishes a series of leaflets containing this information. It is advisable for organisations to keep up-to-date copies of these so that the correct rates can be calculated by staff.

STORAGE AND RETRIEVAL OF DOCUMENTS

Filing

There are five main methods of filing: alphabetical, geographical, chronological, subject and numerical.

ALPHABETICAL FILING

The majority of filing is carried out alphabetically. It is a method that is quick and easy to use and simple to understand. Examples of information that would be filed alphabetically are staff and customer records.

- when filing names the surname is taken first. Therefore Clive Anderson would be filed under 'A' as Anderson, Clive
- short names are always filed before larger ones, for example Jacks before Jackson, Brown before Browne
- if two names are exactly the same they should be filed according to first names, for example Smith, Barry before Smith, Tom
- additional words such as 'the' should be ignored, for example The Ridings Hotel would be filed under 'R'
- numbers should be converted into words, for example 5 Alive Restaurant would become Five Alive Restaurant and be filed under 'F'
- prefixes to names should be treated as part of the surname, for example Du Cane should be filed as if the surname were DuCane
- names beginning with St or Saint should be filed under 'Saint'
- names beginning with Mc, Mc and Mac should be treated as if they are spelt Mac
- qualifications would be ignored when filing but are noted on a person's file, for example Peter Barnes MSc would be filed under 'B'
- if a person has two surnames, he or she should be filed under the first
- titles should be ignored
- hyphenated words should be treated as one, for example Roger Garth-Smith should be filed under 'G'
- names of organisations consisting of initials should be filed before whole words, for example:

M B Supplies Ltd
M B Taxis
M C Motors Ltd

- Apostrophes should be ignored, for example O'Leary becomes OLeary for filing purposes

GEOGRAPHICAL FILING

Geographical filing is used to arrange files alphabetically according to their location, for example by the town, county or country. It is used by organisations who prefer to file by area. For example, sales, exports and mail-order companies use geographical filing as much of their work and correspondence is carried out on an area-by-area basis.

Files are broken into areas or regions; filing is then carried out alphabetically within each. Files can be broken down into towns, counties, districts, cities, countries and so on. Large areas, for example counties, may be subdivided into smaller areas, for example towns.

CHRONOLOGICAL FILING

This is where documents are filed in order of date in circumstances where the date is more significant than other information such as the name or place. Examples of documents filed chronologically would be death certificates and financial documents.

The date style used when filing chronologically should be kept consistent, for example 15 April 1994 or 15/4/94. *Don't* use a mixture of the two. Correspondence received from an organisation will often be kept in a file in order of the date (the most recent at the top).

SUBJECT FILING

Files are arranged in alphabetical order according to the topic or subject. This enables an organisation to keep all related information in a single file. For example: a shop may file according to different types of stock – toys, stationery, clothes and so on – or a bank may file under different types of accounts.

Subjects are filed in alphabetical order, for example:

clothes
stationery
toys

Some subjects may be subdivided, for example:

Clothes
– socks
– tops
– trousers
– vests

NUMERICAL FILING

In this case a file or document is given a number. The numbers follow on consecutively. Examples of documents which may be filed numerically are invoices, orders and customer records. A numerical filing system is easy to expand as numbers can be added indefinitely.

The numbers should be read carefully and copied accurately onto the document before filing.

ACTIVITY

File the following names in alphabetical order:

Freda Marshall	Danielle Fisher
Richard Brown	Joanna Plum
Rebecca Bradford	Tracy McFadyen
Yvonne Jackson	Chris Rowe
Chris Williams	Andrew Wall
Emma Townsend	Joanne Heslop
Scott Wilson	Michell Coope
James McVee	Wayne Dobson

ACTIVITY

File the following in numerical order:

1237	75	33
111	10001	112
152	357	2
2350	95	15
3333	950	437
9.5		

ACTIVITY

File the following in chronological order:

15.7.82	June 8th 1988
1/1/93	16.10.66
10 January 1971	1/10/62
1.1.85	31st July 1994
21/1/94	30th Sep 1950
11th March 1979	8/8/88
25 Dec 1985	10.11.91
1.8.88	10.11.79

Reasons for filing

- so that documents can be referred to
- to deal with queries quickly and efficiently
- to have up-to-date information to hand
- to protect documents from dirt and dust
- to keep documents secure

ACTIVITY

What do you think are some of the problems that may occur if the filing is not kept up to date?

ACTIVITY

Below is a list of some of the different types of files used. Obtain a copy of an office-supplies catalogue and see if you can find a picture of each.

- box file
- lever-arch file
- pocket folder
- expanding folder
- clips
- spike
- manila folder
- ringbinder

ACTIVITY

Below are some filing terms. See if you can match them up with the correct explanations:

- Active or current files — *Files over six years old, rarely required, retained in a storeroom*
- Dead Files — *Files about two years old, maybe required occasionally, usually stored away*
- Inactive Files — *Files used on a day-to-day basis, used frequently*

ACTIVITY

You work as a receptionist for a firm of solicitors in Lancashire. Below is a list of some of their clients.

George King, age 53, a chiropodist from Huddersfield

Caroline Dean, age 52, a care assistant from Market Weighton

Daniel Fletcher, age 40, an engineer from Earls Court, London

Katie Fletcher, age 25, a dentist from Manchester

Florence Worton, age 33, a housewife from York

Toby Crump, age 60, a bookmaker from Bridlington

John Smith, age 45, a butcher from Beverley

Marjorie Hampton, age 24, a plumber from Manchester

Henry McEuran, age 24, a baker from Birmingham

Janet Needham, age 18, a shop assistant from Birmingham

Barbara Needham, age 30, a dietician from Coventry

James Needham, age 53, a pilot from Lands End

Polly Peck, age 27, a teacher from Wolverhampton

Freda Simons, age 43, a beauty therapist from Doncaster

Dennis Maynard, age 42, an electrician from Hull

Susan Quick, age 38, a typist from Sheffield

Kevin Fletcher, age 45, a headmaster from Chester

Denise Springfield, age 37, a carpet fitter from Newcaster

Trevor Forman, age 38, an accountant from Durham

Colin Waterman, age 29, a lecturer from London

Margaret Kinnock, age 40, a civil servant from High Wycombe

Neil Thatcher, age 35, a bricklayer from Cardiff

Hayley Jones, age 17, a typist from Uxbridge

Abdul Singh, age 37, a doctor from Ascot

Jean DeGavill, age 33, a jockey from Liverpool

Marie-Clare Marsaud, age 28, a designer from Bradford

David Stanton, age 31, a market gardener from Cambridge

Frank Varley, age 47, a banker from Birmingham

Sylvia Farnham, age 38, a computer operator from Carlisle

Percy Aldred, age 50, a solicitor from Portsmouth

Denise Morton, age 30, a teacher from Beverley

Copy out the details of each client onto a separate piece of paper and then file the information in the following ways:

1 Alphabetically.
2 By occupation.
3 Geographically.
4 Chronologically (by age).

Filing cabinets

VERTICAL

Files are contained within drawers in pockets that are linked together.

LATERAL

Folders are suspended from rails and are placed side by side.

ROTARY

Files are contained in a rotating stand for easy access.

Tips for filing

- filing should be carried out on a regular basis
- make sure that documents are filed correctly
- groups of documents should be sorted in advance to make filing simpler
- torn documents should be repaired and paperclips or staples removed
- avoid overloading individual files or filing cabinets
- new files should be created as appropriate
- treat files with care

ACTIVITY

Collect the following information from the other members of your group:

- name
- address
- date of birth

For each member of the group record the information on a separate piece of paper as follows:

> Jones, B
>
> 7 Crumb Lane
> Hometown
> HT8 7SX
>
> 28-3-79

When you have completed the above task, have a go at filing the papers in the following ways:

1 Alphabetically (by surname).
2 Chronologically (by date of birth).
3 Alphabetically (by address).
4 Geographically (by post code or area).

Indexing

If you look at the back of a textbook, you will probably notice that it has an index. This is a guide for the reader to use so they can locate information without having to look right through the book. Indexes are often used in offices. Examples of information kept in indexes are: telephone numbers and addresses. An index is really a mini filing system.

ACTIVITY

Below is a list of some different types of indexing systems. See if you can find out what each looks like.

- box index
- strip index
- rotary index
- visible index
- slot index

Possible sources of information are office-supplies catalogues, and office skills/administration textbooks.

Electronic filing systems

Today information can be filed in special software packages purchased for use on computer systems.
The packages allow users to:

- create, update and manipulate information
- construct appropriate formats for files
- add records and update existing ones
- search for information
- sort and organise records
- display the records on a visual display unit (VDU)
- print out information as required

ELECTRONIC TRANSMISSION

Local area network (LAN)

LANs have been created by some organisations. They enable large items of electronic equipment to communicate with each other, and also to share peripheral equipment, for example printers. If an organisation has bought equipment over a period of time, for example the gradual introduction of word processors and computers, the LAN enables them to link together to share information and resources.

Facsimile transmission

Fax machines (as they are commonly known) enable businesses to send exact copies of documents all over the world. The process is much faster than using the post as the document is reproduced immediately at its destination. A fax can be sent locally, nationally or internationally.

ACTIVITY

Ask a member of staff at your school or college if the organisation has its own fax machine. If it does see if they will show you how to use it.

A C T I V I T Y

Obtain a copy of a local office-supplies catalogue and find out the cost of purchasing a fax machine.

REPROGRAPHICS

Reprography involves making copies or duplicates of documents. Before copying can take place a 'master copy' needs to be made of the original document and carefully checked.

Photocopying

Reprography is normally carried out using a photocopier. Photocopiers are relatively simple to operate and produce copies of the original document.

Most photocopiers have a number of features:

- two-(or double-) sided copying
- copying onto different sizes of paper
- speedy printing
- enlargement/reduction facilities
- the ability to collate documents (and in some cases also staple them)
- adjustment buttons to take into account how light or dark the original document is
- an automatic paper-feeder facility
- some machines produce colour copies
- many machines will photocopy onto labels, cards, acetate sheets and so on
- machines often have a special panel that indicates faults to the user

A C T I V I T Y

Have a look at the photocopiers in your school or college. Which of the above features do they have?

THE COSTS INVOLVED

Many copiers are rented on a monthly basis. This means that the model rented can be updated as necessary. Toner or ink and silicone oil need to be used

FIG. 7.8 A PHOTOCOPIER

in the machines. These will normally be included in the rental change, as will the servicing of the machines. Organisations also have to pay a small cost per copy made and have to pay for the paper.

Some large organisations have their own reprographic section. They will often purchase (or rent) quite technically advanced machines and deal with all the multiple copies required by the organisation (for cost effectiveness). Individual departments within the organisation are likely to have their own machines for making one-off copies. These may not be as cost effective and usage may be restricted to a small number of staff.

TIPS FOR MAKING A GOOD PHOTOCOPY

- make sure the original is clean and then place it face down on the glass (check the positioning according to the guidelines on the machine
- alter the copy density control if your original is too light or dark
- if you are making a number of copies, take a single copy first to check the quality
- set the machine for the number of copies required
- if you are copying from a book, press down on the book gently to ensure a good-quality copy
- make sure that you have permission to use the machine

Reprographics request forms

Large organisations who have their own reprographics section often have specially designed forms on which staff can submit their copying request. Below is an example:

RATCLIFFES
Reprographics Request Form

Name: Department:

Number of copies required:
Other facilities required: Sorting
                                        Stapling
                                        Binding
                                        Card
                                        Colour (please state)

Authorised by   _____
Date request submitted: _____
Date returned: _____

....

Name _____   No. of copies _____
Department _____   Date returned _____

FIG. 7.9 REPROGRAPHICS REQUEST FORM

The tear-off slip at the bottom of the form is used as a receipt for the person who has had the copies made.

A C T I V I T Y

Choose an organisation and design a reprographics request form of your own for them. Ask another member of your group to have a go at completing the form.

Some reprographics sections will keep a strict check on the number of copies made by employees. Each employee will be given a monthly limit. On the third week of the month a subtotal is made of copies taken so far and the employees informed of the remaining number of copies available.

A C T I V I T Y

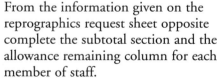

From the information given on the reprographics request sheet opposite complete the subtotal section and the allowance remaining column for each member of staff.

Duplicators

These include spirit, offset litho and ink (stencil) duplicators.

SPIRIT DUPLICATING

This is a cheap method of duplicating involving the use of carbon transfer sheets. It is a rather messy method and only approximately 100–200 copies can be made from each master copy.

INK DUPLICATING

This involves a stencil. Copies are produced when ink seeps through the stencil, which is placed on the drum of the duplicator. Again this method is cheap but can be messy and has a rather unprofessional finish.

OFFSET LITHO

This is the most commonly used duplicating system, as it produces high-quality copies relatively cheaply. The principle that grease (ink) and water do not mix underlies the offset-litho process. The blank parts of the litho plate repel (or reject) the ink and the areas which contain the image attract it.

A C T I V I T Y

Make a list of the advantages and disadvantages of using photocopiers and duplicators.

Reprographics Request Sheet
Copies Made

Month

Name	Monthly limit	Week 1					Week 2					Week 3					Week 4					Subtotal for 3 weeks	Allowance remaining	Monthly total
		1	2	3	4	5	1	2	3	4	5	1	2	3	4	5	1	2	3	4	5			
M Summers	600	10	12	55	1	19	100	110	10	-	-	-	-	10	55	55								
P Brown	1000	150	-	-	-	75	150	-	-	-	75	150	-	-	-	75								
B Little	550	10	92	-	-	-	-	11	20	20	-	-	-	-	17	25								
D Cave	530	-	-	-	200	-	-	-	-	-	-	15	-	12	-	-								
R Bear	300	21	19	-	-	3	-	-	-	-	7	-	-	10	-	20								
L Lines	250	-	-	-	-	-	200	-	-	-	-	-	-	-	-	-								
P Symes	600	-	-	50	-	-	50	-	-	10	-	-	15	-	-	15								
R Wilson	600	-	-	17	-	21	-	-	50	50	-	-	-	-	-	-								
P Bowes	600	-	19	-	-	19	-	-	-	200	-	-	-	3	-	-								
R Peele	450	-	6	-	-	11	-	-	-	25	-	25	-	-	-	25								

Printing

TYPESETTING

This is the method used for professional printing. Sometimes traditional 'hot metal' methods are used, but most common today are computer-based phototypesetting methods. For example, many newspapers have changed from traditional to computerised printing methods. Typesetting produces documents of a professional standard (especially when combined with the use of laser printer). Examples of materials produced by this method are glossy brochures, leaflets, manuals, letterheads and invoices.

DESK-TOP PUBLISHING (DTP)

Desk-top publishing packages can be purchased for use on computers. This is a cost effective way of printing. Staff can be trained to use the packages relatively quickly. The operator can choose from a variety of fonts (print styles) depending on the required result. Examples of material produced using DTP are newsletters, catalogues, forms and manuals.

A C T I V I T Y

You work for a city-centre college with a large administration section and a separate reprographics section. You have been asked to prepare an informal report about suitable reprographics and printing equipment that could be used within the organisation. In groups of two or three carry out some research about the equipment on sale and the costs involved (the college has approximately £6000 to spend) and make a series of recommendations about what should be purchased.

EXAMINE ARRANGEMENTS FOR DEALING WITH INITIAL CONTACT WITH CALLERS

POINTS OF CONTACT

The way a customer or potential customer is treated when he or she first makes contact with an organisation will play a significant role in the overall image or impression that customer will have of the organisation. Because of this it is important that members of staff are carefully trained in the art of dealing with people.

The points of contact will be between members of the public and staff:

- in the reception area
- on the telephone
- outside the organisation, for example at meetings and promotional events

Reception

A receptionist needs to be cheerful, calm, tactful, polite, informed, smart and trustworthy. In addition he or she needs to have a clear speaking voice.

FIG. 7.10 RECEPTION

ACTIVITY

Can you think of any more qualities a receptionist needs?

WHAT DOES RECEPTION WORK INVOLVE?

- dealing with callers
- operating the switchboard and answering the telephone
- dealing with the post
- typing/word processing
- providing information
- making introductions
- dealing with emergencies
- administration
- projecting the image of the organisation
- dealing with callers or visitors

TYPES OF CALLER A RECEPTIONIST MAY HAVE TO DEAL WITH

- people making enquiries
- people making complaints
- those who are lost/asking for directions
- angry customers
- rude visitors
- people in a hurry
- disabled people
- sales representatives
- people with appointments
- interviewees
- adults/children
- foreigners
- elderly people

ACTIVITY

See how many more types of caller you can think of.

TIPS FOR DEALING WITH CALLERS OR VISITORS TO THE ORGANISATION

1 Greet the customer politely.

2 Smile.

3 Find out how you can help them.

4 If you don't understand, politely ask them to repeat themselves.

5 If the visitor has an appointment, ring through to the relevant department and
 – ask someone to collect them *or*
 – give them clear directions to the relevant department.

6 If the visitor does not have an appointment, find out if anyone is available to see them or suggest an alternative time and date.

7 Offer the caller a seat and refreshments if they have to wait to be seen.

8 Be polite and courteous to all callers.

9 Don't disclose any confidential information.

10 Don't leave the reception desk unattended.

11 Don't *ever* be rude to callers even if they are to you.

THE APPOINTMENTS BOOK

This is a special book often kept in the reception area. It contains a page for each day. The following information is recorded in the book: the name of each visitor to the organisation; the company and position of the visitor; the time of the appointment; and the name of the person/people the visitor is visiting.

 Below is an example of a page from an appointments book.

Time	Name	Company	To see
0930	Miss M Moore	Carricks Computers	Mr Perrin
1015	Mr J Burrows	Smiths (sales rep)	Mr Blackman
1105	Miss C Conman	Elle Employment Agency	Miss Clarke
1200	Miss L Ede	Hoods Hardware	Mrs Weatherson
1330	Miss N Woodhead	Peadbury's (managing director)	Mr Burden
1430	Mr A Rands	Hills Engineering Group	Personnel
1500	Mr R Hudson	Lowes	Miss Chambers
1500	Mr L Farmer	Attees Associates	Mr Cutler
1615	Dr C Campell	Peele's	Mr Baker

Wednesday 15 June 19.......

FIG. 7.11 AN APPOINTMENTS BOOK

Draw a blank page of an appointments book. Transfer the following information onto the page.

1 3pm: Mr Jones, a sales representative from Carrs, to visit Miss Hodgson.

2 10.15am: Mrs Wawnes, a computer technician, to visit the administrative section.

3 12.00: Mr Smith, from Smiths Ltd, for a lunch appointment with Mrs Davis, the manageress.

4 Dr Clarry to visit the personnel department at 2.15pm.

5 9am: Miss Jones for an interview with Mr Nephews.

6 10.30am: Mr Hood, from Hoods Hardware, to visit Mr Clarke.

THE VISITORS BOOK

Look at p.146 in Chapter 6 'Business communications' and read about visitor's books.

Draw a blank page from a visitor's book and then enter some information about visitors to an organisation of your choice.

R O L E P L A Y

Reception role plays

You work as a receptionist at Orry's Office Suppliers. Below is a list of visitors to the organisation one morning.

Set up a reception area. Choose one member of your group to be the receptionist and the others to play the role of the visitors.

1 A lorry driver who wants directions to Dodgy Double Glazing.
2 A mother who wants to know if her little girl can use the toilet.
3 A sales rep who has an appointment to see Mrs Perth, the sales manager.
4 A disabled man who requires directions to the lift.
5 A gypsy trying to sell pegs.

6 A young woman who has arrived 20 minutes early for a job interview.
7 An elderly man who is taken ill in the reception area.
8 A woman asking if she can leave a charity collecting-box in the reception area.
9 A young boy making enquiries about Saturday jobs.
10 A young man who appears to be under the influence of alcohol and is causing a disruption.
11 A man requesting an office-supplies catalogue.
12 A woman who wishes to make a complaint about a calculator she purchased recently.
13 A man who has an appointment to see the manager.
14 A young woman who wants to use the telephone.
15 A man selling stationery.

Act out the role plays more than once so that different people can play the part of the receptionist.

As a group discuss how well each receptionist dealt with the callers.

A C T I V I T Y

Here are some examples of job advertisements for receptionists and switchboard operators. Study the adverts carefully and write a letter of application for one of them.

FULL-TIME RECEPTIONIST REQUIRED

To work for **Peeles** a small printing company. Duties would involve switchboard and reception work. No experience necessary.

Call Maureen on 127304 for further details and an application form.

CAVES
An equal opportunities employer

TELEPHONIST/RECEPTIONIST

We are a large building group with a vacancy for a telephonist/receptionist with a cheerful manner to work at our head office, Leeds.

The successful applicant will be working with up-to-date switchboard equipment.

An attractive salary is offered. Applicants should be able to type and have some experience of reception work.

Applications should be made in writing to:

P Wiles
Caves Building Ltd
Lowe Lane
Leeds
LS2 1PT

Closing date: 28 July 19__

JUNIOR RECEPTIONIST REQUIRED

Training given

Tel: 701111

Business cards

When business people visit an organisation for the first time they will often leave a business card. This includes:

- the company name
- the company address and telephone number
- the type of work the company does
- the name of the business man or woman (this may be handwritten)
- a telephone number

Below is an example of a business card.

✳✳ Taylors Toys ✳✳
2 Moss Street, Manchester, MD7 0HP

Timothy Brown
Sales Executive

Tel: 061 392 7061

FIG. 7.12 A BUSINESS CARD

A C T I V I T Y

Have a go at designing a business card for the following:

- yourself
- a friend
- your teacher or lecturer

Dealing with callers on the telephone

The organisation may have a standard greeting, for example 'Good morning, Smiths Seed Supplies. How may I help you?' If it does, make sure that you use it.
Find out who the caller is and the reason for their call.
Decide to whom the caller needs to speak (if they do not already know).

4 Explain to the caller that you are going to transfer the call.
5 If appropriate, take a message.
6 Be polite and courteous to all callers. Use a complimentary close if you are the last person to speak to the caller, for example 'thank you for calling'.

TAKING MESSAGES

1 Make sure that you have a pen and paper to hand.
2 Write down the name of the caller and his or her telephone number.
3 Make a note of the message and whom it is for.
4 Check details you are unsure about by reading the message back to the caller.
5 Make a note of the date and time of the call.

TELEPHONE MESSAGE PADS

Many organisations have their own message pads. When used these save time in taking messages and make it more likely the message will be written down correctly.

TELEPHONE MESSAGES

Date: Time:
Message for:
Callers name:
Message:

Call taken by:

FIG. 7.13 A TELEPHONE MESSAGE PAD

A C T I V I T Y

Have a go at designing your own telephone message pad. Ask a member of your group to complete the message pad.

ROLEPLAY

Telephone role plays

Ritchies is a large DIY store in the centre of town. You are a receptionist and it is your responsibility to operate the switchboard.

The shop has the following sections: administration, sales, customer services and finance. The manager is Miss J Hoggard. Below are a list of calls you have answered. One person in the group should take on the role of the receptionist, while the other members are the callers. For each write down what you would say to the caller.
(With the greeting: 'Good morning/afternoon, how may I help you?')

1 'I had a lawn mower delivered last week and it isn't working ...'
2 'I left my umbrella in your shop yesterday.'
3 'I wish to complain about a rude sales assistant.'
4 'Could you send me a catalogue please?'
5 'I am ringing to see if there are any job vacancies.'
6 'This is Jon Peters. I am a sales representative for Moores Howes.'

7 'I am ringing to thank a sales assistant who helped me when I felt ill in your store yesterday.'
8 'Could you tell me what time you shut today, please?'
9 'Hello this is Miss Hoggard, could you let me have the rota for the switchboard.'
10 'Hello could you tell me when your sale starts?'
11 'Hello I ordered a power drill three weeks ago and it hasn't arrived yet.'
12 'I'd like to make an appointment to see the manager please.'
13 'Hi, Jayne here from admin. Do you fancy meeting up for lunch?'
14 'This is the Job Centre. Can you send us details of any vacancies please?'
15 'Do you stock garden hoses?'
16 'I am ringing about an invoice I have received.'
17 'Hello, can I speak to Trevor please?'
18 'I am a student and would like to do a project on your store.'
19 'There is a bomb in the store.'
20 'I'd like to book a table for lunch.'

Within a group have a go at answering the calls: one member of the group can be the receptionist and the others the callers.

Dealing with people outside the organisation

From time to time employees may be required to deal with members of the public outside the organisation. Examples are attending a meeting or a promotional event. In these circumstances, people should be treated as politely as possible as if they were visiting the organisation itself. They may be existing or potential customers. The employees will be representing the organisation and the impression or image he or she gives is likely to influence the impression that members of the public will have of the organisation for which he or she works.

ORGANISE AND ADMINISTER A MEETING

FORMAL MEETINGS

Documentation

THE NOTICE OF MEETING

This must be sent to all parties entitled to attend before the meeting can take place. Information included will be as follows:

- the title of the meeting
- the date
- the time
- the place

If an agenda (see below) is attached, this will be indicated on the notice.

The notice should be sent by the person who is authorised to run the meeting. It should be sent out well in advance of the meeting.

Robinson's Bank Plc

Notice of meeting: Health and Safety Committee

A meeting of the above committee will be held on Friday 31 March 1994, at 4pm in the large conference room at the Hull branch, Lee Street. Members from all Humberside branches are invited to attend.

Signed *J Cox*
Secretary

Enc.: Agenda

FIG. 7.14 EXAMPLE OF NOTICE OF MEETING

THE AGENDA

The agenda is a list of the matters to be discussed at the meeting. It is sent out before the meeting so that the members have some idea of the format in advance. The agenda will normally be prepared by the secretary in consultation with the chairperson. It should be distributed in good time in order to give members time

to consider the issues to be discussed and read appropriate papers in advance.

An agenda will normally take the following format:

- apologies for absence
- minutes of the last meeting
- matters arising from the minutes
- general agenda items
- any other business
- date and time of the next meeting

Robinson's Bank Plc

Meeting of the Health and Safety Committee to be held on Friday 31 March 1994 at 4pm in the large conference room at the Hull branch, Lee Street.

Agenda

1 Apologies for absence.

2 Minutes of the last meeting.

3 Matters arising.

4 Treasurer's report.

5 Discussion on the motion: That additional health and safety notices should be displayed around branch premises.
Proposed: J L Jones (Beverley branch)
Seconded: E Eagleton (Grimsby branch)

6 Health and safety inspection – to receive a verbal report – T Turner.

7 Any other business.

8 Date and time of next meeting.

FIG. 7.15 EXAMPLE OF AN AGENDA

Minutes of the Health and Safety Committee meeting held on 31 March 1994

PRESENT: A Anderson (chairperson)
               B Blythe (minutes secretary)
               C Carmichael
               D Davis
               E Engleton
               G Godbold
               J Jones
               S Smith
               T Turner
               V Vokes

1 Apologies for absence
Apologies were received from C Clarke, P Potts and R Robinson.

2 Minutes of the last meeting
It was agreed that the minutes of the last meeting were a true and accurate account.

3 Matters arising
There were no matters arising.

4 Treasurer's report
The treasurer provided up-to-date information about the committee's financial position:

a) A total of £375.21 in the current account.
b) £595.02 in the savings account.

5 Health and safety notices
A discussion took place on the motion that additional health and safety notices be displayed around branch premises.

Proposed by: J Jones (Beverley branch)
Seconded by: E Eagleton (Grimsby branch)

It was agreed that additional notices could lead to the improved safety of staff.
G Godbold suggested that a representative should be nominated to display the notices at each branch.
The Chair asked committee members to nominate a branch member before the next meeting.

6 Health and safety inspection
T Turner provided details about the programme of visits to branches planned by the Health and Safety Executive.

a) Beverley and Hull will receive a visit on 30 April 1994.
b) Grimsby and Goole will be visited on 6 May 1994.
c) The visit to the Lincoln branch will be on 16 May 1994.

She pointed out that she was awaiting details about the format of the inspection and that these would be circulated to committee members as soon as possible.

7 Any other business
V Volkes pointed out that fire extinguishers in some branches were quite old and may need to be replaced. It was agreed that committee members should check the extinguishers at their particular branch and forward details to the secretary.

Date of next meeting
The next meeting was arranged for Friday 8 May 1994, at the Hull Branch

Date _____   Signed _____
                               (chairperson)

FIG. 7.16 EXAMPLE OF MINUTES OF A MEETING

MINUTES OF THE MEETING

Depending on the organisation you will find the style of the minutes varies. However, the majority of organisations will stick to the broad headings used in the Robinsons Bank example in Figure 7.16.

Preparation for the meeting

Some useful questions to ask are:

- What size of room do we need?
- Are there enough tables and chairs?
- How should the room be set out?
- Are refreshments required?
- Is there a need for additional equipment, for example a flip chart or overhead projector?

- Are there sufficient copies of relevant papers?

Responsibilities at the meeting

CHAIRPERSON

The chairperson is elected or appointed to the role and is responsible for controlling the meeting. His or her job involves:

- preparation for the meeting – authorising the agenda, checking arrangements
- familiarity with the constitution of the meeting
- opening the meeting and ensuring that sufficient members are present

- accepting apologies for members who cannot attend
- running the meeting — ensuring that it progresses smoothly and efficiently
- closing the meeting and giving details of the next one

SECRETARY

The secretary has a significant role. He or she is responsible for communicating with the members and carrying out all necessary administrative functions. The job involves:

- preparation of the notice and agenda
- circulation of the above (plus additional papers) to all members of the meeting
- supporting the chairperson as necessary
- ensuring that a true and accurate record is made of the meeting (in the form of minutes)
- carrying out all administrative and communication functions linked to the meeting

TREASURER

The treasurer is responsible for controlling the accounts and submitting financial reports. He or she is likely to be asked to make a report to the meeting on a regular basis.

FIG. 7.17 A FORMAL MEETING

A C T I V I T Y

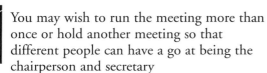

As a group of students have a go at running your own meeting.

- pick a suitable topic, for example the library or sports facilities
- nominate a chairperson and secretary
- prepare a notice, agenda and any other relevant papers
- run the meeting and try writing some minutes

You may wish to run the meeting more than once or hold another meeting so that different people can have a go at being the chairperson and secretary

Internal/external meetings

Sometimes meetings will be held for staff within an organisation. In such cases relevant documentation or papers can be circulated to the appropriate people internally.

On other occasions people from outside the organisation will be required to attend meetings. In these cases it is important that the relevant papers are forwarded in good time in order that those attending can look through them and prepare their comments before the meeting.

Annual general meetings

Once a year members of an organisation all attend a formal meting to discuss the previous year's activities, receive financial reports, debate future developments and reappoint officers and/or elect new ones.

Extraordinary (exceptional) general meetings

On rare occasions when urgent or particularly important issues occur, it may be necessary to call a meeting of all members of an organisation. The members may be required to take a vote on a particular issue or grant special permission to a committee or board of directors.

Follow-up of meetings

Once a formal meeting has taken place it will normally be the responsibility of the secretary to send copies of the minutes to all those who attended (as well as those who sent their apologies). He or she may also be asked to contact those people who agreed to carry out a specific task during the meeting.

INFORMAL MEETINGS

These do not involve the strict formalities discussed previously. For example, there will be no notice or agenda. Despite this people will still need to be invited to the meeting and be given some idea about what is to be discussed. For example, a small staff meeting may take place during a lunch hour. The boss may telephone those who need to be present or possibly send them a memo (indicating any information staff need to bring to the meeting).

In an informal meeting someone is usually nominated to take control. Despite the informality of the meeting, having *no* leader can often lead to problems, for example a lack of order and control.

REASONS FOR MEETINGS

Meetings may be held for all sorts of different reasons. They may be held:

- on a regular basis, for example a weekly staff meeting
- to discuss special issues, for example a trade-union meeting to discuss strike action
- within the organisation, for example a departmental meeting
- outside the organisation, for example a branch meeting

Sometimes you may hear the criticism that an organisation is 'having a meeting for the sake of it'. It is important to remember that a meeting should only be held if there really is something to discuss. If not it is a waste of time, money and energy.

A C T I V I T Y

Make a list of as many different reasons you can think of why an organisation may decide to hold a meeting.

A C T I V I T Y

Think about a situation where you have taken part in an informal meeting (sometimes without even realising it), for example a meeting with friends to discuss a night out.

	FORMAL MEETING	INFORMAL MEETING
What is the constitution?	Written constitution to establish rules and procedures	No formal constitution
Is there any formal documentation?	Yes: notice, agenda, motions, minutes	No: meeting normally arranged informally; sometimes notes may be taken
Is there any special terminology?	Yes. Examples are: proposal, seconder, agenda, minutes, apology	No
Are there any officers or people with special responsibilities?	Yes: chairperson, treasurer, secretary	No
How are decisions made?	A vote is taken	Normally by common agreement, or an individual making a decision after discussion with the others
Examples:	Board meetings Branch meetings	Discussion groups Problem-solving

TABLE 7.1 COMPARISON OF FORMAL AND INFORMAL MEETINGS

COMPILE BUSINESS TRAVEL ITINERARIES AND ACCOMMODATION INFORMATION

ARRANGEMENTS

Itineraries

The majority of jobs will require travel arrangements to be made at some time. It is essential that travel arrangements are well planned and carefully administered.

An itinerary is the first stage in organising a business trip. It is an outline of the places to be visited and the time to be spent at each – a timetable if you like!

MISS RADICE'S VISIT TO LEEDS – JULY 31 1994

0715 hours	Depart Paragon Station, Hull
0820 hours	Arrive Leeds Station
0900 hours	Oldridge Book Supplies Ltd
	Otley Road, Leeds
	Appointment with M Oldridge, sales manager
1200 hours	Queens Hotel, Queens Square, Leeds
	Lunch with F Smith, Smiths Solicitors
1400 hours	Depart Leeds Station
1512 hours	Arrive Paragon Station, Hull

TABLE 7.2 EXAMPLE OF AN ITINERARY

Before making arrangements there will be a number of questions you will need to ask:

- When will the trip take place?
- What/where is the required destination?
- What are the costs involved?
- What method of transport will be used?
- How long will it take to get there?
- Is any accommodation required?
- Is the required transport and accommodation available?
- What sources of information are required?
- What documentation/administration is involved?

Booking accommodation

If accommodation is required a number of factors will need to be taken into consideration: the location; the amount of money available to spend on the accommodation; and individual requirements, such as a bathroom, a room with a telephone and so on.

It is useful to shop around to establish which accommodation is the best value for money. Useful sources of accommodation information are: The *AA Handbook*, travel brochures, *Cromer's Office Companion* and British Rail guides.

A C T I V I T Y

Below is a list of different ways a person on a business trip may choose to travel. Make a list of the advantages and disadvantages of each.

- car
- train
- coach
- plane
- ferry

A C T I V I T Y

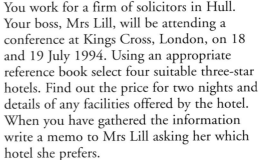

You work for a firm of solicitors in Hull. Your boss, Mrs Lill, will be attending a conference at Kings Cross, London, on 18 and 19 July 1994. Using an appropriate reference book select four suitable three-star hotels. Find out the price for two nights and details of any facilities offered by the hotel. When you have gathered the information write a memo to Mrs Lill asking her which hotel she prefers.

Booking rooms

Booking accommodation may not always be required as a result of a business trip. A simpler situation may occur, for example booking a room within an organisation for a meeting.

If this is the case it is important to find out:

- when the room is required and for how long
- the number of people involved
- the facilities/equipment available in the room
- who to contact to book the room
- any forms/documents which need to be completed

Figure 7.18 is an example of a room-booking form.

BRANDRETHS
Room-booking Form

Room required	Date	Times	Reasons	Booked by:

FIG. 7.18 EXAMPLE OF A ROOM-BOOKING FORM

Planning the route

A business trip should be arranged in such a way that the traveller can reach his or her destination in the quickest and simplest way possible. In some cases, however, the journey may be slightly more complicated.

Costing journeys

The cost of a journey can vary considerably depending on the method of travel and also the time of the journey.

INTERNATIONAL TRAVEL

Some business trips may involve a trip abroad. Foreign travel needs to be organised extremely carefully as there are lots of things to think about, such as:

- dates
- cost
- accommodation
- travel documents
- times (including time differences)
- method of travel
- foreign currency

A C T I V I T Y

Mrs Lill has decided that after attending the conference on 18 and 19 July she will stop off at the Leeds branch on her return journey for a business meeting. She wants to travel by train.

1 Visit your local British Rail station and ask for:
   a a Hull–London timetable
   b a Hull–Leeds timetable
   If your local station does not have a copy of the relevant timetables, you may choose alternative cities for Mrs Lill's journey.
2 Mrs Lill wishes to arrive in London before 11am on 18 July. She has arranged to attend the meeting in Leeds at 12.00 noon on 20 July. Using the timetable work out the following information:
   a the time she will need to catch the train from Hull on 18 July (including the time of arrival in London)
   b the time she will need to catch the train to Leeds on 20 July (including the time of arrival in Leeds)
   c whether she will need to change trains during her journeys

---

A C T I V I T Y

1 *Rail* Find out the cost of a return train journey from Hull to Retford (give details of first-class, ordinary and Apex fares).
2 *Coach* Find out the cost of a return coach journey from London to Doncaster (you should be able to obtain a leaflet from a local coach company that gives details of coach travel to and from London).

If your local coach and train stations do not have copies of the relevant timetables, you may choose alternative journeys for the activity.

Does the cost vary according to the time of the journey?

A C T I V I T Y

Can you think of any additional factors you may need to consider before planning a business trip abroad?

Travel documents

When travelling abroad the necessary documents should be kept in a separate wallet together with the tickets for the trip. The documents may include:

- a passport
- insurance documents
- visas
- health certificates/documents
- travellers cheques

It is also advisable to carry a small amount of foreign currency in cash for purchasing food, drinks and so on when you arrive.

Currency

The majority of countries have their own currency (or form of money), for example in England we have the pound.

As discussed above when travelling abroad it is wise to carry only a small amount of foreign currency in cash. Additional money can be taken in the form of travellers cheques. These can be purchased from banks or travel agencies before the trip. They are signed by the traveller when purchased and again when exchanged for currency in the destination country. They will be replaced by the bank or travel agency if they are lost or stolen.

A C T I V I T Y

Below is a list of countries. See if you can find out the name of the currency used in each.

- Italy
- France
- Turkey
- Holland
- Belgium
- India
- China
- Spain
- Greece

A C T I V I T Y

Have a word with your friends or members of your family who have travelled abroad. Do they still have any foreign currency? If so what does it look like and how does it compare to our currency?

Making international telephone calls

When arranging foreign travel it may be necessary to call businesses and hotels abroad. Before dialling the number it is necessary to dial the international dialling code. Details of the codes can be found in the telephone directory.

A C T I V I T Y

Look in a telephone directory and find out the international dialling codes for the following countries:

- Luxembourg
- Morocco
- France
- Greece
- Hungary
- Turkey

The telephone directory will also provide information about the charge bands into which the calls fit, and details of time differences for each country.

A C T I V I T Y

Look in the telephone directory and find out the time difference for the following countries:

- Austria
- Barbados
- Canada
- Egypt
- Korea
- Poland

A C T I V I T Y

You have been asked to arrange a five-day European trip for a group of business studies students at your school or college. You may wish to work in small groups to complete the following tasks.

1 Select a suitable destination.
2 Find an appropriate hotel and make a note of the following:
  a costs involved
  b facilities available
  c food provision
  d other relevant information
3 Decide the method of travel and note:
  a the times of travel
  b facilities offered
  c other relevant information
4 Prepare an itinerary for the trip.

For more information on business travel in Europe see pp.237–9.

Planning holidays

A good way of planning international business travel is by booking a foreign holiday.

A C T I V I T Y

1 Collect a range of different holiday brochures and select a holiday of your choice (you may need to set yourself a price limit).
2 Make a list of the costs involved, including insurance charges and so on.
3 Write down the dates of travel and the times of flights (including times of take-off and landing, and from which airport).
4 Make a note of the deposit required.
5 Complete the booking form for the holiday.
6 Find out what currency you will require for your trip.

Methods of transport

On pp.11–12 of 'Business organisations and employment', we looked at the different methods of transport businesses can use to transport their goods and the advantages and disadvantages of each.

Methods of travel

As well as transporting goods in the most appropriate way, businesses will need to decide on the most suitable method of travel when members of the organisation have to undertake journeys in connection with their jobs. See Table 7.3.

C H A P T E R   S E V E N

Test Yourself!

1 If a letter begins with 'Dear Sir' what does it end with?
2 What is chronological filing?
3 What is geographical filing?
4 What does 'enc.' stand for at the bottom of a letter?
5 What is recorded delivery?
6 True or false? A franking machine sticks stamps on letters.
7 What is another name for a circulation slip?
8 Give two reasons for filing.
9 What is meant by the term reprography?
10 State three differences between formal and informal meetings.
11 Name two items included on an agenda.
12 Who will normally write the minutes of a meeting?
13 What is an itinerary?
14 List two responsibilities of a chairperson.
15 List five qualities of a receptionist.

TABLE 7.3 DIFFERENT METHODS OF LOCAL AND NATIONAL TRAVEL AND THE ADVANTAGES AND DISADVANTAGES OF EACH

METHOD OF TRAVEL	ADVANTAGES	DISADVANTAGES
LOCAL		
Bus	Cheap Regular service Can be slow	Many routes Not necessarily direct
'little' or 'small' bus service	Offers a local service to areas not covered by main bus routes Cheap Regular service	Only hold a small number of passengers Can be uncomfortable
Park and ride	Convenient Enables the traveller to leave the car at the edge of a town or city and travel directly by bus to the town or city centre Cheap	Slow
Taxi	Direct Readily available Flexible hours	Expensive Can only hold a small number of passengers
Supertram (Sheffield)	Quick Environmentally friendly Cheap Disabled access	Limited routes
Underground (London and Newcastle)	Quick Environmentally friendly	Limited routes
Car	Direct Flexible	Can only hold a limited number of passengers
NATIONAL		
Car	As above	As above
Train	Fast Comfortable Can carry a large number of passengers Facilities, i.e. toilets, buffet car	Limited routes Slow
Coach	Can carry a large number of passengers Facilities, i.e. toilet, snacks	
Plane (national flights)	Fast Comfortable Facilities, i.e. toilets, meals	Expensive

Chapter
8

PROMOTION, SALES AND THE MEDIA

INVESTIGATE SALES

TYPES OF RETAIL OUTLET

Every town and city in the UK will have a variety of shops or sales outlets. Often these can be found in the city centre or town high street and will feature many well-established retail stores such as Marks & Spencer, W H Smith and others.

Many cities now also have shopping precincts or centres (or shopping malls as they are called in the USA where they originated). These new developments contain a number of shop units, often have several floors and are completely under cover. They frequently have restaurant and leisure areas and generally aim to make shopping more of a leisure activity. Well-known shopping centres in the UK are the MetroCentre in Newcastle and Meadowhall outside Sheffield.

In addition to these town-centre developments there are now many out-of-town developments springing up all over the country. These feature large stores, often supermarkets like Sainsbury's and Tesco. They are

FIG. 8.1 ST ANDREWS QUAY

normally found on the edges of towns and offer free parking as well as other facilities such as petrol stations. Occasionally different retailers who need large premises to sell their products will locate together on the edge of town to form a retail park, where you might find, for example, a hypermarket, a do-it-yourself warehouse, a frozen-food store and a carpet retailer.

In business it is very helpful to be able to identify the different type of sales outlets that exist. If you are a manufacturer and want to sell to these shops it will help you to know that large outlets will need a different service from you than small outlets. If you are a consumer, you will soon recognise that each type of outlet is able to offer you a different service.

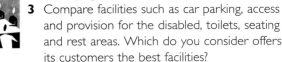

ACTIVITY

Investigate your local shopping facilities.

1 Identify your local out-of-town developments and city-centre shopping precincts.
2 Draw area plans for each development identifying the units.
3 Compare facilities such as car parking, access and provision for the disabled, toilets, seating and rest areas. Which do you consider offers its customers the best facilities?

Independent retailer/unit shop

These will often be run by sole traders and will frequently have local and family connections. There may be more than one shop in the chain, but there will generally be fewer than ten. Independent retailers are frequently found in the local suburbs, as the major retail chains have tended to push them out of city-centre locations.

FIG. 8.2 AN INDEPENDENT RETAILER

ACTIVITY

Check through your local press, including free newspapers. Cut out any advertisements from local independent retailers. What type of products do they sell? Where are they located?

Multiple-chain stores

These are stores that tend to specialise in selling a particular type of product. For example, W H Smith sells stationery, books and records; Currys sells electrical products. These are often very large chains and appear in most high streets. Retailers would need to have more than ten branches to become a multiple-chain store.

Variety chains

In some ways these are similar to multiple-chain stores in that they have a large number of branches. However, they tend to sell a wide range of unrelated goods, often by self-service. They may also sell a range of own-label brands. Examples of variety stores are Argos, Woolworths and Boots.

Department stores

Department stores sell a wide range of goods all under one roof. Different departments specialise in selling particular types of products, for example the women's clothing department or the furniture department. Assistants are active in selling goods and providing customer service.

It is becoming more common to find concessions within department stores. This means that a separate retailer will take space within the department store to sell their own range of goods. For example, you might find Olympus Sports shops in House of Fraser stores and Principles concessions within the Debenhams department store.

Department stores often offer a wide range of services like hairdressing, restaurants and so on. Allders and Debenhams are examples of department stores.

Co-operatives

The co-operative movement was created over 100 years ago. Its aim was for the profits of the co-operative operation to be directed back to its customers, depending on the level of their purchases. In practical terms this has meant that the co-op stores in the high street have paid 'a dividend' back to shoppers, sometimes in the form of saving stamps.

Supermarkets

These are large self-service shops, usually concerned with selling food. The product range will normally focus on fast-selling staple goods for which there is a regular demand. A supermarket will have a sales area of over 2000 square feet, for example Kwiksave.

Superstores

These are much larger versions of the supermarket, with additional facilities. They are self-service stores of over 25 000 square feet and will probably feature at least 20 000 product lines. A superstore will probably also sell non-food products such as kitchenware, books and possibly electrical products. Superstores now frequently have their own petrol stations and always offer extensive parking, for example Sainsbury's, Asda and Safeway.

Hypermarkets

These are very popular in mainland Europe (particularly in France) and are larger versions of the superstore. They will have an area of over 50 000 square feet and offer an extensive range of products, not concentrating solely on food. An example of a hypermarket is Carrefour.

Warehouse clubs

These are a very recent innovation and are popular in the USA. They are now attempting to break into the UK market.

Warehouse clubs are different from normal retail outlets in that customers have to pay a yearly fee (suggestions for the UK fee range from £15–£35). Having paid the membership fee the consumer can then shop in the warehouse, where they can buy anything from baked beans to TVs at a significantly lower price than in the high street. Consumers do, however, have to buy many of the food and household products in bulk, for example a pack of 12 cans of beans rather than a single tin.

Membership can sometimes be limited to certain occupations, such as teachers or civil servants.

Mobile shops

The strength of this type of sales outlet is its mobility, in that it takes the products to the customer, rather than expecting the customer to visit the shop. Mobile shops normally sell food or household items, and are of particular use to those who are geographically isolated from the normal shops, for example rural villages with poor transport links to cities, or to those who are housebound because of age or family responsibilities and who do not own cars. Mobile shops can give customers access to products they might not normally be able to buy, for example fish vans bringing freshly caught fish to inland areas. Another form of mobile

shop is much more common, that of ice-cream and hot-dog sellers who pitch their shops where business is most likely to be brisk.

NON-RETAIL SELLING

Mail-order

There are two different types of mail-order organisations today. The first is where the manufacturer tries to sell directly to the consumer without using a retail outlet. An example of this is the exclusive offers of limited-edition prints or pottery that businesses often sell directly through the press (see Figure 8.3, opposite).

A mail-order house works slightly differently. This sells its goods through its agents who 'run a catalogue'. The agents can buy goods themselves and offer the service to friends and family. The agents receive a commission (typically 10 per cent) on everything they sell. Mail-order houses offer the benefit of being able to buy on credit and the convenience of home shopping. Well-known mail-order houses are Freemans, Grattan and Littlewoods. An example of a mail-order house leaflet is shown in Figure 8.4.

Party plan

The party planner is normally a self-employed person who sells goods for the company in other people's homes. Famous party-plan organisations are Oriflamme Cosmetics and Tupperware. It is the planner's job to and secure as many appointments or parties as possible The host of each party will then invite friends/associa

FIG. 8.3

G. 8.4 A GUIDE TO MAIL-ORDER
OPPING

to view the product range. The party planner will generally receive commission on goods ordered at the party and the host will also receive some benefit (usually a gift) based on the value of orders. The informal and relaxed atmosphere is very good for persuading people to buy products.

Direct mail

Direct mail cuts out the middleman or retailer and goes direct to the customer. Mailshots which have been especially prepared are sent through the post, using customers' names that may have been selected from a mailing list. The mailshots invite customers to order directly from the supplier instead of through retail outlets. The mailshots often use Freepost reader-reply cards.

TV sales

These are currently very limited in the UK. An example would be companies who invite a direct response from consumers to buy an exclusive record advertised on TV. In the USA there are home-shopping channels where all programmes are dedicated to selling products to viewers, who are invited to phone in their order. This system has recently been launched in the UK via satellite TV.

Telephone selling

This is most frequently used by businesses trying to sell to other businesses. For example, a company selling computer paper might ring around customers to see if they wish to re-order. For consumers telephone selling is often used to secure an appointment for a representative to call personally.

Ding-dong, Body Shop calling ...

ANITA RODDICK is taking on the Avon lady in a campaign to reverse a slump in sales.

Doorbells are ringing across the country as the Body Shop moves into the living room, expanding business beyond the green frontage of its High Street branches.

'We are targeting a new market – slightly older women and young mothers who may find it difficult to get out to the shops and choose things at their leisure,' said company spokesman Peter Griffin.

'The initiative will be similar to the way Avon works. It is also a bit like Tupperware but the difference is it will be closely linked with our stores. We also hope it will eventually attract more customers into our shops.

'The idea is to get half a dozen friends together and introduce them to Body Shop products.'

The company is already carrying out trials throughout the country, using home consultants to give demonstrations of make-up, skin and haircare products to gauge the public reaction. The products are the same as those in its shops and are the same price.

Consultants are expected to be 'enthusiastic, confident and possess an empathy with Body Shop values' as well as having their own car and phone.

Mrs Roddick founded Body Shop 18 years ago after she began making lotions

**By VIKKI ORVICE
Consumer Affairs Correspondent**

and potions in the garage of her Brighton home. She and her husband, Gordon, built it into a £365million business with 900 stores in 41 countries.

Earlier this year they admitted there was little room for new outlets in the UK, where there are now 233 Body Shops, although more foreign openings are planned.

The company's British sales have fallen by five per cent in the last year as its environmentally-friendly shopping concept is increasingly copied by High Street competitors including Marks & Spencer and Boots.

US-owned Avon, which stopped testing products on animals five years ago, now operates in 70 countries including Russia and China. It employs 1.5 million representatives, 100,000 of them in Britain.

FIG. 8.5
SOURCE: DAILY MAIL, 21/10/93

Direct selling

The largest and most famous direct-selling organisation is Avon Cosmetics, although there are many different organisations selling goods door-to-door, from kitchens and double glazing to conservatories (see Figure 8.5 on the previous page). This type of selling offers the convenience and comfort of shopping from home. Avon representatives leave samples and a brochure for the customers to choose from and then collect their order later on. The goods are then delivered to the customer by the representative.

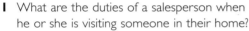

A C T I V I T Y

There has been some negative publicity in the media recently concerning direct selling, particularly in relation to kitchen and double glazing sales techniques.

1 What are the duties of a salesperson when he or she is visiting someone in their home?
2 As a customer how would you expect that salesperson to behave?
3 What services would you expect from him or her?

WHAT IS THE DIFFERENCE BETWEEN DIRECT AND INDIRECT SALES?

Direct sales go straight from the producer through to the consumer without passing through a retail outlet, for example:

Avon ⟶ consumer
Grattan ⟶ consumer

Indirect sales use a retailer to reach the end consumer,

Revlon ⟶ department store ⟶ consumer
manufacturer ⟶ Marks & Spencer ⟶ consumer

A C T I V I T Y

Go back through all the types of sales outlet we have described. Classify them so that you know which are direct and which are indirect.

RECORDING SALES

It is vital that businesses can track their sales and record them accurately so that they can see how well the business is performing. In small individual businesses you may often find that sales are recorded manually. For example, receipts may be written out by hand then used by the business to total up its sales.

It is much more usual these days, however, with the growing popularity of computers to use electronic methods of recording sales. The supermarkets are particularly advanced in this area. The till receipt in Figure 8.6 below not only tells the customer the unit price, for example price per pound weight, and overall price of each item, it also alerts them to the current promotional offer. For Sainsbury's benefit the receipt gives the time of the sale, how many separate items were bought and the debit-card number used for paying for the goods. Large supermarkets use laser scanners to read the bar codes from the products that automatically register on the till roll at the appropriate price. Having this up-to-date information helps supermarkets. If they

```
   J SAINSBURY PLC
   SAINSBURY WAY
      HESSLE
     HU13 9NS
 TELEPHONE NO. 0482 562185

                          £
    PINEAPPLES LARGE    0.95
    JS SKIMMED MILK     0.25
 PLUMS
 0.55 lb @   £0.69/lb   0.38
    DEVON CUSTARD       0.52
 JS ROCHA PEARS
 1.00 lb @   £0.54/lb   0.54
 WTE SDLSS GRAPES
 1.40 lb @   £1.29/lb   1.81
 SATSUMAS
 1.94 lb @   £0.45/lb   0.87
    ROQUETTE            0.65
    BASIL               0.59
 FLAME SDLS GRAPE
 1.35 lb @   £1.89/lb   2.55
 FRESH FIGS
       6 @   £0.19      1.14

   16 BAL DUE          10.25

 EFT                   10.25
    4903 404787 31354205
 CHANGE                 0.00

 825 04  40 1983 15:00 25OCT93

   KEEP RECEIPTS
    OVER £5 FOR
  BA FLIGHT OFFER
```

FIG. 8.6 EXAMPLE OF A TILL RECEIPT

189

know how products are selling hour by hour, they can monitor their own stock levels closely and order in from suppliers at the last possible minute. The information will also help supermarkets to forecast future sales as it enables them to track which products are selling well.

MAINTAINING SALES

Businesses are now becoming very sophisticated and complex. They compete with each other to attract customers and often use self-service or open displays to highlight their wares. This inevitably leads to some security problems. One of the major problems in retailing is that of 'shrinkage'. This means the unnecessary loss of money due to several different problems. It may mean customers and/or staff are stealing from the business, or it could be the result of a shop assistant putting a small item into a very large plastic bag when a smaller one would have done. No matter what the cause, they both result in losses that could have been avoided.

Businesses work hard to avoid having too much shrinkage. Schemes to improve the situation can involve staff training and awareness. In addition many stores now have diverse security systems. They may have very obvious, uniformed security guards as well as discreet store detectives. They may well use security mirrors and cameras. Their merchandise might also carry security tags that have to be removed on purchase so it cannot be smuggled out by shoplifters.

ACTIVITY

Go to a large local store. Note down all of the security methods you can see. You may find it advisable to seek permission from the store before carrying out your survey.

SELLING AND THE CUSTOMER

No matter what type of business structure a company uses, it will share a common aim with other businesses: it wants to satisfy its customers and by doing so hopes to make a profit. Most retail outlets, therefore, share some common goals and use similar selling techniques to keep their customers happy. This section looks in some detail at the selling process in retail outlets.

WHAT ARE THE KEY STAGES IN SELLING SUCCESSFULLY?

Identifying customers

To sell successfully, a business has to demonstrate that it has more to offer to its customers than its competitors have. It is fairly evident that different types of customer exist in any market and these customers can easily be identified or categorised by certain characteristics. These could be age, gender, lifestyle, occupation and so on (see Chapter 3 'Consumers and customers' pp.57–60

for more detail). All of these different target groups will have different needs.

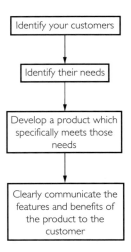

FIG. 8.7 KEY STAGES IN SUCCESSFUL SELLING

Many people have a need to have status or prestige conferred on them by acquiring material wealth, For example, an owner of a Rolls Royce might feel the car is prestigious and therefore gives status to its owner.

If you were shopping in a department store what products would you buy as status symbols for the following customers?

- an 18-year-old student
- a senior citizen
- a 54-year-old bank manager
- an 11-year-old child
- a mother of school-age children

A C T I V I T Y

Many of the items you may have listed above may have been luxury items and not necessities. Is it ethical for stores to persuade people to buy such items?

A C T I V I T Y

If you asked the target groups above what their needs were in terms of entertainment, what answers would they give?

Finding out about customers' needs

It is those outlets that can find out exactly what their customers want and then produce the product the customers require who are most likely to succeed.

How can you find out about customers' needs?

Carry out market research – ask people questions in a survey.

Analyse the outlet's sales figures. Which products look likely to sell well in the future?

Question existing customers – send questionnaires out with account statements.

Listen to customer complaints!

Buy in general research information on retail and buying trends from market-research agencies.

Developing a product and communicating features and benefits

Having gathered the information, it has to be analysed and recommendations made. This should result in an appropriate product being developed. The outlet then has to communicate to the customers why they should buy its product rather than anyone else's. This is often done by promoting features and benefits. This means you not only tell the customer what features a product has, but also what benefits those features will have for the customer. Look at the table below for an example. It shows the features and benefits of a microwave/combination oven.

Feature	Benefit
800 Watts	Cooks more quickly: saves you time
Turntable	Convenient: food does not need stirring
Bell/buzzer	Can leave room and know when food is cooked
Fan-assisted oven	Offers versatility: can roast meat; makes food look more appetising
Easy wipe-clean surface	Ease of cleaning

TABLE 8.1 FEATURES AND BENEFITS OF A MICROWAVE/COMBINATION OVEN

A C T I V I T Y

List the features and benefits of the following products:

- VCR
- camcorder
- mountain bike
- hand-made shoes
- frozen convenience meal

OTHER FACTORS

There are certain other factors that customers may check before purchasing a product, particularly if they are spending a large amount of money. Remember that features and benefits are not always tangible: quick delivery is an intangible benefit that many customers rate highly.

1 *The physical product* The customer will want to be reassured about the function of the product, i.e. that it

does what it says it does. For example, a vacuum cleaner should have sufficient suction to clean a carpet, a fridge should chill food at the right temperature and so on.

2 *Performance* Depending on the price paid, the customer will be looking for a certain level of performance from the product. If, for example, the customer is buying a car he or she would probably expect basic performance from a small, standard model costing less than £6000, and superior performance from a deluxe version of the same car at £12 000 which has a better engine, design and styling and more optional extras.

3 *Quality* Many consumers are particularly looking for quality in a product. The price of the product when linked to its performance gives an indication of the quality and an idea of whether the customer has received value for money. Many retailers and manufacturers try to make their sales to customers on the basis that they offer superior quality to their competitors.

A C T I V I T Y

Review one night's advertisements on TV. How many of the ads suggested their product offered superior quality? Why do you think this idea is so popular?

4 *Appearance* Style and appearance are critical factors in some businesses like fashion and the music industry. Certain customer groupings, like 16–24-year-olds, are much more conscious of appearance than others and a product's style could be a key reason for this group to decide on purchase or non-purchase. The average British consumer has become more design conscious in the 1990s. The major concern here is to recognise which groups respond to what type of product appearance, and to match the two.

5 *Packaging* Packaging has many functions. It can protect the product, add convenience (for example carry-handles on nappy packs), and it can help promote and sell the product, especially if it is sold by self-service.

It is important to develop appropriate packaging for a product. Perfume packaging tends to be innovative, high quality and expensive. As such it is part of the product offering. For some products, excess packaging is seen as wasteful and the consumer may react badly to it. Packaging can even offer an improved product or benefit to the consumer, for example tamper-proof baby-food jars (greater safety) and nitrogen-release beer cans (draught beer).

6 *Reliability* A customer will only be persuaded to buy an unreliable brand or product once. They will not buy the brand again if the product proves unreliable. However, if, for example, a customer has had a reliable Morphy

Richards iron for many years, and is looking for a new kettle, he or she may buy a Morphy Richards again, on the basis that the brand is reliable.

7 *After-sales service/delivery* The sale does not end when the customer hands over his or her money. Many other factors, such as after-sales service and prompt delivery, are part of the offering. Until a recent court case in the USA, Domino's Pizza guaranteed to deliver your pizza within 30 minutes or refund you money. This was a good selling point but it had to be withdrawn in the US because of a road accident involving a Domino home delivery.

Making the sales offer unique

Every retail outlet will want to stand out from the rest, particularly from its own direct competitors. Each will therefore try to make its sales offering unique. This individuality could come from its product range, its pricing strategy, its after-sales service or a combination of all these factors. You can sometimes get an idea of how the retail outlet sees its own unique position by examining its advertising slogan.

A C T I V I T Y

Can you identify the following slogans? Which retailers do they describe? What message do you think the retailer is trying to portray to the customer?

1 'You can't get better than a _____ fitter.'
2 'Good food costs less at _____.'
3 'Miles nearer, smiles better.'
4 'Never knowingly undersold.'

PERSONAL SELLING IN RETAIL SITUATIONS

Most sales assistants are active in trying to help and inform customers, and also in persuading them to buy from their shop. The better trained and motivated the salesperson, the more likely they are to convert an interested browser into a purchaser. There are several recognised techniques and procedures used in personal selling.

Key steps
OPENING TECHNIQUES

- listen to the customer
- establish a rapport
- find out what they want
- use questioning to check needs

- arouse buyer's interest by highlighting proposed benefits

CONTINUE INTERVIEW

- detail features and benefits
- match customer needs to appropriate products and benefits

OVERCOME OBJECTIONS

- establish true reason for objection
- is it real or false?
- reassure customer if uncertain
- check objection not a buying signal, that is, that the customer wants to buy, but the product does not fulfil every requirement

CLOSE THE SALE

- listen and choose sales technique

Overcoming objections

Objections are not always negative: the buyer may have decided to purchase, but be a little worried about one or two points. For example, someone buying a new camera might object that it is rather complicated when all they may be worried about is their ability to focus!

Objections should never be ignored. They can be categorised as follows:

FUNDAMENTAL OBJECTIONS

Here the buyer sees absolutely no need for the product and has to be convinced that he or she has a need for it. The salesperson needs to sell the advantages of having that product tactfully, without letting the buyer lose face. There must be some form of benefit demonstrated to the buyer; if the buyer's objection is valid then it is better for the salesperson to stop.

STANDARD OBJECTIONS

These are much more common. Table 8.2 shows a list of standard objections and ways they might be overcome.

Closing the sale

If the salesperson has successfully overcome the purchaser's objections, he or she is then in a position to close the sale. There are several ways of doing this. The salesperson should always be alert for buying signals, for example 'Do you have this in another colour?' or 'Are you able to deliver?', as these often act as indications of an imminent close of sale.

TABLE 8.2 OVERCOMING STANDARD OBJECTIONS

TYPE OF OBJECTION	WAYS TO OVERCOME OBJECTION
Feature objection – 'but it doesn't have a widget.'	Make sure you have correctly identified the buyer's needs; reconfirm the benefits clearly.
Lack of knowledge objection – 'I don't think this is suitable.'	Demonstrate that the objection is not real: explain the benefits clearly; clear up the buyer's lack of knowledge.
Delay objection – 'I'll have to ask my partner.'	Make sure this is a real rather than hidden objection (see below); explain benefits to convince buyer; vary offer to clinch sale now, e.g. include extra benefits.
Hidden objection	Need to find true objection. Use open question or half-finished ones, e.g. 'If you like the product and the price is not a problem, you can't commit to buying now because ...?' The buyer then may well provide the true objection.
Loyalty objection – 'I've bought this brand for five years and don't want to change.'	Never criticise the competing brand. Show your benefits over the competition. Invite the purchaser to try. Tact is needed.
Price objection – 'It's way out of my league.'	Focus on value for money. Point out benefits against cost – is it effective in the long term? Break down cost into small terms, e.g. the moisturiser works out at just 25p a day for rejuvenated skin.

A C T I V I T Y

In class take turns to participate in a retail simulation exercise. In pairs try out the roles of salesperson and customer. Devise and agree on a list of products you will be involved in selling and buying. The salesperson needs to be able to overcome objections.

The class should observe and write brief summaries of each performance.

Very often open questions, where a customer is not able to answer simply 'yes' or 'no', are used during the closing period to move the customer towards purchase.

Type of close	Example
Trial close	'If I can demonstrate to you that this dishwasher will save you money and effort, would you be interested?'
Alternative close	'Would you like the hairdryer with or without a diffuser?'
Direct question	'Is there anything else I can help you decide?'
Summarise benefits	'So we can see this washing powder is cheaper, less harmful to the environment and easier to handle.'
Confirming details	'So it's the 14" TV to be delivered Tuesday, paying by interest-free credit?'
Value-for-money statement	'This furniture represents the best value for money on the market, which I'm sure you're interested in.'

TABLE 8.3 CLOSING THE SALE

WHAT HAPPENS AFTER THE SALE?

AFTER-SALES ACTIVITIES

If a business is to grow and prosper it needs a steady supply of customers, and most businesses hope their customers will be loyal and come back to buy from the business again and again. In order to keep their customers satisfied, most businesses try to maintain a good level of customer service. This means that they do not forget about the customer once the sale has been made, but have a structured programme that will help them look after the customer in every way. This is called after-sales service. Table 8.4 outlines some typical after-sales activities.

A C T I V I T Y

You are the supervisor of a local car-repair garage. What do you think will be the main areas you will need to cover to provide good after-sales service?

Why is after-sales service so important?

Looking after a customer's total requirements shows a responsible and caring attitude from a business. It does, after all, hope that the customer will become loyal to it. A reputation for good customer service can enhance a business's reputation, for example Marks & Spencer, or just as easily destroy it.

A C T I V I T Y

Draw up comparative lists of businesses who have either good or bad reputations for customer service. What advice would you give to those with poor reputations to help them improve their after-sales service?

COMPLAINTS

How should complaints be handled?

Despite all of the best efforts listed above, it is inevitable that customers will need to complain from time to time and some complaints will come to light from a few of the after-sales activities above.

In dealing with complaints there are two key factors to consider:

1 The business should have an official procedure to follow in the case of complaints. This avoids confusion, lays down a clear path forward, makes sure everyone knows what to do and is the simplest way to arrive at an appropriate solution to the problem.
2 There should be a timescale attached to the solution of the problem. If a complaint is allowed to drag on and or

ACTIVITY	TYPE OF COMPANY THAT USES IT	CUSTOMER BENEFIT
A follow-up call to the customer who has bought the product.	Business-to-business companies, e.g. office supplies company selling to another business.	The customer gets reassurance. A good link is established between the supplier and the customer; this can iron out teething problems with the product. Enhances the supplier company's quality and image.
Guarantees.	Manufacturers of electrical products, etc.	The customer has contact if the product fails. Reassurance of quality builds customer confidence. Retailers can offer extended guarantees. With a guarantee-registration system, the customer can receive details of offers, etc. from the company if the company has a database of customer names and addresses from guarantee cards.
Servicing agreements.	Gas/electrical.	For a fee a business may agree to service your product, e.g. central-heating system, every year. The customer is persuaded by the reliability of the service so that he or she can avoid future problems developing.
Information and advice service.	Financial institutions, retailers, manufacturers, software houses.	Many manufacturers have customer-service departments who will advise on how to get the best from a product. This gives customers help and reassurance. Many software houses (who develop computer systems for other businesses) have helplines for any client who has a problem with the system and who needs instant advice on it.

TABLE 8.4 TYPICAL AFTER-SALES ACTIVITIES

this can be a waste of time and effort and result in great consumer dissatisfaction. Many businesses have a policy of responding to complaints within a certain number of hours or days. For example some phone companies guarantee to mend faults within 48 hours.

How to complain

As a customer the method you use to complain will very much depend on the severity and nature of your complaint.

LETTER

Customers can formally lay down their grievances in a letter. This is a useful way to complain as it is an official record of the complaint (the customer must always retain a copy of the letter). The letter needs to be addressed and copies sent to the appropriate personnel.

A letter is sometimes used for a serious complaint that may take some time to investigate. On the other hand, a letter containing a simple complaint can often result in a quick response! The letter must be brief, polite and include your preferred resolution to the complaint.

TELEPHONE

A telephone call is very quick and direct, but it is unlikely that you will receive an instant solution to your problem. The complaint may need further investigation or the person you need to speak to may not be available.

A telephone call could form one step in a complaints procedure. Write down the main thrust of the conversation and **always ask for the name of the person you are speaking to** in case you call again.

FACE-TO-FACE

A face-to-face conversation can be very effective as long as the complaint is not delivered or handled in a confrontational manner. It is a useful method if you have a faulty product with you and can actually show the nature of the complaint to the salesperson. This type of complaint is very often handled by customer-service desks these days.

A C T I V I T Y

You have bought a personal stereo that persistently breaks down. How would you complain about it using the steps listed above?

MAKING SURE YOUR COMPLAINT IS LISTENED TO

There are several steps involved in making sure your complaint is listened to and dealt with promptly to your satisfaction. Take the product (or refer the service) to the retailer who sold it to you. If the goods are under guarantee you can also contact the manufacturer, but the retailer is the best first port-of-call, as your contract is with them.

Step 1 Make sure you have all the information you need and that it is correct. Do not worry if this means writing conversations down to remember them. Make your complaint promptly!

Step 2 Take the product back, if possible with evidence of purchase (your receipt). Do not hand this over.

Step 3 Explain the nature of your complaint politely and calmly to the manager or owner or the appropriate customer-services personnel.

Step 4 State your case clearly, pointing out that you would like a repair, refund or whatever your required solution is (provided it is your legal entitlement).

Step 5 If you leave faulty goods with the retailer, make sure you get another receipt for them.

Step 6 Be persistent and firm.

If you still receive no satisfactory solution, your next step would be to seek help from either the Citizens Advice Bureau or Trading Standards Office.

A C T I V I T Y

You are the customer services manager for a large, well-known chain store. Draw up a procedure for staff to follow when handling complaints.

MANAGING SALES AREAS

MAKE THE MOST OF THE AREA

Having looked at after-sales service, it is worth while examining what shops do to look after customers while they are in the process of buying.

As business becomes more and more competitive it is vital that shops make the most of their sales areas in order to attract customers. There are some key factors that all retailers must consider before they decide on the layout of their shops. They are:

1 How to make the best use of counters, shelving or display areas to attract customers and make sales.

2 How to ensure that displays are safe and that the customer is shopping in a safe environment.

3 How to minimise any losses in the shop and ensure that the display is secure.

Many retailers will have a plan to overcome any problems and to get the best results from their sales area. They will want to review the sales area from three different perspectives: business, presentation and legal.

Business checks

All businesses will want to know how each area is performing, i.e. how many sales are being made. If the organisation is a supermarket it can find this out fairly easily via the till laser-scanning equipment that reads barcodes. Information from the tills will be fed into a central computer that registers all of this information and calculates a total sales figure. The computer will then automatically re-order stock when it realises that current stock levels have fallen below a certain level.

This system works best in supermarkets. If, however, the business is a department store, then the system may well be very different! All department stores not only sell own-brand goods, for example House of Fraser knitwear, they also sell products from other manufacturers, for example Clinique make-up. Each House of Fraser store will want to record all sales for its own records, but sales assistants may also be required to send sales records back to the manufacturers. In this case, stock levels may simply be monitored by counting stock manually. The normal system for this would be to record all deliveries, add them to existing stock levels and then deduct sales for the period concerned. Table 8.5 illustrates this method.

EXISTING STOCK 30/11/93	DELIVERIES IN DECEMBER	TOTAL STOCK	SALES IN DECEMBER	STOCK 31/12/93
54	30	84	21	63

TABLE 8.5 STOCKS OF WATCHES

Sales paperwork is often completed on both a daily and weekly basis and can be very important when sales consultants/assistants are working on a commission basis.

Stores will also have periodic stock checks/counts (perhaps every three or six months) to check the stock levels in the company.

The form in Figure 8.8 is a typical piece of paperwork that a sales consultant might have to fill in. The form reports back on sales and will also help to monitor stock levels. It is fairly detailed.

1 What are the pros and cons of having to fill in this type of paperwork? Could you suggest a computerised system that might help to solve the problems.
2 How might the form be redesigned to make the task easier?

Presentation checks

All sales areas need to be checked frequently to make sure the merchandise is displayed to its best effect. The sales assistants should be responsible for maintenance of a sales area and managers will also oversee checks. Depending on the type of organisation checks will be made on a daily/weekly basis.

FIG. 8.8

CRYSTAL FASHIONS — Daily Sales Report

Brand _____ Store _____ Town _____ Consultant _____ Date _____

Customer Number	gold p.e.	gold c.e.	colour p.e.	colour c.e.	stone p.e.	stone c.e.	pearl p.e.	pearl c.e.	gold necks	gold bracelets/ bangles	gold pins	colour classic	stone classic	pearl classic	rhodium classic	total classic	total fashion	sale stock	Monet 2	grand total	non CFL sales
1																					
2																					
3																					
4																					
5																					
6																					
7																					
8																					
9																					
10																					
11																					
12																					
13																					
14																					
15																					
16																					
17																					
TOTAL																					

Daily Target	Weekly Target	No. Of New Customers On File	Products Out Of Stock	Sleeping Beauties
£	£			

MD/T 02 94

A C T I V I T Y

Visit your nearest department store and look at all of the perfume and jewellery counters.

1 What methods and equipment do they use to display their products effectively?
2 Which counter works best in your opinion? Why?

A C T I V I T Y

On a different visit to either a department store or multiple chain, draw out a plan of where groups of products are displayed and describe the techniques used to display them effectively.

Consider stands, posters, signage and so on. How do you think the management decide on where to position merchandise?

You will probably need to ask permission from the store before you attempt to draw the plan.

A C T I V I T Y

Your company supplies high-quality costume jewellery to department stores. The jewellery is on display in cabinets and on stands. Draw up a set of instructions to your sales consultants, advising them how best to display the products and of any free gifts they may be promoting.

A C T I V I T Y

Clothes are very difficult to display to their best effect. On a shopping visit to the high street select the store you think displays its merchandise best. Give reasons for your choice.

Shops have a difficult balance to find. They need to allow customers to sample and view the products, but are at risk of losing merchandise to pilfering if they are too lax in their presentation. High-value items (particularly if they are small and easy to hide) are often kept in locked cabinets; other items may be electronically tagged to prevent shoplifting.

Legal checks

All businesses have obligations towards the customer in terms of safety as well as towards their own staff. All retail outlets should make frequent safety checks in their stores to make sure there are no hazards. Obvious dangers need to be looked out for, like stacking products too high, not wiping up spillages, and leaving stock and boxes in the aisles where people could fall over them.

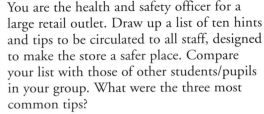

A C T I V I T Y

You are the health and safety officer for a large retail outlet. Draw up a list of ten hints and tips to be circulated to all staff, designed to make the store a safer place. Compare your list with those of other students/pupils in your group. What were the three most common tips?

A C T I V I T Y

On your next visit to a supermarket identify the danger areas for customers. Were there any visible signs that the supermarket was aware of potential problems?

LEGAL AND ETHICAL CONSTRAINTS ON BUSINESSES

All retailers have duties to operate in an ethical and responsible way when serving customers. Some of these duties are laid down by law, others are voluntarily followed.

Code of practice

This tends to be an agreement on standards of behaviour and actions to be followed. A code of practice is an agreement between businesses in the same industry. It offers consumers a reassurance that a business will operate according to the code. It is a voluntary agreement.

Trade associations

These are formed by individual businesses coming together and agreeing to work together as a trade association. For example, SEAMA is the Small Electrical Appliance Manufacturers Association and a company like Moulinex would be a member. These associations often form their own code of practice that members have to adhere to. For example, ABTA (Association of British Travel Agents) members have a common code for dealing with customer grievances.

Draw up a code of practice for businesses selling double glazing. How would it change the way the companies do business? Design an A5 sized leaflet to include your code, making sure it is attractive and easy to read.

The Trading Standards Department

The Trading Standards Department enforces criminal consumer law on behalf of local authorities. Its consumer protection or consumer services departments (previously known as weights and measures) are active in enforcing the law. They deal with areas such as food labelling, weights and measures, and trades descriptions. For example, sausages labelled 50 per cent beef must

FIG. 8.9 EXTRACT FROM A CODE OF PRACTICE

contain 50 per cent beef, a pint of beer must not be less than a pint and a waterproof coat should not let the rain in! The correct labelling of goods is a key area to monitor. Even major reputable firms sometimes get it wrong.

ACTIVITY

You are the public relations officer for Comet following the case below. Write a press release that indicates your future company policy on labelling. Then design a 10-point guide to give to all store managers to ensure their prices are displayed correctly

National legislation

As well as the local authority checks, there is also national legislation that companies have to be aware of. Two of the most important laws are outlined below.

SALE OF GOODS ACT 1979

This covers contracts for the sale of goods. It helps to clarify the buyer's and seller's rights under the contract. There are three rules:

1 The goods must be of 'merchantable quality', i.e. they must be fit for their normal intended purpose. For example, a new pair of tights should not have a hole in them.
2 The goods must be fit for any particular purpose made known. For example, if you told the seller you were buying boots to hike in and he or she sold you lightweight fashion boots, assuring you they would do the job, the seller would have contravened the law.
3 Goods must be as described, for example jewellery that is described as solid gold should not be gold plated.

Daily Mail Reporter

The truth about the amazing sale at Comet was revealed yesterday.

Some goods at three of the electrical giant's branches were dearer than usual, a court heard.

Nearly half of 97 items labelled as sale goods were incorrectly priced. Among them were:

A 'clearance special' microwave labelled £299.98, which was on offer at £50 more;

A jug kettle billed as 'Special price! Hurry while stocks last' which was £2.01 more, and a £699.98 electric cooker in the 'clearance' section which was reduced by just one penny.

Complaints

The firm was fined £11,000 by Swansea magistrates after admitting ten charges of giving misleading prices and one of displaying a false notice.

Assistant county consumer protection officer Bob Egan told the court: 'It is an horrific case.

'This is either a deliberate attempt to deceive gullible consumers, or gross negligence or incompetence from the top of the company down.'

The case followed investigations by consumer protection offcers at the three stores in Swansea last January after complaints from two membiers of the public. Mr Leslie Slade, for the company, said: 'We

£11,000 fine on store where sale 'bargains' cost more than before

give no mitigation. We'd like to apologise to our customers.'

After the case trading standards officers urged the public to be extra vigilant for misleading prices in other stores during the January sales.

Mr Egan urged: 'They should compare the actual selling price, not the one which the sales card says the item has been reduced from – that could be misleading.

'Shoppers shouldn't be conned by what seems a massive saving. They might get the item for £20 less next door.'

Customers should also check the model number on the item in case it is old stock.

'Quite often we find, particularly with electrical goods, which people don't know much about, that last year's models are being sold as new. Shoppers should check to make sure the super washing machine they've seen advertised is actually the same model as the one in the sale.'

Mr Egan, a consumer protection officer for 18 years, said the offences were among the worst he had seen.

Noel Dardis, communications director for Comet, which has 302 branches and showed profits of £17.9million for 1989–90 said: 'It was an isolated incident and a mistake.

'We are trying to be consumer friendly. We want to be honest with people and get them to come back to our shops. We don't want to con them.

'We have changed our sale price notices to try to avoid any more mistakes.'

FIG. 8.10.

SOURCE: DAILY MAIL SEPTEMBER 90–JUNE 9

The Act helps to clarify the rights and duties of both buyer and seller. If the seller has broken the law, the Act lays down the remedies available to the buyer, for example what the buyer is entitled to claim against the seller.

WEIGHTS AND MEASURES ACT 1963 AND 1979

This is concerned with the provision of food and is enforced by the Trading Standards Office. If a retailer breaks these laws he or she can be prosecuted. The types of law are as follows:

1 It is an offence to sell short weights of food, for example selling 90 grams instead of 100 grams.
2 If the food is pre-packed in tens, it is an offence to sell only nine per pack.
3 All packs should be marked with weights and ingredients.
4 Meat, fish, cheese and sausages should have the weight written on the packs or verbally communicated to the buyer before the purchase is made.

The Trading Standards Department has the power to seize goods if, for example, they are faulty or dangerous, as in the case of toys with spikes.

BUSINESS AND THE MEDIA

WHO ARE THE MEDIA?

Businesses often have to use other businesses to help them promote their goods and services to the customer. These 'helpers' could be advertising agencies, TV companies and public relations agencies amongst many others. They are all usually specialists who can provide skills that the original company does not always have. The media are often quoted as being very important in helping companies to promote.

The phrase 'the media' (the plural of 'medium') covers all of those publications or channels that allow a business to communicate with a mass audience. The media are normally classified as print media, electronic information, outdoor advertising, broadcast media and film media.

A C T I V I T Y

Fill in the table here with examples of each type of media.

MEDIUM	TYPE	EXAMPLE
Print	National newspapers	
	Local newspapers	
	Magazines	
	Journals	
	Directories	
Electronic information	Database publishing	
	TV databases	
Outdoor advertising	Billboards/posters	
	Adshels (advertising displays for posters at bus stops)	
	Buses/tubes	
	vans/taxis	
Broadcast media	Television	
	Radio	
Film	Cinemas	

Which media would you use to communicate the following messages? Give your reasons why.

1 You are a manufacturer anxious to recall some faulty electric kettles.

2 You are a candidate canvassing for votes in a general election.

3 You are a high-street bank launching a new telephone banking service.

4 You are a touring theatre group announcing a set of forthcoming dates.

5 You are a small, regional furniture store announcing a sale at your showroom.

WHY DO BUSINESSES USE THE MEDIA?

As we have already stated, the media allow companies access to a wide audience. Therefore, if a business has any important news, it is likely to use the media to get its message across. The main reasons for using the media are:

1 To make the public aware of a product or service.

2 To make the public aware of or to change the image of a company.

3 To stimulate demand for a product, leading to increased sales and profit.

4 To launch a new product.

5 To recruit staff.

At any one time there will be hundreds of businesses all using the mass media, all jostling for the public's attention. How can they ensure that theirs is the message that is picked up?

Common messages

There are some common messages that businesses will want to communicate to an audience. Most businesses will focus on one particular aspect of the business and try to make the public aware of why they excel at this.

BRANDING

Many businesses concentrate on promoting their brand to consumers with the idea that their brand, with its particular name, design and qualities, says something unique to a consumer, that other brands don't (see p.209).

Try these simple recall and recognition tests.

1 *Recall test*

Get into groups of three and see how many advertisements you can remember from your TV viewing yesterday evening. Which messages did you clearly receive? Were they advertisements you liked? Why do you think they worked?

2 *Recognition test*

Write down brief details of the advertisements you see on TV one evening. In class, in groups of three and, using your list, ask the other members of the group if they have seen the advertisements, once you have prompted them with the name of the product.

How much can they remember? Have they remembered correctly? Why do you think they have remembered certain advertisements?

What do the following brands suggest to you? Why have you drawn those conclusions?

- Sainsbury's
- Heinz
- Levi's
- Virgin
- Nintendo
- St Michael
- Nike
- Chanel

DESIGN

The design of a particular product or its packaging can often be an area businesses want to highlight, in the belief that their design is better than the competition's.

A C T I V I T Y

The following advertising slogans come from advertisements that emphasise a product's design. How many brand names can you put to the advertising slogans?

1 '_____, the appliance of science.'
2 'The ultimate driving machine.'
3 'If anyone can, _____ can.'
4 'Handbuilt by robots.'

QUALITY

As business gets more and more competitive, businesses have to give consumers reasons why they should buy their particular product. A recent emphasis has been on quality. Companies are keen to state that their product is more reliable, dependable and durable, better designed and so on.

A C T I V I T Y

How many promotional campaigns can you think of that emphasise quality? Which message about quality works best in your opinion? In a group discussion give reasons for your selection.

CUSTOMER SERVICE

As goods and services become more similar, it is very often only the level of customer service provided that makes one business stand out from another. For example, the new competing multiplex cinemas tend to show similar films and charge similar prices. They will win customers from each other by offering good customer service: polite and helpful staff, good transport and parking facilities, a telephone advance-booking service, and a good supply of food and drink.

A C T I V I T Y

Can you decide on the most important customer service elements the following businesses could provide?

- a boarding kennels/cattery
- a motor repair garage
- a department store
- the housing section of a local authority

Recruitment

Many businesses use the media to advertise when they are recruiting staff. Advertisements can be very expensive and it is important that the right form of media is used to attract the right candidate. Some media specialise in certain types of recruitment or focus on different types of jobs on different days. For example, *The Guardian* often has special features on public-sector and creative and media appointments. Local newspaper advertisements may be appropriate for regional companies. Specialist journals, for example *Computing* or *Marketing Week*, focus on jobs in their own particular industries.

CAN THE MEDIA INFLUENCE BUSINESS?

Although businesses usually pay to use the media to promote and advertise their products, it is not only a one-way system of communication. The media can often influence businesses and they therefore have an interdependent relationship with each other. Newspapers (particularly the broadsheets like *The Independent* or *The Times*) often write about businesses; TV channels and radio stations make documentaries about businesses or report on them in the news.

A C T I V I T Y

Many people now get their business news from the TV. How many TV programmes can you name that specifically relate to businesses and their customers? You may need a TV listings guide to help you to compile your list.

What form does media influence take?

Consumers tend to see TV channels and newspapers as having authority and being believable. They tend to be less cynical about information supplied by the media than they would be about straightforward advertising by a company. The media have large numbers of viewers and readers. A very negative or positive report from them can often have sweeping effects on consumer demand for or acceptance of a product.

ACTIVITY

Review the job advertisements below.

1 Which newspaper do you think the jobs should be advertised in?

2 Are the job descriptions clear and detailed enough to secure the right types of candidate in your opinion?

INFORMATION AND THE MEDIA

The media do an excellent job in providing clear and extensive news to the public. They can provide information in an interesting and entertaining way, for example in women's magazines. They also supply more detailed information in review programmes and documentaries. In doing this, they can very often influence public opinion. By making people aware of a story they are having an effect on the story. It is vital, therefore, that the media are either neutral and present

---

WILLIAMS plc
Information Systems Manager

Leeds   To £30,000 plus car and benefits

This highly successful and rapidly expanding company which has gained a high market profile and position by its quality service is continuing to enhance that service by the introduction of a new computer system into its 100-plus store network.

To manage the company's IS requirement and to ensure the effective implementation of the system chosen, the Company requires to recruit a highly skilled IS Manager. Candidates will probably be graduates with a computer science or related degree who can demonstrate a successful track record in implementing large systems preferably in a distribution/wholesale/retail environment. Experience of a high volume of transactions and multi-site operation would be an advantage.

They will be self-starters who can work with the minimum direction and who are capable of contributing to the overall success of the business. Applicants will be expected to take a hands-on role and yet be capable of defining the IT strategy. They will be fully conversant with the hardware and software systems in the market place for their relative merits.

The succesful applicant will display drive and initiative and have excellent presentation and interpersonal skills. This is a key appointment within the company and offers excellent career enhancement prospects.

If you believe it provides the challenge you are looking for then please write enclosing a copy of your CV to:

The Personnel Manager
Williams plc
1 Smith Street
Leeds LS1 6TR

WILLIAMS plc

DEMONSTRATION FLEET SUPERVISOR

Godalming   **c£17,000**

We have an opportunity for an experienced transport professional to take responsibility for our demonstrator fleet of over 100 commercial vehicles. This includes the physical preparation and administration of the fleet; maintainance scheduling; planning and staging driver training; introduction tours for dealer and customer groups and assisting in PR events.

Candidates will need to be CPC holders and HGV1 licenced. The position demands some out of hours commitment, including weekends, and therefore candidates will need a high degree of flexibility and the ability to motivate others. Proven organisational and communication skills are essential together with good technical knowledge.

For an application form please telephone 0483 962731 between 9.00am and 5.00pm Monday to Friday.

SOUTH RIDING

Chief Executive

training & enterprise council

South Riding TEC, with an annual budget of £22m and a staff of 90, works to build partnerships between the private and public sector by facilitating education, training and business support in a diverse and challenging industrial and cultural environment.

• RESPONSIBILITY is to the non-executive Board for the management and direction of the TEC in its aim to play a significant role in the provision of training and support to business.

• THE NEED is for proven management talent at a senior level probably from the private sector, with excellent leadership and interpersonal skills, and an ability and willingness to adopt a high profile in the area.

South Riding TEC is an Equal Opportunities Employer and welcomes applications from all sections of the community.

Please write or fax requesting an application form quoting ref: 93277

High Profile Personnel
14-16 The High Street
South Riding SR1
Tel/Fax:: 07721 643882

FIG. 8.11

both sides of a story or, if they do represent one side, that they clearly state this!

A C T I V I T Y

The Sunday Times was influential in campaigning for justice for the victims of the thalidomide drug. Do you think it is right for a newspaper to be involved in such campaigns, or should they just stick to reporting the news?

A C T I V I T Y

Select the appropriate media (giving an example of a TV programme or the name of a newspaper) where you would look for information on the following:

- a manufacturer's goods
- competing (with the above) goods
- financial news and information
- economic news and information
- political news and forecasts

CONSUMER DEMAND

Media influence can have quite a dramatic effect on consumer demand. For example, when the BBC chose to re-run the *Thunderbirds* series, this stimulated consumer demand for new *Thunderbirds* products. And when Edwina Currie was interviewed on TV and stated that many British chickens were infected with salmonella, the consumption of eggs dropped rapidly. These examples give an indication of the power of the media.

There are certain key areas where businesses may take extra care to ensure that their operations are fair and are fairly represented in the media as shown in Table 8.6 below.

Having looked at the key players in the media and reviewed how they can help businesses, we now need to look more closely at promotion as a whole and its influence on sales.

TABLE 8.6 INFLUENCE OF MEDIA ON BUSINESS

KEY FACTOR	IF GIVEN POSITIVE MEDIA COVERAGE	IF GIVEN NEGATIVE MEDIA COVERAGE
Quality control	Reassures consumer.	Scares off consumer.
	Improves corporate image.	Tarnishes company image.
	Can stimulate demand.	Sales may fall.
	Encourages brand loyalty.	Encourages brand switching.
Price control	Gives fair image of company.	Can lead to accusations of profiteering.
	Can help value-for-money statement.	Consumer may feel 'ripped off'.
	Can stimulate demand if price cut communicated effectively.	
Promotion	Can help awareness, stimulate demand, enhance image.	Can lead to loss of reputation, sales and profit.
Health and safety	Can improve standard in companies.	Media can highlight shortcomings, damage business reputation.
Customer and employee care	Can improve standards, reassure public and employees.	Can damage reputation.
	Provides more customer and employee satisfaction.	Could make customers switch brands.
		Could result in high staff turnover or low morale.
	Could result in increased sales, profits or productivity.	Depresses sales, profits and productivity.

WHICH PROMOTIONAL ACTIVITIES CAN ACHIEVE SALES?

WHY DO BUSINESSES USE PROMOTIONAL ACTIVITY?

There are several reasons why businesses use promotional activity. If the business is advertising it may want to make the consumer aware of a good or service it is offering. It will be focusing on *communicating* with the consumer or customer so that the business will build up a favourable reputation and/or impression over time in the customer's mind. Advertising generally works best over a long period of time.

Sales promotions are much more likely to be short-term projects (sometimes called 'tactical' promotions). Their aim is usually to give a short-term boost to sales. They can encourage customers to buy more of a product, for example 'Buy two, get one free', or buy at different times, for example 'Cinema tickets cheaper before 6pm'.

A cautionary tale from the marketing department

Do you guzzle coupons? I gather that the practice of taking in competitors' coupons and redeeming them is known as guzzling – but be careful how you word your offer, in case it backfires.

Unfortunately, this happened to the Co-op, when the Yeovil Leo's decided to redeem anyone's vouchers. Using the newspaper ad shown here, the chain invited local shoppers to: "Bring along any money off coupons* issued by any foodstore in this area and we'll honour them here at Leo's. No catches. No conditions. Just every special offer in Yeovil under one roof." And the asterisk? Ah yes, the small print. "*Valid until further notice. Subject to the same conditions." Well, it ought to be clear. "It was intended to mean only redeemable as the terms stated on the coupon," a CRS spokesman told a colleague.

"However, the words 'No catches. No conditions' which applied to the redemption of other

food stores' coupons was misinterpreted by customers to mean that vouchers could be redeemed against any purchase.

"We decided to accept coupons in the interest of customer goodwill. The promotion certainly succeeded in attracting new customers."

And so it did. In a four-day blitz, bargain-hungry shoppers from as far afield as Newcastle-upon-Tyne and Scotland descended on the place in a spree.

Brothers Brian and Andy Ashton emerged from the store with shopping worth £8,000! The two builders drove 500 miles around the region collecting vouchers before arriving in two vans and settling at the checkout with a mountain of tokens.

Mother-of-two Beverley Waugh travelled from Gosport, near Southampton, and made four visits to the besieged store.

Packing the best part of a case of wine, a distinguished champagne and a 10 year-old-malt into the boot of her car, she said: "There were dozens of people at the checkouts waving their vouchers." She went home with £500 worth of shopping.

No-one knows the final cost: a guess of £100,000 has been hawked about.

FIG. 8.12
SOURCE:
THE GROCER,
22/2/92

Types of promotional activity

It is important to remember that there are many different ways of promoting a product and that, therefore, many different types of promotional technique are available. It is unlikely that any business will have unlimited funds to spend on promotions or to undertake lots of different types of promotion at the same time. The important thing from a business point of view is that you choose the appropriate type of promotion for your business, that it appeals to customers, that it achieves the goals it set out to and that it is put into action effectively. It is very easy to get promotions wrong (see the example in Figure 8.12 on the opposite page).

The most common types of promotion are:

- advertising
- point-of-sale advertising/display material
- press releases

Sales promotion techniques include:

- competitions
- banded offers – where two products are banded or taped together and sold together as a special offer
- free products
- 'money-off' offers
- free premiums
- samples
- personality promotions
- coupons
- trading stamps
- trial offers
- price discounts
- sponsorship

WHICH FACTORS AFFECT THE CHOICE OF PROMOTIONAL ACTIVITY?

Before creating any type of promotion there are several factors for a business to consider.

Audience targeting

The business must decide which type of customer it wants to reach before choosing a method of promotion. Very few businesses or organisations would want to speak to the whole population about their product. (An exception to this might be the different political parties when they are campaigning in a general election. Even then they are probably likely to concentrate their efforts

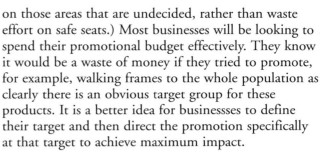

ACTIVITY

Visit your local high street and list the number of promotions you can see there.

1 Is any particular type of promotion popular?
2 Do the promotions you find in the high street differ very much to those you can find in your local supermarket?

on those areas that are undecided, rather than waste effort on safe seats.) Most businesses will be looking to spend their promotional budget effectively. They know it would be a waste of money if they tried to promote, for example, walking frames to the whole population as clearly there is an obvious target group for these products. It is a better idea for businessses to define their target and then direct the promotion specifically at that target to achieve maximum impact.

There are several different ways of identifying a target audience. It could be by:

- age
- gender
- occupation
- income
- geographical area
- ethnic/religious group
- lifestyle/taste

A NOTE ABOUT ETHNIC/RELIGIOUS GROUPS

Certain groups have distinct characteristics for which businesses may wish to cater. For example, cosmetic and toiletry companies sometimes produce special products for black hair and skin and certain religious groups have limitations on the types of food they may eat so food companies often produce different ranges of food to cater for these needs.

LIFESTYLE/TASTE

There are many ways to consider lifestyle. Examples of different lifestyles could cover students, people with a definite green lifestyle or the 1980s image of a 'yuppie'. A yuppie is a young, urban professional, said to have a high income that is spent freely on status-conscious items and brand names, such as Porsche and Gucci. Yuppies are young and live in the city. Many products are marketed as being suitable for this lifestyle, for example Filofaxes and portable phones. This lifestyle is now outdated but will undoubtedly be followed by other trends.

The important thing for any business wishing to sell to these various customers is to recognise that they are different, have different tastes and will spend their money in different ways. The business then needs to provide goods that satisfy the different needs of these different groups. If a company wanted to sell holidays to any of the above lifestyles it would provide a different type of holiday to satisfy each of the various needs. For example, it might sell a holiday backpacking around Europe to the student, a holiday in the countryside to the green consumer and a trip to the Far East to the yuppie.

SOCIO-ECONOMIC PROFILE

This is a way of classifying customers by their occupation and income.

Businesses assume that people in the same **occupation** earn similar amounts of money, but more importantly spend their money on similar products and have similar lifestyles. The standard classifications are:

A Higher managerial, administrative or professional, for example a solicitor.

B Intermediate managerial, administrative or professional, for example a middle manager.

C1 Supervisory or clerical, junior managerial, administrative or professional, for example a bank clerk.

C2 Skilled manual workers, for example a carpenter.

D Semi-skilled and unskilled manual workers, for example a labourer.

E Subsistence level, for example pensioners, widows, the unwaged.

Often higher incomes are earned in the A–C1 group, but this is not a hard and fast rule. There will be many self-employed skilled plumbers and electricians in the C2 group who, perhaps, earn more than the teachers in group B. The key factor is how the groups spend their money. Groups A and B often spend their money on forward-looking projects, for example savings plans, pensions, school fees and so on, whilst C1s, C2s and Ds might buy cars, hi-fis and TVs. Members of a family are put in the same group as the head of the household.

You can see that businesses can draw some general conclusions from socio-economic classifications. Senior managers found in group A will probably own their own homes, buy second cars and may have investments. Skilled tradespeople in C2 may buy new cars and have a high level of ownership in new home-entertainment products, such as satellite dishes, CD players and other consumer durables.

ACTIVITY

As a small travel agent in a market town you need to increase your holiday sales. The town is fairly prosperous with a large farming community in the surrounding area and a new science park estate that has attracted many high-tech firms (both consultancies and manufacturing outlets) into the area. You are aware there are many young adults and more mature families moving into the area.

1 What type of holidays would you try to sell to them and why?
2 How would you attract their attention?

It would help you to complete this task if you visited a local travel agent first and examined the current types of holiday available to different types of consumers. Better still, write to your local travel agent, requesting an interview to help you with your studies.

ACTIVITY

In a class discussion, examine the socio-economic classifications.

1 Do you think they are useful in business?
2 Are they relevant today?
3 Have you any criticisms of this system?

ACTIVITY

Devise your own way of classifying consumers that may be of help to business. Use visual material and a chart format to make your classification easy to understand. Present your findings to the rest of the class.

A C T I V I T Y

Socio-economic profiles are useful in business, but must be used carefully alongside other information. There is a danger of identifying people as 'stereotypes'. Write a paragraph explaining what a stereotype is and whether this term is relevant to businesses selling products to consumers.

One important link to occupation is the level of income people earn. This can be defined in several ways.

1 *Gross income* This is the level of income before any stoppages (i.e. tax and NI payments) are deducted from the salary or wage. This is the sum you will see advertised in the job section in newspapers. For example, 'Sales assistant required, salary £8000 p.a.' ('per annum' or per year).

2 *Net income/disposable income* This is sometimes also called 'disposable' income. It is the sum left after tax and NI has been deducted. Disposable income gives businesses an idea of how much potential customers have available to them to spend.

3 *Discretionary income* This is the level of income you have once you have paid for essentials out of your disposable income. Essentials are rent/mortgage, heating, lighting, food and so on. Your discretionary income will always be the lowest level of income and it is what is truly left over after your expenses have been covered. You can choose to spend your discretionary income on whatever you like. Remember that someone might have a large disposable income that is severely reduced by large mortgage and council tax payments. If the property is large then there may be large heating and lighting bills. It is often the discretionary income levels that businesses wish to find out so that they can persuade those customers with more discretionary income to buy their products.

See Chapter 3 'Consumers and customers' pp.57–60 for a further discussion of age, gender, geographical area, and lifestyle/taste.

BRANDING

Businesses are particularly keen for customers to buy from them again and again. This type of customer is known as 'brand loyal'. They become brand loyal for a number of reasons.

They have used the product already and are highly satisfied with its performance.

2 They see the brand name as being a guarantee of quality/satisfaction.
3 Their peer group (friends, neighbours and family) also use the product and recommend it.

A C T I V I T Y

How important are brand names to you? In groups draw up lists of brands you would not be prepared to substitute for a different make. For example, would you be prepared to swap your current pair of jeans for those with a different label? Give reasons why/why not.

WHO IS THE DECISION-MAKER?

It is quite clear that businesses need to clearly define the different types of customers so that they can produce products that meet those customers' needs. It is also very important that businesses identify exactly who within a household or family makes the decision about which product to buy. This won't necessarily be the same person who is paying for it! For example, in choosing a family holiday both parents and children might contribute to the decision, with the parents possibly having the final say. Identifying the true decision-maker is important as it means that businesses can direct their communications and advertising messages at him or her.

BUSINESS-TO-BUSINESS CUSTOMERS

Private individuals are not the only customers or consumers of a business's product or service. If you are a business selling to other businesses you need to be able to classify these businesses as well. This is done in different ways to consumer classification:

1 *Geographic* You could have export or home customers, or split home (domestic) customers up into regions, for example north, north-west, south-east and so on.
2 *Usage* Your customers may be heavy, medium or light users of your product. For example, if you sell office stationery you might feel a stationery retailer is a heavy user who orders frequently, a drawing office a medium user and a small manufacturing business a light user.
3 *Type of industry served* You may well sell the same product to different types of customer. China clay is a type of material used in paint, pottery and cosmetics! Each of these customers represents a different type of industry.
4 *Standard industrial classification* Government departments use this to classify industries. These classifications help if the government departments are compiling statistics.

ACTIVITY

Look at the advertisement below. What type of customer was the business trying to attract? Give reasons for your choice. Describe the socio-economic profile of the potential customer.

ACTIVITY

Read the newspaper article opposite.

1 Do you agree with it in general?
2 Should children be able to influence their parents?
3 Should advertisers take advantage of this fact?

Lose yourself in our private paradise.

DISCOVER the meaning *of* luxury. Sample *pure* indulgence. Experience nothing but *pleasure.* Imagine yourself on PRINCESS CAYS, our own PRIVATE ISLAND *hideaway* in the Bahamas.

Where blue, blue sea mixes with pure white sand giving you a cocktail of delight.

And palm fringed beaches lie before you, stretching out as far as the eye can see.

Then when it's time to come back down to earth, you'll find nothing but heaven back on board.

On a Princess Caribbean Cruise, there is so much more on offer.

Fine food, first class service, intimate bars, Broadway style shows.

Everything is laid on for you and nothing is too much trouble.

Then, when you go ashore, a whole host of exotic locations await your discovery.

Places that up until now, you've only

PRINCESS CRUISES
FIRST CHOICE *in the* CARIBBEAN

ever dreamt about, like Grand Cayman, Montego Bay or San Juan.

For £945 this all inclusive nine night journey to paradise can be yours.

You know where you can find us.

For further information and a copy of our 1994 Caribbean brochure, just see your local ABTA travel agent, or telephone us on 071-831 1881 (24 hours).

P&O

FIG. 8.13

Advertisers bank on parents falling prey to pester power

By Michael McCarthy

MARKETING and advertising industries are aiming campaigns at the "pester power" of children – their ability to persuade parents to buy particular products.

The development is attracting increasing interest, study and excitement in the marketing world and is thought to be worth hundreds of millions of pounds a year in potential sales. However, it is also attracting intense criticism.

"The wilful exploitation of children as commercial levers is positively obscene," Jackie Miller, deputy general secretary of the Professional Association of Teachers, said. "People should wake up to the fact that it is happening. It is time we put a stop to it." Instead of being given sound and caring values, children were being treated as "greed bags".

The 1990s version of pester power goes far beyond children's classic nagging and crying at the supermarket checkout. Young people, mar-

■ **The marketing wizards are enticing young voices to shout for their products, a ploy attracting praise and condemnation**

keters believe, are increasingly influential across the whole range of family shopping, including many goods that have no obvious connection to childhood, such as pet food, televisions, cars, stereo equipment, furniture and household cleaners.

The reasons lie in the changing nature of the family. More cases of both parents working, one-parent families and couples having fewer children are all thought to result in young people being given more possessions and more influence over family decisions.

Family relationships are being scrutinised to identify the points at which parents are likely to give in to children's requests. Last month, 150 of Britain's leading advertising and marketing professionals

packed a London seminar to hear a paper on "Family dynamics and the shopping experience" by Sally Ford-Hutchinson, planning director of the agency DMB & B. She talked at length of how pester power could be used, saying: "The power and influence of children can be harnessed by both manufacturers and retailers alike." There was thunderous applause.

Angela Humphries, a director of The Research Business, a market research consultancy, estimated that in total the commercial vales of pester power was likely to run into hundreds of millions of pounds annually.

"Children are starting to have a huge and increasing influence in ways people don't realise," she said. "They might come back from a

friend's house having seen a TV set with digital stereo, and say 'Why haven't we got one like that?' They might want their parents to buy environmentally friendly cleaners, or even furniture.

"The implication for marketers and manufacturers is that children are extremely important as persuaders, and can't be ignored."

Advertisements explicitly encouraging children to persuade their parents to buy things are unlikely, as both the Advertising Standards Authority and the Independent Television Commission forbid it in their codes of advertising practice.

The marketing approach is more subtle. Typical promotions directed at children, said Mrs Ford-Hutchinson, were the Kids' Club launched by the Burger King chain, and the school computer promotion being run by Tesco, which offers a voucher towards classroom computer equipment for every £25 of groceries bought.

Fig. 8.14
Source: The Times, 10/5/93

CONSUMER PROFILES

Often businesses will use a combination of consumer characteristics to identify their target audience. For example, a business marketing baby food might target women between the ages of 20 to 40 with children under two years old. Having defined the typical customers, the business might find that this group can be reached via magazines and breakfast and daytime TV. They may also discover that this type of consumer is particularly responsive to 'money-off' promotions and therefore provide coupons for this purpose either in magazines or pushed through letter boxes.

ACTIVITY

List all of the advertisements you can see on Channel 4 on Friday evening. Compare them to the ads you can see on ITV on the same evening.

1 What are the different products advertised?
2 Who do you think these are targeted at?
3 Why should Channel 4 and ITV attract different target audiences?

Although items such as confectionery can be classified as a mass-market product, companies still try to reach specific target audiences with their products. Who do you think the following products are targeted at? Describe each product's typical consumer. Can you think of any promotional activity that would appeal to each type of consumer?

- Cadbury's Tribute
- Terry's Chocolate Orange
- Rowntree's Quality Street
- Elizabeth Shaw's After Dinner Mints
- Cadbury's Dairy Milk
- Thornton's Continental Selection
- Selection boxes, which include a selection of products from the same company to be sold together

What different types of holiday would you promote to the following target audiences?

- single male/female, under 25, employed
- family with three children, low income
- couple with no children, high income, adventurous tastes
- couple whose children have left home, high income, very conventional

Timing of promotions

Different types of business will want to promote their products at different times. TV advertising is particularly popular in the period leading up to Christmas as companies compete for the gift-giving market. The perfume companies are particularly active at this time. Other promotional activity can often take place around gift-giving events like St Valentine's Day, Easter or Mother's Day. There are now fairly frequent price promotions taking place, with January, July and mid-season sales a regular occurrence. These are all examples of promotions that happen at specific times of the year.

It is also critical that the timing of the promotion fits in with the availability of the product. It could be a disaster for a business if they advertise a new product but are unable to supply it because of a production problem.

When many businesses promote at the same time, for example Christmas, it can be very difficult to stand out from the crowd, so it is worthwhile considering quieter periods. The golden rule is that the time must be right for your product/business so that you will truly benefit from the promotion.

The other aspect of timing is that if you are going to advertise on TV you need to decide how frequently your advertisement will appear and how long the whole campaign will be. For example, if you launch a new product, your advertisement for this might appear every other evening for a period of six weeks. Each 'spot' might appear around the most popular programmes like *Coronation Street* and *News at Ten* (these are the most expensive 'spots' as they have the largest audiences). They will also appear at other times during the day. Your aim will be for your target audience to have the best chance of seeing your advertisement. Timing is important in this respect as you can estimate the viewing habits of your target audience, and, working with an expert from an advertising agency, plan the timing of your TV campaign to closely follow the times when your audience should be watching.

Cost

It is very difficult to check if some forms of promotion have been good value for money for the business.

There are several methods of deciding how much money you should spend on promotion each year.

PERCENTAGE OF TURNOVER

You can decide that, come what may, you will keep back a proportion, say 5–10 per cent, of your turnover (the money you receive in your till from sales) to cover the cost of your promotion. This is a good method in that it gives you a clear idea of what level you will be working to and a rough idea of how much cash you will have to spend. However, 10 per cent might be far too much, and you could, perhaps, be using that money more effectively somewhere else. On the other hand suppose 10 per cent was not enough and all your competitors were spending 15 per cent – you might be left behind.

THE SAME AS YOUR COMPETITION

This sounds like a sensible option, in that you will neither be overlooked nor left behind if you spend the same amount as your competitors, and so you will maintain your presence in the marketplace. The first difficulty with this is finding out just how much your competitors are spending! This information can be obtained from official sources, but it could be a lengthy process. Also, if your competitors are much larger than you, you may not be able to spend as much as they do!

WHAT YOU CAN AFFORD

This is a common method, but not necessarily the right one. Businesses will use what money they have spare after covering all of their other expenses. This suggests that promotion is not that important and comes after everything else. Whilst you should not decide to spend huge amounts of money on promotion if your business cannot afford it, you do need to plan ahead and decide quite clearly whether you seriously intend to promote and how much you are prepared to allocate.

WHAT IT TAKES TO DO THE JOB PROPERLY

This is probably the best and most effective method to use. It is probably the most difficult to control and can at times be the most expensive, so it is not surprising that it is not the most popular! It simply means that you look at what you are trying to achieve with the promotion and then allocate however much money it takes to do the job properly. Companies tend to dislike this method as it is difficult to know just how much money they will be spending each year.

Once you have an idea of how much you intend to spend you can then look at the different forms of promotion available, check how much they cost and decide which one represents value for money for you.

TV ADVERTISING

This can be very expensive. You have to pay for:

- the time on the TV channel when the advertisement is shown (known as 'airspace')
- an advertising agency, for their expertise in researching your customers, coming up with ideas for a campaign, developing a theme and writing a script
- a film production company to make the advertisement for you

PRESS ADVERTISING

This is less expensive than TV, but still costs a large amount of money. You will have the same sort of costs as for TV advertising, apart from the film production company, but instead you will have to pay someone to produce the press advertisement for you. Generally, colour advertising is more expensive than black and white, and pictures are more expensive than writing (known as 'copy'). Popular publications can charge more for advertising space than specialist ones.

RADIO ADVERTISING

This can also cost a lot of money, but can be effective if you use local radio.

POINT-OF-SALE ACTIVITY

The cost of this depends on how sophisticated your point-of-sale material is. It could be a small, A5, black and white leaflet with just copy on it. It could also, however, be a glossy brochure with a free sample attached, plus a complex display stand (see pp.217–218).

OTHER FORMS OF SALES PROMOTION

There are many other forms of sales promotion that can be extremely cost effective, such as coupons, the offer of an extra product and so on. All businesses should forecast how much each of these would cost before they launch the promotion.

Competitions, for example, might involve the cost of the prizes, the cost of the competition leaflets and the aid of a 'handling house' (a company that specialises in handling promotions, who will receive the entries, check the forms and help sort out the winners). This might sound very expensive, but has to be balanced by the increase in sales. To enter the competition shown below you have to include a till receipt for either four or twelve 330 ml cans of Budweiser. So even though Sainsbury's is offering some very attractive prizes, part or all of that expense will be offset by the increased sales of Budweiser!

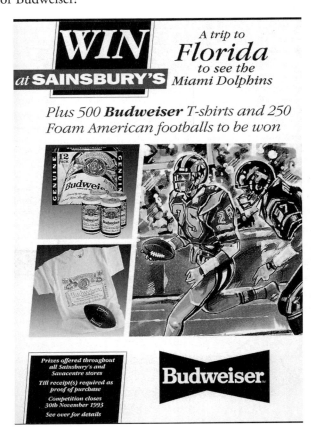

FIG. 8.15

On a visit to your local supermarket check how many leaflets you can find for competitions.

1   How many of them require the consumer to make a purchase?
2   Make a list of the costs you think the supermarket has to pay for.

SPONSORSHIP

This is a form of promotion that is becoming more and more popular. A company will agree to pay a sponsorship fee to, for example, a football team or a Formula 1 racing team. The team can then use the money to support itself. In return for this fee the team will display the name of its sponsor, for example Leicester City are sponsored by Walkers Crisps and wear the Walkers name on their shirts, and the sponsor then receives free publicity. It can be a very cost-effective way of reaching large audiences, particularly if the advertisement (and therefore your team) appears frequently on TV or billboards.

Other businesses, who are forbidden by law to advertise on TV are also quite active in sponsorship. For example, Embassy, a cigarette manufacturer, sponsors a snooker championship. The players don't wear the Embassy logo, but the company's name is mentioned on TV and it is discreetly displayed around the auditorium.

In a group discuss whether this type of sponsorship is ethical and should be allowed on TV. In your opinion should cigarette companies be allowed to sponsor sporting events?

1   How many sports team sponsors can you identify?
2   Have any of these sponsors any special link with the team?
3   Is there any particular type of company that sponsors sports teams? Why do you think they have chosen to promote in this way?

Impact

Any business that is active in promoting its product is looking to cause the maximum impact with its promotion, particularly with advertising. The promotion can only be deemed successful if you can remember it and it causes you to act in a particular way. It is not important that you particularly like an advertisement, only that you remember it. If you do, when it comes to buying a product you will probably remember the brand from the advertisement which may well appear in the choice of products in front of you. This is no guarantee, of course, that you will actually buy it. Other forms of promotion do need to appeal to you. You must feel it is worth buying a product to receive the free gift. In trying to cause the maximum impact, however, some companies can cause a great deal of uproar.

Read the article opposite on Yorkie bars. Do you think this is an acceptable form of promotion? Hold a class discussion on the ethics of such a campaign.

Product

The type of product you wish to promote also has an effect on the type of promotion you choose. Obviously TV is a good choice for most products where you need to highlight the visual aspect of, say, cars, with colour, sound and movement. You may wish to support this at dealership level with different forms of promotion, such as detailed brochures that include the specification and limited period offers of 0 per cent finance (or interest-free credit).

If, however, you were selling specialised or expensive furniture to a person in the 55–64 age group, you might wish to advertise via a magazine or newspaper, where you could include more information and detail. This might give the older purchaser more reassurance than a flashy visual image on TV.

Using sales-promotion methods, mass-market products often try to increase their value-for-money aspect to the customer, for example 'Get 450 ml of shampoo for the price of 300 ml' or 'Buy two packs of spaghetti and get one free'. On the other hand more

ITC proves no block to 'obscene' Yorkie ads

By Juliana Koranteng

The most recent Yorkie bar TV campaign is about to make history – not because it produced record sales for manufacturer Nestlé Rowntree, but for causing the most offence to TV viewers last month.

According to the ITC's latest Complaints Reports, the "Wild West" ad, featuring "a woman wearing large plastic imitation breasts and showing a lot of false cleavage", drew 93 complaints.

The ad also showed a man ripping off his trousers to reveal red satin boxer shorts enscribed with the words "marry me".

Viewers objected to the "sexist" portrayal of the woman, to the man's "obscene" actions, and to the ad's transmission during children's programming.

But the ITC rejected the complaints on the grounds that the commercial was made in a traditional bawdy seaside postcard style not likely to offend a majority of the audience.

Nick Symington, senior brand manager for Yorkie, denies that the £1m ad was pulled off air because of the criticisms. "It was meant to last only six weeks," he says. The campaign ended last month.

The company did remove the film from children's programmes, and later restricted it to programmes transmitted after 7.30pm. The number of complaints then dropped dramatically.

John Ward-Zinski, account director for Yorkie at J Walter Thompson, says there are no plans to repeat the commercials.

FIG. 8.16
SOURCE: MARKETING, 11/92

complex, expensive products might emphasise the same idea in a different way, for example 'Extended three-year warranty free when you spend over £1000 on one of our computers'.

If you were a business selling to another business, for example a photocopier company installing copiers in offices, your promotion might take the form of leaflets and brochures, sending round a sales representative to the office to explain your products or even giving the offices extended credit facilities, such as allowing them to pay you in three months' instead of one month's time.

Image

This is a very important factor in deciding what type of promotion to use. You must be very careful with promotions, as using price cutting frequently and without careful thought may detract from your image. If you come across a business that has non-stop sales which were supposed to be for a limited period, then you might begin to disbelieve the sale itself – perhaps the consistently low prices are an indication of the poor quality being sold.

If you have an exclusive, upmarket image then you would be unlikely to be promoting 'crazy prices' on a regular basis, although you might be involved in some discreet price reductions. Companies want to be seen as offering good value to the customer, regardless of their image. They might choose to offer free gifts rather than cut prices if they are upmarket. The important thing is that they pick the right form of promotion that enhances (improves) their image to the consumer.

A C T I V I T Y

Make an observation survey of local stores. Check all the advertisements in your local press for sales notices over a period of three months. Are there any that keep appearing? What type of image does that store have? Which store, in your opinion, has the most effective sales notices and why?

Design your own sales notice for a sports shop.

WHAT ARE THE DIFFERENCES IN APPROACH AMONGST THE DIFFERENT TYPES OF ACTIVITY?

It is worthwhile at this stage examining each type of activity, checking which type of organisation uses it and illustrating the advantages and disadvantages of each method.

Advertising agencies

Advertising is paid for by the business or organisation wanting to communicate with the public. A business will sometimes use an advertising agency to help it. The agency might carry out market research to find out what customers want from a business. It will then come up with some creative ideas of how to get the message about the product across to the consumer. For example, an advertising agency helped to create the love story of the Gold Blend coffee made by Nestlé. The agency will also advise the business on where to advertise. Should the advertisement be on TV, or in newspapers and magazines? Which channel or paper is right for the product? Should billboards or cinema advertising be used?

TV advertising

TV advertising is very effective in reaching mass audiences, and communicating simple messages or reminding people about products. It can have a lot of impact because of its visual nature and its use of music, colour and so on. TV advertising is often used by major companies selling well-known brands, for example Nestlé selling KitKat, Birds Eye selling fish fingers, Ford selling the Mondeo car.

ANY DRAWBACKS?

It can be extremely expensive. Businesses with nationwide TV advertising campaigns that run for several months face bills running into millions of pounds. Regional businesses can cut down on these costs by advertising only in their own TV region.

With the advent of video recorders, anyone who has missed a programme and then records it is likely to fast forward through the advertisements without paying much attention to them. People may well miss an advertising campaign that is brief and short-lived.

It is very difficult to assess how successful a campaign has been and whether it was worth investing the money. If your sales rise during an advertising campaign, how do you know whether the increase is due to the advertising, to your keen prices or to the fact that your competitor has failed to promote?

Radio advertising

Again this has the potential to be expensive if a campaign is long running and perhaps uses famous people for the voice overs. It can, however, be very cost-effective for local and regional businesses who are trying to communicate with a specific target audience to use local radio. This means that a local business wanting to attract the attention of housewives between the ages of 25 and 44 might consider advertising on a regional radio station.

Radio stations also tend to attract specific types of listeners. For example, the radio stations that play 'Classic Gold' music often have slightly older audiences than independent radio stations like Kiss FM.

ANY DRAWBACKS?

Radio lacks the visual impact of TV. It may be more difficult to make memorable advertisements for radio, but there is scope for great creativity through script writing. Some critics say that the rush hours, when people are driving to and from work and are listening to the radio in their cars are the only worthwhile times to advertise on the radio, as at all other times people do not really concentrate on the message being broadcast.

A C T I V I T Y

Listen to your local radio station.

1 Which types of business advertise?
2 What type of good/service are they promoting?
3 Why do you think they have chosen radio?
4 List the advertisers and try to identify which type of customer they are trying to attract.

Press/magazine advertising

Advertising in the press works well where customers require more detailed information about products. Advertisements could be placed in local or national newspapers, for example the *Hull Daily Mail* or *The Independent*. They could be placed in glossy supplements (the colour magazines that often accompany newspapers at weekends) or in general interest magazines like *TV Times*. There are also hundreds of women's and men's magazines that cater for various specialist interests, such as *Vogue, Woman's Own, GQ, Good Housekeeping, Just 17, Mizz, PC User, Gardening Week*. The list is endless.

The advantage about having such a wide choice of magazines and papers to advertise your product in is that you can pick one that your potential customer is likely to buy. This gives a business a better chance of reaching the right customer with the right message.

ANY DRAWBACKS?

Advertising in black and white newspapers means it is quite difficult for your advertisement to stand out and catch the consumer's eye (although many newspapers now have colour). Also some magazines carry pages and pages of advertisements. Unless your advertisement occupies one of the key or most eye-catching areas in the magazine (near the front, a double-page spread in the middle or on the back page) it is quite easy for an advertisement to get lost in the crowd.

A C T I V I T Y

Try this on your friends. Once they have read their favourite magazine ask them to try and remember which advertisements they have seen and for what products, without looking at the magazine.

1 How many can they remember?
2 Where were these advertisements positioned?
3 In your opinion, does this mean the advertisers who cannot be recalled have wasted their money?

Point-of-sale advertising

This is information or advertising that is positioned where a consumer is buying or selecting a product (called the point of sale). It does not always have to be where the money is handed over for the purchase. For example, there may be point-of-sale leaflets attached to the shelves in a supermarket next to a product that is being promoted. Point-of-sale advertising can take many forms. We will look at each of these in turn.

BROCHURES/LEAFLETS

These vary enormously in appearance and therefore expense. Generally, the more colours that are used in a brochure, the glossier and heavier the paper is and the more pictures that are used, the more expensive the brochure becomes. So, if you are a small business you might choose to use a small, single-page black and white leaflet and distribute it directly to your potential customers. This should be a very cheap exercise. If,

however, you are an international business and you want to describe and show your new hi-fi range to attract potential customers in retail outlets, you will spend a great deal of money.

FIG. 8.17 AN EXAMPLE OF AN ADVERTISING LEAFLET

A C T I V I T Y

On a shopping outing collect as many brochures and leaflets from the shops you visit as possible. Try and make sure you visit a mixture of retail outlets, for example supermarkets, variety stores, multiple-chain stores and department stores. Then collect two weeks' worth of leaflets and brochures you have received through your letterbox or in local newspapers.

1 Compare the two sets of leaflets.
2 How do they differ?
3 Why do you think these differences exist?

A C T I V I T Y

Most schools and colleges now have brochures that explain the courses available to potential students. Find a copy of your college brochure and analyse it.

1 What do you think of its cover and contents?
2 Was the information easy to find and follow?
3 Did it contain all the information you needed?
4 Was it attractively presented?
5 Design a new cover for the brochure that you think would appeal to students like you.

SHOWCARDS/POSTERS

Showcards often feature a special promotion on them. For example, they may have a small pad of leaflets on them that the consumer is invited to tear off to send away for an offer. The cards are often A4 or A3 size and are designed to stand alongside products and catch consumers' eyes.

Large posters are also used to make the surrounding area and the potential purchases more attractive. This is often the case in supermarkets, where large pictures of food are displayed to make the food seem more exciting, or in video stores, where posters from films will try to catch the consumer's attention.

MOBILES/SHELF WOBBLERS/SHELF TALKERS

Most point-of-sale advertising is aimed at grabbing the customer's attention. Anything that has impact and stands out from the rest of the display therefore has a head start on winning attention. Businesses can use mobiles, shelf wobblers (a piece of point-of-sale material such as a pointing finger, arrow or product image, attached to the shelf, which wobbles to attract attention), or shelf talkers (a display stand with point-of-sale material), which are all display stands that display the products attractively. Cosmetics companies are particularly keen on attractive display material.

It is important to remember that point-of-sale advertising can take many different forms. Even the beer and brewers' names and logos on pub beer-pumps are a form of point-of-sales advertising.

Sales promotion

This is an activity that is designed to give a short-term boost to sales. As we have already mentioned on p.207 there are many forms of sales promotion.

One type of sales promotion deserves special mention here: competitions. These are growing in popularity. Businesses like using them as they are reasonably easy to control (especially if a handling house runs the competition for you), and you can calculate how much each competition will cost fairly accurately. Competitions often have a great impact and will generate a lot of interest in your product and brand. Generally, the more difficult you make the competition (particularly if you ask for a slogan) and the more money a consumer has to spend to enter the competition (e.g. if they need to send in 20 pack-tops to enter), the fewer entries will be received. If the competition is easy to enter, with little required in terms of qualifying the entry, then it will be very popular.

Here is a list of typical promotions. Find a real-life example of each one. See if you can find evidence of each promotion (e.g. a leaflet, sticker, empty bottle, etc.) and bring them to your class. Compare your list with fellow students. Can you build up a picture of the most popular types of promotions?

- 'buy two, get one free' or multibuy (see p.219)
- competitions
- free prize draw
- money-off coupons
- free premium
- price promotion
- extra product free
- instant-win pack

There is a magazine called the *Competitors' Companion* that lists all the current high-street competitions, helps to provide any answers required and gives hints and tips on how to win competitions.

In a group discussion decide whether, if you were a business, you would want this type of magazine to encourage interest in your competition or not. Give reasons why.

PROMOTION DEVELOPMENTS

Promotions have changed over the years. They were initially very simple, for example free plastic flowers with washing powder, but as consumers' tastes changed and became more sophisticated, so did promotions. Promotional campaigns have changed a great deal since the simple 'money-off' offer.

Loss-leaders

One of the original promotions was the 'loss-leader' and this is still used in some outlets. The promotion works like this. A supermarket, for example, would select a product or group of products each week and c prices drastically. This would often be on staple products that everyone needed and that were very popular, such as bread or baked beans. The price wou be cut so much that the shop might make a loss on each loaf of bread sold.

The shop would advertise these low prices to attract customers into the shop, who would then spend money on a wide range of goods. The shop would hope to make a high enough profit on all of the other goods sold to make up for the loss made on the bread.

Bulk buys

Some supermarkets, like Sainsbury's, run multibuy systems where you either get a price discount or a free product when you buy more than one of a type of product, for example 'buy three cans of milk and get the fourth free'. Other outlets try to encourage consumers to 'bulk buy'. This means each customer will buy multiples of any one product, for example 24 cans of baked beans at one time, 50 kitchen rolls and so on. Bulk buying can be very cost effective, as each roll will work out cheaper. However, buying 50 at a time means having to pay a large bill. This method is often most attractive to large families. The discount warehouses (see p.186) being built in the UK, like Costco, encourage bulk buying (see Figure 8.18 below).

No-fuss packaging

There have been many worried voices raised over the past years over the amount of natural resources wasted by unnecessary packaging. A certain amount of packaging is undoubtedly essential for most products in that it protects them from being damaged. It is also used to promote products, as it is attractive and displays product features and brand names. Packaging can often enhance the image of a product. At times, however, it can seem excessive.

No-fuss packaging has been a response to the concerns raised. Sometimes used by supermarkets for their own-label products, it provides the minimum packaging to preserve and protect the product without wasting money on fancy, additional decoration. The cost savings are then passed on to the consumer in the form of lower prices. Other retail outlets have made a determined effort to cut down on excessive packaging and will ask customers whether they require plastic bags or not.

ENVIRONMENTALLY FRIENDLY IMAGE

This is a growing trend, first started in the late 1970s and early '80s, that has fast become a major promotional focus for many businesses. The image can be found in practically any area of business, from cosmetics with The Body Shop and Beauty Without Cruelty, and washing machines that use less water and energy, to tuna caught with dolphin-friendly nets. Lately there has been uneasiness expressed that some businesses have jumped onto the green bandwagon and are making false claims about their products, interested only in making a profit and not in truly helping the environment.

Shopper's paradise: Inside a U.S. Costco

The price war starts here ...

BRITAIN'S first Costco warehouse looks more like an aircraft hanger than a supermarket.

Inside the windowless barn, a team of American workers are preparing for next month's opening beneath a 60ft ceiling which is a mass of steel piping and girders. Yesterday, they were busy surfacing the 812-space car park.

The building is half a mile from the M25 on a shopping estate already home to branches of B & Q, Dixons and a multi-screen cinema.

Shoppers from nearby Grays complain that they have to negotiate a three-mile network of roundabouts to get there.

'The roads get snarled up at weekends,' said grocer John Edwards. 'There are so many large stores out there already. I don't think one more will make much difference.'

FIG. 8.18
SOURCE: DAILY MAIL, 28/10/93

ACTIVITY

Collect information from The Body Shop and BWC.

1 Is there any difference in their approach to environmentally friendly products?
2 Why in your opinion has The Body Shop been more successful in getting its image across?

ACTIVITY

On a visit to your local supermarket list all of the environmentally friendly claims you can find. Remember not to look just at food, but review detergents, cosmetics, drinks, household goods, paper towels and so on. How many of these claims do you think make a serious contribution to maintaining/improving the environment?

ACTIVITY

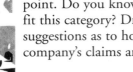

Have a class discussion on the previous point. Do you know of any businesses who fit this category? Draw up a list of suggestions as to how you can check if a company's claims are true.

ACTIVITY

Look at TV ads. How many businesses are claiming to help or be concerned about the environment? Write a paragraph on each of them and sum them up by giving marks out of ten for:

- honesty
- credibility
- effect on the environment
- which is making the most effort so far

CHAPTER EIGHT

Test Yourself!

1 What is the procedure for making a complaint?
2 Name seven different promotional methods.
3 What is the difference between a feature and a benefit?
4 List and describe common objections raised in selling.
5 Provide ways to overcome the objections raised in selling.
6 What is a customer profile?
7 How do you identify:
  a a consumer market
  b an industrial market?
8 List five ways of closing a sale.
9 What is the difference between a supermarket and a superstore?
10 List four ways of non-retail selling.

11 What is the difference between direct and indirect selling?
12 How many types of retail outlet can you list?
13 What is a Trade Association?
14 What are the main points of the Sale of Goods Act 1979?
15 Name four types of after-sales service.
16 List four ways of deciding how to calculate your promotional budget.
17 What does audience targeting mean?
18 Why is timing important in choosing when to promote?
19 What outside organisation can help you if you have a complaint against a retailer?
20 What are the major drawbacks of TV advertising?

Chapter

9

BUSINESS IN EUROPE

THE STRUCTURE OF THE EUROPEAN UNION

WHAT IS THE EUROPEAN UNION?

The European Union (EU) is becoming more and more important in world trade and politics. It came into existence in 1957 under the Treaty of Rome. You may also have heard it referred to as the European Economic Community (EEC), the Common Market or as the European Community (EC). The name 'European Union' has been used since the Maastricht Treaty extended the role of the EC.

After the Second World War (1939–1945), the continent of Europe needed rebuilding in terms of both industry and housing, as both had been destroyed during the war. This was an enormous task. The USA offered to help Europe finance the rebuilding under the Marshall Plan. The Americans insisted, however, that the different European countries work together in deciding how to spend the finance in rebuilding the continent. The EEC was born from this initial co-operation.

What did the EEC hope to achieve?

The EEC hoped to build a Europe of the future. The original member states intended to work together as a group and had several aims. They thought that a Europe based on co-operation would:

Avoid further outbreaks of war.
Provide stability in Europe.
Become a world power like the USA or the former USSR.
Be able to manage its own affairs and bring the peoples of Europe closer together.
Thrive and become a trading power bringing prosperity to its citizens.

Who belongs to the EU?

The original member states were:

- West Germany (now unified) (D)
- France (F)
- The Netherlands (NL)
- Luxembourg (L)
- Italy (I)
- Belgium (B)

In 1973 the six states added three new members:

- The United Kingdom (UK)
- Denmark (DK)
- Ireland (IRL)

In 1981 one new member joined:

- Greece (GR)

In 1986 two new members joined:

- Spain (E)
- Portugal (P)

In 1995 three new members joined:

- Austria (AUS)
- Finland (FIN)
- Sweden (SWE)

This makes a total of 15 member states.

ACTIVITY

1 The UK joined the EC in 1973. Why did we join then and not in 1957? Check your library for information.
2 In 1975 the UK had a referendum asking whether the general public wanted to remain in the EC.
3 a What was the result?
   b Why do you think people voted that way?
   c What, in your opinion, would be the result if a referendum was held today?

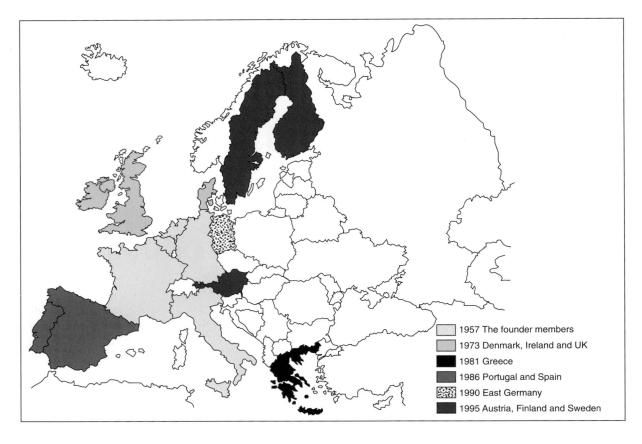

FIG. 9.1 MAP OF EUROPE

Map legend:

1957 The founder members
1973 Denmark, Ireland and UK
1981 Greece
1986 Portugal and Spain
1990 East Germany
1995 Austria, Finland and Sweden

How does the EU work?

There are four major bodies (usually called institutions) that run the EU. They are:

- the European Commission
- the European Parliament
- the Council of Ministers
- the European Court of Justice

Figure 9.2 shows how these institutions work together.

THE EUROPEAN COMMISSION

The European Commission is rather like the civil service of the Union. There are 20 commissioners. Germany, France, the UK, Italy and Spain each appoint two commissioners; Portugal, Denmark, Ireland, Luxembourg, Greece, The Netherlands, Belgium, Austria, Finland and Sweden all appoint one commissioner. Commissioners are appointed for four years by their own national governments, but they work for the Union and act in the interest of Europe as a whole, not for their own country.

ACTIVITY

Can you find out who the two current British commissioners are? What are their particular responsibilities on the European Commission?

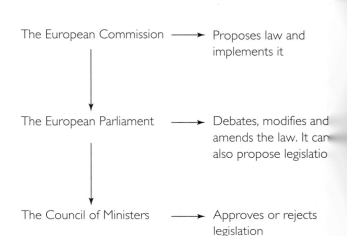

The European Commission → Proposes law and implements it

The European Parliament → Debates, modifies and amends the law. It can also propose legislatio

The Council of Ministers → Approves or rejects legislation

FIG. 9.2 HOW THE INSTITUTIONS WORK TOGETHER

Each commissioner has a particular area of responsibility, for example there is a commissioner for agriculture, one for regional policy, and one for energy and transport.

A C T I V I T Y

There are a number of specific areas of responsibility for the Commission. Three are listed above. Can you find out the others? Which in your opinion is the most important?

The European Commission:

1 Makes sure the rules of the Union are followed and respected.
2 Suggests policies that will help the Union to develop, for example on the environment, energy or industry.
3 Helps to implement policies already agreed.
4 Manages the Union budget.

THE EUROPEAN PARLIAMENT

This has 577 members who are elected every five years in elections where everyone in Europe aged over 18 votes.

A C T I V I T Y

1 Who is your local European Member of Parliament (MEP)?
2 When will the next elections be held?
3 Will you be able to vote?
4 Do you think your vote will count?

The 577 deputies are made up as follows:

81 from each of Germany, France, Italy and the UK
60 from Spain
25 from the Netherlands
24 from each of Belgium, Greece and Portugal
22 from Sweden
21 from Austria
16 from each of Denmark and Finland
15 from Ireland
6 from Luxembourg

The European Parliament:

Helps to make legislation. It debates laws and may modify or propose them.
Helps to decide on the Union budget.
Represents the voice of the people of Europe.

A C T I V I T Y

1 Looking at the figures listed above, how do you think the numbers of seats were allocated to the countries?
2 Is this a fair system?
3 Can you suggest any other methods of allocating seats?

THE COUNCIL OF MINISTERS

This is a very important institution within the EU. The Council is really the key decision-making body within the Union. The Council does not have a set membership: the ministers involved change depending on the policy area to be discussed. For example, if farm prices are to be discussed, the agriculture ministers from all 15 member states will meet to form the Council, or if unemployment is to be discussed the Council will be made up of the minister for employment from each member state.

The European Council is a slightly different body. Meetings of the European Council occur two or three times a year. These are attended by the head of state or government, for example the UK prime minister, the German chancellor, the French president and so on.

The Council of Ministers:

1 Makes the key decisions in the EU. It decides which laws are adopted or rejected.
2 Co-operates on major international problems.

THE EUROPEAN COURT OF JUSTICE

This has 13 independent judges, who are appointed for a six-year period by the member states.

The Court:

1 Interprets points of Union law.
2 Resolves disputes between any member state and the Commission.

Do we have a 'United States of Europe'?

Some sections of society in the UK and other countries worry about belonging to the European Union. They are scared that member states will be ruled from Brussels and lose the right to run their own country. They fear becoming lost in one big 'Euro pool' where they will lose their national identity.

Much of this fear is based on lack of knowledge of Europe. In fact, all the countries in Europe are free to enjoy the spirit and flavour of each other without having to suppress their own identities. Where would we be in the UK without French wine, German cars, Italian fashion, Dutch cheese, Belgian chocolates, holidays in Greece, Spain and Portugal, and Danish bacon? Being a member of the EU can add a richness to a country's culture.

There are obvious differences between the member states and many of these should be valued as part of a heritage worth keeping. Membership of the EU should bring the member states closer, whilst still preserving each country's individuality.

A C T I V I T Y

Using travel brochures as a model, create your own brochure for the EU, with a section on each member state. Include information on climate, major areas/cities of interest, rivers, lakes, mountain ranges and so on. Give each country a small descriptive paragraph and your own star-rating as a holiday destination. Don't forget to include maps.

A C T I V I T Y

List famous football teams from each member state. How does their approach to the game differ from the UK's? Does this reflect anything about that country's culture or way of life?

A C T I V I T Y

Read the 'tongue in cheek' article below on body language. Taking the role of a personnel manager for a large company, write a list of dos and don'ts for executives travelling overseas to do business.

A C T I V I T Y

How many languages of the EU can you list? Why do you think that French and English are two of the most commonly spoken ones?

Fig. 9.3
Source: Daily Mail, 23/1/91

A kiss for the manager

When in Rome do you kiss the bank manager, or simply shake his hand? It is difficult enough to know precisely what to do in Britain, but the wrong handshake or kiss on the cheek can separate European nationals for a lifetime, such is the formality of Community business and social etiquette.

Here is a simple country-by-country guide to making the right impression on the right person when you have your traveller's cheques stolen, lose your banker's card, or simply wish to conclude a business deal:

■ BELGIUM: always use English, or at least never speak French to the Flemish – or

Flemish to the French. Formal suits are customary for business meetings, so are punctuality, the exchange of business cards, and shaking hands. Throughout Europe you shake hands until you know somebody really well.

■ DENMARK: Toasts should not be acknowledged in booze unless you know what the hosts promise. Choose sparkling water instead, and never respond until after the host has answered.

■ FRANCE: Like Belgium, what matters is how heavy a 'big vegetable' you are. As they say, the heavier the turnip, the bigger is the door it opens.

That door depends on how you kiss the cheek. Once means acceptance, and twice that you are a member of the family. Stop there.

■ GERMANY: They still click heels … and shake hands, but casual clothes are acceptable in all but the most formal circumstances. Never forget the formal titles of Doctor or Professor when addressing people – with Herr, Frau or Fraulein added at the front.

■ GREECE: Always dress well, and never nod – it means No. Although Greeks smoke like chimneys, it is against the law to smoke on public transport or in public places, let

alone at a business meeting.

■ HOLLAND: The Dutch are the most laid-back of the Europeans. They are also the most formal. Invitations are official, and business suits mandatory. Tolerant of jeans on students, they look for white shirts, tasteful ties, sober suits and visiting cards from their foreign visitors.

■ ITALY: Do not forget that this is the centre of civilisation … according to the Italians. Worship the three gods of food, family and religion and you will not go far wrong. In business, they will still expect you to demonstrate impeccable taste – from your tie right

down to your underwear.

■ SPAIN: By far the most difficult European country to read, with a legal system which has already defeated many international companies. In business, exchange cards frequently and hire a good lawyer.

■ PORTUGAL: Very similar to Spain to deal with.

Which leaves us with Britain, Ireland and Luxembourg. All countries where your word is your bond.

ROGER BEARD

A C T I V I T Y

Look at the chart below on how other countries spend Christmas. If you had to swap, which other country would you want to spend Christmas in and why?

All of these exercises, including the one following, should demonstrate that Europe has a rich culture to be enjoyed by all member states. None of the member states' cultures have been diminished by membership: the French are no less French, the Greeks no less Greek.

There are undoubtedly some countries that have had long-standing relationships and friendships and who share common goals, for example the British and the Danes, the French and the Germans. Regardless of whether these countries are in total agreement or complete disagreement on the best way forward for the Union, the EU provides a peaceful and constructive organisation for co-operating for the future.

Jean Monnet, who was one of the people responsible for creating the EU, said: 'We are not merging states, we are uniting people.' For anyone worried about the future of Europe, this statement should set their minds at rest.

FIG. 9.4

SOURCE; THE DAILY MAIL 24/12/92

	FOOD & DRINK	GIFTS	COST	HOLIDAYS	BONUS	CUSTOMS	TELEVISION	WORSHIP	OPENING
BRITAIN	Turkey, cranberry sauce, Christmas pudding, sherry, port and wine	Super Nintendo Game Boy, Sindy/ Barbie, opened on Christmas Day	Average cost £358	Bank Holidays; Christmas Day, Boxing Day, New Year's Day	No fixed amount, employers pay bonuses at their own discretion	Carol singing, Boxing Day hunt	Blockbuster films, comedy specials, religious services, soap opera specials	Midnight Mass, Christmas Eve. 16 per cent of population attend church	Resturants, some pubs, petrol stations, some newsagents
FRANCE	Oysters, foie gras, turkey, cheeses, white wine and champagne	Computer games, cuddly toys for tots, gifts opened before meal	A family of four would budget £550 for presents	A long break of five days	None given	National seasonal customs no longer exist	Hours of game and variety shows, and circuses	Only 10 per cent of population attend Christmas mass	Nothing is open
GERMANY	Carp or herring on Christmas Eve, roast goose on Christmas Day	Playmobil, a Lego type toy, Christmas plate of sweets, biscuits and fruit	Average cost £385	December 25, 26 and Jan 1 are national holidays	Month's salary is paid, this is known as the 13th month's pay	Christmas Eve, parents decorate the tree for children	Nostalgic re-runs of popular old films, folk music and cartoons	Midnight Mass on Christmas Eve, church on Christmas morning	Mostly everything stays open
ITALY	Christmas 'dinner' served on 24th, steamed fish, cod or bass, white wine	Video games. Gifts are not dispensed before midnight on Christmas Eve	Average cost £275	Christmas Day and St Stephens Day (Boxing Day)	A month's extra pay	Mistletoe given by guests visiting another family for luck	National lottery talk show, followed by 'classic' films	Most people attend Midnight Mass, which begins at 11.30pm	All shops and offices are closed on Christmas day and Boxing Day
NETHERLANDS	Rabbit, game and venison, served on Christmas Day and Boxing Day	Teddy bears and family games opened on Christmas morning	Average spending for family of four is £132	Christmas Eve to the first week of January	Amounts vary from about £100 to an extra month's salary	No special traditions, fir trees, holly and Father Christmas	Short family Christmas shows, but mostly a normal TV service	Christmas Eve service, known as Kindje Wiegen, which is popular	Nowhere apart from police stations
BELGIUM	Veal sausage, like black pudding, apples, sparkling Luxembourg wine	Toys on St Nicholas, Dec 6, clothes, slippers on Christmas Day	Family of four spend about £275	Two days off work - December 25 and 26	Pay bonus given in December, called 13th month (1/13th of salary)	No particular customs – they eat a lot of chocolate and marzipan	Religious and musical programmes, cartoons	Majority go to church on Christmas Morning, most are Catholic	Small corner shops are usually open from 9am to 1pm
LUXEMBOURG	Blood sausage, like black pudding, apples, sparkling Luxembourg wine	Gifts given on St Nicholas, Dec 6, clothes, sweets on Christmas Day	Family of four spend about £220	Two days off work - December 25 and 26	Extra month's pay given by most companies	Colourful outdoor street markets on Christmas Eve	Musical shows, plays performed in the Luxembourg language	Midnight Mass on Christmas Eve, most people are devout Catholic	Nothing open at all
DENMARK	Duck, goose stuffed with fruit, rice pudding with cinnamon	Pregnant doll, presents opened after dinner on Christmas Eve	Average cost £440	24th, 25th and 26th, most people take time off until after New Year	Non-compulsory, but employers usually give something	Children put out rice pudding and almonds for the Christmas pixies	Pixies' Christmas calendar series counting up to Christmas Day	Nearly everyone attends Midnight Mass or Christmas Morning service	Everything closed
IRELAND	Turkey and ham on Christmas Day	Gameboy computer game, gifts opened on Christmas morning	Average cost £550	Bank Holidays are December 25, 26 and 27	Pay bonus varies, usually one week's pay	No special customs, same as Britain	Christmas Day films, special editions of popular soap operas	90 per cent church attendance	All shops and offices are closed
SPAIN	Shellfish, roast lamb, turkey, suckling pig	Small presents on Christmas Day, big presents given on Jan 6	Average cost £900	Holidays are 24th, 25th and 26th, Jan 1st and Jan 6th	Minimum of one month's salary	Eating turron, a sweet almond toffee	Festive films, big TV specials	Nearly everyone attends Midnight Mass	Christmas Day is like a Sunday with most places open
PORTUGAL	Salt cod eaten at a meal called the Consoada, sweet port wine	Toys and video games, opened on Christmas Eve	Family of four spend about £275	Two days, Christmas Eve and Christmas Day	An extra month's salary paid at end of November/ early December	Most families put up a manger and a Christmas Tree	No big specials over Christmas, usual programmes	Midnight Mass on Christmas Eve is traditional service	Shops and offices are closed on Christmas Day
GREECE	Turkey served with wine	Video games, presents opened on Christmas morning	Average cost around £220	Christmas Day, Boxing Day, New Year's Day and Epiphany	Compulsory one month's pay, extra month's pension for pensioners	A traditional gamble	Variety shows on Christmas Eve, repeated on December 25/26	Church attended by elderly people. Christmas is not as popular as Easter	Cake shops and greek kiosks

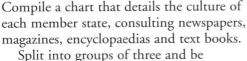

Compile a chart that details the culture of each member state, consulting newspapers, magazines, encyclopaedias and text books.

Split into groups of three and be responsible for one to two countries. Each chart should include written and visual material. You need to give examples of famous people for each country. These could be politicians, film stars, musicians, writers, entertainers, sportspeople and so on. You also need to compile a list of famous items of each country's culture. This could include music, food, architecture, painting, literature, films and institutions.

Compare and contrast the different cultures when all the charts are completed.

TRANSPORT

Doing business in Europe or even holidaying as a private citizen depends very much on the transport links that exist in the various countries. The major methods of transport are air, road and rail.

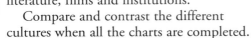

A C T I V I T Y

In order to sample the different European cultures, you need good transport links to travel about. Using the current *Statesman's Yearbook* (Macmillan, ed. B. Hunter) as a reference document, compare the different travel systems in Europe.

1 Which countries have the most developed systems?
2 Why do you think this has happened?
3 Are there any improvements you could suggest?

A C T I V I T Y

The UK is now joined to mainland Europe by the Channel Tunnel. In a class discussion debate whether the tunnel is a good thing or not.

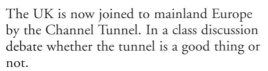

Air

All EU countries have major airports and national airlines. Air travel is frequently used, particularly by business travellers, although there has been some criticism that air fares in Europe are more expensive than in other parts of the world.

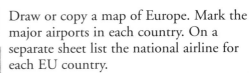

A C T I V I T Y

Draw or copy a map of Europe. Mark the major airports in each country. On a separate sheet list the national airline for each EU country.

Road

Road links are fairly good in Europe, with a particularly good motorway network in northern Europe. All countries, in particular large cities, have 'rush hours' or periods that are very busy. As an individual driver you can avoid these, though for business purposes you will have to work around them. The times of the busy periods will vary depending on which country you are in. Motorway tolls are common in Europe.

Rail

This is used extensively throughout Europe, for both passengers and freight. Many countries have developed their version of a high-speed train. In France it is the *train de grande vitesse* (TGV), the Spanish train is the *AVE* and the German intercity express is the *ICE*. It is envisaged that over 30 000 km of high-speed track will be built by European train companies over the next 25 years! Rail undoubtedly has a large part to play in the transport system of the future in Europe, despite national differences in stock and track.

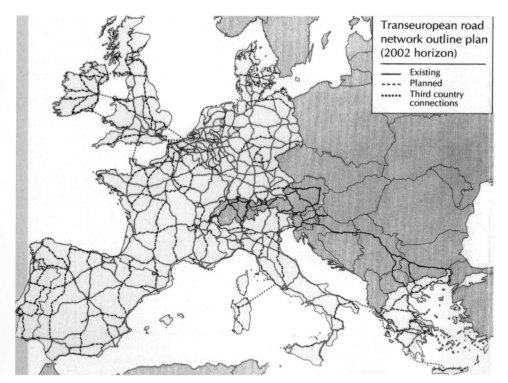

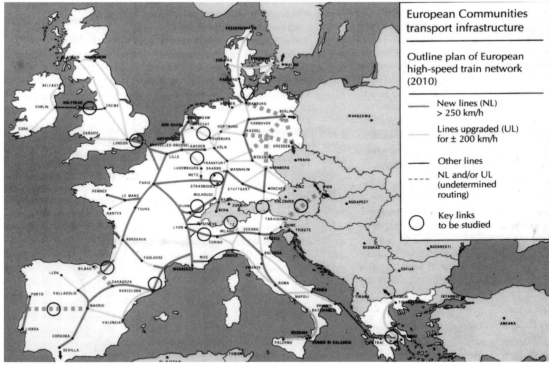

FIG. 9.5

WHAT ARE THE EFFECTS OF THE EUROPEAN UNION ON BUSINESS?

THE SINGLE MARKET

We have already mentioned that one purpose of the original EEC was to increase trade in Europe. This was achieved by reducing or eliminating tariffs (taxes on imports and exports) on goods in Europe, which made goods cheaper and therefore encouraged people to trade. This policy was very successful and by the late 1960s many tariffs had been abolished.

By the early to mid-1980s, however, there was a feeling within the Community that the EC had lost its direction, and was stagnating. The president of the Commission, Jaques Delors, devised a reform package that would take the EC into the next century. The reforms were formalised in the Single European Act of 1986. The main points of the Act were:

1 To create one large market in Europe where people, goods, services and capital (money) can all move around freely.
2 To develop policies to help the poorer regions and areas to improve their standard of living.
3 To encourage all countries to co-operate on research and technology.
4 To develop monetary co-operation within the European Monetary System (see p.231).
5 To make sure that ordinary citizens benefit from the single market, that their living and working conditions are protected.
6 To co-operate on protection of the environment

Freedom of movement

Creating a single market is perhaps the objective that has received the most coverage in the media. It guarantees some fundamental freedoms in terms of movement.

PEOPLE

You can travel to any member state. Border controls and checks are infrequent. Customs have added a blue channel for EU citizens alongside the red and green. You can live and work in whichever country you like providing you can support yourself.

GOODS/SERVICES

You can buy anything you like (there are special arrangements for tobacco and spirits) in the EU and take it home without having to pay duty on it. A business can sell its products wherever it likes.

CAPITAL

You are free to invest money in whichever country you choose or to raise money from another country. For example, you can apply to an overseas insurance company for insurance cover.

A C T I V I T Y

There are certain restrictions on the amount of tobacco and alcohol you can bring into the UK. If you want to bring back more than 800 cigarettes, 90 litres of wine, 100 litres of beer and 10 litres of spirits you will have to prove they are for your personal consumption.

1 Why do you think there are special restrictions on these products?
2 Are these restriction fair in your opinion?

A C T I V I T Y

Reducing border controls is a very positive move for law-abiding citizens. There are a number of advantages to this reduction shown below.

- easier to travel
- saves time
- cheaper for businesses to move goods, so goods may be cheaper to buy
- more consumer choice
- new job opportunities

1 Can you think of any disadvantages in reducing border controls?
2 How would you solve these problems?
3 List the possible disadvantages of your solutions.

CURRENCY TRANSACTIONS

All of the measures under the Single European Act that created the single market (all 15 member states treated as one big market with no dividing borders) will help to increase trade between member states. One specific objective within the Single European Act that could bring the countries of the EU even closer together is achieving monetary co-operation and creating a European Monetary System.

There are still certain obstacles to trade in Europe. One obvious problem to overcome is that of the language barrier. Another problem is dealing with all the different currencies within the Union. International companies that trade in other countries also have to deal with this currency problem.

A C T I V I T Y

Which countries do the following EU currencies belong to?

- krone
- punt
- deutschmark
- Blg franc
- guilder
- peseta
- schilling
- drachma
- pound Sterling
- Fr franc
- lire
- Lux franc
- escudo
- markka

Exchange rates

An exchange rate is simply the price of one currency in terms of another, for example £1 is worth roughly $1.50.

Currencies and their exchange rates can go up or down for several reasons:

1. The pound can rise in value if there is a great demand for pounds. If everyone wants to change their money into pounds, pounds are therefore in demand and become scarcer. This makes the value rise and it could move from, say, £1 = $1.50 to £1 = $1.60.
2. The pound can fall in value if demand falls for pounds. If no one wants to buy pounds and there is a surplus of pounds available, the value of the pound will fall and could move from, say, £1 = $1.50 to £1 = $1.40.

If a British chain of off-licences wants to buy some French wine from a French vineyard, the wine producer will probably send the buyer an invoice with the amount owing in French francs. The buyer will then have to go to the bank to change their pounds sterling into French francs to pay the vineyard. The British off-licence will want to know what the exchange rate is, i.e. how many French francs each pound will buy. The off-licence will also have to pay the bank some commission for changing their pounds into francs.

Exchange rates go up and down. This means that businesses can never be sure exactly how much they will end up paying or being paid if there are foreign currencies involved.

A C T I V I T Y

Most broadsheet newspapers print the most common exchange rates every day. Select one currency to check over a number of weeks. Is the rate going up or down? What does this mean if you want to change some pounds into this currency?

Many people are involved in buying and selling currencies. On a small scale individuals might want to exchange their pounds for pesetas if they are going on holiday to Spain. On a larger scale businesses often buy foreign currencies so they can buy raw materials and goods from overseas. They may also want to invest money overseas.

There are also people called currency dealers. They operate on the money markets. The major money-market centres are Frankfurt, London, New York, Tokyo, Hong Kong and Paris. The dealers buy and sell currencies to make profits for companies or individuals. They can be very powerful and influence exchange rates. If they all decide a currency is weak and undesirable and sell this currency to get rid of their holding, this can push its value down.

Governments can act in the same way to protect their own currency or to help another country to protect theirs. If the pound is weak the British government can instruct the Bank of England to start buying pounds to make it less available and therefore more desirable, which should push up its value.

Changing money within the EU

There are many different ways of changing money into another currency. Overseas travellers need to weigh up the pros and cons for each one and decide which method is best according to their circumstances.

EUROCHEQUE

This is a system that allows you to buy goods abroad using a cheque. You cannot use the same cheque book you use at home, but instead your bank will issue you with a number of Eurocheques. You also need a special Eurocheque bank card (much the same as a normal bank card) to back up your cheques. Under this system if you are on holiday, say in Portugal, and want to buy some pottery, you would take the following steps:

1 Complete the cheque in the normal way.
2 Complete the amount to be paid in escudos (the Portuguese currency).

The bank in the UK will then convert the escudo amount into pounds sterling when the cheque is received, and withdraw that amount from your account. The pottery shop receives its payment in escudos and you have pounds debited from your account. Eurocheque bank cards can also be used as debit cards and cash-machine cards.

currency is converted into pounds. This goes towards the cost of the overseas bank. The UK bank also makes a small charge on each cheque.
3 Any withdrawal from an overseas cash machine will attract a small charge.

AUTOMATIC TELLING MACHINES (CASH POINTS, CASH MACHINES, AUTOBANKS)

Some banks and their cards (normally Eurocheque cards, see previous section) allow you to withdraw cash in foreign currency from cash points overseas.

Advantages
1 It is quick, easy and convenient. The machines are simple to use and avoid queuing in banks.
2 You can draw out cash from your account at home.

Disadvantages
1 Not all countries in Europe have this service.
2 It may require a special Eurocheque card for which you will have to pay a fee.

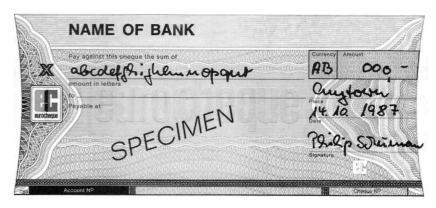

987654321   89012345<

No writing or stamping in this space

FIG 9.6 A EUROCHEQUE

Advantages
1 They are widely accepted in shops, restaurants hotels and petrol stations in over 40 European countries. In some countries they can also be used to obtain local currency from cash machines.
2 They are convenient to use and allow you to draw money from your account at home.
3 They are fairly secure. If any cheques or a card is lost or stolen, there is a 24-hour telephone service to notify the bank in the UK. The Eurocards also have a PIN number to use when withdrawing cash.

Disadvantages
1 There is an annual fee payable for the Eurocheque service, currently £7.50.
2 Each cheque is subject to a handling charge when the

3 Each withdrawal will attract a charge.
4 Cash is less secure than cheques. If you have cash stolen, it may well have gone for good. Cheques can be stopped if the banks and police are notified in time.

CREDIT CARDS

These are a recognisable and popular way of paying for goods abroad. The most common are Access/ Mastercard and Barclaycard/Visa. When paying for goods or services in shops, hotels and restaurants, the customer offers the credit card and the amount for the product is converted into sterling and added to the nex statement. Interest will be added to the amount. Some banks now levy an annual fee for the use of a credit card (see Chapter 4 'Financial transactions' p.97).

Advantages

1 They are widely accepted.
2 They are quick, easy and convenient to use.
3 They allow you to put off payment for a certain length of time.
4 In case of theft, notification to the company involved will stop the owner's liability if the thief uses the card.

Disadvantages

1 There may be an annual fee payable.
2 They are attractive to thieves.

TRAVELLERS CHEQUES

These are usually purchased in advance of overseas travel from a UK bank. The buyer can choose which currency the cheques are to be issued in. For example, they could be dollars, sterling or deutschmarks.

Each cheque is signed when purchased in the presence of the bank employee who sold them. They are later counter-signed again in the presence of a bank employee, when they are cashed in the overseas bank. This helps to counter theft and prevent people attempting to forge signatures. Travellers cheques are normally cashed in banks on production of a passport and the cheque itself.

Advantages

1 The counter-signature system helps security.
2 By keeping a note of the number of the cheque issued, notifying the authorities is an easy process if cheques are stolen.
3 It is a secure method of keeping money.
4 They are widely accepted.

Disadvantages

1 Overseas banks' hours are sometimes inconvenient. In certain countries long queues are the norm.
2 Cashing cheques means passports and cheques have to be carried around.
3 The purchaser is charged a percentage commission, currently 1–2 per cent, when buying the cheques.
4 If you return to the UK with unspent cheques and wish to convert them to sterling, this may involve a further charge.

BUREAUX DE CHANGE

These bureaux are businesses that exist to change money. They normally buy and sell a wide range of currencies. They will also change travellers cheques and Eurocheques and carry out credit-card transactions. The bureaux display their current rates to customers on a chart that changes from day to day.

Advantages

1 They are normally quick and easy to use.
2 They are convenient. They always have much longer opening hours than banks, and can deal with all types of transactions.

Disadvantages

1 They normally charge a higher rate of commission for any transaction than a bank.
2 Their exchange rates may not be as favourable as those in a bank.

BANKS

Many of the above currency transactions require the services of a bank. When using a bank overseas you may find them to be very similar to British banks. Occasionally their opening hours and practices are different, and the traveller must take care to be aware of these.

THE EUROPEAN MONETARY SYSTEM (EMS)

You can see from the above that currency transactions can be fairly complicated for the individual traveller. Imagine how complex the process becomes for a business buying and selling goods in many different countries! The European Union has been looking at this problem for some time to try and find a solution. One possible answer to this is the European Monetary System.

What is the EMS?

The European Monetary System is a system that was created in 1979 to try and avoid the many changes and fluctuations in the values of European currencies. It is an attempt to bring the European currencies (and therefore economies) closer together, to make them more stable and introduce ultimately, perhaps, one single currency for Europe. If currencies are more stable, this makes it easier for businesses to plan ahead, it helps them to cut costs (which may bring down prices for customers) and encourages them to take advantage of the single market and increase trade in Europe. Member states of the EU may join the EMS if they so wish.

The EMS has two major components:

- Exchange Rate Mechanism (ERM)
- European Currency Unit (ECU)

EXCHANGE RATE MECHANISM

This is the method used to try and bring currencies together in a stable band. When a country joins the EMS a value is fixed for its currency linked to the deutschmark (the deutschmark was selected as the strongest currency in Europe). So when the UK joined the EMS in October 1990, it was decided that £1 was worth DM2.95. It was then agreed that the pound would be allowed to increase or decrease by 6 per cent, i.e. its value could increase to DM3.13 or decrease to DM2.77, before further action (see below) would be taken. The same percentage allowance was given to the other new entrant, Spain, with its peseta. All the other currencies that were already well established in the ERM could only fluctuate by 2.25 per cent. It was expected that the pound and peseta would eventually fit into this band as well.

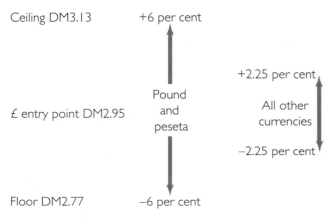

FIG. 9.7 THE CURRENCY BAND FOR THE POUND WITHIN THE EMS

If the pound were to hit its ceiling of DM3.13, all of the European central banks would, in theory, act in the same way. They would flood the market with pounds by selling the pounds they held, therefore creating a surplus of sterling, and so pushing its value down. If the pound hit its floor of DM2.77 they would, in theory, again act together. This time they would all buy as many pounds as possible to reduce the number of pounds generally available. This would make sterling scarce and therefore push its value up.

The system was not really tested until autumn 1992, when the European banks failed to prevent the value of the pound falling through its floor to DM2.40. The currency dealers working together in the money markets proved more powerful than the European banks working together, and so the ERM did not work. Several currencies (including the pound) withdrew from the ERM and the system was temporarily suspended. The EU is now in the process of devising a new monetary system.

A C T I V I T Y

In a class discussion debate whether it is a good thing for Europe to have weak and strong currencies that change rapidly or whether we should have stable currencies linked together.

THE EUROPEAN CURRENCY UNIT

If a new EMS and ERM are resurrected then they will rely on the future development of the ECU. The ECU is the potential single currency in Europe. It is not yet legal tender, as no coins or banknotes have been issued. All 15 member states have put some of their currency and gold reserves into a 'basket' to establish the value of the ECU. The stronger the country's economy, the greater the contribution they make to the ECU.

Eventually the ECU could take over from all the other currencies in Europe. This is currently predicted for the year 2000, but will probably take much longer.

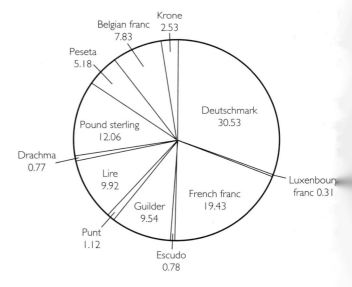

FIG. 9.8 COMPOSITION OF THE ECU (1990) – PERCENTAGE SHARE OF EACH CURRENCY
SOURCE: EUROSTAT

ACTIVITY

In January 1993 the ECU was worth about 70p. Find out the current valuation of the ECU.

ACTIVITY

Design an ECU coin and set of banknotes. What type of design would you pick? Who would you feature on the notes? Give your reasons why.

ACTIVITY

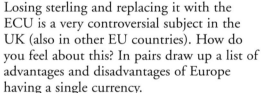

Losing sterling and replacing it with the ECU is a very controversial subject in the UK (also in other EU countries). How do you feel about this? In pairs draw up a list of advantages and disadvantages of Europe having a single currency.

ACTIVITY

Review the following statistics resulting from a Eurobarometer survey carried out in December 1990.

1 What do the figures tell you?
2 Can you explain why some countries are more in favour than others?
3 In your opinion, would there be any change in these figures if the survey was held today?

COUNTRY	IN FAVOUR (%)	AGAINST (%)
Italy	72	11
Greece	64	10
France	62	19
Belgium	61	18
Netherlands	61	25
Ireland	58	17
Portugal	55	16
Spain	53	10
Germany	50	27
Luxembourg	47	26
UK	38	43
Denmark	35	50
EC Average	55	23

TABLE 9.1 ATTITUDES OF EUROPEAN CITIZENS TO A SINGLE CURRENCY

SOURCE: EUROBAROMETER

BUSINESS PRACTICES

Action checklist for business

Doing business in Europe involves much more than simply learning a language and sailing forth, expecting to meet the same conditions as exist in the UK. Apart from the differences in culture in different European societies, a businessperson will undoubtedly have to get used to different procedures as well. Anyone wishing to do business abroad needs to prepare thoroughly, to be aware of the potential difficulties that lie ahead and to be prepared to accommodate them. Before giving the go-ahead, any business must be able to answer the following questions:

1 Do we have the language skills to cope?
2 Do we understand the culture?
3 What are the normal working hours?
4 How are appointments made?
5 How formal will the contract be?
6 How are meetings used? Are they simply a forum for discussion or are decisions made and expected?
7 What form should entertainment take?
8 What subjects can be safely discussed?
9 Are business gifts expected/frowned on?
10 What form of dress is expected?
11 When are the public holidays?
12 How will they react to senior businesswomen?
13 Is there a difference in attitude in the regions?
14 How are businesses structured?
15 What is their attitude to overseas buyers/sellers?
16 What is the trade-union influence?

In fact a company profile needs to be built up alongside a profile of the country you intend to do business with. This can be a long and arduous process, but there are certain agencies who can help.

Sources of information

Many organisations can help with information on European countries. The British government is particularly keen to help British exporters, and is therefore a rich source of advice for those companies thinking of entering the single market. The Department of Trade and Industry (DTI) publishes a guide to sources of information. This breaks the UK down into regions and gives the name and addresses of many organisations who can help businesses. The types of organisation include:

- representative organisations, for example trade associations like the Advertising Association
- research and technology organisations (RTOs), for example the Furniture Industry Research Association
- professional bodies, for example the British Computer Society
- small-firms organisations, for example the Federation of Small Businesses
- international chambers of commerce, for example the German Chamber of Industry and Commerce in the UK
- local chambers of commerce – these provide advice on documentation, exporting, trade exhibitions and so on
- local business organisations – these can take many forms and tend to give advice
- European information centres – established by the European Commission, these give information on sources of finance, technical standards, research and development initiatives, market intelligence and public contracts
- language-export (LX) centres – designed to help local firms with language training, translation, trade information and advice
- local authorities – many have economic development units who give advice
- European documentation centres – hold all community documentation
- training and enterprise councils – will help to support new small firms with information and advice

The DTI publishes many guides to exporting for small business. Prior to the launch of the single market on 1 January 1993 it set up a telephone hotline for any exporting queries. There are other, professional advisers who can provide information for exporters.

The major high-street banks all provide a wide range of international services, including help and advice for businesses. They can provide help on a one-to-one basis and publish many helpful guides to specific EU countries.

CONSULTANTS

Certain organisations run consultancies that may give free or paid-for advice, for example the Institute of Management Consultants. Other organisations that may be able to help are:

- the British Standards Institution
- Trading Standards Office
- Institute of Directors
- Simpler Trade Procedures Board (SITPRO)
- European Business Institute
- the Confederation of British Industry (CBI)

The CBI deserves special mention. It has over 250 000 companies as members. It can provide help and information on the single market and Europe from expert sources.

There are of course many other sources of information. Trade journals like *The Grocer* or *Campaign* can provide specialist information for a narrow section of industry. Good broadsheet newspapers like the *Financial Times, The Independent* and *The Daily Telegraph* carry a lot of helpful information. The important factor is that the information is used constructively to help improve business within the European Union

How can the UK build business within the Union?

As more and more of UK trade is involved in Europe, it is important that businesses take steps to improve on that performance, both in the short and long term. This will involve:

1 A great deal of market research to find out
  – the state of the current markets
  – the opportunities available
  – the preferences and needs of overseas customers.
2 The development of the appropriate goods and services to satisfy overseas customers' requirements.
3 The setting up of systems and procedures to enable businesses to export smoothly and efficiently.
4 A change of mentality, so that a UK firm begins to 'think European'.

The business should then begin to interact with Europe. Many European companies have seen the opportunities in the UK following the advent of the single market to set up here, for example supermarkets like Aldi and Netto. It is vital that the UK also takes advantage of opportunities on mainland Europe.

EU legislation affects businesses on a day-to-day basis. It allows all companies to operate along similar lines, so that they all work to the same rules. Legislation from the EU may help or hinder any one particular company. The important thing is to be aware of, act on and implement the legislation, adapt to the new circumstances and take advantage of the existing environment.

THE PATTERN OF TRADE BETWEEN THE UK AND THE EUROPEAN UNION

TRENDS IN TRADE

All of the opportunities the single market has presented as well as membership of the EU since 1973 has meant that UK trade with the EU has become more and more important.

The following 1992 figures show how dependent we have become on the Union for our trade.

	UK IMPORTS FROM (%)	UK EXPORTS TO (%)
Germany	17	12
USA	11	13
France	9	10
The Netherlands	8	7
Japan	6	2
Italy	5	5

TABLE 9.2 UK IMPORTS/EXPORTS 1992
SOURCE: EBIU

The UK's major exports covered both goods and services. They included chemicals, engineering, aircraft production, motor vehicles, oil and gas, banking, insurance and financial services. Around half of all our total imports come from the EU and half our exports end up in the Union.

A C T I V I T Y

Looking at the list of exports on the left can you think of the names of any UK firm who might be involved in exporting? Why do you think the type of British product/service this firm offers is in demand overseas?

The growing dependency on other EU countries is not purely a UK phenomenon. It is happening all over the Union.

	1980	1991	±%
Portugal	44.9	73.1	+28.2
Belgium/Luxembourg	65.6	72.8	+7.2
Ireland	74.5	71.9	−2.6
The Netherlands	62.2	67.5	+5.3
France	49.4	63.9	+14.5
Spain	41.7	62.5	+20.8
Greece	49.4	62.2	+12.8
Italy	45.4	58.3	+12.9
Denmark	49.5	54.2	+4.7
Germany	47.5	54.2	+6.7
UK	45.2	53.0	+7.8
All 12 EU member states	50.2	60.1	+9.9

TABLE 9.3 TRADE WITHIN THE EU AS A PERCENTAGE OF TOTAL EXTERNAL TRADE
SOURCE: EUROSTAT

You can see from the figures in Table 9.3 that all the EU countries sell at least half of their exports to other EU countries. All of them have increased exports significantly, apart from Ireland.

A C T I V I T Y

The Portuguese and Spanish have increased trade by a greater percentage with other EU members than any other country. Can you think of any reasons why this should be so?

A C T I V I T Y

Apart from the EU, the UK's other major trading partner is the USA. What type of goods do we sell to and buy from them? Why should we have such strong links with America?

WHY HAS THE UK'S TRADE GROWN?

Our trade with the EU has grown for many reasons. Our political links have meant it has made sense to do business with our partners. The single market has opened up opportunities for expansion and growth for many businesses. If a business has more customers to serve (remember there are 372 million potential consumers in the EU – it is the largest single market in the world!) and increases its production, it may benefit

from economies of scale, i.e. each unit it produces will cost less as the business can make cost-savings. The factory will only need to set up a machine once, whether it produces 200 or 20 000 irons. The cost of setting up a machine can be spread over the number of products produced. The more units produced, the thinner the costs can be spread. It is therefore in many businesses' interests to serve as many customers as possible and so enjoy these reduced production costs.

In the same way distribution costs may be better controlled by sending full lorry-loads of irons to customers in France and Italy, rather than have a half-empty lorry visit one customer in France! Most EU countries are within a reasonable delivery area for UK businesses and products can therefore be delivered efficiently.

Recession

During the late 1980s and early '90s many European countries were affected by a worldwide recession. A lot of countries had high interest rates at this time. This meant the cost of borrowing was high, so that if a business needed a bank loan to expand, it would have to pay a large amount of interest on top of the loan. This discouraged borrowing and sometimes growth.

By 1993/94 interest rates had dropped significantly in some countries, particularly the UK. This means there is now a favourable climate for businesses to borrow money, and many may do so if they are considering expanding, which should act as a stimulus to trade.

BUSINESS TRAVEL IN EUROPE

As the UK becomes more and more dependent on other Union countries for trade, it is becoming more common for UK managers and sales personnel to travel frequently throughout Europe. These journeys must be organised in a thorough, orderly and effective manner. Forward planning and clear communication are the keys to ensure that such journeys are trouble free.

Itineraries

Itineraries are documents that fully detail all travel arrangements for a business journey. An itinerary should itemise times of arrival and departure, method of travel, relevant names and addresses, time spent at each venue and so on. A copy should always be given to each of the people making the business journey.

<u>Mr R Paxton's visit to Bristol</u>
<u>Friday 14 January 199</u>

0630	Depart Paddington Station, London
0845	Arrive Bristol Temple Meads
0915	Kingston Hotel
	Kingston Square
	Bristol
	Telephone (0272) 659721
	Breakfast meeting with Ms Rhona Eli, journalist
1030	Williams Partners (Accountants)
	33 Wigmore Street
	Bristol
	Telephone (0272) 779922
	Appointment with Mr B M Williams followed by lunch with partners
1510	Depart Bristol Temple Meads
1655	Arrive Paddington Station

FIG. 9.9 SAMPLE ITINERARY

The example above is a very simple itinerary. You can see that it involves travel in the UK only and uses the 24-hour clock.

ACTIVITY

Draw up a sample itinerary for Mr Paxton. Imagine he has the same number of meetings to fit in as on the example, but with the destination changed from Bristol to Aberdeen. What are the new factors you will have to consider for a longer journey?

Steps in organising a journey effectively

There are some obvious pointers that can help you to organise a journey effectively. The key questions you need to ask in order to obtain the appropriate information are:

1 Who is travelling?
2 Which method of travel is preferred/required? For example, an air journey is fast but expensive. Sales representatives with bulky sales samples may need to travel by road.
3 What budget is available?
4 Who must be visited?
5 How much time is involved? For example, does the journey involve an overnight stay and therefore require accommodation to be booked?
6 Are there any special requirements for this journey?

The people travelling should be able to supply the general information before detailed plans are drawn up.

Methods of travel

Journeys can be made by road, rail, air and sea.

ROAD

You will need to check if a company, pool car or even a personal car is to be used. There may be a need to hire a car. If driving in Europe, the driver will need a green card and you need to consider the problem of left-/right-hand drive cars, making sure you have GB stickers, and checking that the car meets all technical and safety requirements. For example, you need to check the direction of the headlights and consider carrying warning triangle signs.

Road journeys can also be undertaken by coach.

RAIL

Depending on the length of the journey you may need to book sleeping accommodation. You may well be involved in planning a journey in Europe that involves rail companies in different countries. Facilities and train connections will be important here. You will need to consider what class of accommodation your travellers require.

AIR

Air journeys may be either internal, within the UK, or international, in Europe. You will need to consider how your traveller will journey to and from the airport. Most airlines have different classes of flight; first, business and economy. Air travel is expensive, but very fast.

SEA

Ferries and hovercraft offer a different mode of transport for business travellers. This is appropriate if people want to take their car abroad of if they are carrying heavy, bulky, fragile or confidential products with them.

For all of the above methods there are two key factors:

- What is the time-scale involved?
- How expensive is the journey?

These need to be accurately estimated. Don't forget that at certain times of the year the UK and some other European countries operate in different time zones. Your itinerary will need to accommodate this! For long journeys the most likely method of travel is by air.

Whatever arrangements are made they should always be confirmed, either by letter or fax, and the appropriate details kept on file. If hotel rooms are required these bookings should be confirmed by fax.

The confirmation must include the number and type of rooms with required facilities, times of arrival and departure, and meal and any car-hire requirements.

Sources of help

Journeys in Europe can be very complex so it is important to identify those agencies who can help you.

TRAVEL AGENTS

These will have lots of information and can be very helpful in organising complex European journeys. They have all the necessary charts, maps and, importantly, time tables that are required for effective journey planning. Travel agents can be particularly effective if your journey involves different travel methods, for example rail and air.

TRAVEL CENTRES

Many of the transport networks themselves have travel centres that give help, information and advice on their own transport, sometimes around the clock, for example British Rail travel centres.

TOURIST OFFICES

If the journey involves one particular country or region, the tourist offices representing that country in the UK can give up-to-date advice and information, without any language problems arising.

REFERENCE MATERIALS

Businesses who have a great deal of business interests in Europe will need to build up a library of their own information. This could include any of the following:

- local, national and international rail and air timetables and maps/charts
- international directories (phone and fax)
- AA/RAC handbooks
- Michelin guides
- atlases
- underground/metro maps

The final touches

You need to remember that anyone travelling in Europe may need:

- a current passport (even EU citizens). Whilst technically not required for travel it can facilitate it. It is needed for travel in non-EU Europe and useful for identification. For example, when changing cheques.
- a visa (for some countries, but not EU member states)

- health vaccinations
- an amount of foreign currency together with other means of payment acceptable, for example Eurocheques, travellers cheques, credit or charge cards
- adequate insurance for the visit

People who have travelled in Europe on business may find at some point in the future that they wish to take up permanent residence and employment in another European country. The next section examines that possibility in more detail.

EMPLOYMENT OPPORTUNITIES WITHIN THE EU

WORKING IN THE UNION

One of the benefits of the Single European Act for ordinary people is that it enables them to work in any member state, providing they have the qualifications and experience for the job.

Types of employment

There are many different types of employment that can be pursued.

FULL-TIME EMPLOYMENT

This is a permanent job where an employee works a full week. In practice this would be around 35 hours a week. Some businesses regard anyone working more than 30 hours a week as a full-time employee.

PART-TIME EMPLOYMENT

There are no hard and fast rules as to what constitutes part-time work in Europe, apart from in The Netherlands, where anyone working fewer than 35 hours a week tends to be classed as a part-time employee. In practice, part-time work tends to cover any job where an employee works fewer hours than the norm. Generally speaking in the UK, anyone working fewer than 16 hours may be classed as a part-time employee.

PERMANENT EMPLOYMENT

This is where an employee has an on-going contract of employment with no specified finish date. Employment is therefore continuous and will cease either in the case of voluntary curtailment of the contract, when the employee finds another job, or redundancy, where the job no longer exists.

TEMPORARY EMPLOYMENT

This covers temporary positions where the employer and employee have agreed that the employment will cover a limited period, for example one year, or the time taken to complete a task such as a computer installation project, or to temporarily replace an employee on maternity leave.

Types of workers

Workers are often classified into different categories to make job finding and the allocation of wage rates easier.

SKILLED WORKERS

These tend to be craftspeople who may have served an apprenticeship. They are involved in non-repetitive work and have a wide range of skills and knowledge that they use. They will work without supervision, for example a carpenter.

UNSKILLED WORKERS

This is a term used for workers who do not have specific occupational skills or qualifications. They may be employed in repetitive tasks or manual labour and will need supervision, for example a labourer.

How can you find employment in another EU country?

1 Buy overseas newspapers or check *The European* and other UK broadsheets.
2 Contact agencies who specialise in overseas jobs.
3 Contact The Overseas Placing Unit Employment Service,

Rockingham House, 123 West Street, Sheffield, S1 4ER. This organisation will help and give information to anyone wanting to work overseas and has specialised brochures for each EU country.

4 Use your Job Centre, which can call on the European Employment Service (EURES). This is a computerised service with current information on job vacancies throughout the EU. All application forms must be completed in the language of the overseas country!

5 There are many publications that may help. Below are just a few:

- *Directory of Jobs and Careers Abroad*, Alex Lipinski
- *Work Your Way Around the World*, Susan Griffith
- *The Au Pair and Nanny's Guide to Working Abroad*, Susan Griffith and Sharon Legg

NB Some countries insist their civil servants are nationals of that country. This type of job therefore would not be open to other EU citizens.

A C T I V I T Y

Visit your local library and check any overseas vacancies in the broadsheet newspapers.

1 What types of job are listed?
2 What skills are sought after in the European job market?

A C T I V I T Y

Students are often interested in temporary holiday jobs, such as grape-picking, that they can combine with a holiday. What are the benefits of living and working in an overseas country this way rather than simply taking a package holiday?

A C T I V I T Y

Trade unions are still influential in Europe, but have much more influence in some countries than others. Look at the graph opposite. Can you think of any reasons why the figures vary so much for each country?

Wanting to work in the EU and having the right qualifications are not in themselves a guarantee of success. You need to be very flexible to survive in a completely new environment. Apart from the obvious language skills needed, you should also try and learn about the countries you are interested in to appreciate their culture. It is perhaps easiest to start your investigations from your home base.

A C T I V I T Y

Carry out a survey of local businesses in your area.

1 How many of them are owned by European businesses?
2 How many of them own European companies?

You can start your desk research by using the *Yellow Pages* to find likely businesses; those with 'international' in their name, those involved in import/export or transportation and those with foreign language names. You could then perhaps compile a simple questionnaire covering business links abroad.

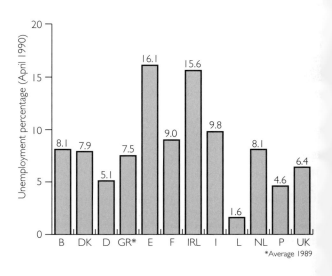

FIG. 9.10
SOURCE: THE EUROPEAN 21–24/10/93

A C T I V I T Y

1 Ask anyone in the class who has been on an educational exchange to describe their experience. Was it beneficial?
2 Find out what the Central Bureau for Exchanges and Visits does.

A C T I V I T Y

Is your town or suburb twinned with any European town or city? Prepare an information sheet on your twin. Why do you think the twinning partners suit each other? Are there any towns you think would make appropriate twins? Draw up a proposal, giving reasons for your nomination.

A C T I V I T Y

With your lecturer or teacher, make a video about your town that would be suitable for showing to a prospective twin.

A C T I V I T Y

Your local paper may carry a business section. Compile a scrapbook of articles that feature local businesses with European links.

Any of the activities outlined on p.240 might lead to the opportunity of working abroad. If not there are several obvious areas that could offer potential employment:

1 The tourist industry is a major employer in Europe and, as part of the service sector, often has part-time or temporary opportunities. The major tourist areas in the Union are Spain, Portugal, the UK, Greece, Italy and France.
2 The large conurbations (or centres of population) will also be attractive to employees.
3 Major manufacturing areas may also be worth investigating. The job opportunities here are more likely to be full-time, permanent, skilled jobs.

TRENDS IN THE EU LABOUR MARKET

It is worthwhile examining the current level of opportunities within the EU.

1 There has been a general movement from industry into the service sector across Europe. Some countries like Greece and Portugal still have a large percentage of their population working in agriculture, but generally the service sector offers the most employment opportunities (see Figure 9.13).
2 Unemployment is still a problem across Europe. This may influence the country you choose! (see Figure 9.11)
3 Certain countries are much more popular than others in attracting EU nationals.
4 Part-time work is generally growing in popularity. This type of work is often more popular with women (see Figure 9.12).

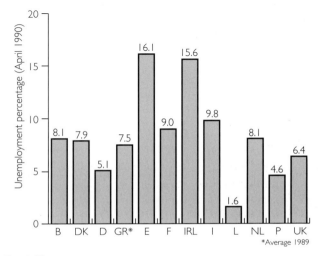

FIG. 9.11
SOURCE: EUROSTAT

Part-time work is more readily available within the service sector. In Denmark, the UK and The Netherlands around one-third of the employees within this sector work part time.

Belgium	4.8
Denmark	0.5
Germany	2.7
Greece	0.2
Spain	0.1
France	3.1
Ireland	2.2
Italy	Not published
Luxembourg	31.0
The Netherlands	1.5
Portugal	0.1
UK	1.6

TABLE 9.4 PERCENTAGE OF EMPLOYEES WHO ARE NATIONALS OF OTHER EU COUNTRIES
SOURCE: EUROSTAT

A C T I V I T Y

The figures above for Belgium and Luxembourg are fairly high. Can you think of any reasons why this is so?

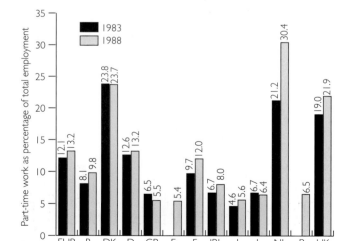

FIG. 9.12
SOURCE: EUROSTAT

Employment according to economic sector and sex in the EU – 1988

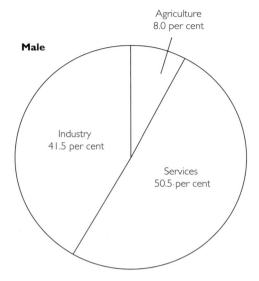

Male

Agriculture 8.0 per cent

Industry 41.5 per cent

Services 50.5 per cent

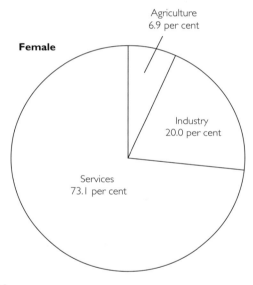

Female

Agriculture 6.9 per cent

Industry 20.0 per cent

Services 73.1 per cent

FIG. 9.13
SOURCE: EUROSTAT

Working conditions

These will vary from country to country and within each sector.

HOURS OF WORK

There has been a general trend downwards over the past 20 years in the numbers of hours worked by paid employees. Self-employed people who work full time tend to work longer hours than paid employees, an average of 50.8 hours per week against an average of 40.5 for paid employees (see Figure 9.14).

EARNINGS

These vary enormously throughout the EU and have to be considered alongside the cost of living in each country. Figure 9.15 therefore uses purchasing power standard (PPS) to compare earnings. PPS eliminates the distortions between each country that are caused by different price levels.

The average earnings of Union employees have tended to rise since 1970. This increase has not been halted by economic crises.

It is worthwhile looking at earnings again from a different point of view: how much net income is left once employees have paid income tax and made their social security contributions (National Insurance payments) in the UK.

You can see by comparing Figures 9.15 and 9.16 that those countries with the highest earnings often have the highest rate of deductions too!

A C T I V I T Y

Referring to Figure 9.15 give reasons for the low level of earnings in Greece and Portugal.

Training and qualifications

The Treaty of Rome guarantees the right to work or set up a business in any European Union country. This means that you should be treated exactly the same way as nationals of that country with respect to pay, unemployment training, trade-union membership and so on. It also means, of course, that you have to pay the appropriate taxes and social security contributions.

QUALIFICATIONS

The Union has a flexible approach to qualifications and assumes that all national diplomas and degrees are of equal worth. A potential employee may be asked to sit an additional course or test if he or she lacks sufficient professional practice in his or her own country. The EU has passed a number of directives (laws) that cover the different types of qualifications listed below.

Higher education – professional degrees completed at university over a period of at least three years, for example architecture.

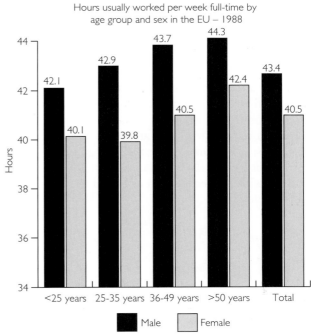

FIG. 9.14   SOURCE: EUROSTAT

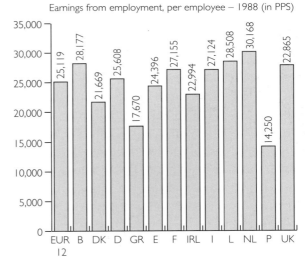

FIG. 9.15   SOURCE: EUROSTAT

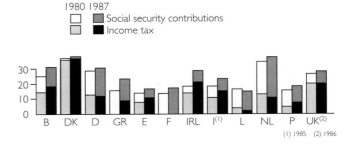

FIG. 9.16   SOURCE: EUROSTAT

2 All other professional diplomas of one to three years duration in higher education.

3 Secondary courses completed following minimum school-leaving age, plus any professional training or experience.

It is clearly a major task to detail and recognise all professional and vocational qualifications, but the Union is continuing the process and extending recognition to include NVQs and other qualifications. There is also a National Academic Recognition Information Centre (NARIC) in each member state that deals with the recognition of academic qualifications.

In groups select one of the training programmes below and investigate it. Prepare a short presentation to the class that explains the main points of the programme. In addition, prepare a single-sheet handout to give to members of the class, again covering the major points of the programme.

Community programmes and budgets – useful addresses

Programme or initiative	Target group	Budget (million ECU[1])	Address
Lingua	Students and teaching staff in vocational training (secondary level); business and industry personnel	200 (1990-94)	Equipe d'assistance Lingua Place du Luxembourg 2-3 B-1040 Brussels
Erasmus	Students in higher education	192 (1991-93)	Bureau Erasmus Rue d'Arlon 15 B-1050 Brussels
Comett	Students in higher education; business and industry personnel	200 (1990-94)	Bureau Comett Av. de Cortenbergh 71 B-1040 Brussels
Petra	Young people undergoing initial training and persons with responsibility for training	15 (1991)	Ifaplan Square Ambiorix 32 B-1040 Brussels
Tempus	Young people in Central and Eastern Europe		Rue de Trèves 45 B-1040 Brussels
Force	Training staff and persons with responsibility for ongoing training	13 (1991)	Rue du Nord 34 B-1000 Brussels
Eurotecnet	Young people or business and industry personnel	2.2 (1991)	Rue des deux Eglises 37 B-1040 Brussels
Youth for Europe	Young people between 15 and 25	6.5 (1991)	Jeunesse pour l'Europe Place du Luxembourg 2-3 B-1040 Brussels
Arion	Education experts and persons with responsibility in the field		Equipe d'assistance Arion Pädagogischer Austauschdienst Nassestrasse 8 D-5300 Bonn 1
Action Jean Monnet	Centres of higher education		EC Commision-DG X – University Information rue de la Loi 200 B-1040 Brussels
Cedefop	Vocational training specialists		Cedefop Bundesallee 22 D-1000 Berlin 15
Eurydice	Persons with responsibility in education		Eurydice Rue Archimède 17 B-1040 Brussels

[1] 1 ECU (European currency unit) = approximately £ 0.69 on the basis of rates applying at the end of May 1991.

FIG. 9.17

TRAINING

Training is a very important part of the Union's strategy and the EU has devised many different programmes that young people can benefit from.

The programmes cover higher education, young workers exchanges and specialist areas. The body responsible for creating training programmes is the Centre for the Development of Vocational Training (Cedefop). This was created in 1975. Figure 9.17 on p.244 shows some previous and current training programmes, but the EU is developing new programmes all the time. One of its most recent is the IRIS programme, which is focused on women's needs for training. Language training is vital for the prosperity of the Union and the Lingua programme concentrates on this.

Further information on current programmes can be obtained from the European Commission and Cedefop.

THE COSTS AND STANDARD OF LIVING ACROSS EUROPE

Having investigated the possibility of finding employment in Europe or in receiving further training with overseas employment as a goal, let's look at what it's like to live abroad.

STANDARD OF LIVING

Living in another country can be an exciting and rewarding experience. There will be many new aspects to get used to, quite apart from mastering the language. The standard of living varies across member states. There are many ways of measuring it, but there is no absolute rule. Certain features give an indication of the standard of living. One is wage levels which we have already looked at in the section on employment on p.243. Another is the level of ownership of consumer durables. Generally, the higher the ownership level, the higher the standard of living is assumed to be.

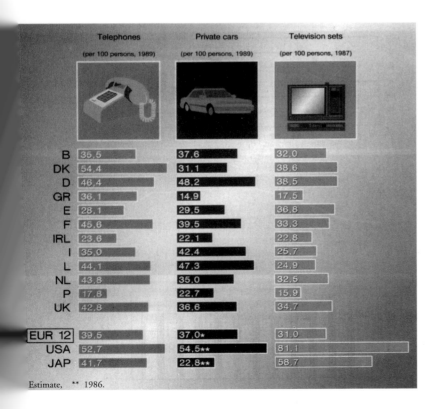

	Telephones (per 100 persons, 1989)	Private cars (per 100 persons, 1989)	Television sets (per 100 persons, 1987)
B	35.5	37.6	32.0
DK	54.4	31.1	38.6
D	46.4	48.2	38.5
GR	36.1	14.9	17.5
E	28.1	29.5	36.8
F	45.6	39.5	33.3
IRL	23.6	22.1	22.8
I	35.0	42.4	25.7
L	44.1	47.3	24.9
NL	43.8	35.0	32.5
P	17.8	22.7	15.9
UK	42.8	36.6	34.7
EUR 12	39.5	37.0*	31.0
USA	52.7	54.5**	81.1
JAP	41.7	22.8**	58.7

Estimate, ** 1986.

FIG. 9.18

A C T I V I T Y

Can you explain the differences in the figures in the chart on the previous page?

Types of accommodation and facilities give an indication of the economic health of a country. Citizens of countries often show a tendency to prefer either rented or owned property. This can be viewed as a national preference. What is important is the facilities these properties have.

	BATHROOM OR SHOWER ON THE PREMISES	CENTRAL HEATING ON THE PREMISES	INTERNAL WC
B	73.9	79.0	:
DK	85.1	95.8	54.6
D	92.3	96.0	70.0
GR	69.3	70.9	:
E	85.3	:	22.5
F	85.2	85.4	67.6
IRL	82.0	84.5	39.2
I	86.4	87.7	56.5
L	86.2	97.3	73.9
NL	95.9	:	66.1
P	58.0	58.7	:
UK	98.0	97.3	:

TABLE 9.5 BASIC AMENITIES (%) – 1981–82 CENSUSES
SOURCE: SOCIAL EUROPE

The standard of living can also be measured by the wealth of the country. The more it produces per head of population, the greater its output (this is normally called the gross domestic product or GDP) and the higher the standard of living is said to be (see Figure 9.19).

The amount of money people have to spend on leisure in Europe also indicates their standard of living. We can assume that people going on holiday have covered their basic needs of food, shelter and heat and are therefore choosing how to spend their disposable income.

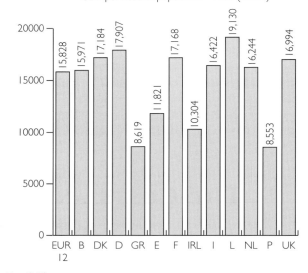

FIG. 9.19
SOURCE: EUROSTAT

A C T I V I T Y

The standard of living does not always reflect the quality of life. Look at the table above: the people in Portugal and Greece have the lowest standard of living. Does this lack of material goods necessarily mean an unhappier life? Would you like to try living in one of these countries?

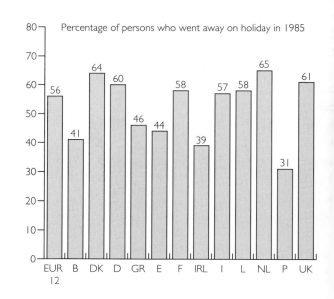

FIG. 9.20
SOURCE: EUROBAROMETER

Expenditure on leisure as a percentage of our total household income shows a definite increase over the past few years. This trend may indicate that the standard of living has gone up. It may also reflect lower prices on other items of expenditure.

THE COST OF LIVING

From the tables provided it would be easy to decide that the most attractive country is the one with the highest salaries, most cars and so on, but we have to stop and consider how much everything costs (see Table 9.7).

	B	DK	D	GR	E	F	IRL	I	L	NL	P	UK
1970	4.1	7.1	8.3	5.2	6.4	5.7	8.3	6.5	3.6	7.5	:	7.4
1975	4.9	8.4	9.7	4.8	7.0	6.3	8.2	6.4	3.6	8.7	:	8.7
1980	6.0	9.2	9.3	5.4	6.8	7.3	10.1	7.9	3.4	9.7	5.0	9.5
1985	6.0	9.7	8.8	5.9	6.6	7.1	9.6	8.1	3.4	9.3	5.8	9.4
1987	6.4	9.6	8.9	6.5	6.6	7.3	9.7	8.2	:	9.6	:	9.5

TABLE 9.6 TRENDS IN HOUSEHOLD EXPENDITURE ON LEISURE, ENTERTAINMENT AND EDUCATIONAL AND CULTURAL PURSUITS AS A PROPORTION OF TOTAL EXPENDITURE (PERCENTAGE)

SOURCE: EUROBAROMETER
TOTAL OVER 100 OWING TO MULTIPLE REPLIES

Country by country, how prices compare

ITEM	FRANCE	UK	SPAIN	GREECE	PORTUGAL
40 ltrs petrol	£28	£17	£22	£24	£24
1 day's car hire	£37	£37	£30	£37	£30
Average hotel room	£49–£74	£40	£45–£57	£30.58	£67
Expensive hotel room	£184–£368	£200	£156–£340	£142	£157
Fast food meal for two	£9	£5	£7	£3–£6	£7
Expensive meal for two	£98–£245	£120	£68	£55–£61	£63
Bottle of wine	£1.10–£2.33	£4–£10	85p–£1.28	£4.59	£2.24
Large beer in a bar	£2–£5	£1.20	£1.13	£1–£2	67p
Cup of coffee	59p–£1.84	50p	58p	76p–£1.53	27p
Ice cream cone	£1.47	60p	58p	61p	67p
Loaf of bread	33p	50p	34p	37p	58p
250g of butter	£1.14	60p	£1.13	£1.07	£1.57
500g of local cheese	£4.17	£2.26	£4.25	£1.99	£2.91
1 ltr milk (1.75 pints)	82p	55p	54p	73p	63p
Four apples	99p	40p	58p	92p	39p
Four tomatoes	£1.26	35p	85p	61p	63p
Museum admission	£4	£4	£3.40	£4.59	89p
Cinema ticket	£5	£5	£2.84	£3	£2
Nightclub admission	£18	£5–£10	£8.50	£4	£7
20 cigarettes	£1.40	£2.40	91p	£1.30	£1.16
Souvenir T-shirt	£9.20	£10	£5.67	£3.67	£11
Cheap sunglasses	£6–£15	£10–£15	£3	£2–£6	£8.95
Suntan lotion	£6.75	£5–£10	£8.51	£4.89	£2.68
Postcard	31p	30p	9p	9p–15p	13p
Postage of postcard	27p	24p	16p	28p	31p

Exchange rates, equivalent to £1: France 8.15 Francs, Spain 176.25 Pesetas, Greece 327 Drachmas, Portugal 223.5 Escudos.

TABLE **9.7** COMPARATIVE BASKET OF GOODS SOURCE: DAILY MAIL 1/5/93

There are wide variations in the purchase price of goods over Europe from cars to houses. Even renting is a precarious business. Look at Table 9.8. This shows that Greek rents have trebled over six years whilst German rents have only increased by 26.4 per cent. The Greek rate of increase is nearly ten times that of Germany!

Even VAT rates differ, as can be seen from Table 9.9.

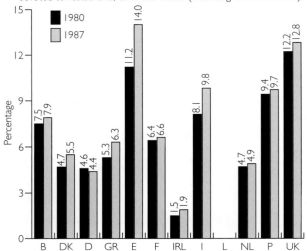

Trends in the proportion of total household expenditure devoted to restaurants, cafés and hotels (excluding alcoholic drinks)

■ 1980
▨ 1987

FIG. 9.21
SOURCE: EUROSTAT

ACTIVITY

Reviewing the information supplied on both the standard of living and the cost of living, which two EU countries would you like to live in? Give your reasons why.

	1980	1981	1982	1983	1984	1985	1986
B	100.0	108.1	116.4	126.3	132.5	136.1	140.9
DK	100.0	107.8	118.3	129.5	139.7	147.0	153.2
D	100.0	104.4	109.7	115.6	120.0	123.9	126.4
GR	100.0	124.9	153.5	172.2	198.3	230.1	281.5
E	100.0	111.2	125.4	136.0	146.2	152.9	159.9
F	100.0	113.3	125.4	137.9	148.9	158.7	167.5
IRL	100.0	107.9	125.5	134.6	148.8	156.6	161.0
I	100.0	115.6	135.0	160.4	196.2	207.9	226.1
L	100.0	:	:	:	:	:	:
NL	100.0	107.0	114.6	122.4	127.9	131.9	135.6
P	100.0	:	:	:	:	:	:
UK	100.0	129.4	149.3	160.5	170.3	184.1	202.3

TABLE 9.8 INDEX OF RENTS FROM 1980 TO 1986 (BASE 1980 = 100)
SOURCE: SOCIAL EUROPE

Denmark	25
Ireland	21
Belgium	19.5
Italy	19
Greece	18
France	18.6
The Netherlands	17.5
UK	17.5
Portugal	16
Spain	15
Germany	15
Luxembourg	15

TABLE 9.9 VAT RATES (%) IN THE EU

WHAT ARE YOUR RIGHTS AND RESPONSIBILITIES IF YOU CHOOSE TO LIVE IN ANOTHER EU COUNTRY?

RIGHTS AND RESPONSIBILITIES

Any EU citizen has the right to live and work in another member state. In exceptional cases, you can be refused entry on the grounds of health, public security or finance. This rarely happens. There are certain conditions to consider, however.

1 You can stay in another member state for about six months to look for a job. Longer periods are allowed if you are genuinely looking and seem likely to secure employment.
2 You can take a job or set up your own business without a work permit. However, you should apply for a residence permit. This lasts for five years. It can be renewed and is normally given automatically.
3 Between three months and one year into your stay you will be granted a temporary residence permit on application.
4 Anyone employed in an EU country can bring their family to live with them.
5 Students, pensioners and those of independent means can live in another state providing they are registered with their own national health service.

All of these rights, however, are counterbalanced by duties that you have as an EU citizen. You must abide by the laws and customs of the country you are living in. Even when the laws are different to those of the UK you are still subject to them and must obey them. You do not have the right to ignore those laws you disagree with. You must also adhere to any customs regulations that exist. Although the single market allows free movement of goods, as we have already specified special conditions apply to alcohol and tobacco.

A C T I V I T Y

Are there any problems associated with the free movement of people across Europe? What problems did earlier border controls help to contain?

Identity cards

European passports were introduced in 1985 as a common identity document. However, passports are not essential in the EU. If stopped at a border crossing, a Union citizen need only show a national identity card. As the UK does not have a national identity card system, British citizens do have to use a passport. By displaying the EU green sticker on a car windscreen, a driver can cross Union borders with no problems. Visas are required for non-Union nationals.

A C T I V I T Y

The UK has not had a system of identity cards since the early 1950s. Do you think it would be a good idea to have such a system, as in some other European countries? Design a card. It could be a simple card or machine-readable (like a credit card) with information stored on computers. Which system do you think is best?

BENEFITS

Social security

Member states are understandably worried about the prospect of other EC nationals moving into their country and becoming a burden on their own social security system. Therefore, students have to be enrolled at an educational establishment and prove they can support themselves to get a permit. Pensioners and those of independent means receive a permit, but must prove they have sufficient funds to live on. If you are unemployed you have the right to have your unemployment benefits transferred to another EU country for up to three months.

Will I be eligible for any benefits in another EU country?

You will be eligible for the social security benefits of any EU country, providing you have already made the appropriate contributions in the UK or another EU country. This means you will have access to that country's health service as well as other benefits. In some countries, the health service may operate slightly differently to the service in the UK. For example, you may be asked to pay a percentage of the treatment's cost and then get some money reimbursed later. You may need to top up your health cover with a private insurance scheme to cover these extra costs.

You will need to register for social security on your arrival in the EU country. Not all countries have identical benefits, but the most common ones you could expect to find are:

- unemployment benefit
- retirement pension
- maternity benefit
- accident-at-work insurance
- medical treatment

Help and advice

If you need information and advice within the EU then UK embassies and consulates may be able to help you. They can supply general information on passports, voting rights and so on. They are a good point of contact if an emergency arises, for example serious illness. Their role is an official one, however, and their services in an emergency would focus on giving advice and help; they would not pay for any emergency services.

CHAPTER NINE
Test Yourself!

1 Name the 15 EU member states.
2 Name the four institutions of the EU.
3 List three objectives of the Single European Act.
4 What does the SEA ensure free movement of?
5 What is an exchange rate?
6 Name six non-EU European countries.
7 Name three methods of changing currency abroad.
8 What are the two major components of the EMS?
9 List four sources of information for potential exporters.
10 Who are the UK's major trading partners?
11 Why has UK trade with the EU grown?
12 What is the difference between part-time and temporary employment?
13 List three sources of information on job opportunities in Europe.
14 Which countries have the highest standard of living in Europe?
15 Name the major centres of population in Europe.
16 Name four Union programmes for training.
17 Which countries have the lowest cost of living in Europe? Why?
18 Who has the right to live in another EU country?
19 Which countries in Europe have the highest and lowest GDP?
20 What services can an overseas embassy provide?

Chapter

10

BUSINESS AND ENTERPRISE

ENTERPRISE PLANNING

WHAT IS ENTERPRISE?

Every year many ordinary people decide to go into business for themselves. Sometimes this is a result of a life-long dream, at other times they may be pushed into it by enforced redundancy. Whatever the cause it is becoming an option for many people, and the more skills and knowledge they can bring to the project the more likely it is to succeed. Many small businesses fail every year despite the best intentions of their owners. The failure might be due to lack of research, lack of planning or just a lack of cash.

Enterprise, that is creating businesses, jobs and wealth from your own ideas, is now part of the British business culture. Many major businesses, like Richard Branson's Virgin empire, started as one-man bands. As a student of business you may have the opportunity to take part in enterprise schemes within your school or college. These should be good preparation for the world of work outside.

Why do people go into business for themselves?

We have already mentioned two reasons why people might want to run their own business. Another reason might be to escape from an unfulfilling job or to pursue a hobby that they think can provide a livelihood for them.

Running their own business is a big risk for many people to take so they need to carry out a great deal of research and preparation before deciding whether or not to try their hand at being their own boss.

We must not forget that making good profits may also be one of the key reasons for people to launch a new business – they would not be contemplating it with a view to making losses!

Preparing and contributing to a plan

There are three key areas to consider in setting up a small business:

1 Planning.
2 Implementing the plan and managing the business.
3 Assessing how well the business is performing.

None of these areas should be neglected.

PLANNING

Many new businesses fail as they do not plan, despite having many orders. Most banks will require you to provide a business plan before they will consider granting any loans. Plans help companies to prepare for any unexpected problems or opportunities.

IMPLEMENTING THE PLAN AND MANAGING THE BUSINESS

Business plans should be reviewed frequently. They need to be used as working documents and be often referred to so it becomes easier to see how the business is performing and how to manage it.

ASSESSING THE BUSINESS PERFORMANCE

This can be done in many ways. You can check sales and profit levels or ask your customers for feedback. Your actual sales and profits should be measured against any forecasts.

WHAT RESOURCES DO YOU NEED TO GO INTO BUSINESS?

The resources you require will fall into three main areas:

1 Time.
2 Materials and equipment.
3 People.

All of these will of course require the additional and most critical resource of money or finance.

Time

This is a critical factor in any business. You need time to plan your business properly before rushing anything onto the market. You also need to allocate enough time for your business to become established before you can expect to start making profits.

Writing a business plan will help you make decisions on time, people and materials. The following list discusses what should be contained in a business plan.

BASIC ELEMENTS OF A BUSINESS PLAN

1 The business name and address.
2 A description of the business organisation. Will it be a limited company, partnership or sole trader (see Chapter 1 pp.1–3 for descriptions).
3 A section that describes the main activities and products of the business.
4 The date the business started trading.
5 The objectives of the business.
6 Its capital structure, for example the share value and amount of capital in the business if it is a partnership or limited company.
7 Some details of key personnel, their ages and qualifications, their positions and salaries.
8 Details on your product/service.
9 Statistics on the market you are entering and information on your potential customers' buying habits.
10 Comparative information on your major competitors.
11 Your projected turnover (sales revenue) for year one.
12 Information on any market research you have carried out.
13 Details of any marketing campaigns you intend to carry out.
14 Information on your suppliers.
15 Any production details.
16 Details of your business premises, rent, rates and so on.
17 Details of your plant and machinery.
18 Information on any assets held as security. For example, if you require a loan from the bank, will you offer your house as a guarantee against non-payment of the loan?
19 A breakdown of the finance required to fund your project and its sources.
20 Details of any loans/funding you may require from the bank.
21 A cash flow forecast to cover your first year of trading.

The above list seems pretty extensive, but if you look carefully at the information required, you can see it falls into general areas of staff, finance and business details. The business plan can be used to show you have a viable business proposition and to help persuade the bank to loan you money to help your business. The plan must be reviewed frequently to make sure your business is on track.

As we have already said, time is an important resource. You can see by the amount of information required for the plan just how much preparation you have to do before you can launch your business.

Contingencies

Sensible business plans allow for contingencies. This means that plans are prepared in advance suggesting action to be taken if anything abnormal should happe

For example, if you rely on importing goods from mainland Europe by sea, what would you do if the ferries were to go on strike? A good business plan would contain the contingency of using the Channel Tunnel, flying in goods or switching to a UK supplier. The problems a business is most likely to meet are:

- disruptions, for example a strike of employees or a cut in supply of energy or vital materials
- emergencies, for example a fire
- health and safety issues, for example a leak from a nuclear plant or an outbreak of salmonella in the egg supply
- normal insurable risks such as theft, flood damage or accidental damage

Contingency action should always be stated in the plan even though a business may normally insure against the risks above. For example, in terms of health and safety there needs to be an emergency plan detailing responsibilities allocated to key personnel in case of an emergency.

A C T I V I T Y

A good business plan should be clear and easy to read, but still have enough information to show how the business will run. Using the list of information required on p.252, design your own blank business plan that small businesses could fill in. Remember this document may run to four or five pages, so make sure you leave enough space for each section.

A C T I V I T Y

The major high-street banks often provide information or starter packs for small businesses. Many of these packs contain business plan documents. Gather as many as you can and compare them with your own design. You could use one of the bank's or your own blank plans for your own enterprise project.

What are the sources of information?

Adequate information is a key element of any business plan. You should check the sources in the following table to see if they provide any kind of student information packs.

INFORMATION REQUIRED ON:	SOURCE
General business start-up	High-street banks
	Business advice centres
Tax	Inland Revenue
VAT	Customs and Excise
National insurance	DSS
Building regulations	Local authority planning department
Public health	Environmental health services
Trading practice	Trading standards
Grants	European Commission

TABLE 10.1 SOURCES OF BUSINESS INFORMATION

NB Local reference libraries are an invaluable source of information. They hold directories on suppliers, competitors, market-research statistics and local information.

Materials and equipment

These will vary enormously depending on the type of business you are setting up. If you are thinking about a service such as window cleaning, your equipment will probably be limited to your cleaning equipment and transport. If, on the other hand, you are going into manufacturing, you may find you need a great deal of money to acquire the resources you need. A brief check concerning your equipment will cover the following points:

1 If I need raw materials can I get hold of them easily? Is the supply of these materials constant? Is the price subject to wild fluctuation?
2 What type of premises do I need? Could I work from home? Should I buy, lease or rent premises? How much will the premises cost to run? Am I eligible for any grants for premises as a small business?
3 Plant and machinery – Do I buy new or old machinery? Can I lease some of it? Will it need to be replaced frequently? Can my machinery levels cope if the business grows?

People

Staff may be a key factor in making your new business a success. You may start out on your own, but at some stage it is likely that you will need to employ someone. This can be quite a complicated area of business. You will need to consider:

1 How many staff will I need? Are there any key posts that have to be filled?

2 Could I employ outside consultancies and agencies on individual projects, for example pay an accountant to prepare the accounts, rather than employ full-time staff?

3 How will I find the staff with the right skills? Am I prepared to do any training?

4 How will I pay staff? What will their terms and conditions be?

5 Do I have the expertise to deal with staff and trade unions?

Estimates

In order to assess how much money and other resources you will need, it is sensible to prepare an estimate of what income you will receive from your business venture and what you think your costs will be. You will need to be able to calculate breakeven point. Breakeven point is where a business does not make a profit or loss. This means once a business has earned enough money from its sales to cover its costs it has reached breakeven point. Any money received after breakeven point has been reached is profit. For example, your total weekly costs including material, wages, etc. for your sandwich business are £250. All of your sandwiches cost £1. You need to sell 250 sandwiches per week to reach breakeven point. If you sell 300 sandwiches you make £50 profit.

Budget statements

This type of statement will list all of the material and human resource needs of a business and allocate a cost to them. It also includes income. A budget statement should therefore list expected income and expenditure item by item for a stated future period.

INVESTIGATING RESOURCES

Resources and their correct use are so critical to the success of a business venture that it is worthwhile looking at them in some detail. You may well notice significant differences in how businesses use resources between small businesses/enterprise ventures and larger businesses. The first factors to affect the use of resources are the business goals of the venture. A goal is a future aim which the business is trying to achieve. These will vary depending on whether the business is a profit-making one, for example a food manufacturer, or a non-profit-making venture, for example a local art gallery. Some common business goals are as follows:

ACTIVITY

You are running a car cleaning serice. Your prices are £3 per car and £5 per van and you employ four staff. Over a 10-week period you clean the following vehicles.

Week number	No. of cars	No. of vans
1	7	2
2	6	2
3	5	3
4	13	0
5	19	0
6	10	6
7	7	3
8	12	4
9	4	5
10	7	10

You have spent £16.95 on cleaning materials over the 10-week period and you pay each car cleaner £1 per vehicle (regardless of whether it is a van or car). You have also paid £3.87 back to your car cleaners as expenses to cover their bus fares to the cleaning site. You must:

- calculate your income for the 10-week period
- calculate your total costs for the 10-week period
- calculate how many cars and/or vans you need to clean to reach breakeven point
- prepare a budget statement for your enterprise
- calculate how much profit you have made

- to increase profits
- to increase market share (your sales in relation to your competitors)
- to control your costs (normally this means to keep them down)
- social goals, for example the transfusion service might have a goal of securing more blood donors for the benefit of local patients
- to look after the health and welfare of employees (past and present) and customers
- to care for and be responsible towards employees, customers and the general public

All the goals listed above require human, physical and financial resources to make them achievable. Different types of resources will be important to different industrial sectors (as discussed on p.6 of Chapter 1, 'Business organisations and employment').

Primary sector

Primary-sector businesses, for example farming and mining, are sometimes described as being extractive industies as they take natural resources from the earth. They might sometimes produce raw materials, for example oil to go into petrol. They are not generally labour intensive (this means that many people are employed to do a job). For example, many large farms in the UK have few employees. Instead they often rely on a great deal of machinery and equipment which can be expensive. Examples of equipment are tractors and combine harvesters for farming, mining equipment and refining and processing plants for oil.

Secondary sector

This sector covers manufacturing and construction. Businesses within this sector make products using raw materials and parts from other industries. An example would be a car manufacturer like Ford. The type of resources they use will vary depending on the product they produce and how far that prodution process can be automated. For example, car manufacturers use fewer and fewer production workers as they can replace them with robots. However, the business will still employ skilled designers, marketing, finance, sales and other production staff. Staff will be used in the most cost effective manner and most manufacturers will want to control staff costs to help them in their goal of making profits. The human resource department (personnel) will help with controlling employment costs as well as looking after the overall welfare of employees. Alternatively if you are a business making hand-made chocolates you will need to employ a large number of people to keep your production lines rolling. Manufacturers tend to have to spend a large amount of money on physical resources such as production machinery, vehicles for transportation, component parts and factory buildings. This will require a great deal of investment so the business may well take up loans and grants to fund the business. This is one of the most expensive types of business to set up and run as it often requires a lot of investment at the beginning and needs a lot of cash to keep it going.

Tertiary sector

This is sometimes called the service sector. The key resource used here is people. Staff are normally employed to deliver the service customers are buying, for example a hairdresser cuts hair, a sales assistant helps with a purchase, an accountant will draw up a set of accounts. More than 50 per cent of the UK workforce is now employed in the service sector. As staff are vital in the process it is important that they are well-trained. One of the main expenses in running this type of business will be staff costs, however there will be other costs. If the service business is a retailer, they will need premises which can be expensive, good sales staff and stock to sell. There will be some service businesses where staff are the main resource used. For example, a cleaning business might need a central office, a number of vans for transport, cleaning materials, a few central administrative staff and also a whole army of cleaners to do the job. Quite often service industies do not have to invest as much in machinery, equipment or physical resources as manufacturers do, they may therefore be a little less expensive to start up and run, but this is not a hard and fast rule.

Obtaining resources

We have already discussed how expensive it can be to run a business. It is unlikely that any business will have enough money of its own to start up and run so it is important for businesses to know the best methods available for them to acquire resources.

Physical resources, for example equipment, can be purchased or leased. Leasing means that the equipment is rented out and monthly payments are paid (this system is similar to hire purchase). At the end of the leasing period the equipment does not belong to the business who has leased the equipment (the lessee) but still belongs to the business renting it out (the lessor). This way the business is able to use the asset, but does not buy it. There will normally be some kind of service agreement for the equipment.

ACTIVITY

Draw up a list of advantages and disadvantages to a business of leasing equipment, for example a photocopier, rather than buying it?

Human resources can be employed by a number of methods, for example advertising, interviewing and then recriting staff. You may not wish to employ staff on a regular or full-time basis, but may need them short term for a special project where a particular type of expertise is needed. For example, engaging the services of a roofing firm and its employees for six months if you are a housebuilder and need to finish a new development of houses. This is called subcontracting. Subcontracting means that although one business has overall responsibility for completing a contract, the business can farm out parts of the contract to other businesses and buy in its expertise.

All businesses require financial resources. This is normally in the form of funds that businesses use to purchase equipment etc. Capital is provided by the owner or business at the start of trading, and this could come from the owner's own money. Working capital (the funds used for the business to operate) could be in the form of shareholders' funds, an overdraft provided by the banks or from creditors (those people who have provided the business with goods and services, but who have not yet been paid for them). Banks and finance companies are normally active in providing loans for businesses, usually for large purchases.

PLANNING RESOURCES FOR SMALL BUSINESSES

Smaller organisations will have some shared goals with larger organisations. However, they have some distinct features which need to be examined as these will affect how they use their resources. Their business goals may include the following:

- increasing profits
- improving productivity
- increasing sales
- maintaining and/or improving quality control
- controlling costs
- social goals, for example sponsoring a litter bin outside a shop to help the environment
- to look after the health and welfare of employees and customers
- to care for and be responsible towards employees, customers and the general public

ACTIVITY

'Controlling costs' is vital for both large and small businesses. Draw up a list of things which might happen if a business were to fail to control its costs.

ACTIVITY

Why is 'increasing sales' key for a small business? Design a newspaper advertisement for a small business which you think will help to increase sales.

Resource requirements for small businesses

The financial resources required will again be capital (to start the business) and loans, like larger organisations, however they are likely to be on a much smaller scale. Physical resources could take a variety of forms such as:

- site/location (for example where the business is to be found)
- buildings (for example workshops, offices, factories)
- equipment (for example production machinery, office equipment)
- materials (for example components, raw materials)
- services (for example, power, water)

Human resources play a critical role in a small business's success. The business is unlikely to have excess funds so the staff it employs must work effectively. Often a small business owner will carry out many roles him or herself. As the business grows it will need to employ more staff to take on specialist roles. If staff do not already have the skills required when recruited, the business will need to provide the right type and amount of training. Specialist skills may be needed in the following areas:

- to manage and administer the business
- to produce the goods
- to promote goods/services
- for security purposes
- to train and develop staff
- to ensure health and safety

Not only is it important that all these areas are covered, but there also needs to be the right number of staff to carry out these roles. In some small businesses it may be tempting for the owner to think he or she can control costs by employing low numbers of staff when they really need more. This is a short-term view which could well hinder the performance of the business.

When obtaining resources, small businesses have the same options open to them as larger organisations:

- physical resources – purchase or lease
- human resources – recruit or sub-contract
- financial resources – capital or loans

However, although the methods available are the same, it may be more difficult to obtain the financial resources for a new business as it may be seen as a greater risk to a bank than a larger, well-established business. If it is not as well-known as larger organisations it may also be more difficult to attract good staff.

Not all of the above has to be taken into account for a student enterprise scheme. However, it is important to understand just how vital the use and planning of resources is to the success of a business regardless of its scale.

STUDENT ACCELERATED SCHEME

Starting a business is a very complicated process and many small businesses take years in getting to even this stage. If you are students setting up a business for an enterprise activity, you will not be able to take this amount of time, so you need to take the fast track!

You should never attempt to cut corners in business. All too often it will lead to grief and failure. We have already shown in this chapter just how much planning is required to make a business successful. However, if you are a student you may have to concertina your business activities into one academic year, so below you will find a list of hints and tips which may help you to find information or make decisions more quickly.

Finding an idea for a business – potential ventures

This is one of the most difficult areas of all. Ideas that are original, appealing and easy to manage and fund are difficult to come by! Try not to be tempted into 'me-too' ideas that have been done many times before and where it would be difficult to make your mark, for example designing T-shirts or a sandwich delivery service. Instead try the following approaches:

- Carry out a survey to really find out what people would like, rather than just assuming you already know what they want.
- Review you local paper's business section to see what new ideas are succeeding.
- Hold brainstorming sessions to come up with as many ideas as possible. Do *not* discount any ideas even if they seem outrageous and completely out of the question. These wild responses may lead you onto a good idea,

and they can always be screened out later. Make sure someone leads the sessions and records all of the ideas.
4 Do some desk research to see if there are any local customer groups whose needs are not being satisfied. This may mean checking in local papers.

Are there any local causes you could tie in with? A T-shirt project might be viable if it were to promote a 'Save our school' or 'No to the M81' cause!

Instead of going into business for yourself, you might consider working as part of a team. This will be particularly relevant for any student taking part in an enterprise activity. Remember that some ventures can be adapted for individuals and teams. Perhaps you have been involved in baby sitting before. If so, would you be able to organise a baby-sitting service with a team of students available on a rota basis? Another idea for an individual or a team might be to organise an event such as a sponsored walk for charity or run a stall at a local fête. Ventures do not have to be large profit-making concerns.

Selecting your venture

Once you have decided on two or three potential ventures you will need to select your preferred business. You may wish to draw up a list of criteria against which you can assess each venture. Questions you may wish to ask yourself are:

- Do we have the resources to run the venture?
- Is it a venture that will need a lot of money to start up?
- Is the good/service easy to produce and/or buy?
- Do we have the skills to run the business?
- Is there a demand/market opportunity for our good/service?
- Do we have enough time to start the business effectively?
- Will there be adequate rewards at the end of our venture?

What will the major constraints be?

These are quite often the same as the required resources. You need to acknowledge immediately that the following will cause problems:

1 Allocating the right amount of time to each part of the business. Finding enough time to run the business effectively, and making sure all of your staff dedicate enough time to the business.
2 Finding people with the right skills to do the job effectively.

3 Being able to secure the right equipment at reasonable rates (particularly if it is specialist equipment).
4 Controlling the costs of the business. This is one of the major causes of business failure in the UK. New entrepreneurs let the costs of the business spiral out of control without checking them. They may have seriously under-estimated how much it would cost to get the business up and running in the first place. It is a key area that must be carefully controlled.

A C T I V I T Y

Good planning beforehand will help you to avoid the problems listed above.

1 With other members of your group discuss how businesses could avoid these problems.
2 Draw up a list of actions businesses could take if the problems do arise.

LEGAL CONSTRAINTS

It is vital that your business venture is legal and does not contravene any equal opportunities. For example, baby minders must be registered with the local authority. If you advertise for staff you must be careful not to use terms like 'salesman' which deny equal opportunities to certain sectors of society. Food production must take into account hygiene and health and safety regulations.

Business objectives and goals

BUSINESS GOALS

A business goal is a future aim which the business is trying to achieve. The type of business goal will depend on the nature of the business you are setting up. Your goal could be to create a profit-making business and therefore make profits, where one of your key objectives will be to make profits which can be used to develop the business and/or to give back to investors. Alternatively, it could be to create a non-profit-making business whose goal is to spread awareness of a cause, for example a charity. This does not mean that the business does not wish to make profits under any circumstances, it means that making profit will not be the primary objective of the business. For example one of Oxfam's main objectives is to reduce suffering and hunger in developing countries. In order to achieve this Oxfam makes profits from its shops which it uses to achieve its main objective of reducing hunger.

A C T I V I T Y

How many local non-profit-making organisations can you identify? Remember these can include charities, art galleries, museums, churches and religious organisations.

When an organisation wants to be more specific and detailed about what it wants to achieve, it will set objectives. These must be agreed within the business so that the business team can set about achieving the objectives in a constructive manner. Objective setting is a very difficult area that many new businesses struggle with. There are a couple of tips that will help you to establish logical business objectives:

1 They must be realistic. You will not become the largest business in the area overnight. If your target is unattainable, it will be difficult to maintain you and your staff's enthusiasm if you fail.
2 They should be measurable. 'To be successful' is not an objective. Who will judge what success means? 'To expand' is not really a proper objective either. If you sell 1,000 cars one year and 1,001 the next you have expanded, but would it be judged a success?

There are several ways of stating objectives. These could be in terms of:

- sales
- profit
- customer take-up
- product/service promotion

SALES

Sales objectives can be measured in terms of volume, i.e. number of products sold, or revenue, i.e. the total value of all products sold. An example of this would be:

Our objective is to sell 300 mugs at £3 each and have a turnover of £900 over one year.

NB Objectives must always have a time-scale to show how long it will take the business to achieve them.

PROFIT

This is a key objective and one on which most commercial organisations will focus. It does not matter how many mugs you sell each year if you do not make a profit! Your objective will therefore be:

To make £300 profit for the year January 1996 to December 1996 (assuming we sell £300 mugs retailing at £3 each and costing £2 each to buy).

CUSTOMER TAKE-UP

This can be difficult to measure. If you know the total potential market size, i.e. the number of actual and potential buyers of a product, you can estimate your take-up. For example, if the total market for blue Rolls Royce cars in the UK is 300 people and you sell 30, you will achieve a 10 per cent customer take-up. This is more usually referred to as market share.

Some businesses do not consider the potential buyers of a product, but instead limit the market to the number of *actual* buyers. So, if 18 million kettles are sold in the UK every year and your company sells 6 million, you have a 33 per cent market share.

Your objective, as a new small business, would need to be very modest initially, say under 1 per cent take-up of your product. This will grow later on.

PRODUCT PROMOTION

As well as general business objectives, you may wish to highlight specific promotion objectives. These could be:

> To inform the people of the city of Bath about our new service we will spend £5,000 on poster sites around the city. The campaign will last for one month.

or

> To boost sales by 5 per cent over the Christmas period we will offer a 'buy one and get 50p off your next purchase' promotion.

You must be very careful when deciding on these types of promotional technique. They can be very costly if not controlled correctly and may not have the desired effect if carried out incorrectly.

UNDERTAKING ROLES IN ENTERPRISE

HOW CAN THE BUSINESS BE MANAGED EFFECTIVELY?

The key to running a business well is good planning, supported by skilled and well-motivated staff who are clear about their own roles and responsibilities. Allocating roles must be done in an ethical, orderly and agreed manner. There is no point in forcing a colleague to take over a role. How do *you* feel when ordered to do something? People will be much more productive if roles are co-ordinated and agreed.

For many students an enterprise project will be the first time they have the opportunity to take on the different roles they might enjoy later in the world of work. Other students might already hold down part-time jobs so they will be able to bring that experience to the enterprise project. In all matters, the important thing is that everyone is aware of their specific role and understands their overall obligation to support all the other members in the team.

The most likely functions you will need to fill are:

managing director
finance and accounts
human resources
production
sales
marketing

The main roles (each undertaken by an individual, such as a personnel manager) for each function (the department where that person works, such as the personnel department or function) are listed in the table overleaf. This will obviously differ depending on the type of business you intend to run.

You can see in the table that there are some common responsibilities which all functions carry out such as allocating resources, decision-making and recording and reporting progress, particularly in a large business. This is not always the case with a small business.

A C T I V I T Y

Can you identify which role should deal primarily with the following responsibilities?

- advertising
- customer service
- allocating resources
- making decisions
- recording and reporting progress
- administration
- security and safety
- production and scheduling

Function	Roles
Marketing and sales	Allocating resources
	Making decisions
	Recording and reporting progress
	Helping to write the plan
	Deciding objectives
	Market research
	Promotion
	New product development
	Customer service
	Pricing decisions
	Distribution decisions
	Selling
Human resources	Allocating resources
	Making decisions
	Recording and reporting progress
	Recruitment
	Training and development
	Terms and conditions of contract
	Dealing with trade unions
	Disciplinary action
Finance	Allocating resources
	Making decisions
	Recording and reporting progress
	Finding capital
	Shares issues
	Cash flows
	Operational budget management
Managing director and overall administration (to include accounts)	Allocating resources
	Making decisions
	Recording and reporting progress
	Deciding business structure
	Insurance
	Managing payroll
	General office administration
	Monitoring legislation that will affect the business
Production	Allocating resources
	Making decisions
	Recording and reporting progress
	Purchasing
	Production
	Quality control

TABLE 10.2 ROLES OF FUNCTIONS IN ENTERPRISE

WORKING METHODS

Good working methods will prove an asset to your organisation. It will become much easier to run and be more productive if your working methods are organised, logical and well controlled. If you do not agree how you and your colleagues should work this could lead to conflict, a breakdown in communication and poor business practice.

What methods are available?

BY FUNCTION

A group can simply stick to the tasks that are allocated to them, for example sales personnel performing selling and no other function, accounts personnel sticking solely to preparing accounts and so on. This system allows each function to develop expert skills in its own area. It is quite clear which responsibilities lie with which personnel. There may be a problem, however, if staff are ill or away and one function grinds to a halt. This system does not help the flow of information in a company and does not build team spirit.

BY MATRIX

Another option is for people to work in mini-teams on small projects. This means a mini-team of staff from each function (one each from marketing, finance and so on) will be responsible for a number of tasks for the enterprise team. This works well at building team spirit and getting everyone involved, but can become rather messy and confusing if it is not controlled properly.

Checklist for organisation

You need to answer the following questions:

1. How often will you meet and who should attend?
2. Where will you meet and how long should the meetings last?
3. How will you record the meetings – will you take minutes?
4. How will you communicate decisions to other members of the team?
5. Who will take decisions? What type of voting system will you use? Will anyone have a casting vote?
6. Will you draw up a time schedule to make sure the enterprise activities are running to plan?
7. What systems do you need to establish to make the business work well?

Team work and supporting others

In any type of business or enterprise activity it is vital that everyone is supportive of each other so that the business objectives can be achieved. The other personal skills you will need are to be adaptable and flexible in your role as there will be several different types of demands on your time from different sources. No matter what your role you will probably need to consider how you will act with regard to:

1. Customers – How will you deal with them? Who will be your public relations spokesperson? What will your customer care policy be?
2. Resources – Who will be handling them? Who will make decisions regarding resources? Will all personnel be involved?
3. Decision-making and reporting decisions – Who will have the final say in making decisions? How will you handle routine and non-routine problems? What system of passing decisions will you adopt? What type of management style will suit the company best? What provision will you make to change the structure or decision-making powers of the business? How will you make the information on businesses available and accessible to the company and outsiders?

Once these decisions have been made and roles allocated it will be easier for the business to achieve its objectives of improved customer take-up, achieving profit and/or sales or promoting goods and services well. The business is more likely to be effective. This will also happen when resources are used appropriately: where best use is made of staff skills, equipment is well maintained and used efficiently and productively, good planning makes good use of time and materials are used correctly with little waste.

WHAT ARE THE GENERAL RESPONSIBILITIES OF EACH ENTERPRISE MEMBER?

One of the major commitments that everyone has to supply is to make a willing and positive contribution. Work colleagues should not be expected to carry a colleague who is not prepared to pull his or her own weight. Another responsibility in business is to act in an ethical way at all times and to behave with integrity. Business is not about cheating or short-changing a customer.

One key area is to make sure that everything you do is done with health and safety in mind.

Health and safety requirements

This is a vital part of managing any business. All personnel should consider the health and safety implications of their actions and the possible consequences for themselves, their direct customers, and the general public. This is equally important if you are manufacturing a product or delivering a service.

A C T I V I T Y

Businesses may need to appoint a health and safety officer.

1. Can you define this role?
2. How will health and safety affect your venture in particular?
3. Design a poster to alert everyone to the implications for health and safety.

INFORMATION ON HEALTH AND SAFETY

There are several government departments who produce leaflets on health and safety and who can give advice on related problems:

- Trading Standards Office
- the fire prevention department attached to your local fire brigade
- the Department of Employment
- the Health and Safety Executive
- the Factories Inspectorate

The Environmental Health Department, run by local authorities, can also help.

Remember your duty includes protecting yourself, other employees, your customers and the public at large. This is a major requirement and needs to be tackled seriously.

Security

Security is another area of concern. How will you store and locate stock? Who will be responsible for handling money and signing cheques?

ACTIVITY

Devise a security system suitable for a small business. It will need cross-references and checks to make sure everything is sorted and handled in the correct fashion. These could include having two signatories for signing cheques. Cross-referencing will take place through proper accounting procedures. How will you deal with any breaches of security?

Goodwill

This is a vital ingredient for any successful business. If an organisation loses goodwill it can suffer many problems.

Loss of goodwill from staff can result in low productivity, low morale, resentment and high staff turnover.

Loss of goodwill from suppliers may end in loss of suppliers, poor trading terms, loss of credit facilities and even the end of a business agreement.

Loss of goodwill from customers can affect sales and profitability, long-term growth, lead to a poor company image and to the failure of the business.

Loss of goodwill from the general public may result in a poor company image, loss of credibility and loss of sales and profitability.

HOW CAN GOODWILL BE MAINTAINED?

This can be done in many ways. Good communication is vital. Joint projects with the local community can help, as does being seen to act in a fair and proper manner. Listening to the public and your customers and acting on their feedback is essential if goodwill is to be nurtured.

ACTIVITY

In a group discuss and list as many businesses as possible who have lost the goodwill of their customers.

1 Why has this happened?
2 In your opinion, is there any solution to this problem?

EVALUATION ACTIVITIES

IMPLEMENTING THE PLAN

Running a business can be a very exciting experience, and it is very easy to be swept along by the deadlines you have to meet and the new roles you are experiencing. However, you must make provision for evaluating or assessing the performance of your own business. You need to check how the business is running at regular intervals, so that you can modify plans if you are not quite meeting targets or standards, or take advantage of an opportunity that has presented itself to your enterprise.

Many small businesses make the fundamental mistake of assuming the business is running well because it appears to be doing so. They rely on 'gut feelings' for the market, which is very dangerous. You cannot be everywhere, overseeing your overall operation at all times, so how can you know if there is a problem or not? If you simply rely on your own instincts, there may be a problem of whether or not you are impartial enough to judge your own performance.

Not only will you want to assess just how the business is performing, you will also want to check on how well all the other members of the team are faring, so that the opportunities for improvement can be identified. This is a very sensitive area, so you need to be careful and approach it constructively. The human resources function could make a valuable contribution here, particularly in terms of suggesting training and development needs. You may find the team members are a little inhibited at first at discussing each other's performance. Try the activity (Step 7) on p.264, which will act as a stimulus for further discussion.

Where will the development needs be?

There are bound to be some general areas that some of the team could be picked up on, perhaps in terms of punctuality and attendance. If commitment and contribution are a real problem then the student needs to really think about whether an enterprise project is right for them. Other common areas are difficulties over handling accounts and/or production difficulties for manufacturing companies. These are practical areas that will require specialist help. Other lecturers may be able to help with accounting problems and the banks carry lots of free literature containing financial information. Production problems will be specific to the product you are selling, but your first queries may be to your lecturing staff. One difficulty that students often have is talking frankly but diplomatically to each other when assessing skills. They tend either to give praise where none is due or to keep quiet and silently fume about colleagues who are not pulling their own weight.

Business performance

It may be easier to gather information about the performance of your business than about your colleagues' performance. This is because some factual information should be available and the area you are evaluating is less sensitive than individuals' feelings.

A C T I V I T Y

Enterprise Activity

In groups of four or five, plan an enterprise activity to be carried out alongside the rest of your GNVQ studies. Here are some suggestions:

- a car-cleaning service
- a CV-typing/word processing service
- selling second-hand text books
- helping out with your school or college tuck shop

Step 1 Hold an initial meeting to:

- elect a leader
- decide the idea for the enterprise activity
- allocate roles and responsibilities
- agree the aims and objectives of the group
- discuss any start up costs
- forecast your sales

Make sure you keep a record of the meeting.

Step 2 Carry out some market research (possibly a face-to-face questionnaire) to find out if there is a demand for your product or service.

Step 3 Draw up a basic business plan.

Step 4 Obtain the necessary finance to get the activity off the ground.

Step 5 Carry out the activity for at least two months.

NB Hold regular meetings to discuss progress and record details of sales. Make sure that any money you make is kept in a safe place.

Step 6 After your enterprise activity has been carried out hold a meeting to discuss:

- the financial position – did you breakeven, make a loss or even a profit? Did you achieve your forecasted sales?
- whether the group achieved its aims and objectives
- whether people carried out their roles and responsibilities effectively
- what to do with any profits

Keep a record of the meeting.

A C T I V I T Y

Enterprise Activity Step 7

All members of the group should take part in this exercise and all of their views should be considered equally. Write down a list of all of the qualities you consider necessary for someone to work well on your project: they could include things like helpfulness, ability to meet deadlines, research skills, reliability, punctuality and attendance and so on.

Once you have all agreed on the list each member should then give all other members marks out of 10 for each of the skills. This can be a written exercise and should be carried out in confidence and anonymously.

Once all of the team have completed the ratings, the human resources function should add up the scores for each individual, and the scores should be discussed at a group meeting. The ensuing discussion should highlight reasons for any particularly low or high scores.

A C T I V I T Y

Enterprise Activity Step 8

Assessing colleagues is a very difficult task, as is being assessed yourself. Evaluation sessions can easily turn into arguments if they are not properly controlled. Try some of the following techniques to help colleagues through an evaluation session.

1 Always give positive feedback before negative, for example 'The posters you designed were terrific, but you need to apply the same sort of hard work to your reports.'

2 Ask the colleague if they are aware of any weakness – most people will answer honestly.

3 Avoid confrontational statements. Ask a question, for example 'How do you feel you have performed this term?'

4 Be honest, not hurtful, for example 'Your accounts have been great, but your continued absences have let the group down.'

5 Say why you have made the evaluation, for example 'It's very difficult for the business to function if the accountant is always missing.'

6 Give colleagues a chance to respond. There may be an authentic reason for the problem.

7 Don't prejudge the situation.

8 Decide on the solution together.

Remember that whilst assessing colleagues is very important, there are a number of key factors you must always implement (action) correctly and review continually:

- Have resources been provided and allocated correctly, are they being used effectively or wasted? Make sure the right staff are allocating the resources in the correct manner.
- Check the roles have been allocated appropriately individually and throughout the group.
- Ensure that you have made the right provision for any colleagues and/or customers with special needs.
- Action the advertising plan in close co-operation with your marketing staff.
- Have the correct administrative support systems laid down and communicated so everyone knows what to do.
- Progress the production/delivery schedule so your company has a good/service to market.
- Devise and follow through on your customer care policy.
- Draw up and action your strategy for security and safety.

For all of the above points, to make the plan work you must allocate responsibilities, communicate them and evaluate continually to assess performance.

SOURCES OF FEEDBACK

Your customers should be a credible source of information.

You need to make sure that you managed to achieve your business objectives. If you did not, do you understand what the problems were and how you would solve them the next time?

A C T I V I T Y

Enterprise Activity Step 9

Draw up a questionnaire to distribute to your customers. Keep the document short and make it easy to fill in. Make sure you ask your customers to give you ratings on a scale of 1–5, where 1 is very poor and 5 is excellent. Areas you may wish to include on the questionnaire are customer service, product quality, advertising effort and so on. Once you have completed the survey collate and analyse the information. Use the information you have collated to assess how well you are performing. What do the statistics show? Be honest about the results.

One very interesting source of information would be the people who decided not to buy from you. By interviewing non-buyers you will be able to find out what were the weaknesses or flaws in your operation. The important thing to learn from evaluation is that it should provide information to help you to plan for the future. This means that next time your business should be bigger and better, and you will be able to avoid the pitfalls you met in your first attempt.

It is worthwhile comparing your actual results with the objectives you initially set for the business in your plan. How do the results compare with your objectives?

- Were customers satisfied?
- Did you gain new customers?
- Did profits increase or did you at least break even?
- Did sales increase?
- Were your promotions successful?
- Were your general aims met?
- Did your production and scheduling run smoothly?
- Did your organisation and administration work well?
- Were there any breakdowns in communication?
- Were you successful in dealing with contingencies?

A C T I V I T Y

Enterprise Activity Step 10
Draw up a series of bar charts that show your forecasted sales volume compared to your actual sales volume by month. Give reasons for your excess/shortfall on sales. Discuss these with the whole team at a company meeting.

A C T I V I T Y

Enterprise Activity Step 11
The person responsible for finance needs to draw charts that illustrate how actual profit and turnover differ from forecast profit and turnover. Discuss these with the whole team at a company meeting.

A C T I V I T Y

Enterprise Activity Step 12
Once you have gathered all of your information, hold a company meeting to discuss the results. From the findings of this meeting, draw up a list of recommendations that would improve your operation should you continue to run it.

A C T I V I T Y

Enterprise Activity Step 13
Do you know any other groups of students involved in enterprise activities? If you do, ask them to review your team critically (but diplomatically!). You can, in turn, review their performance.

C H A P T E R   T E N

Test Yourself!

1 List the qualities a person needs to go into business.

2 What are the three key areas any entrepreneur needs to consider?

3 Name the key elements required in a business plan.

4 What type of information will you require about your competitors?

5 What services do the high street banks offer small businesses?

6 List staffing considerations for a new business.

7 Name three sources of ideas for a new business.

8 Where will you find information on VAT?

9 Where will you find information on public health?

10 What major problems do most small businesses face?

11 Name four key business objectives.

12 Describe two promotion objectives.

13 Name the major functions within a company.

14 Who is responsible for managing payroll within a company?

15 What is a matrix organisation?

16 Name six sources of help and guidance for health and safety at work.

17 What is meant by goodwill?

18 What do we mean by evaluation?

19 What qualities should a good team member have?

20 What are the sources of feedback for a small business?

INDEX

Hopwood Hall College